ISBN: 978-0-9679947-5-8
What Is It Series start date: 11-26-2001
Book (3) revised on: 07-20-2018

Description: What Is It Book 3, Drawings 501 to 750
eBook ASIN: B07FN5WCHN, ISBN: 978-0-9679947-5-8

The What Is It Series of Books is a compilation of over a thousand drawings by Sebastian De Angelis. The drawings are interesting, fascinating and sometimes humorous. They're in black & white and are available in paperback. The whole family should enjoy hours of viewing these detailed drawings. De Angelis' unique, unusual style will leave you wondering What Is It?

Although there doesn't seem to be a rhyme or reason as to what the artist is drawing, small creatures appear randomly throughout the books. These humanoid looking beings (unnamed or purpose described) come in all shapes and sizes. They typically are involved with things of a malicious nature, throwing levers, pressing buttons and all-out getting in the way of normality.

So where do all the wild ideas come from that sets the artist's pen in motion? Most of the work tells me that De Angelis is delivering a message that life is not as perfect under the facade surface as we imagine. And that situations in the world around us are a lot more ironic then we assume. The nuts & bolts, chewing gum & duck-tape that holds it all together is the World's way of evolving. Then the practicality fades due in part to those pesky humanoids! So be careful (xiao xin) out there, it's much more precarious then you think! Heee heeee...

Books in the What Is It Series

Book (1) Drawings 1-250
Book (2) Drawings 251-500
Book (3) Drawings 501-750
Book (4) Drawings 751-1000

What Is It

Book 3

Drawings 501 to 750

Sebastian De Angelis

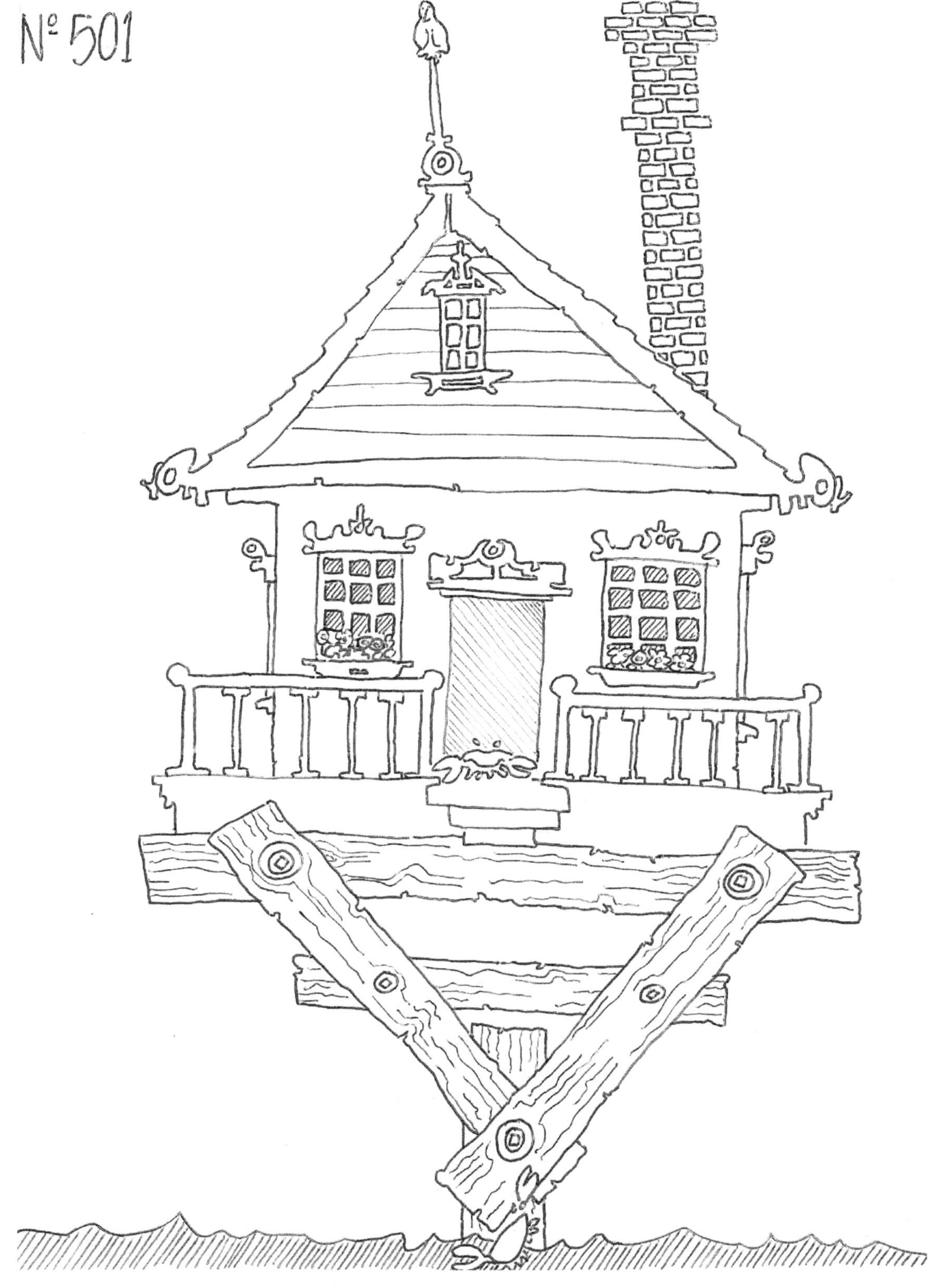
Nº 501

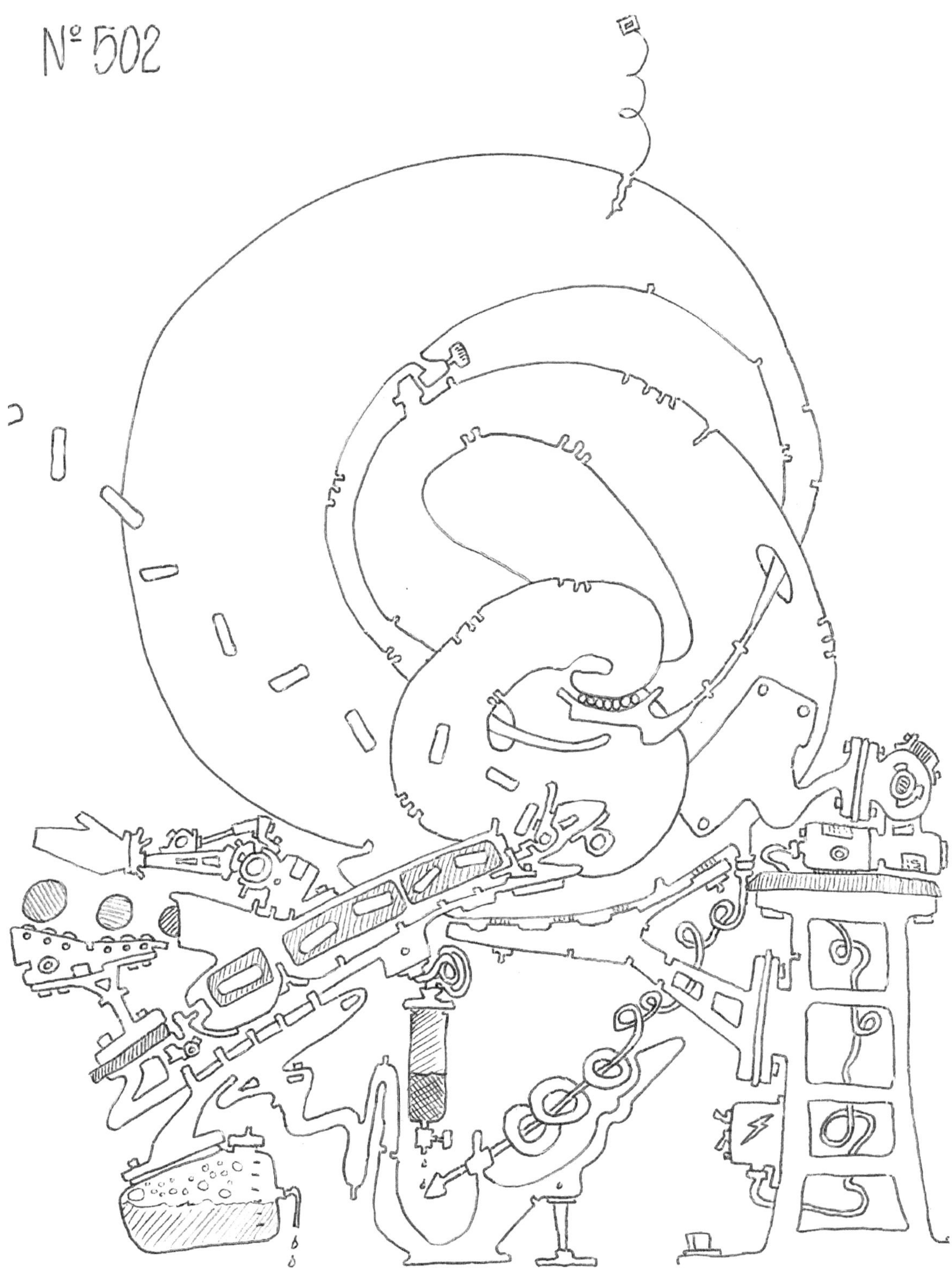
Nº 502

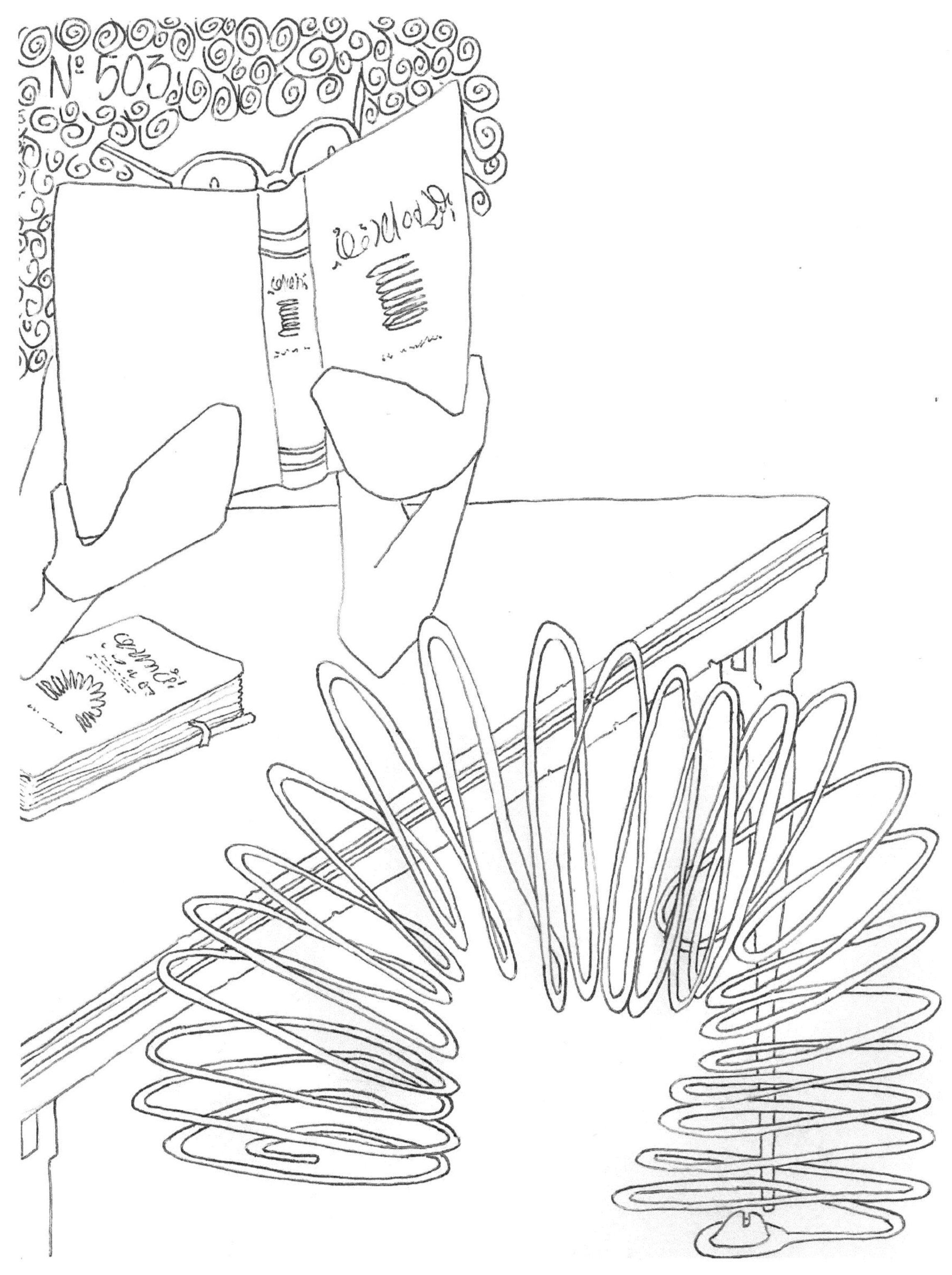
N° 503

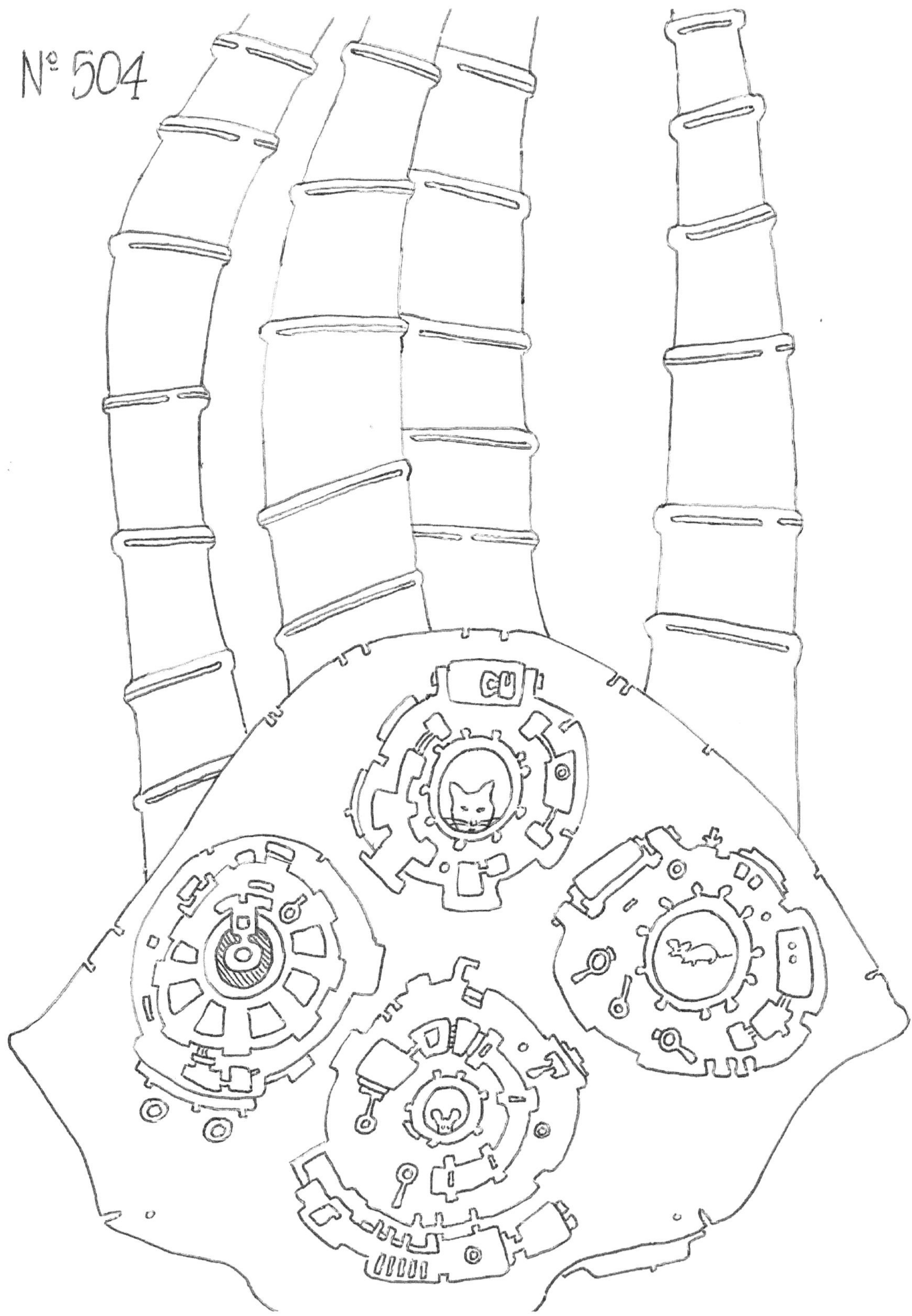
Nº 504

№ 505

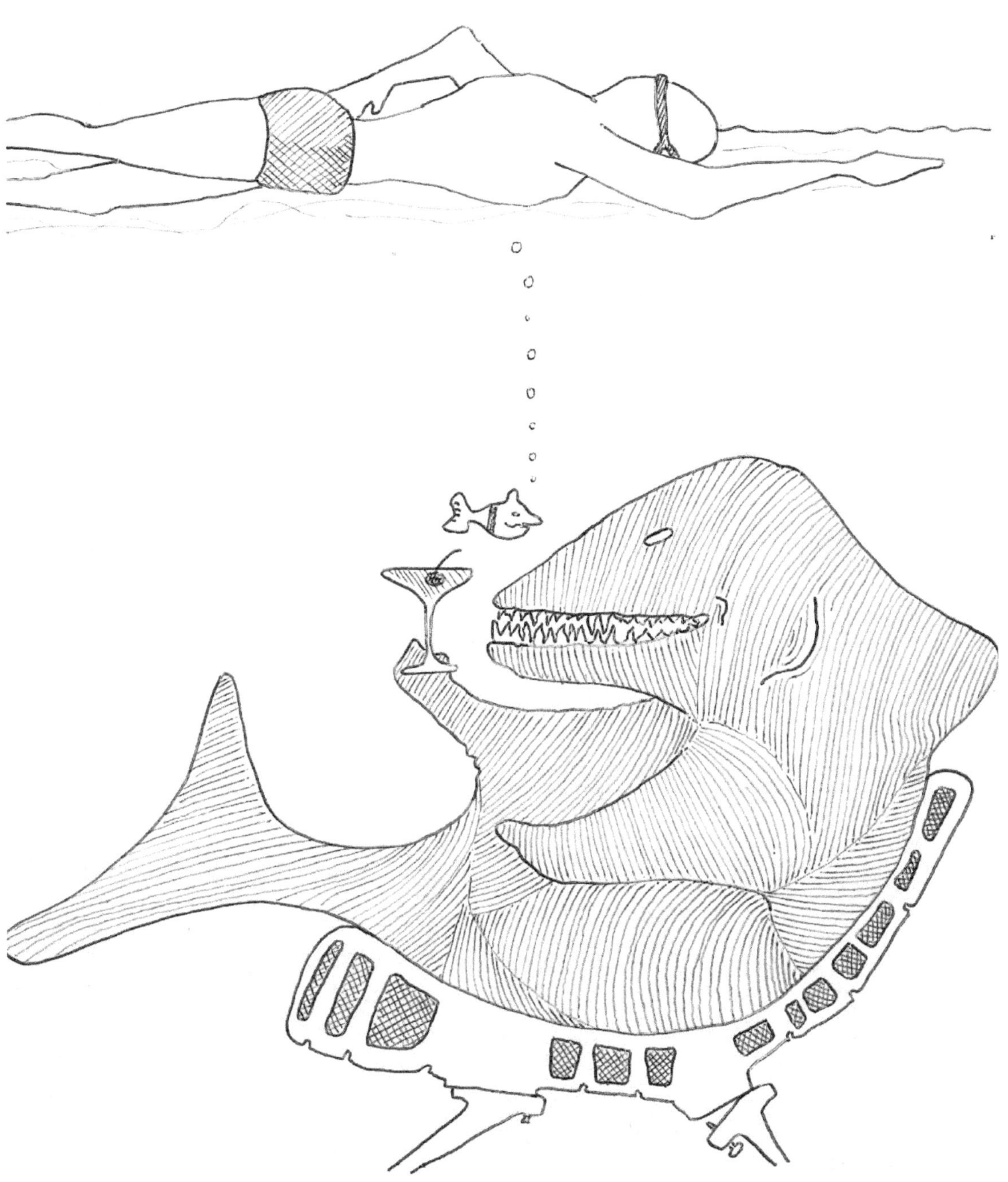

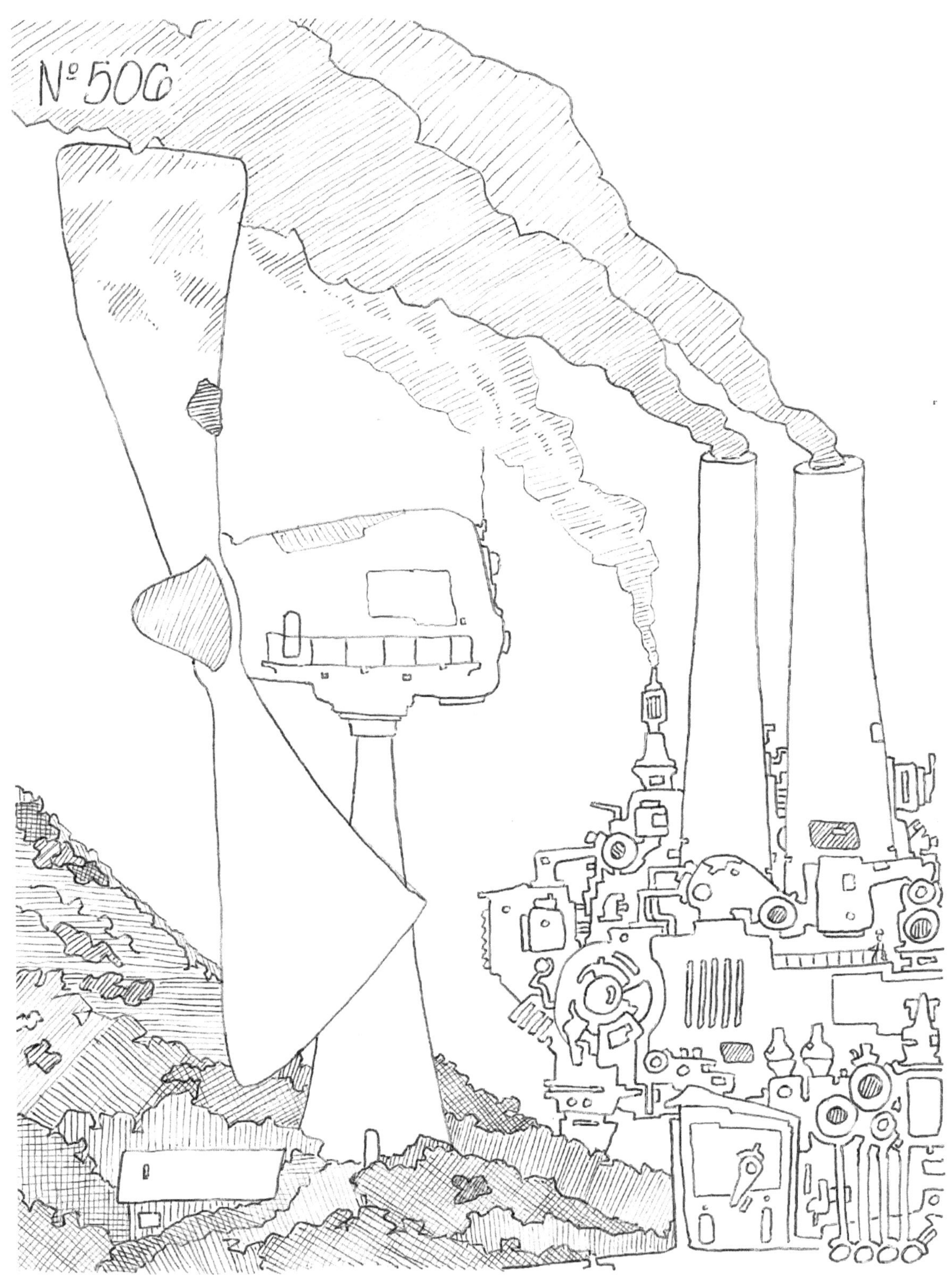
№ 500

№ 507

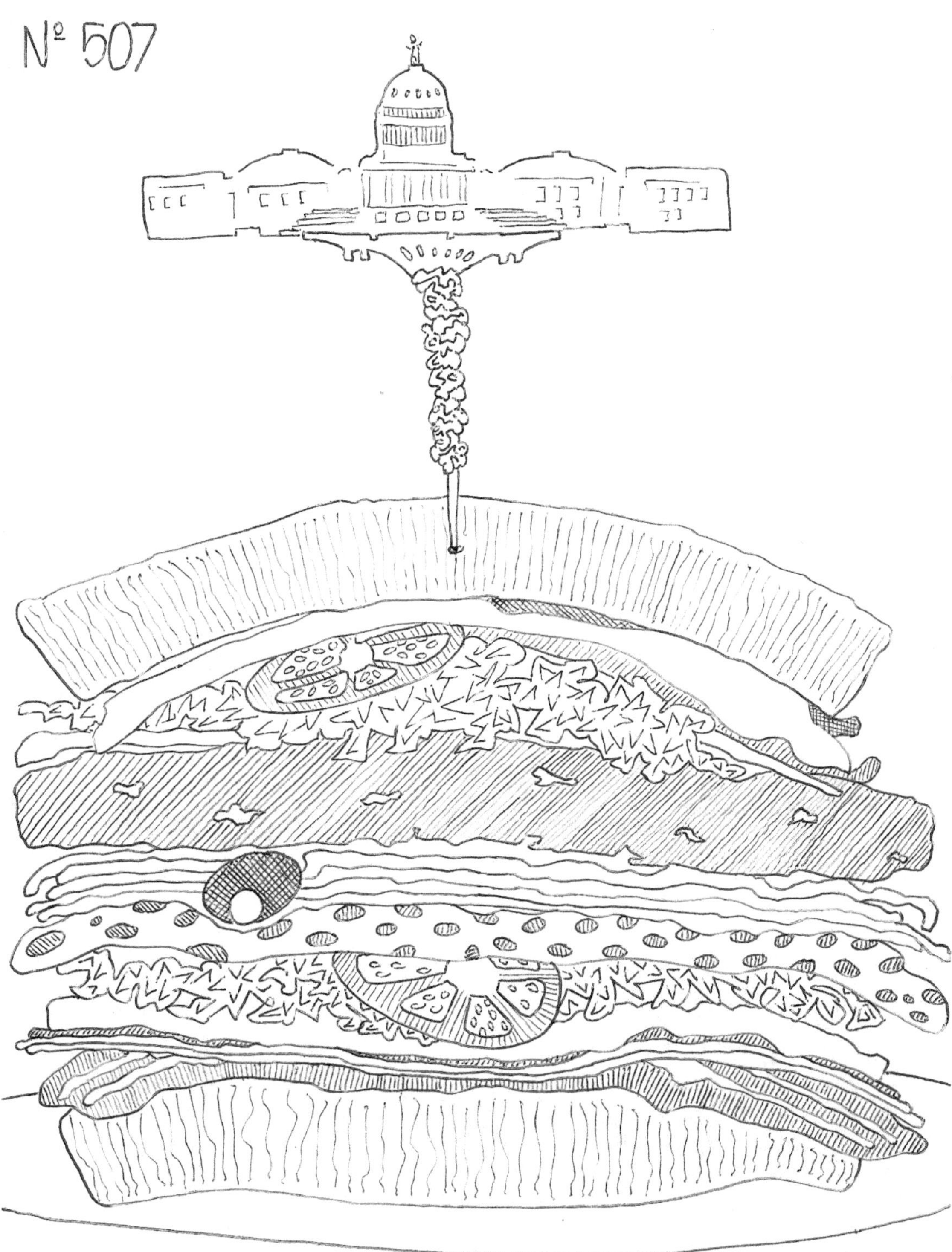

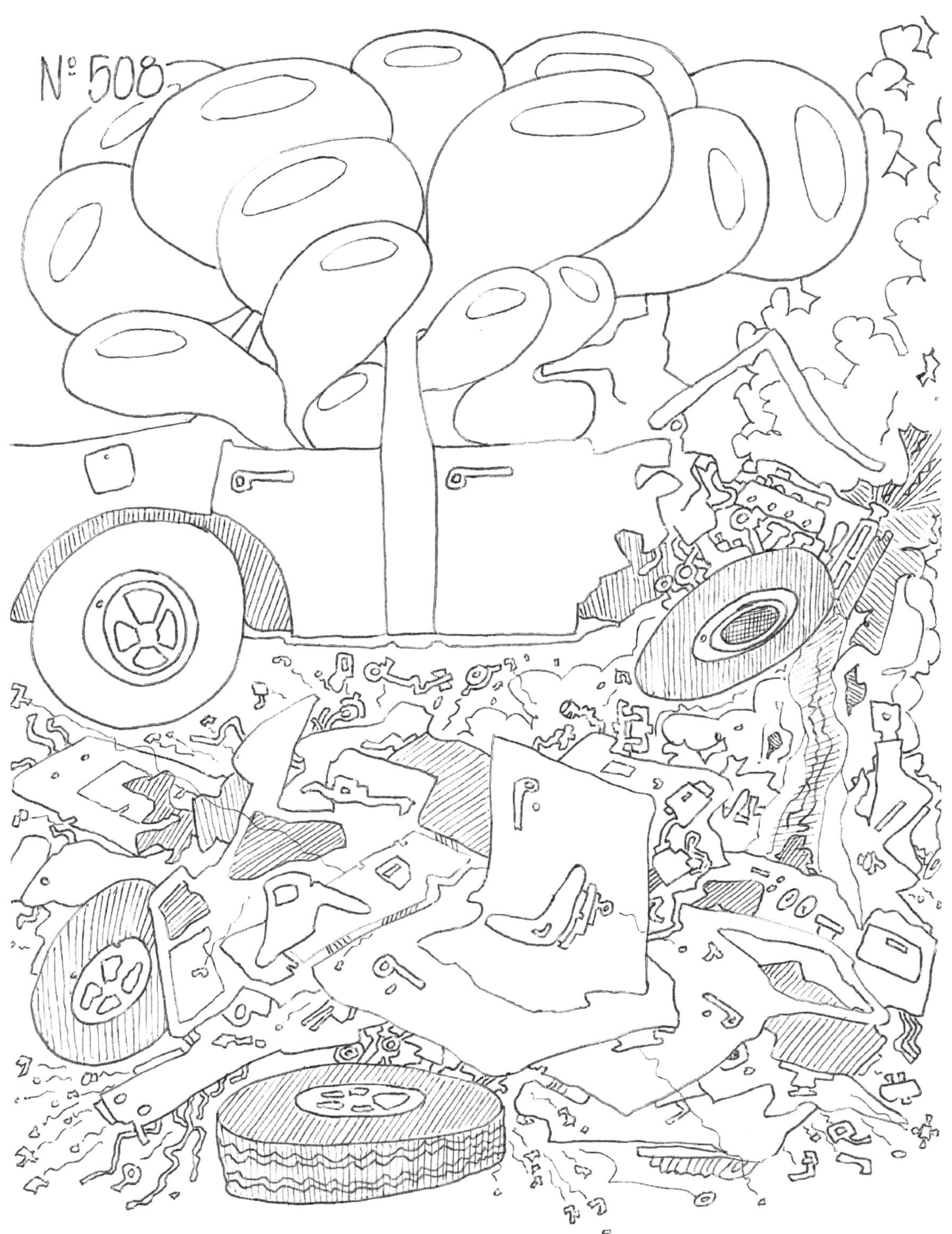
№ 508

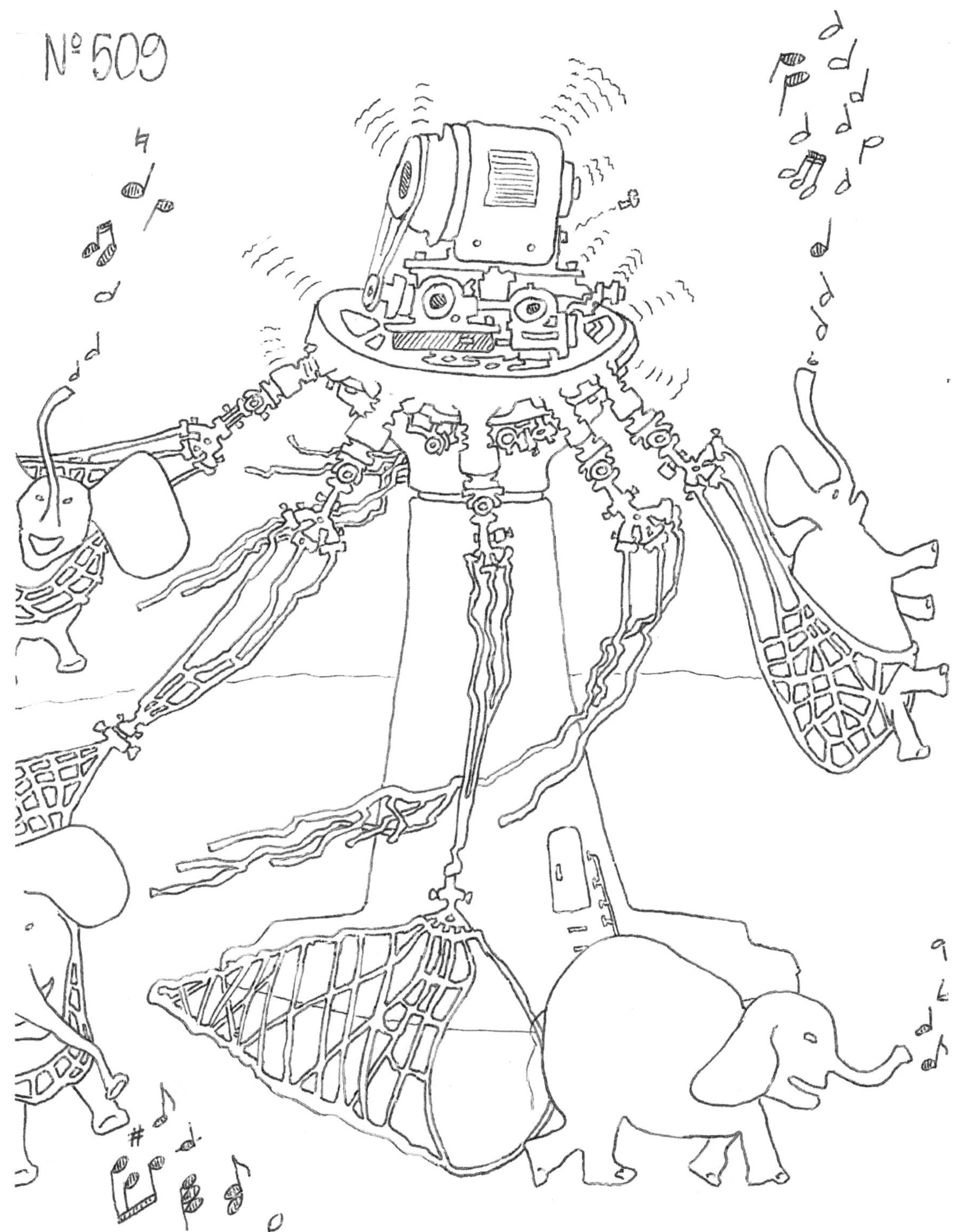
Nº 509

N°510

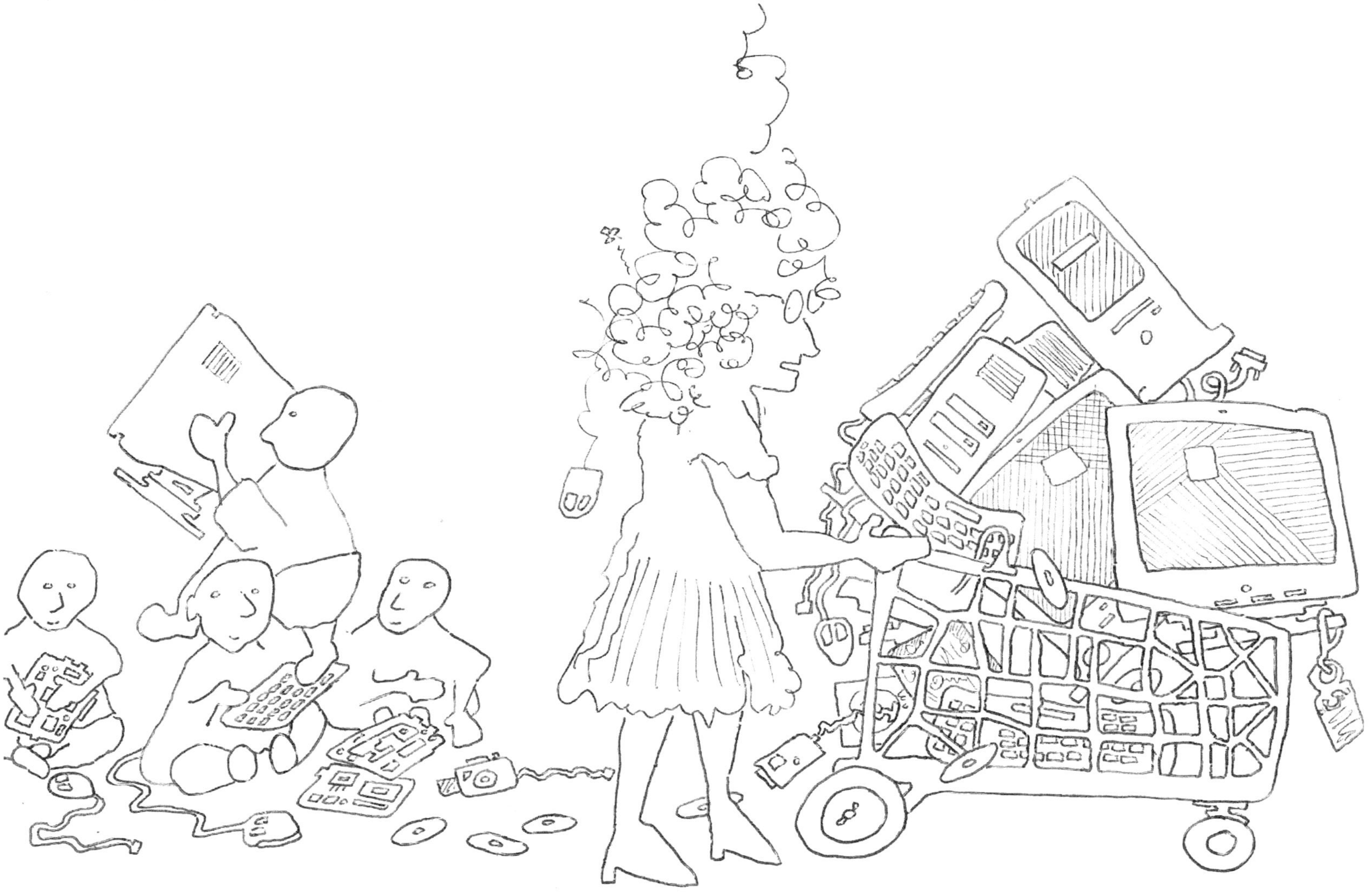

No. 511

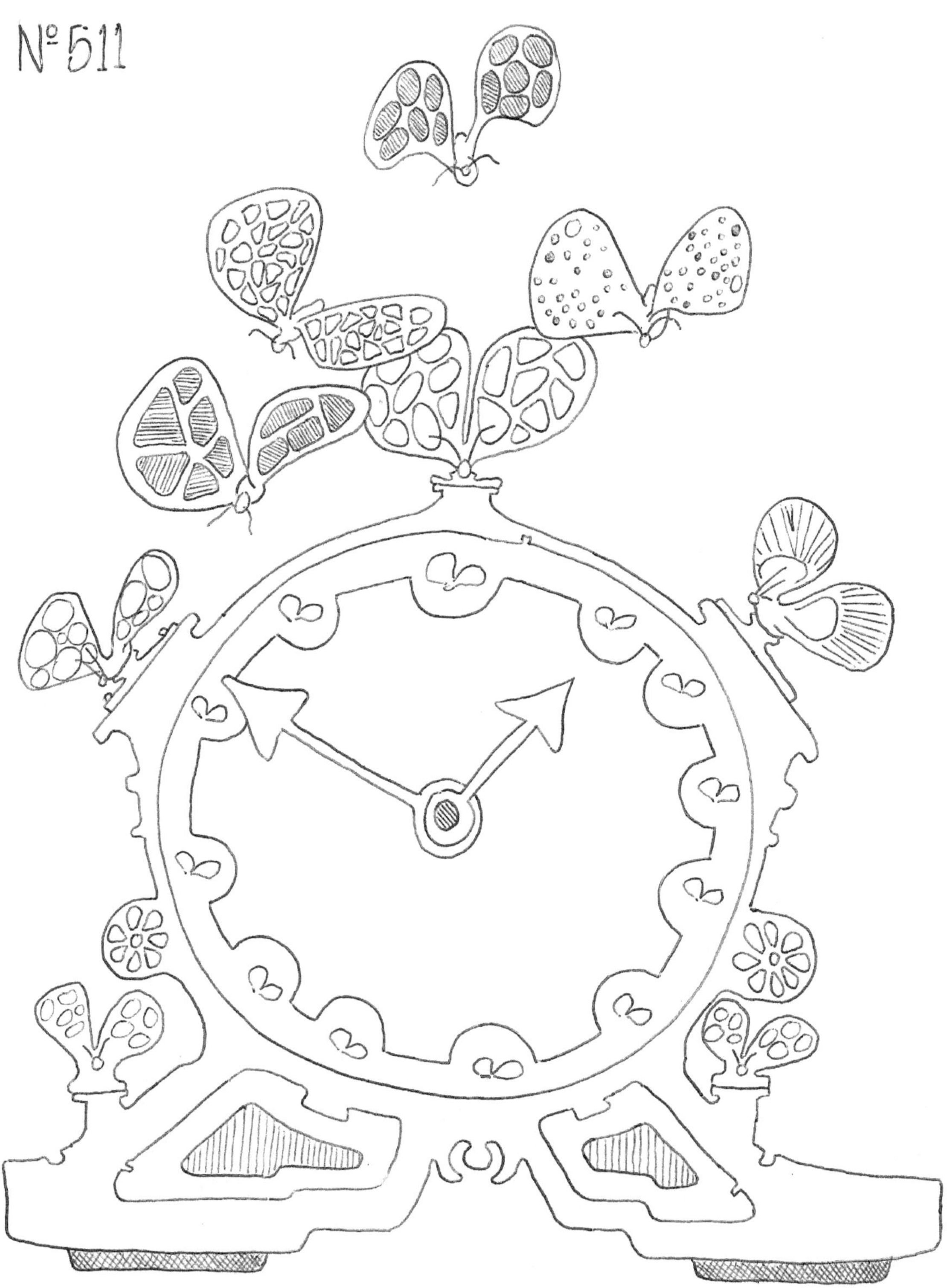

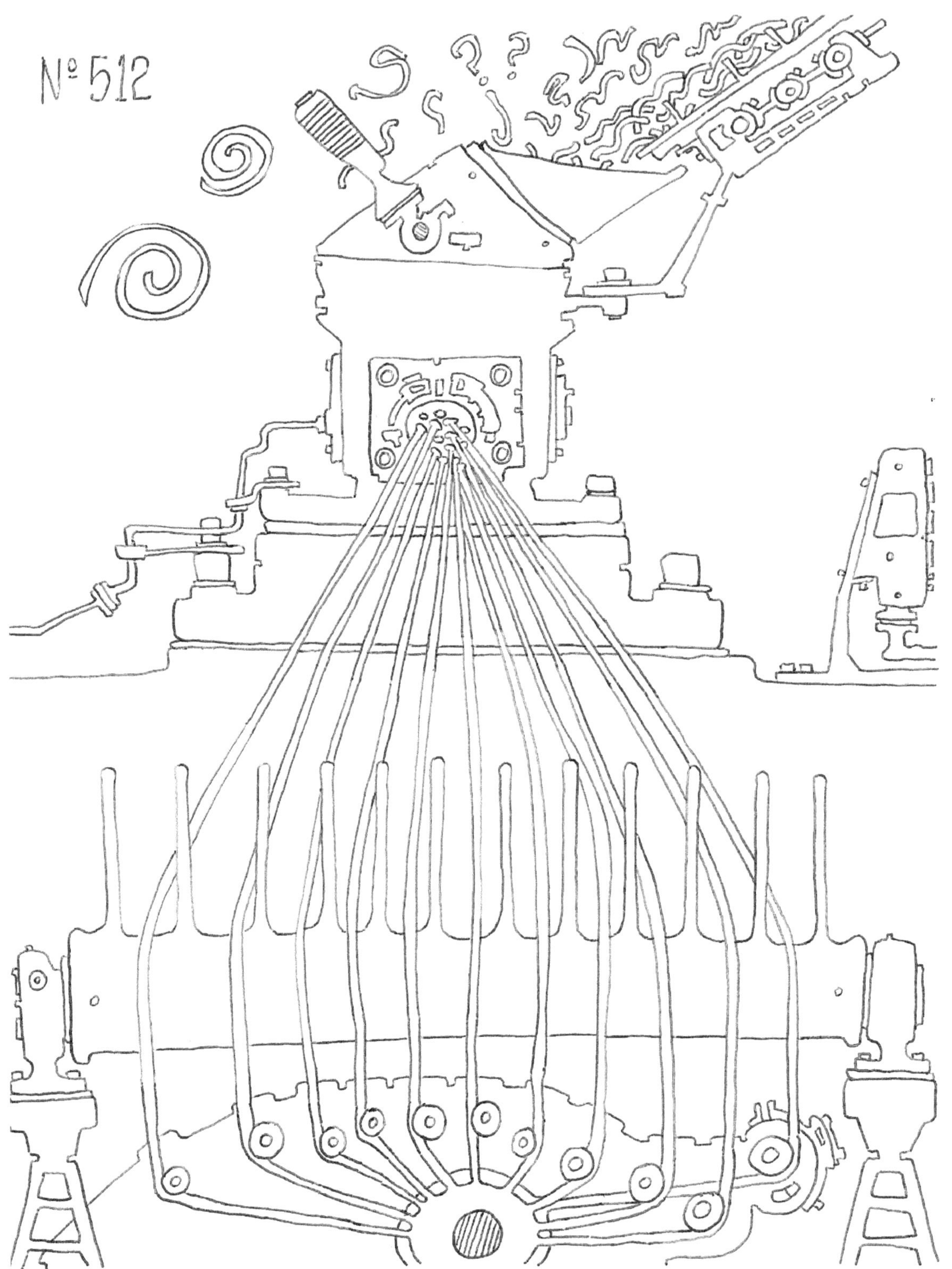
№ 512

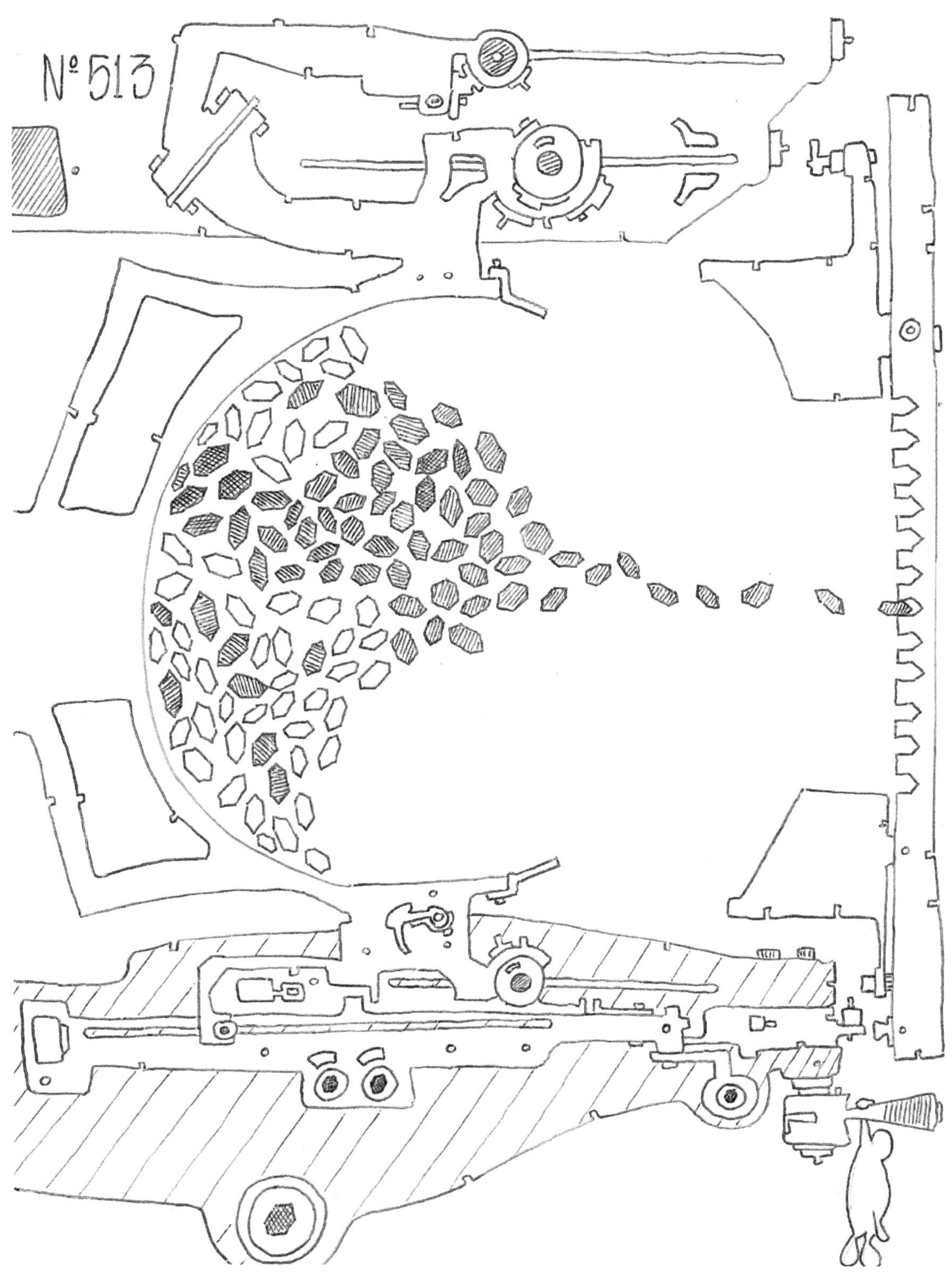

№ 513

№514

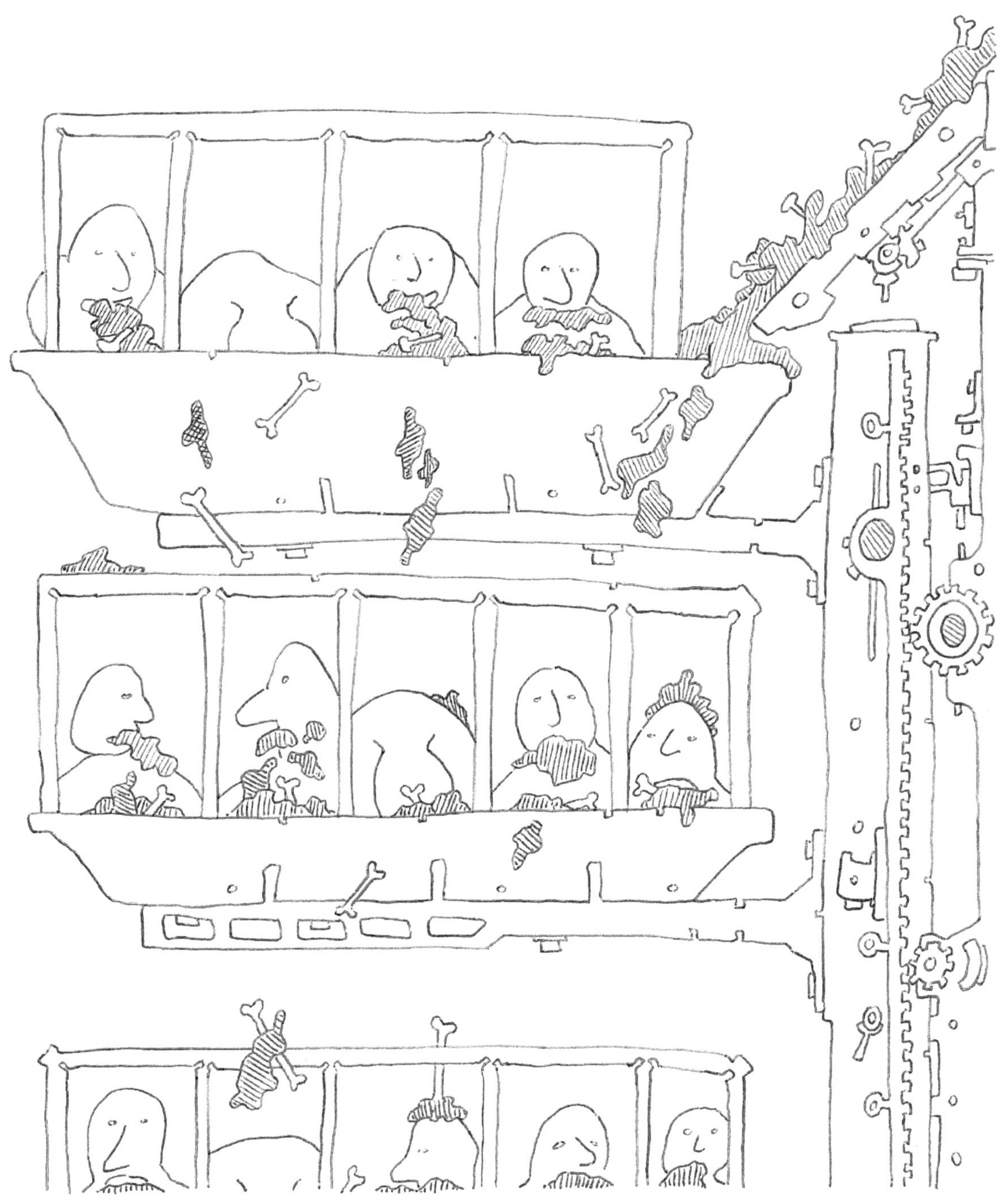

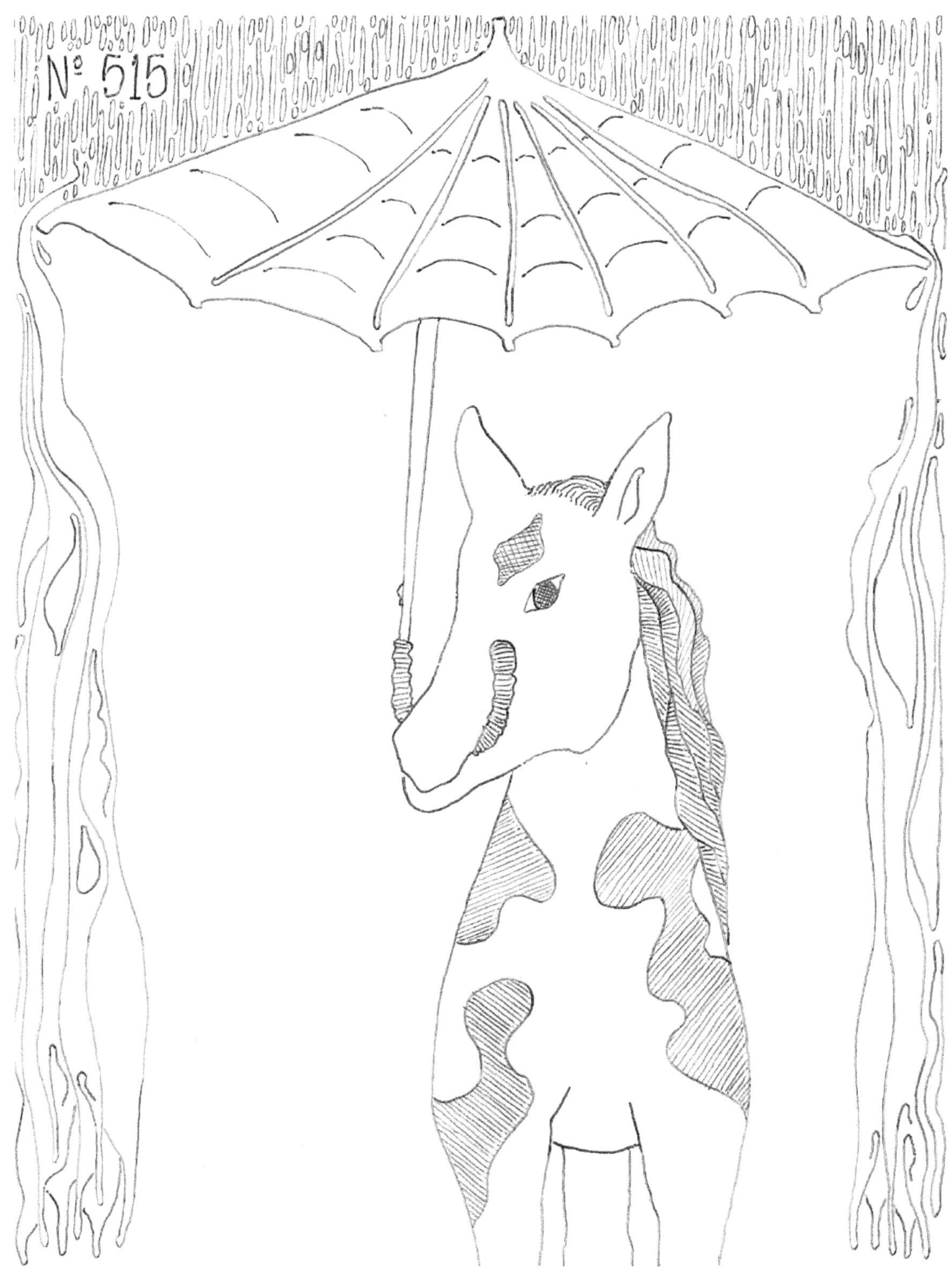
Nº 515

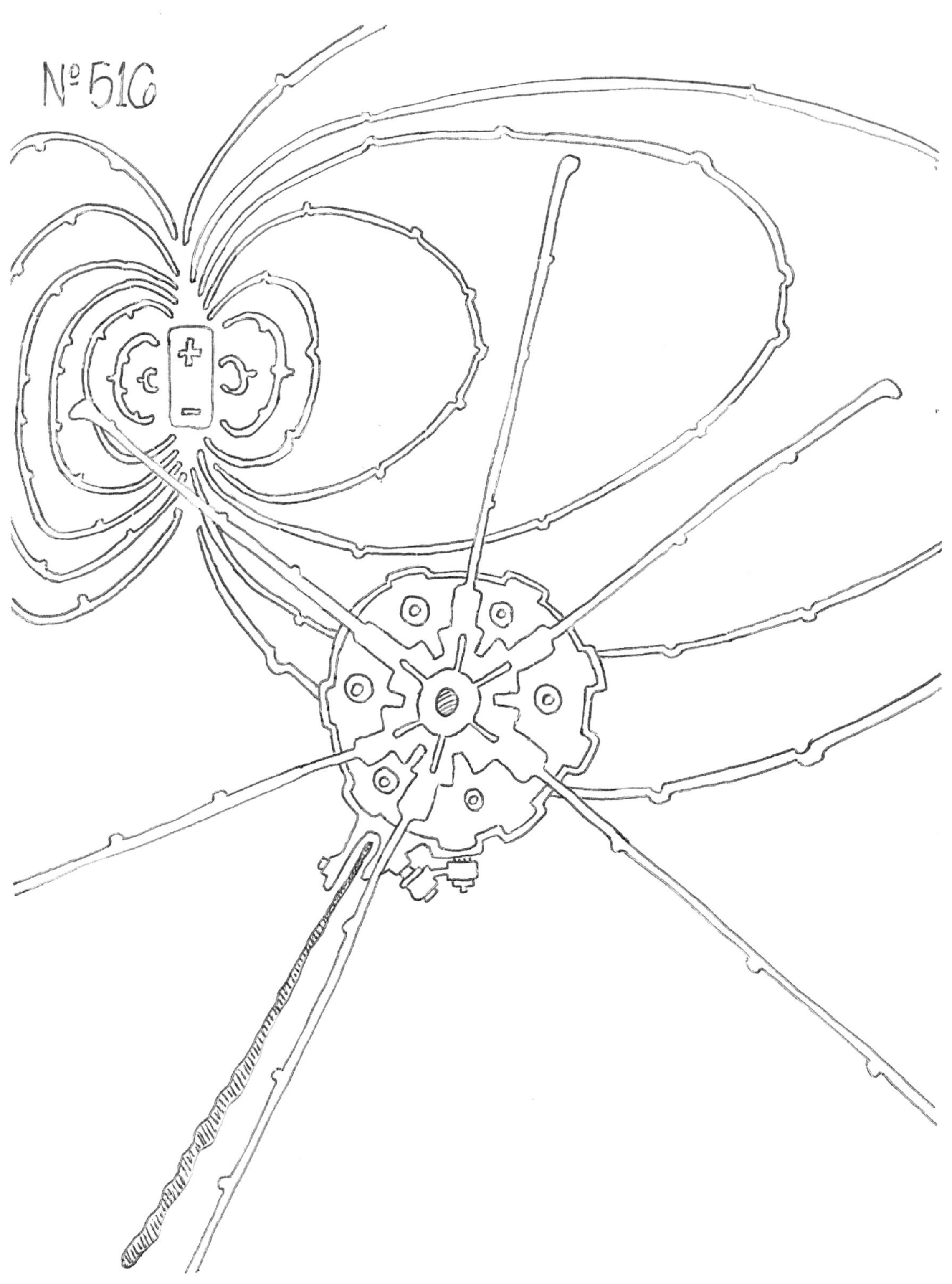
№ 516
+
–

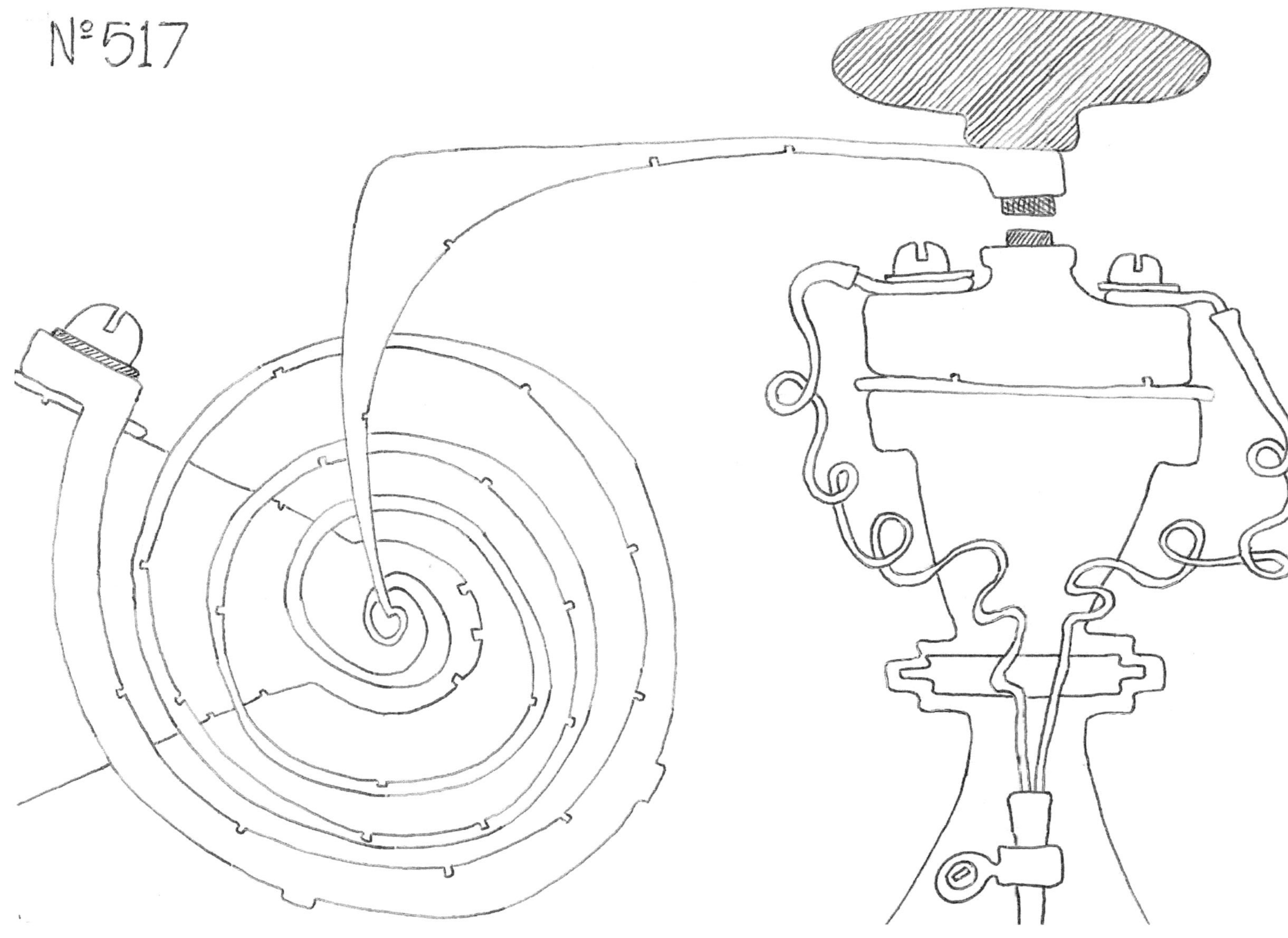
N°517

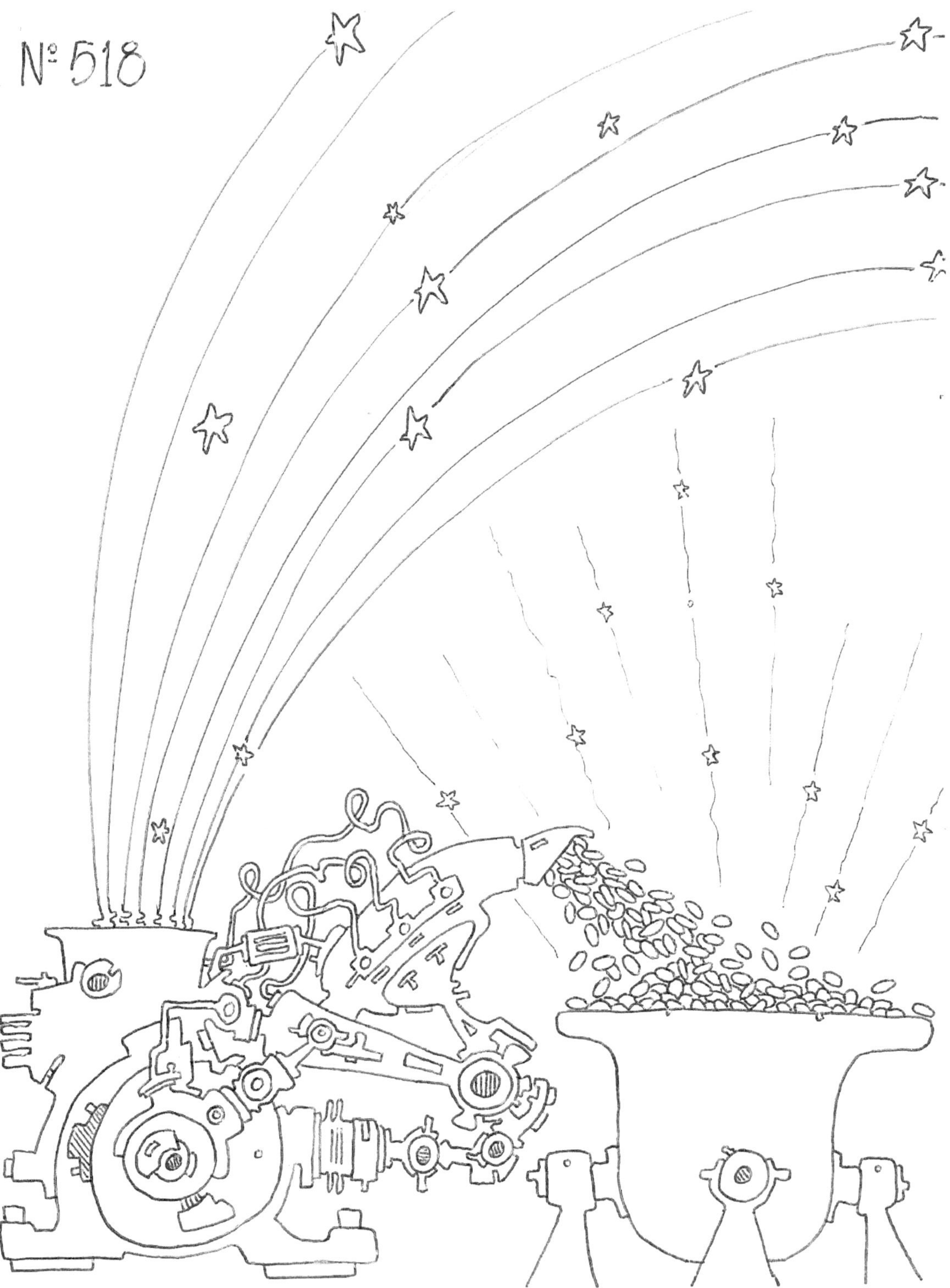
Nº 518

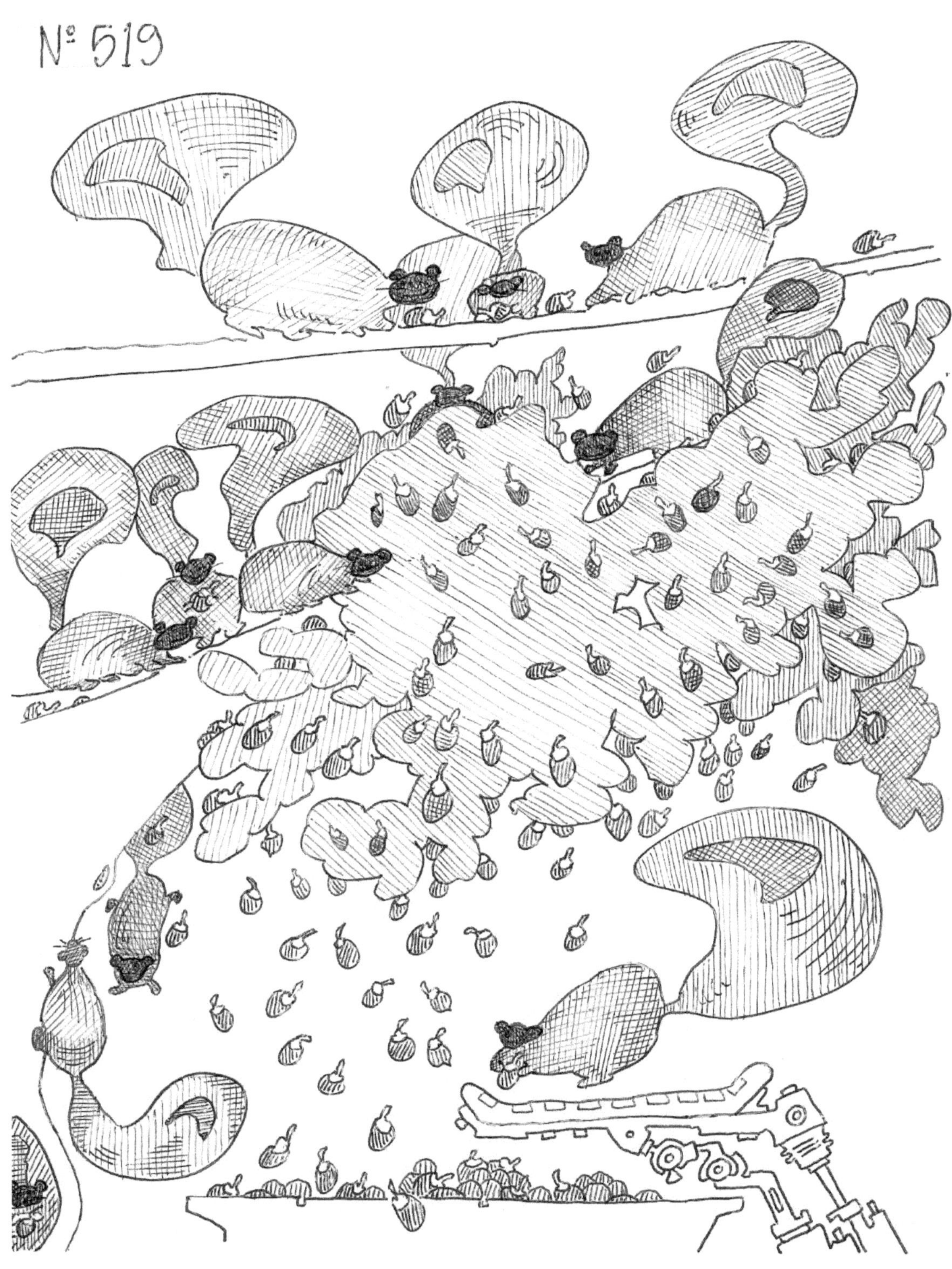
№ 519

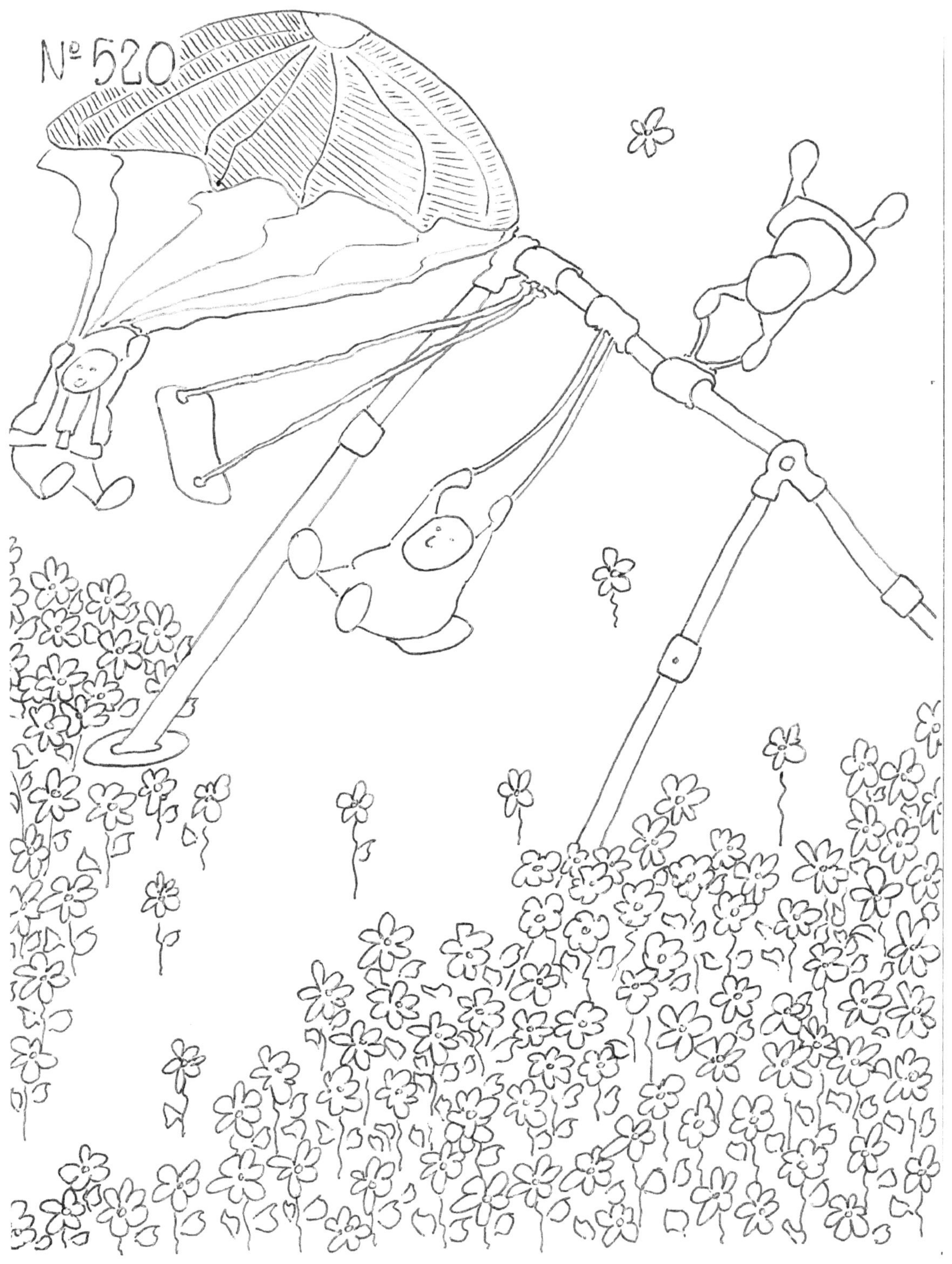
Nº 520

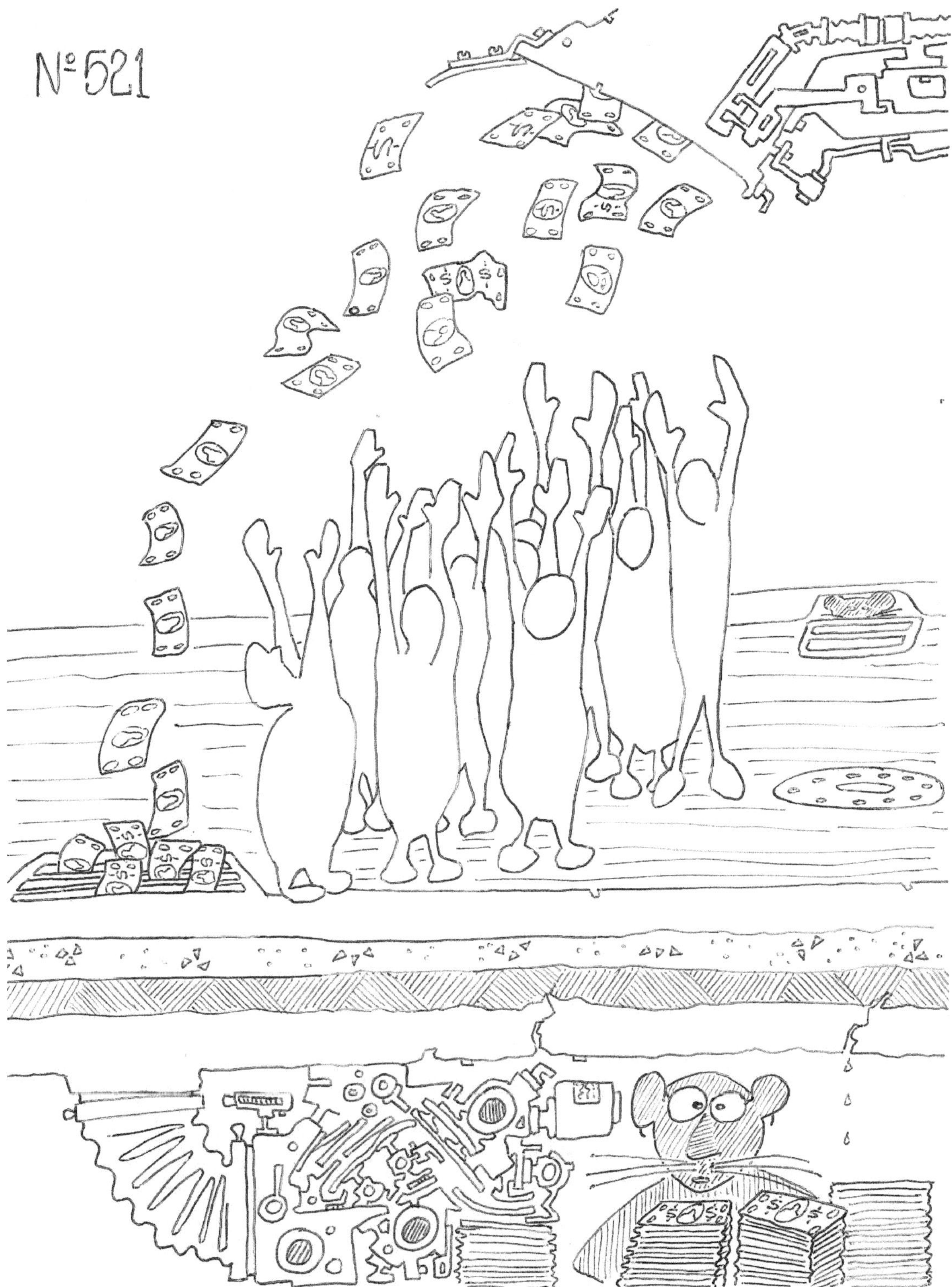
№521

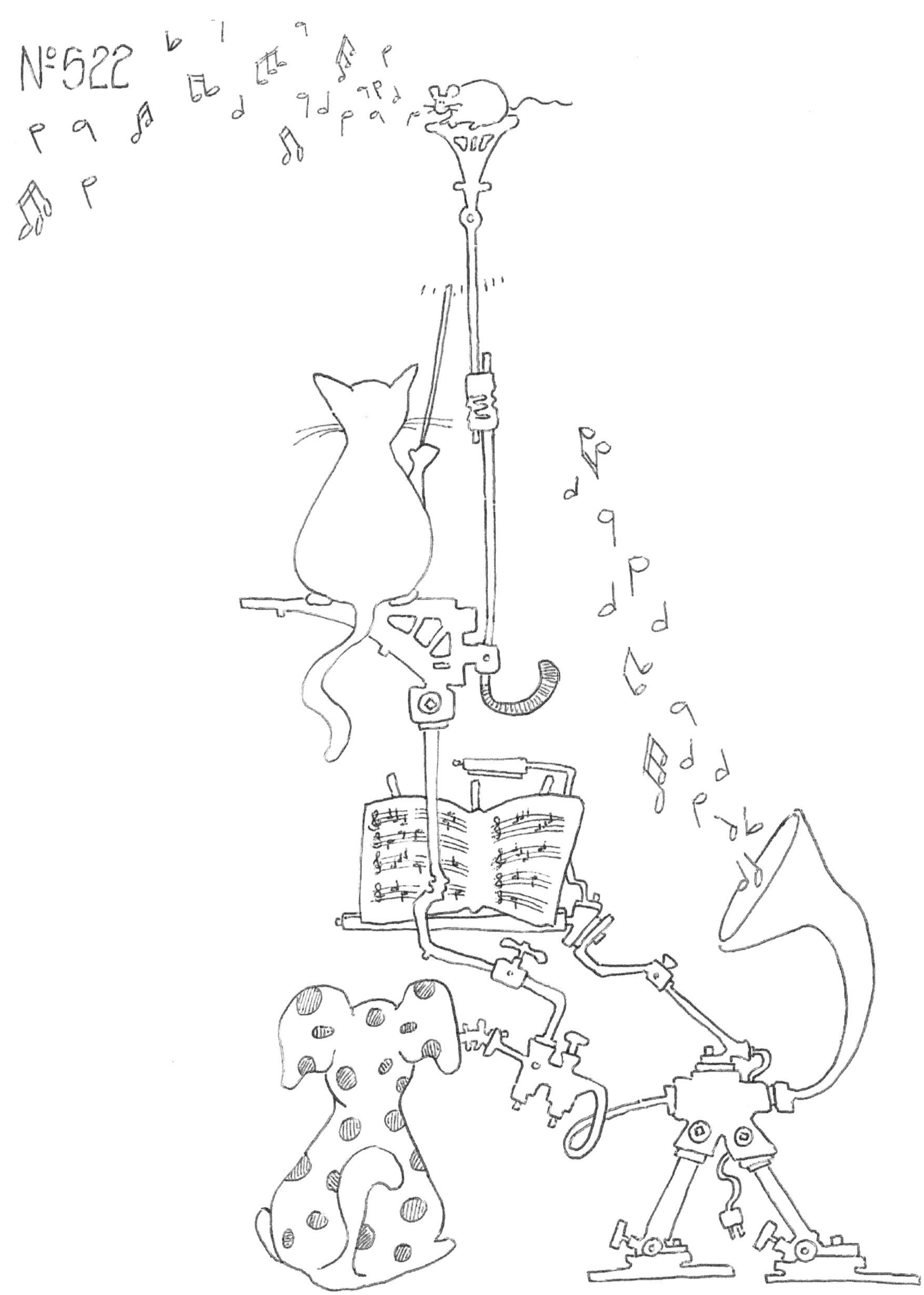
№522

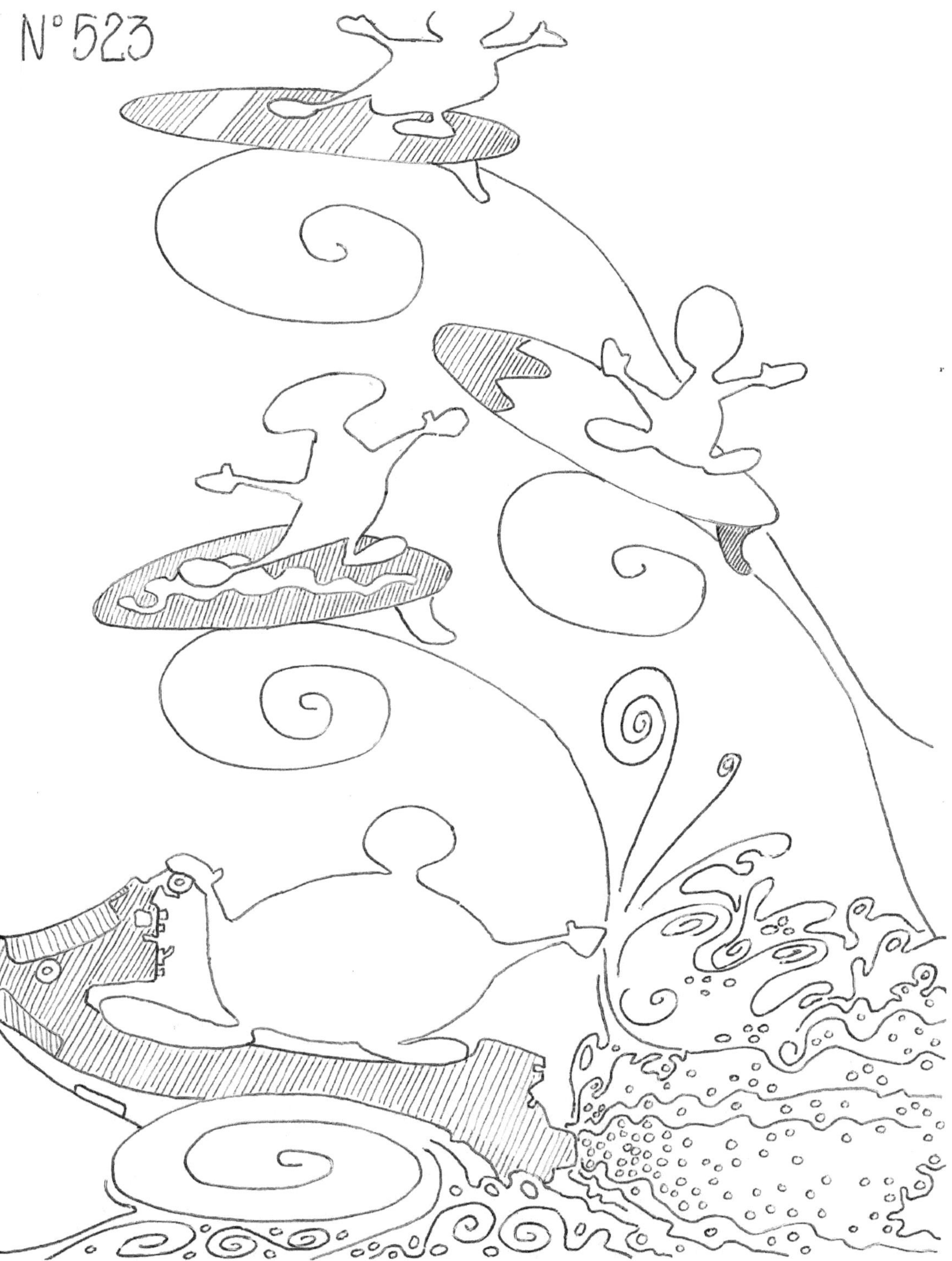
N°523

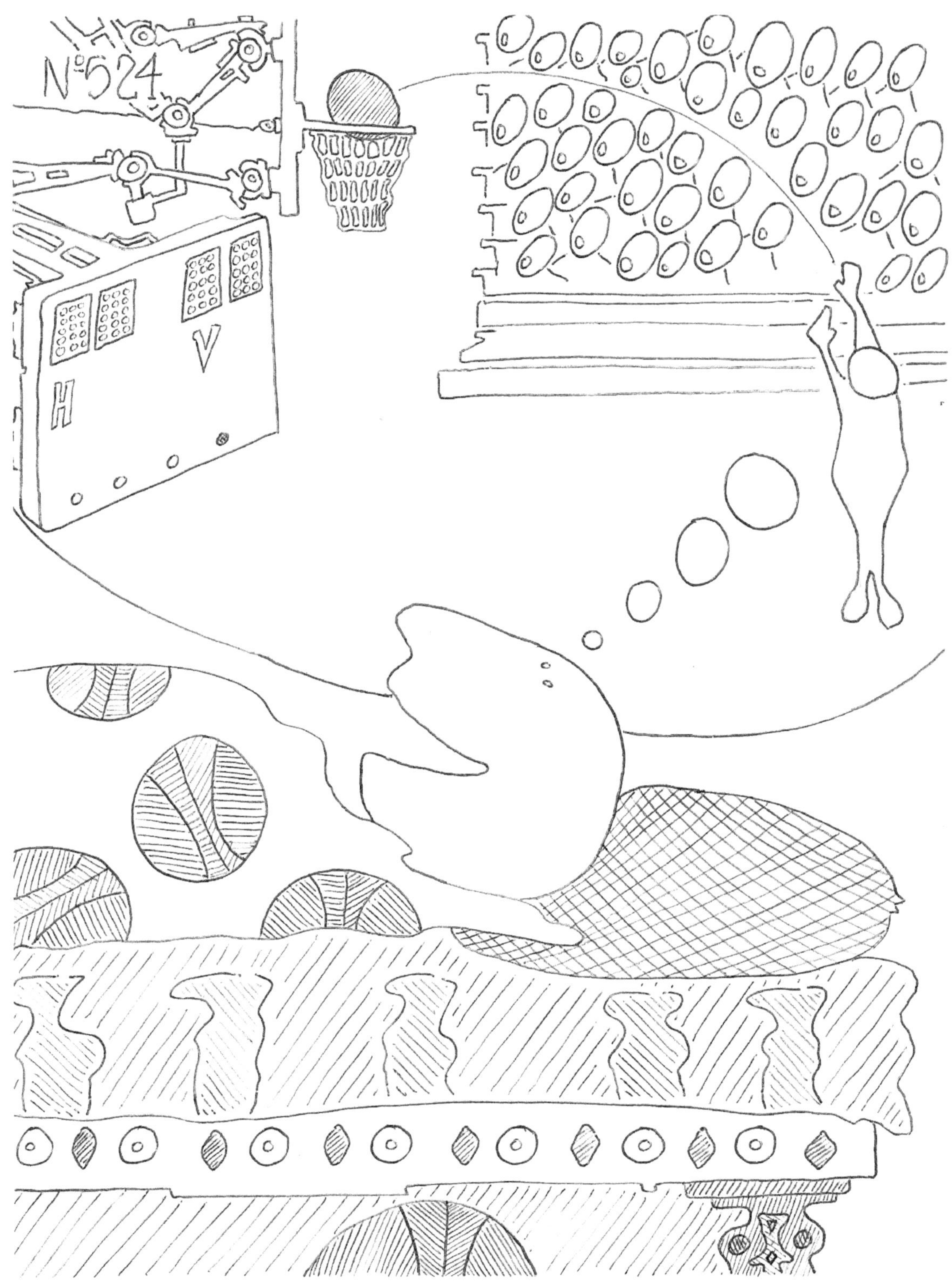
N°524
H
V

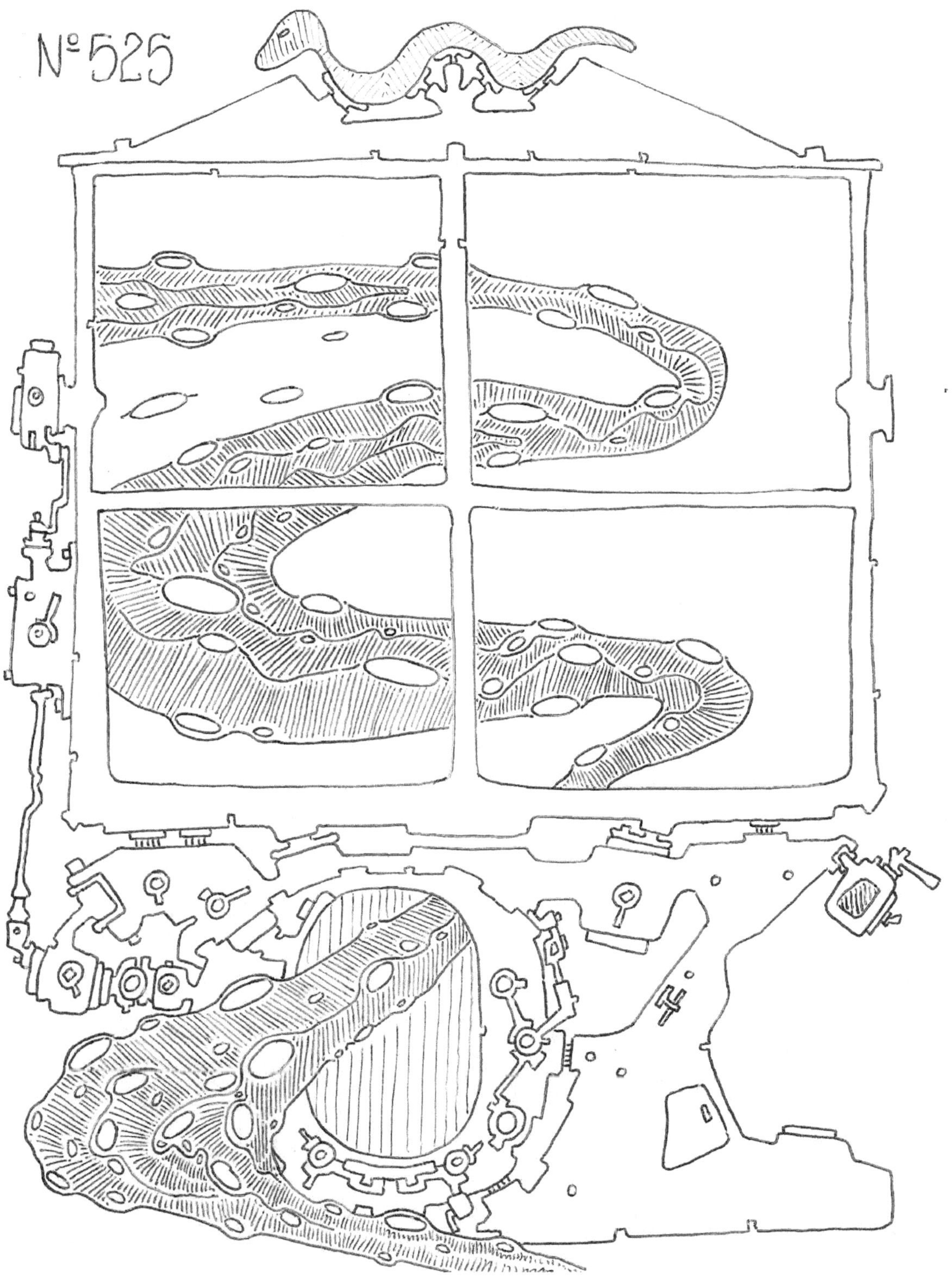
Nº 525

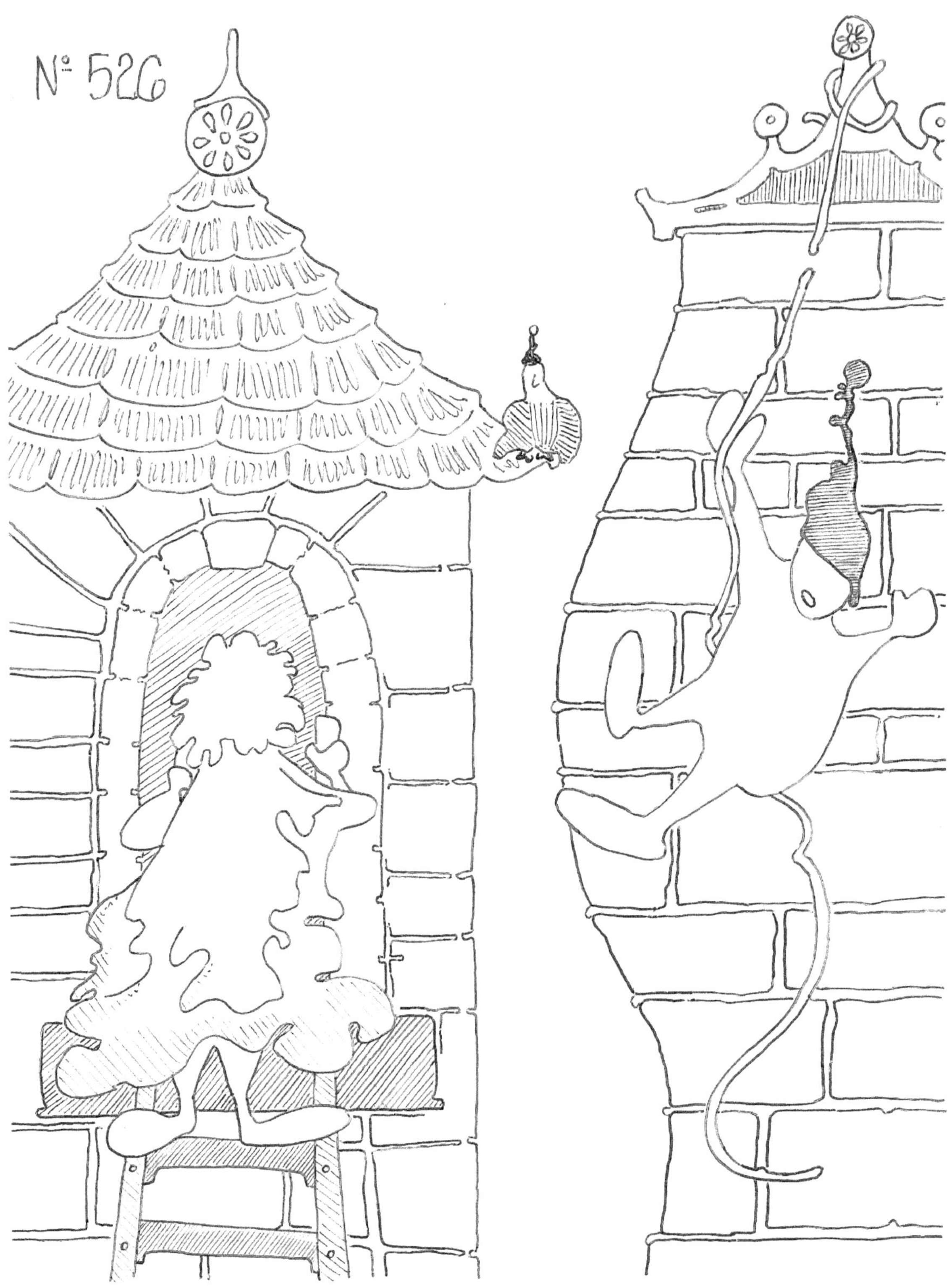
№ 526

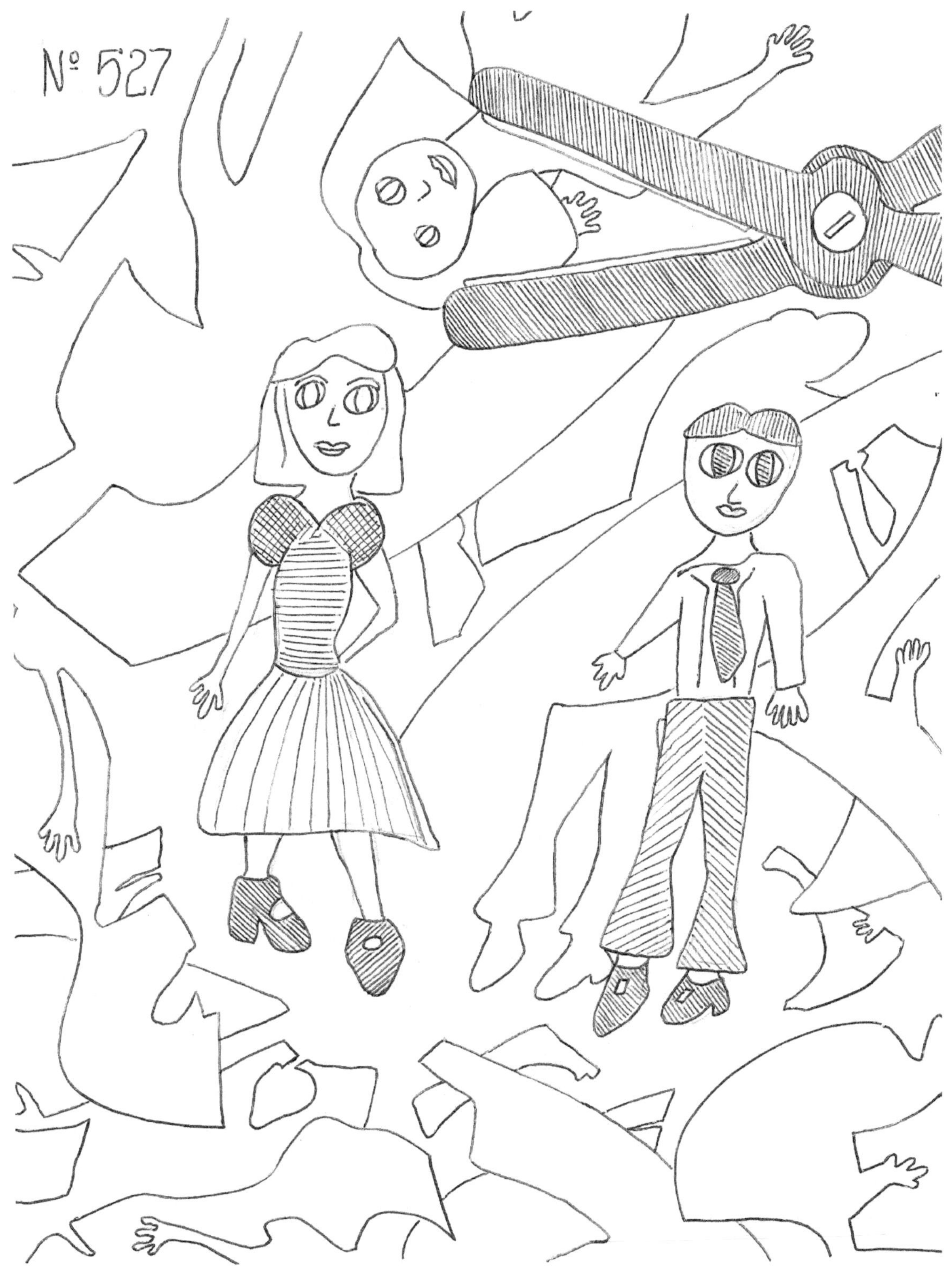

№ 527

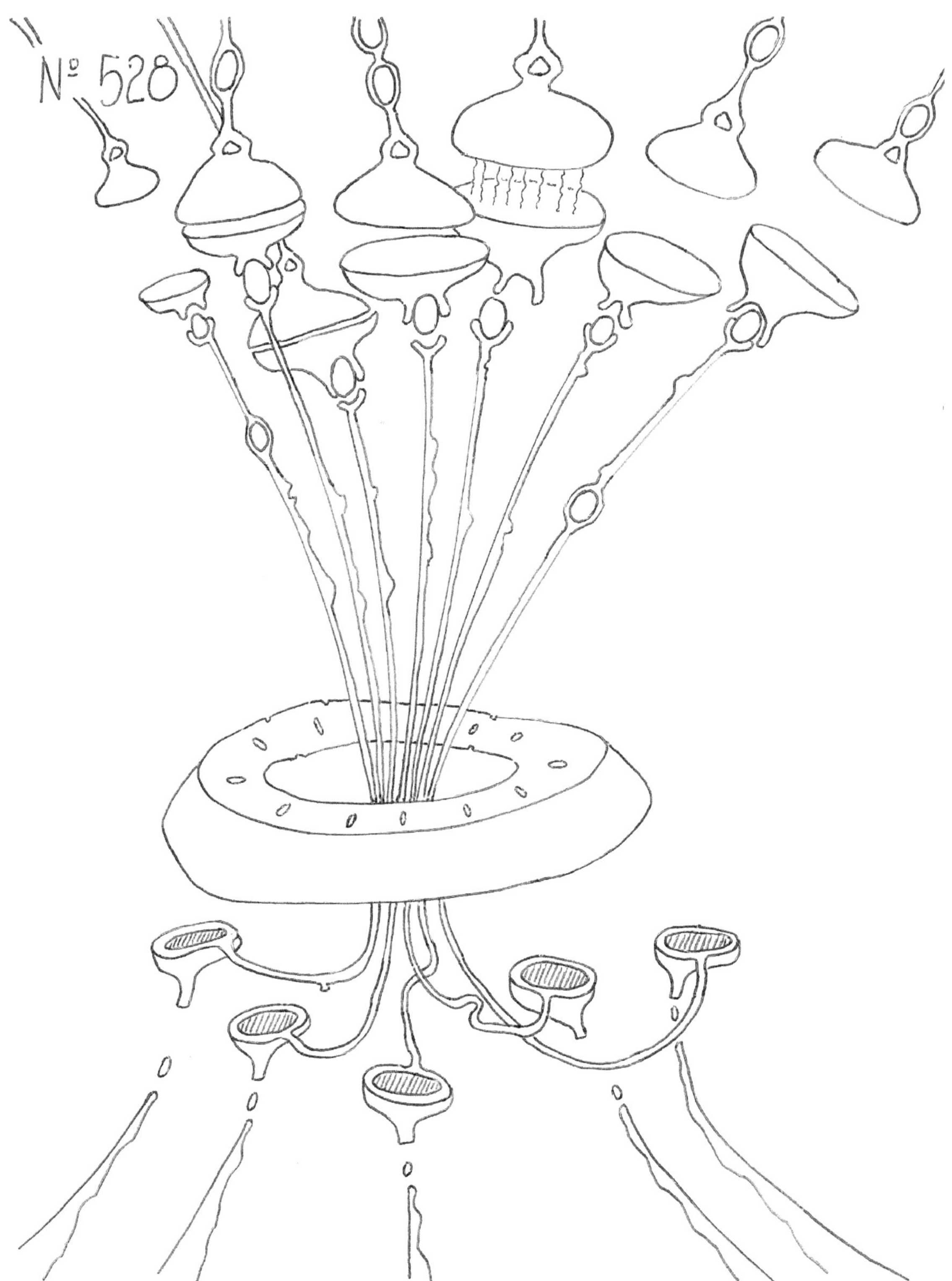

№ 528

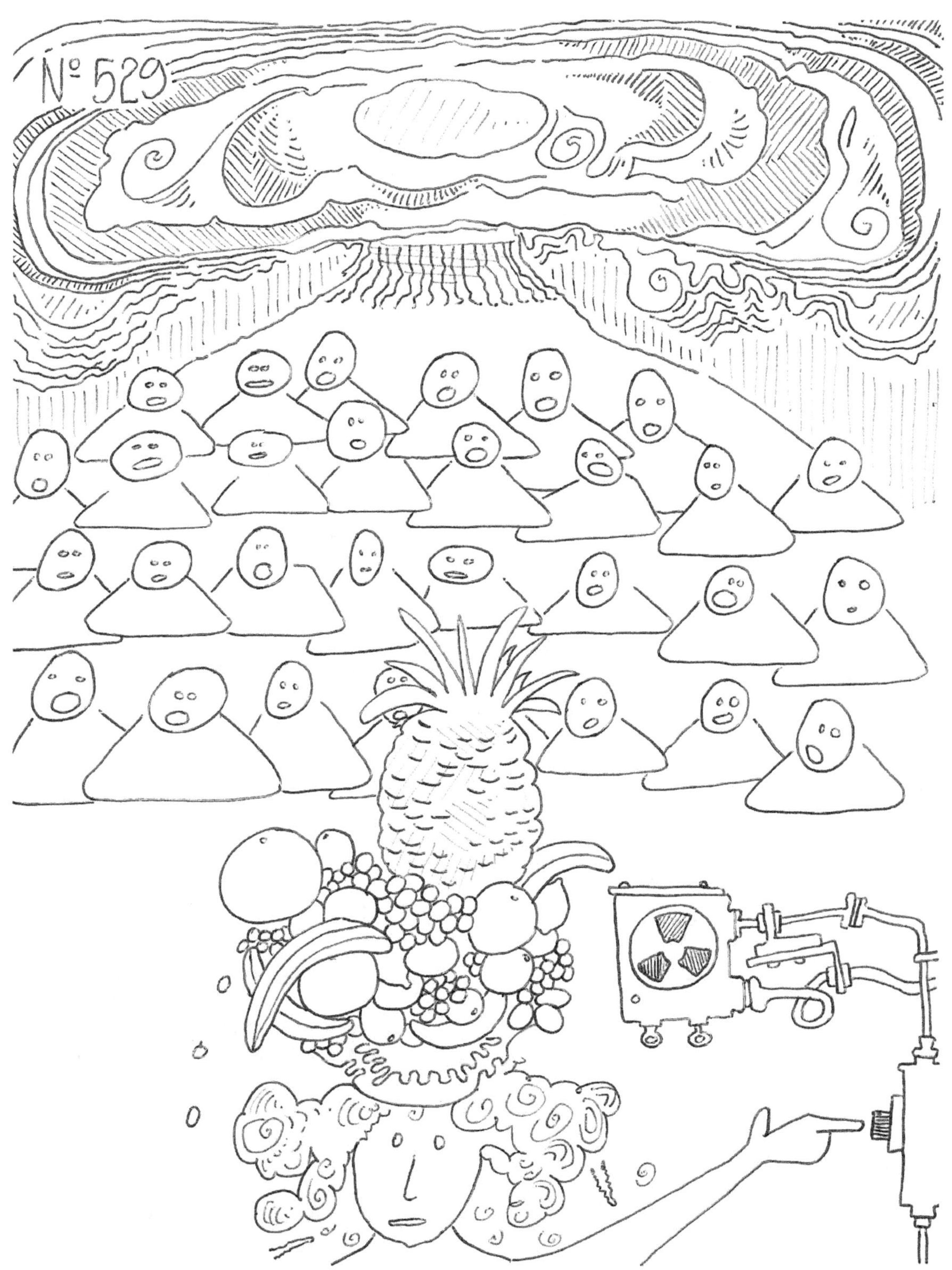
Nº 529

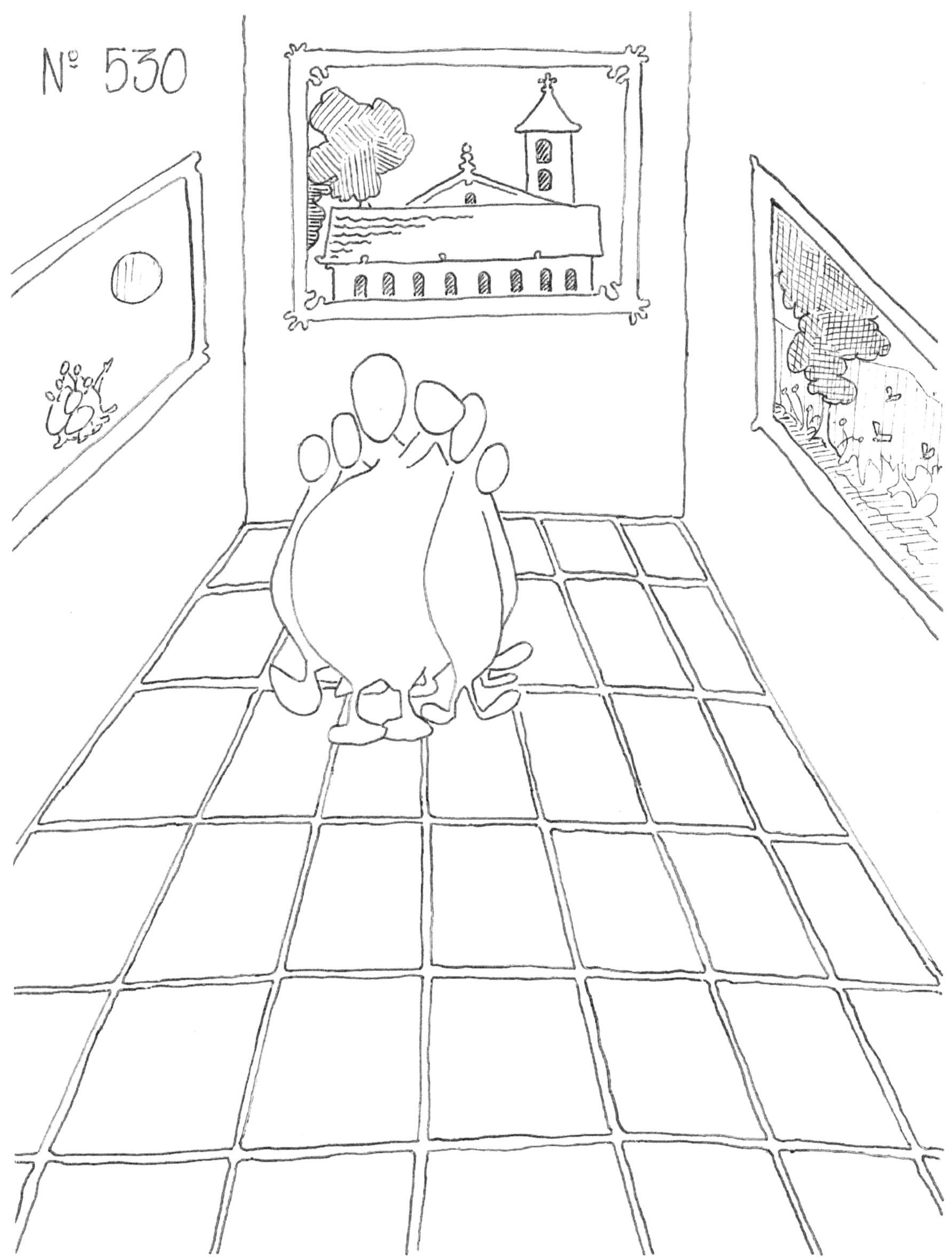
Nº 530

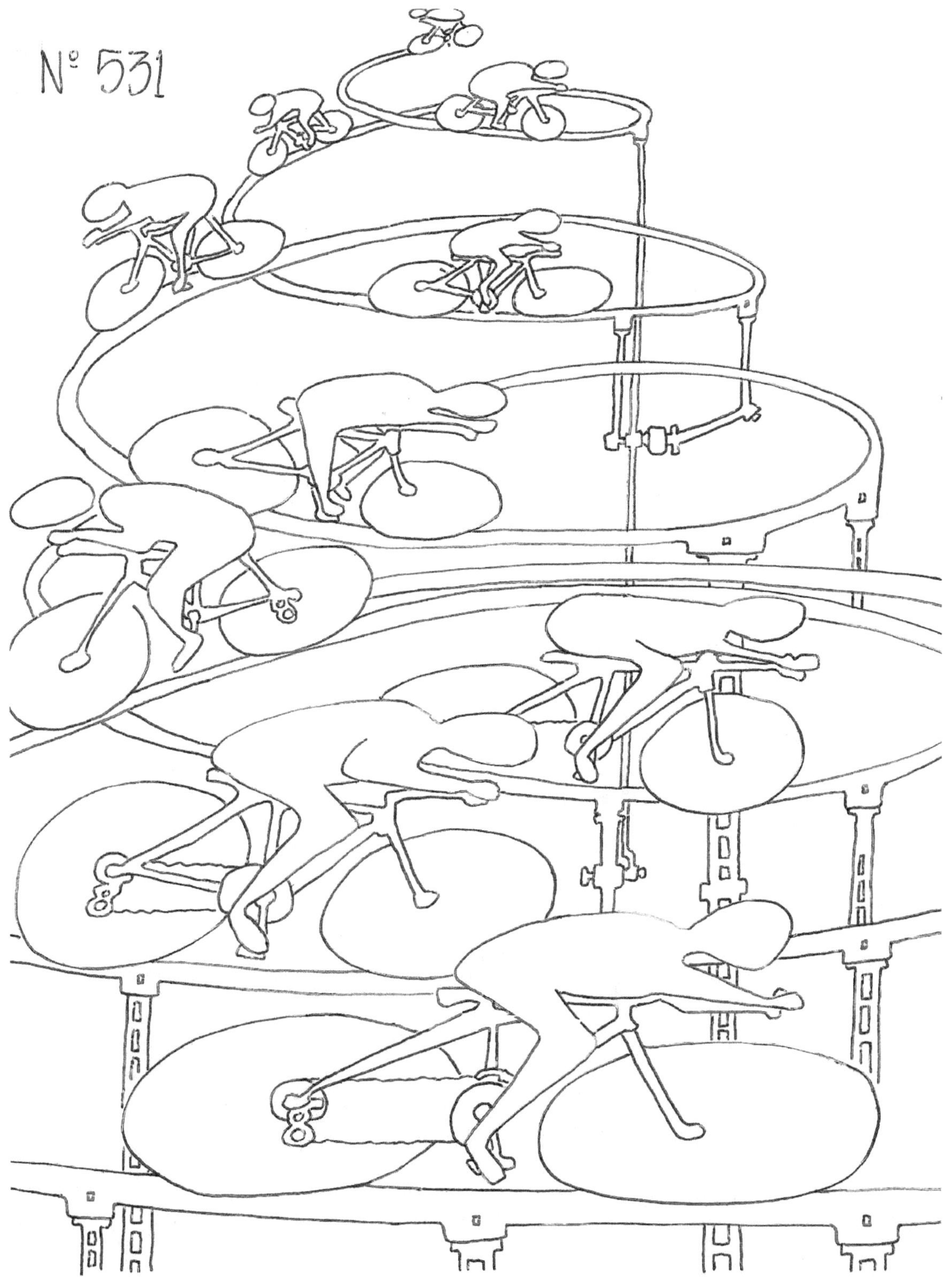
Nº 531

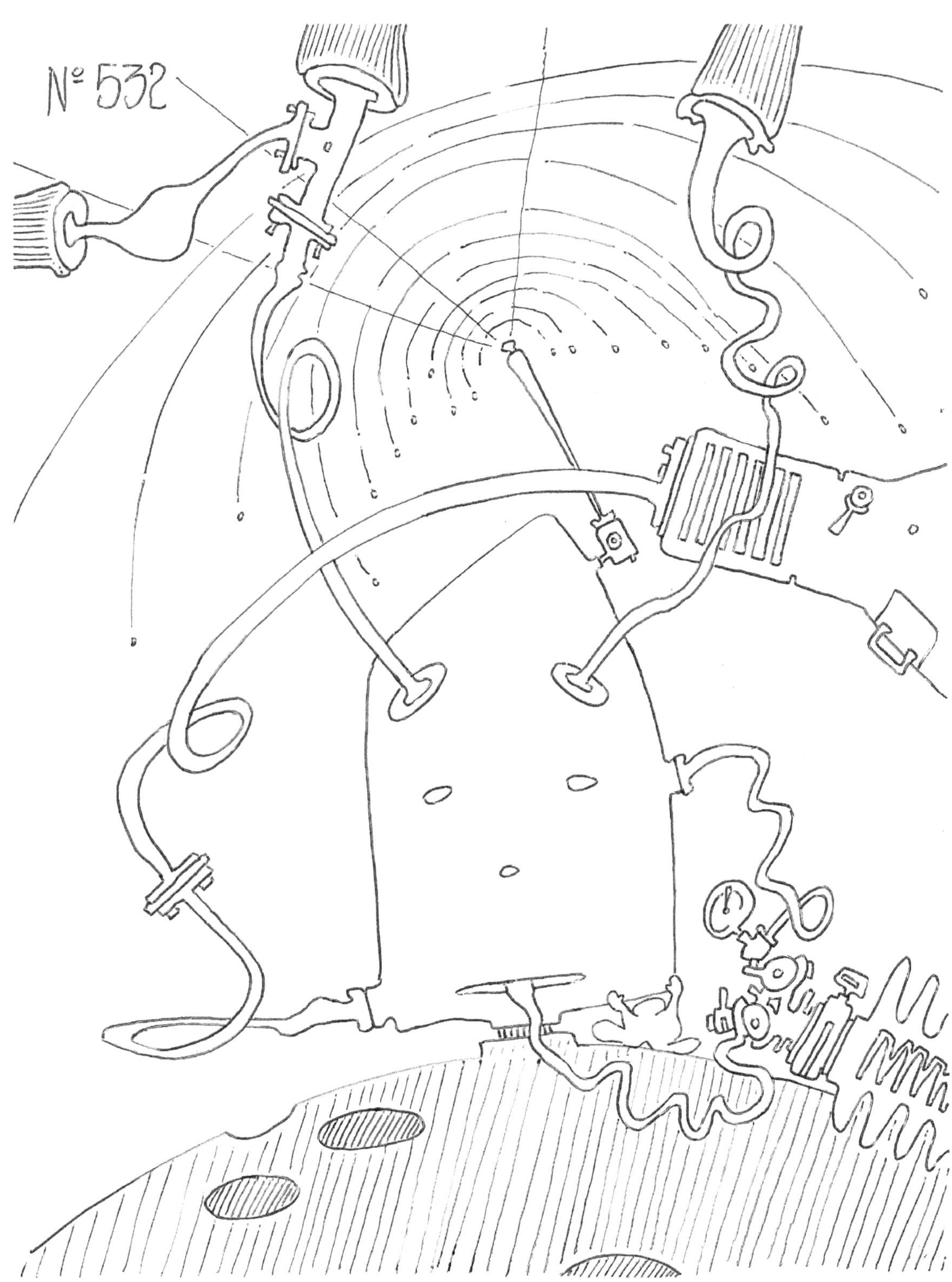
Nº 532

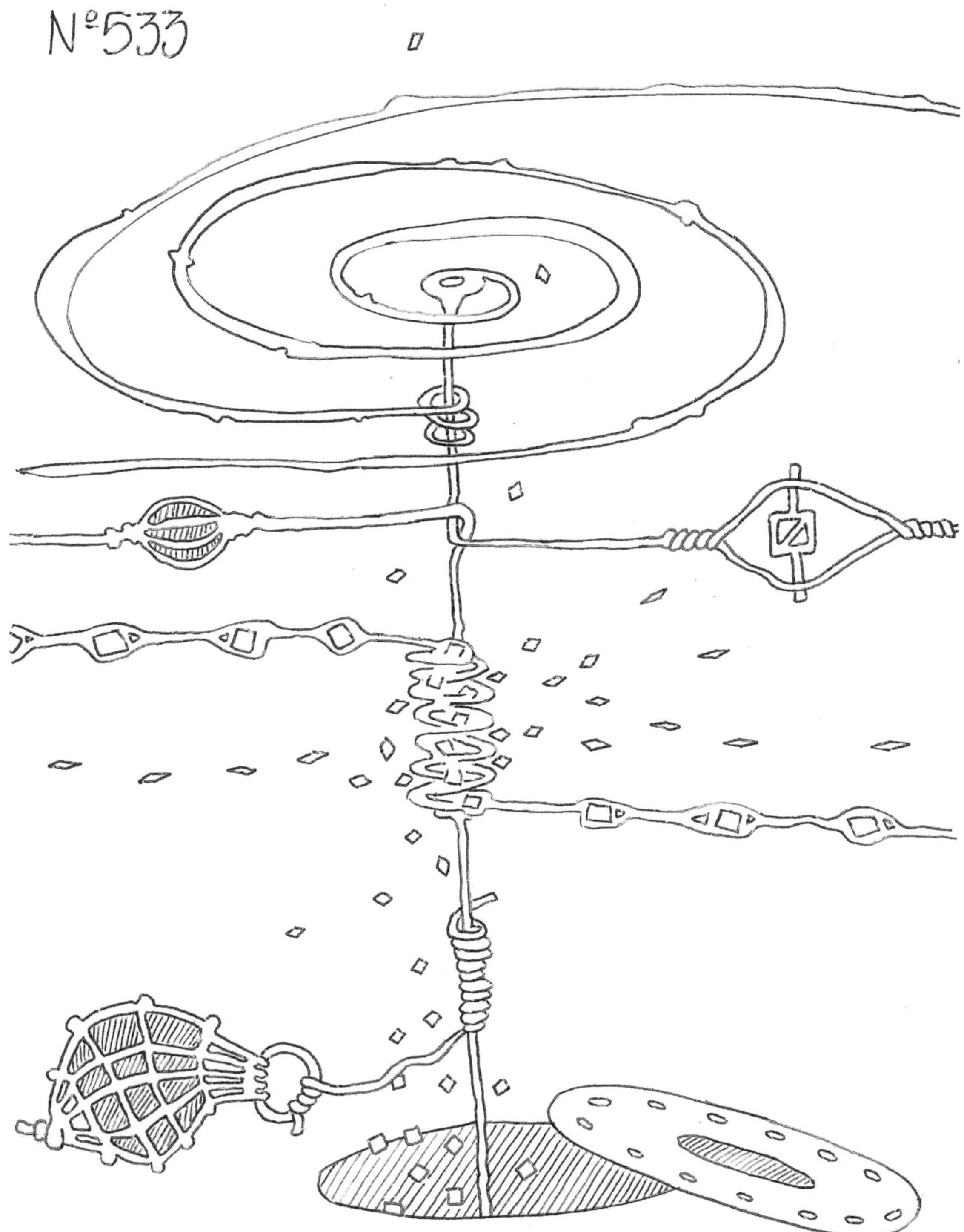
Nº533

Nº534

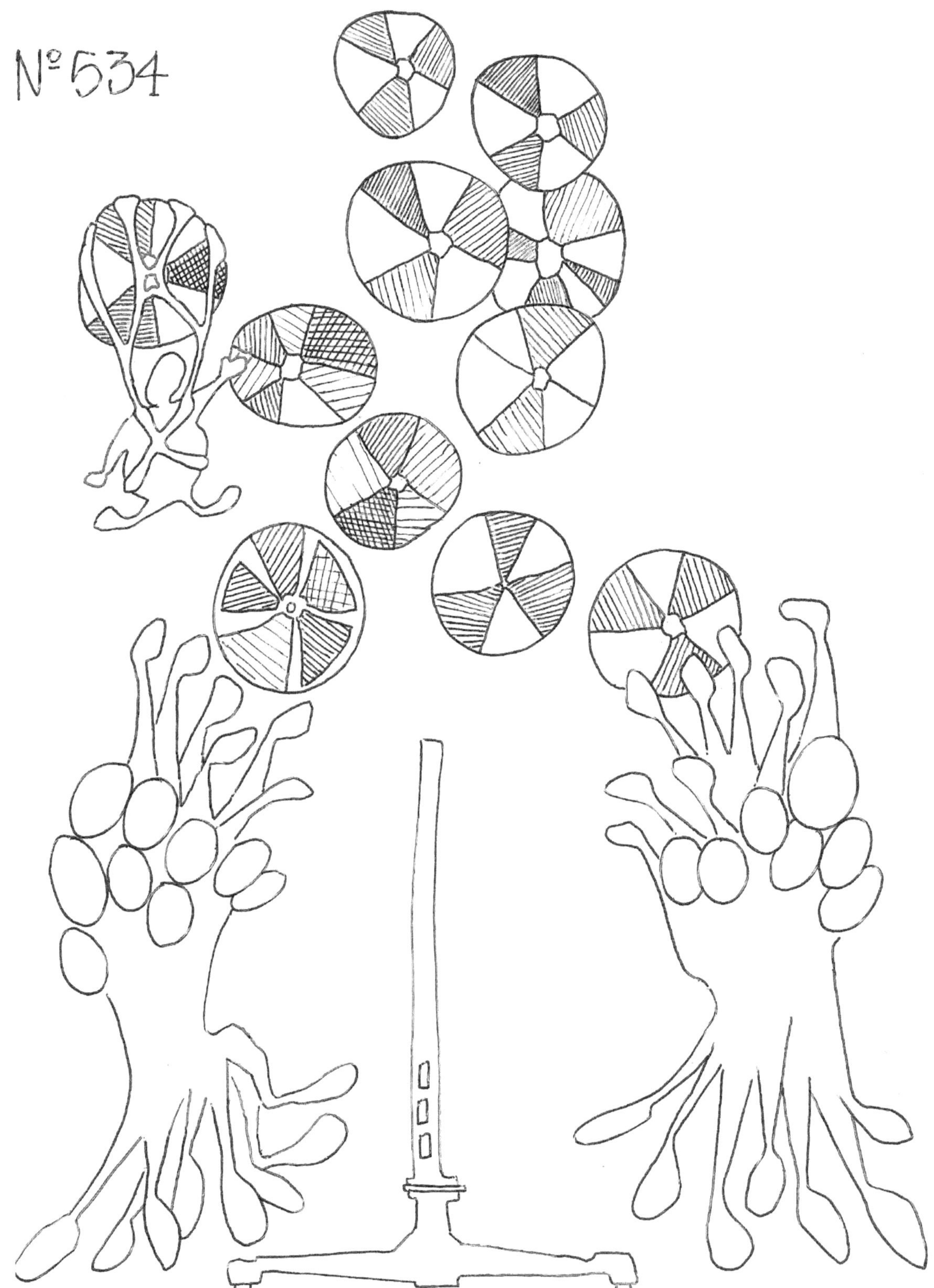

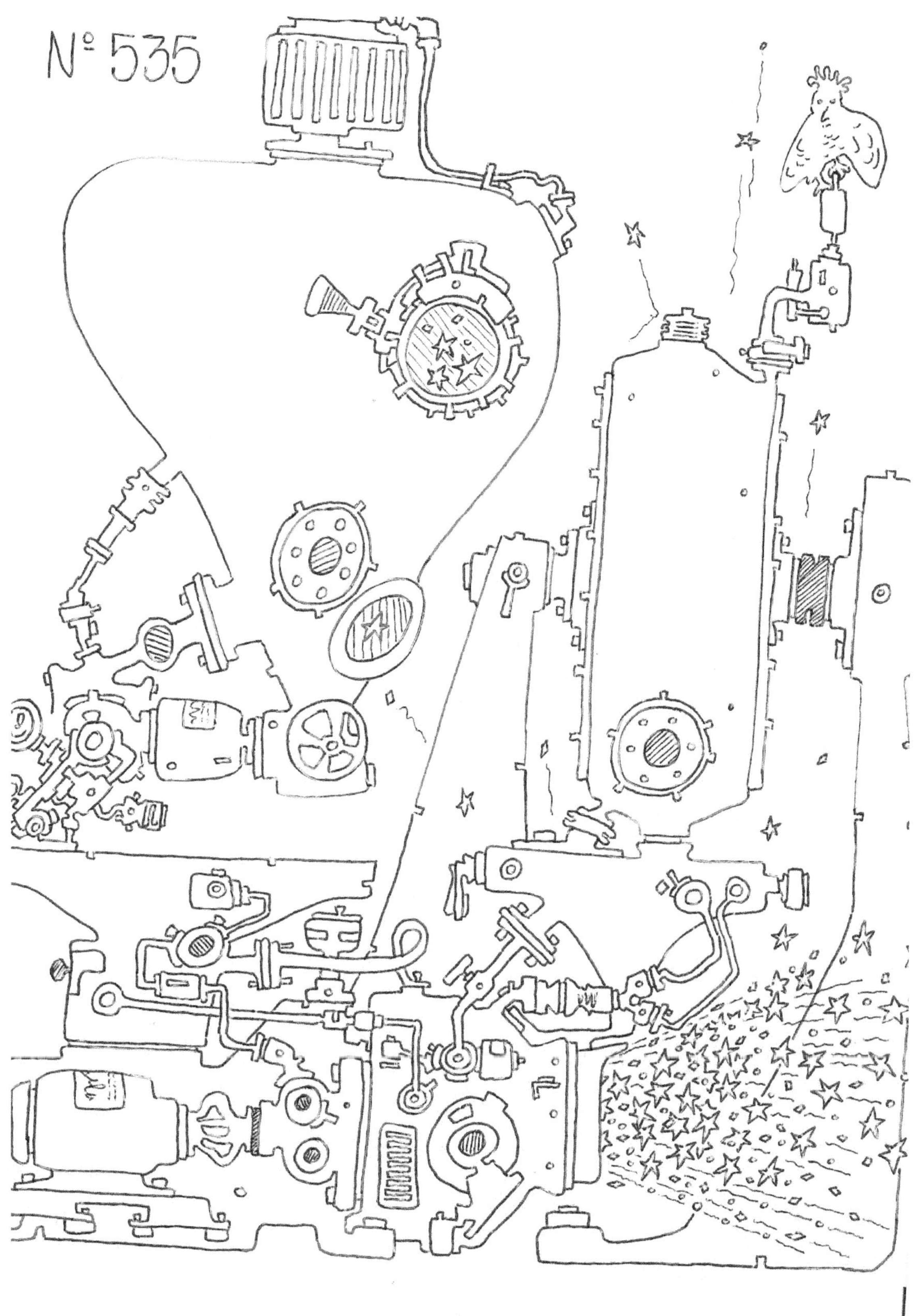
Nº 535

№ 536

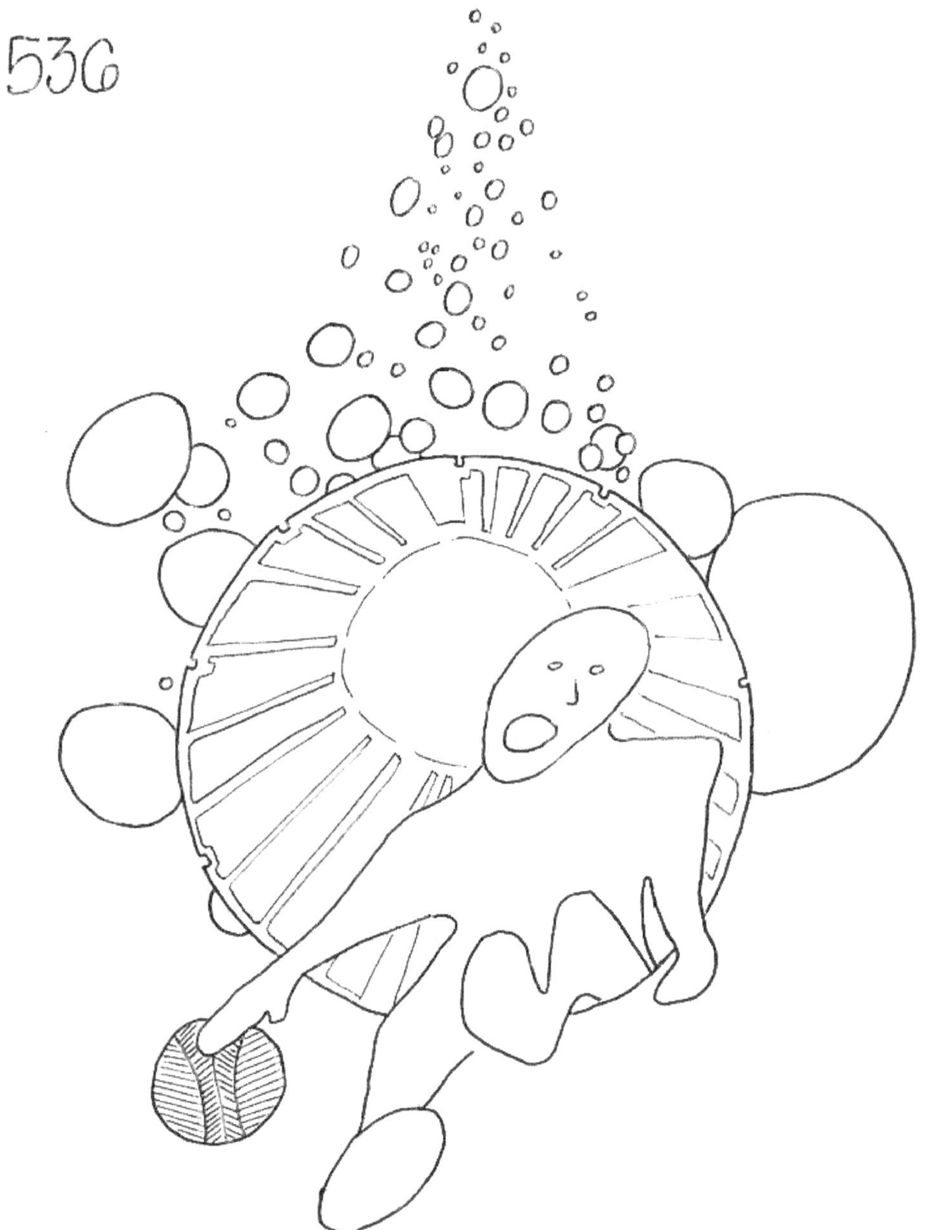

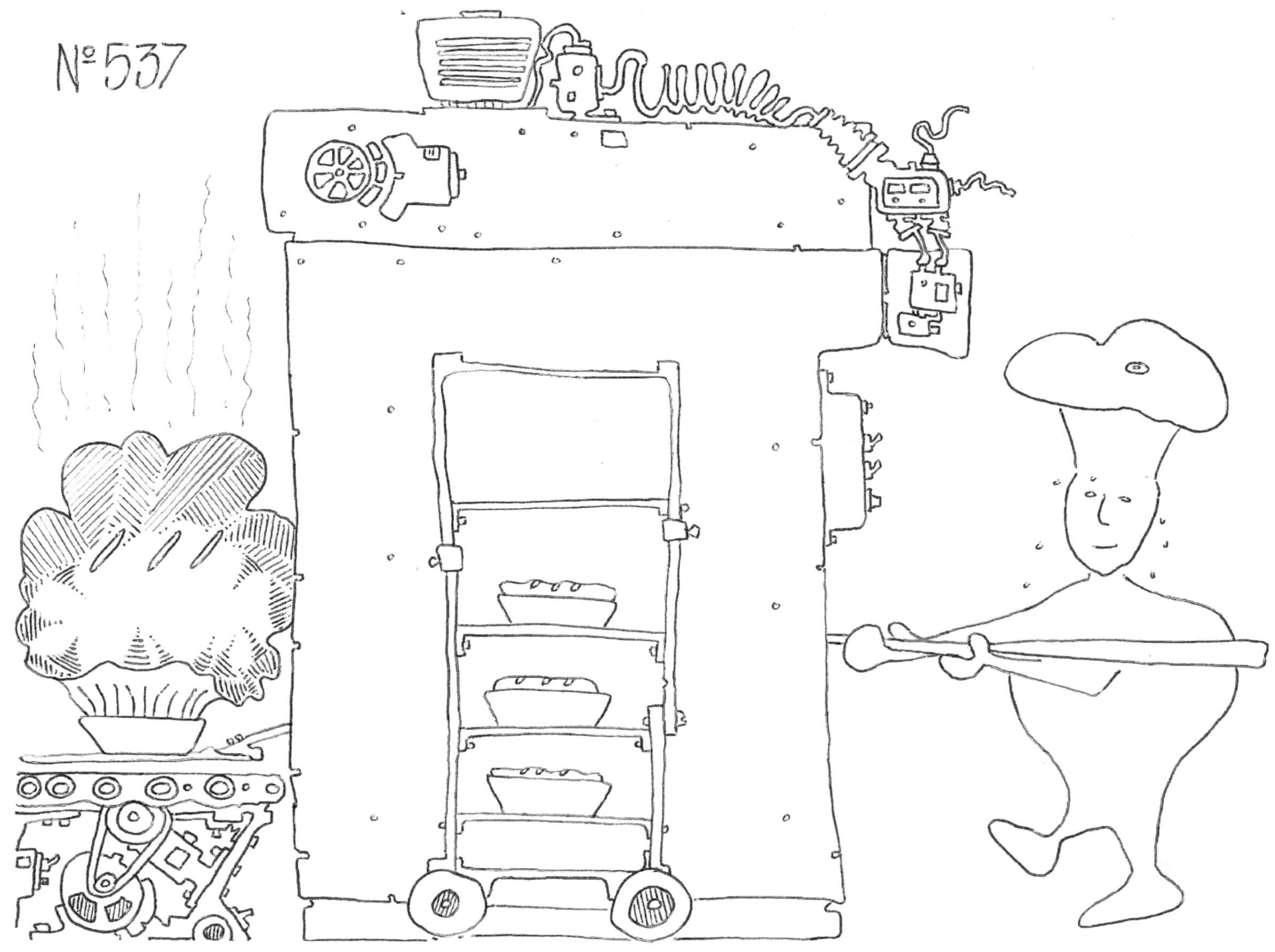
№537

№ 538

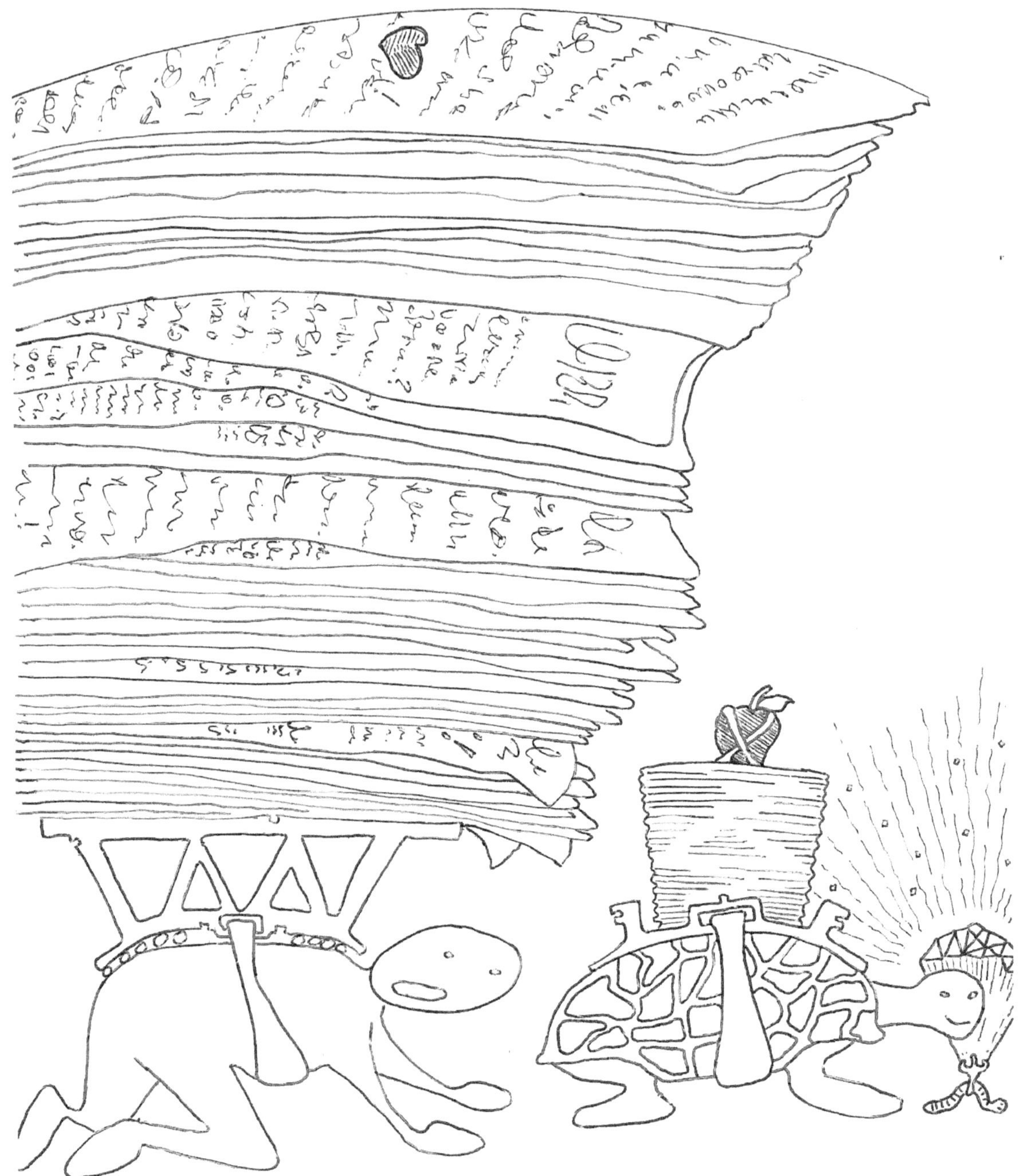

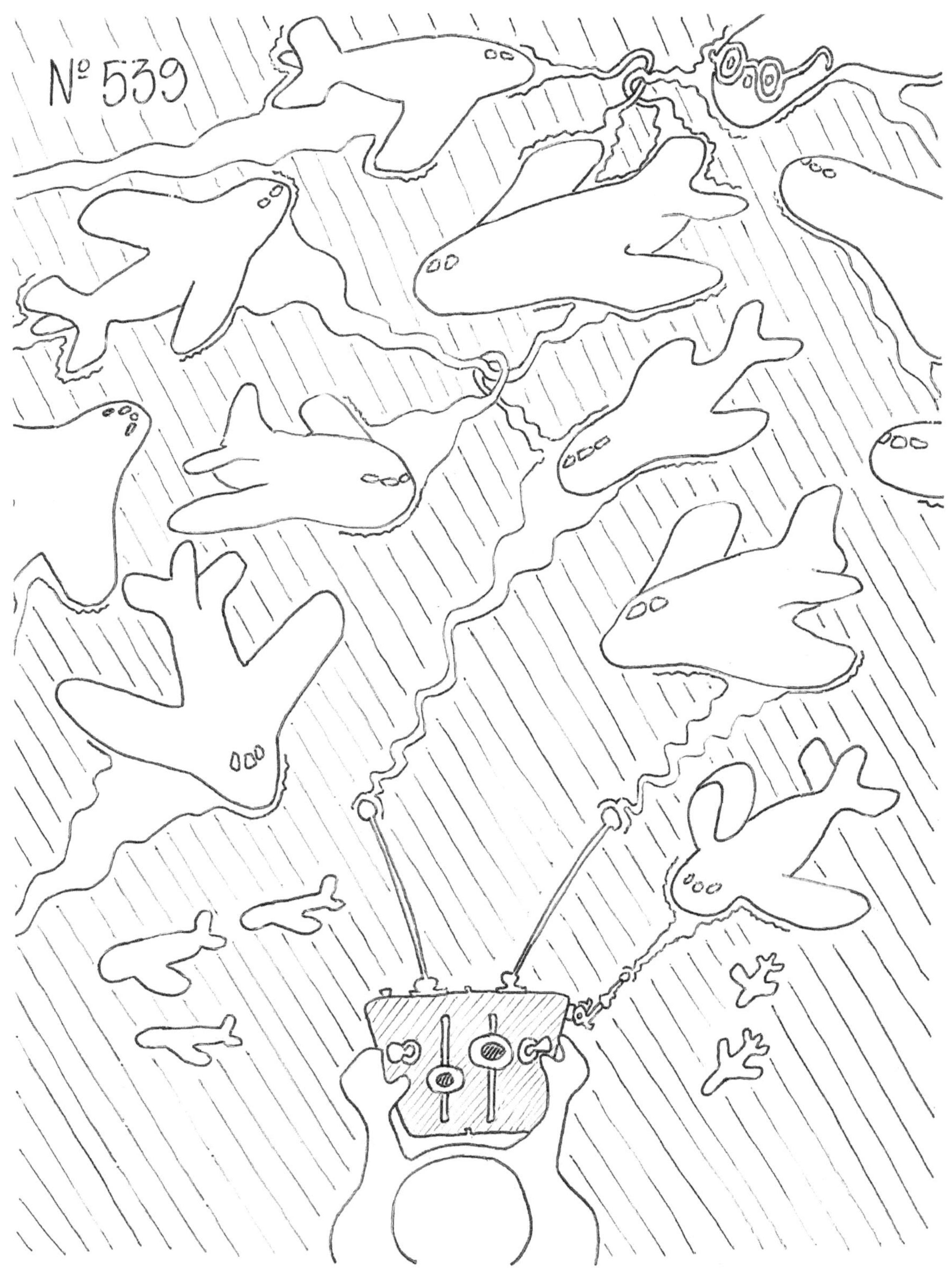
№ 539

N°540

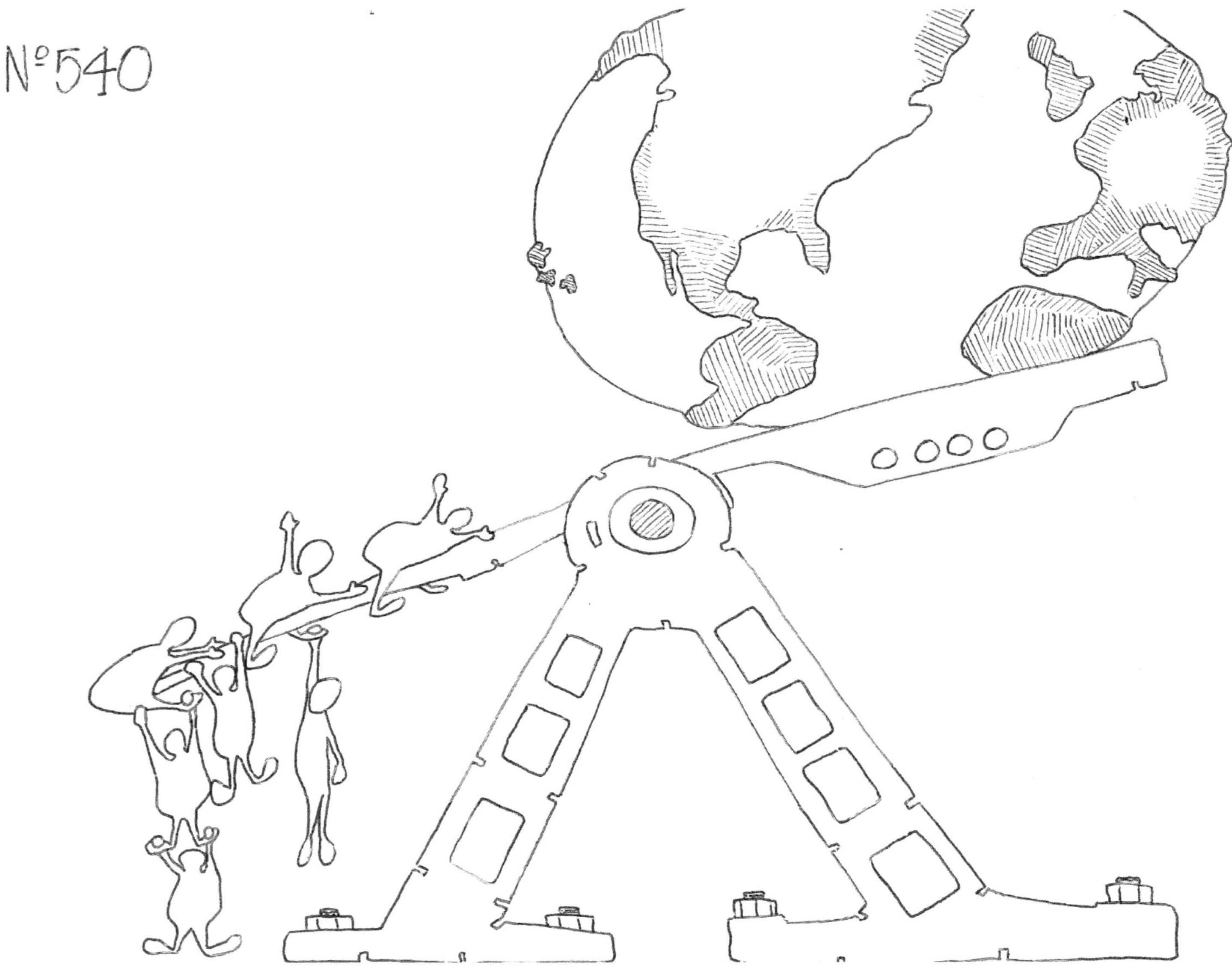

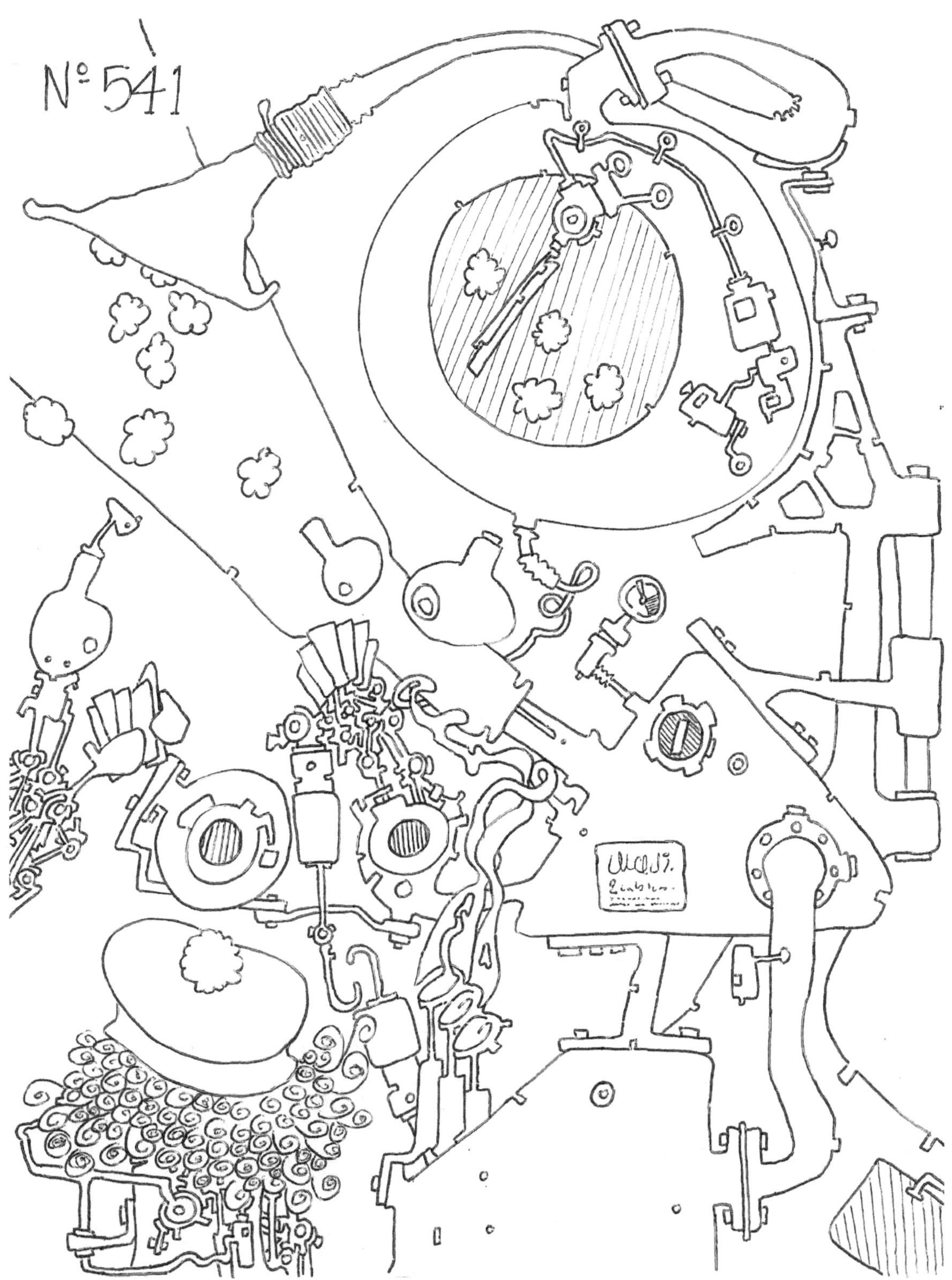
Nº 541

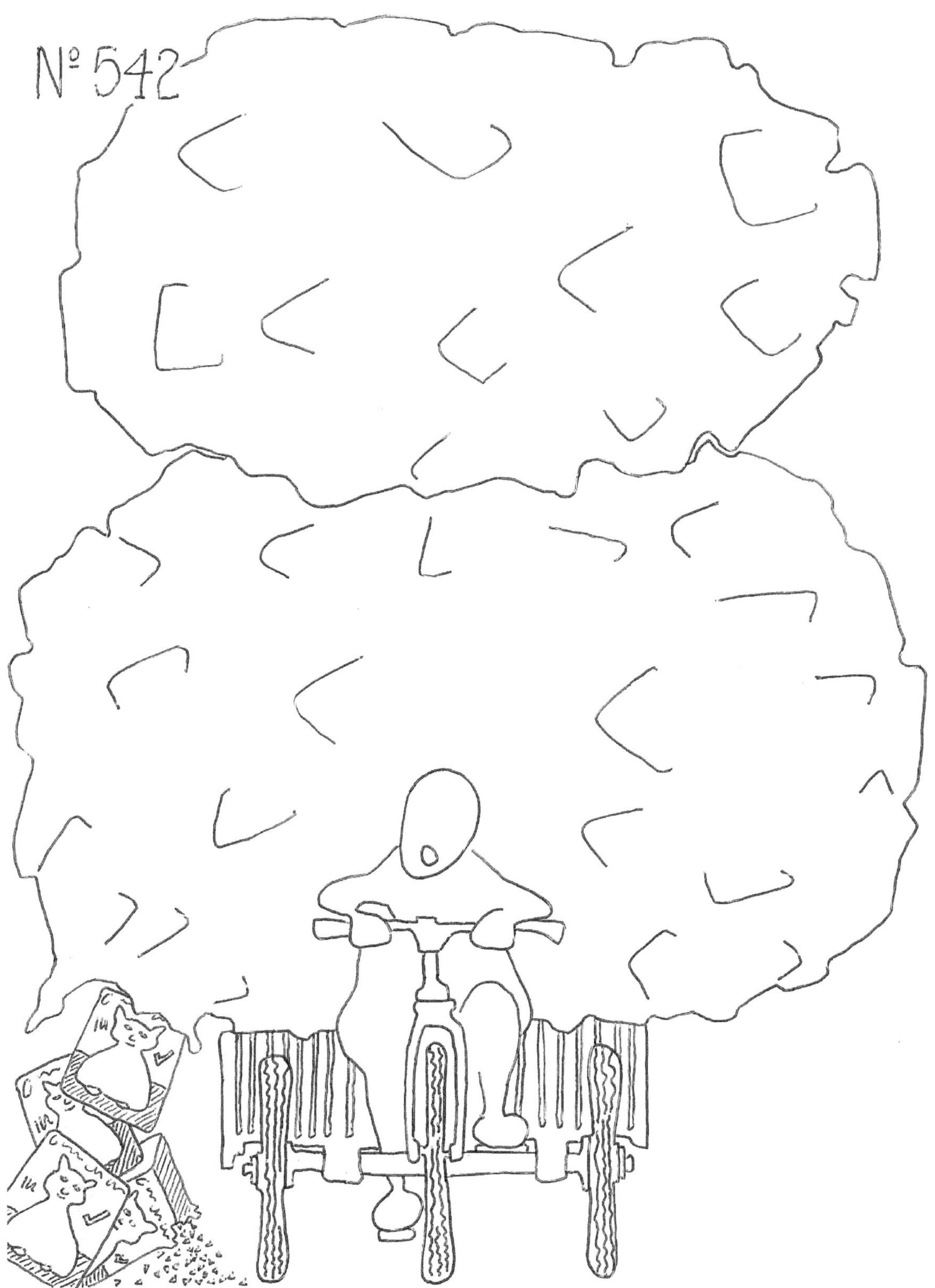
Nº 542

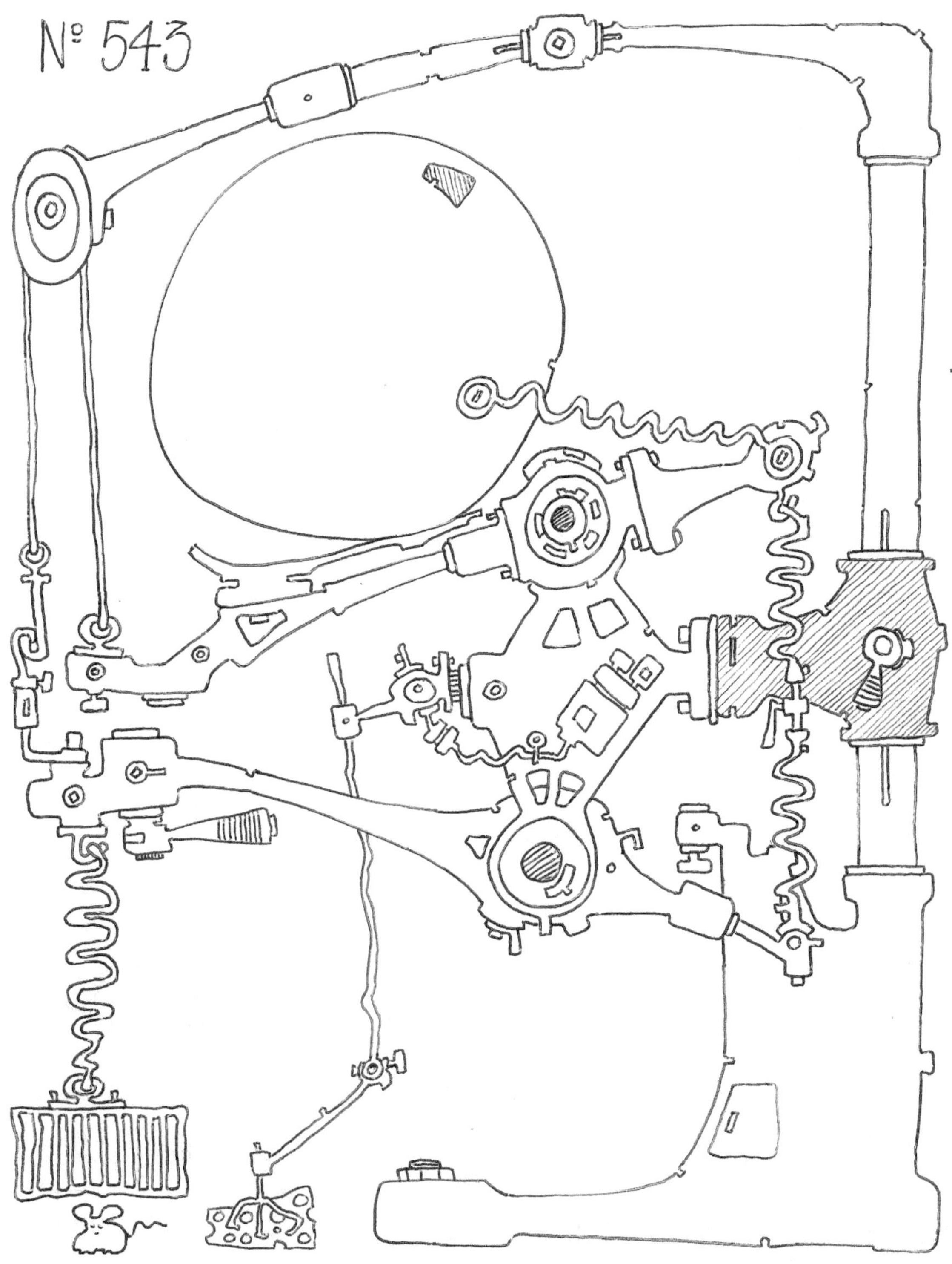
№ 543

Nº 544

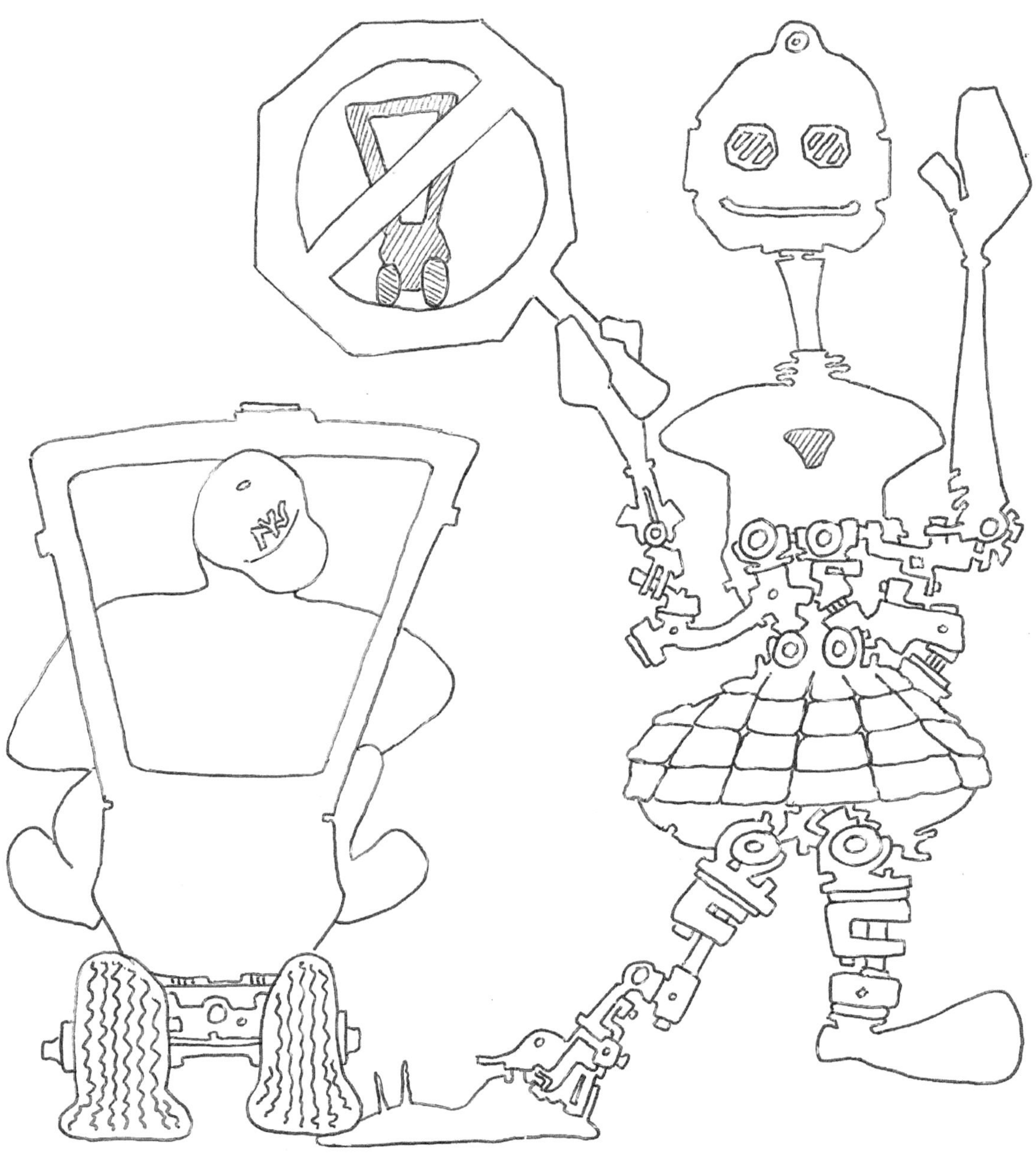

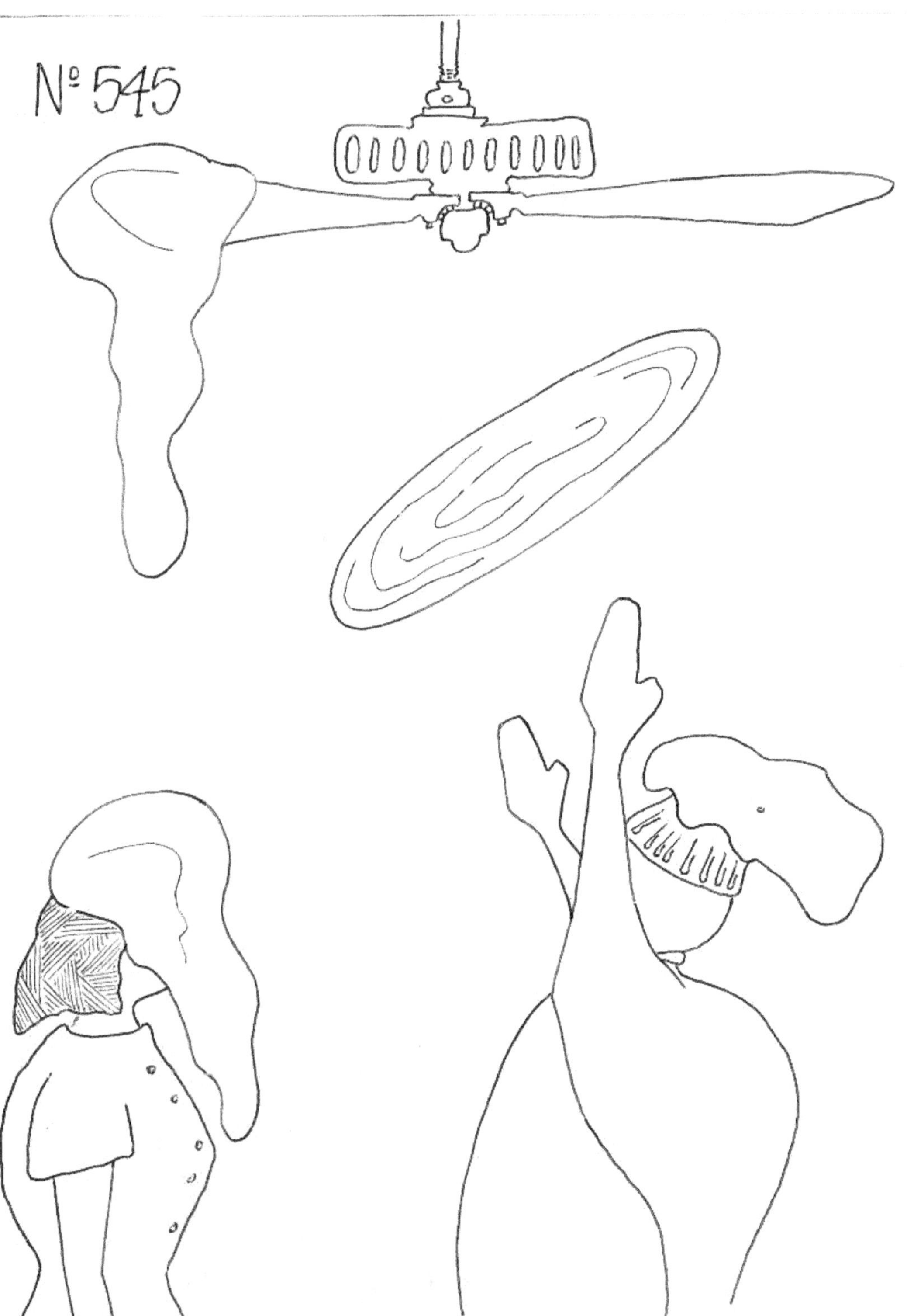
Nº 545

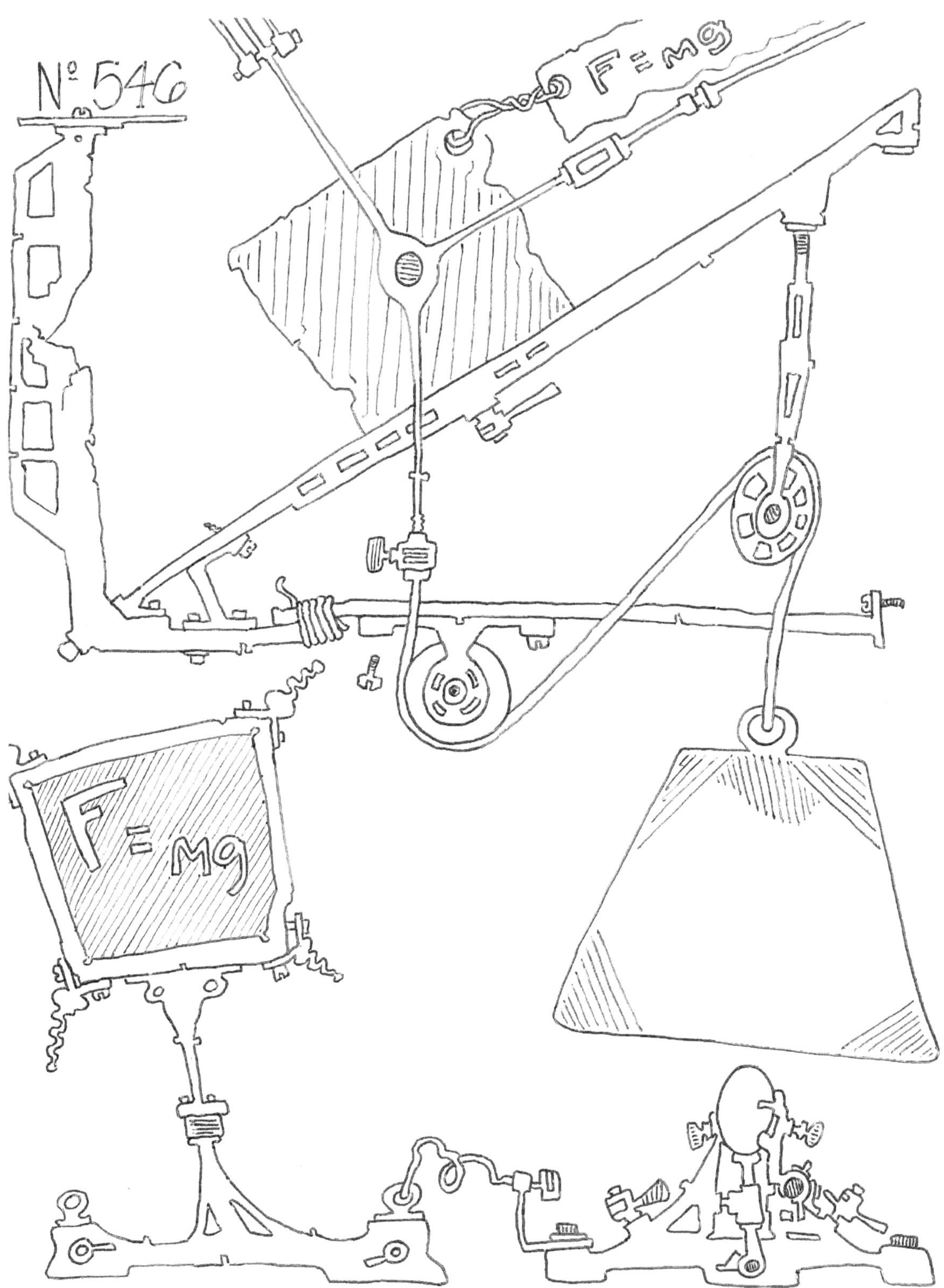

N°. 546
F = mg
F = mg

№ 547

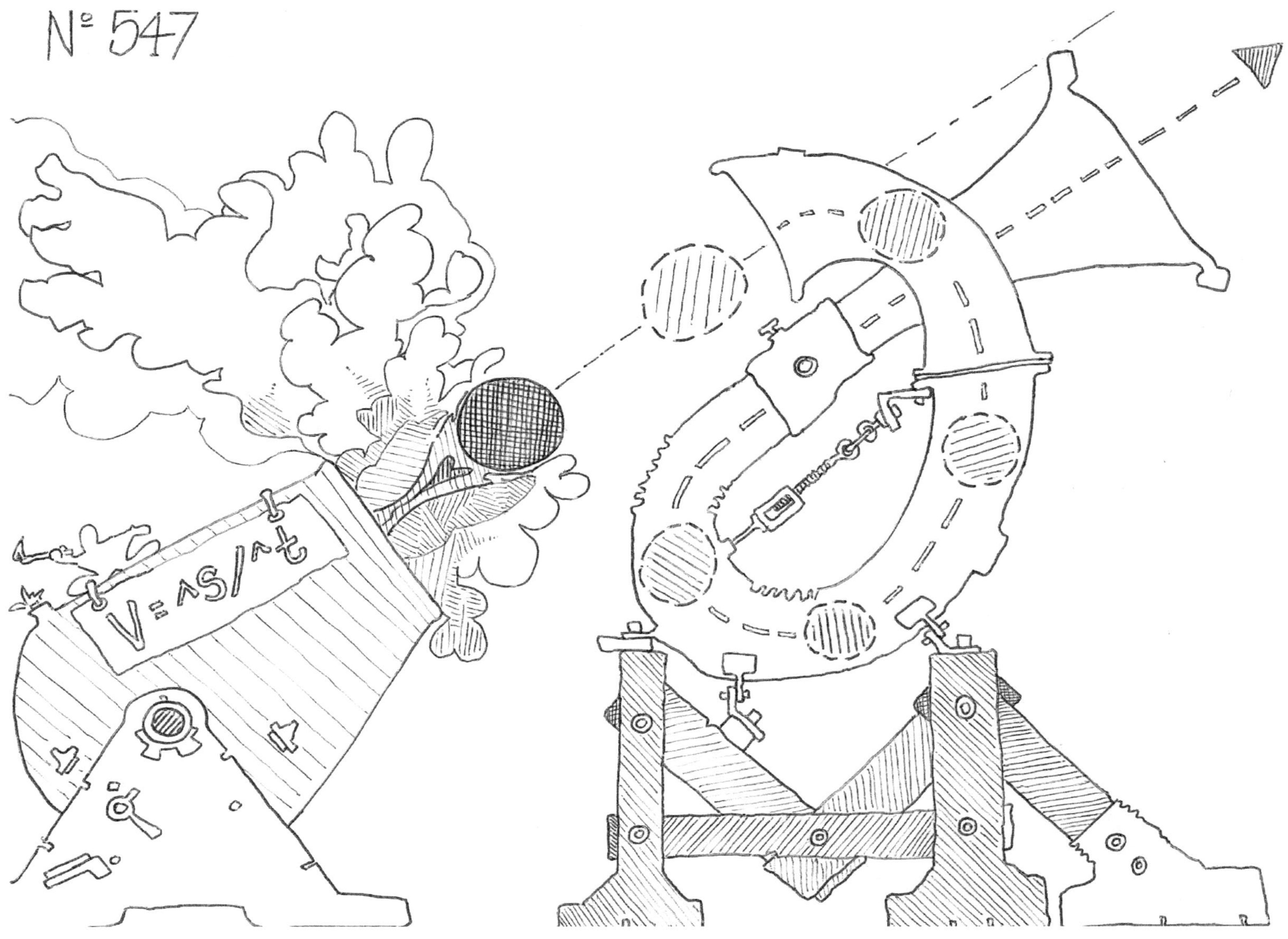

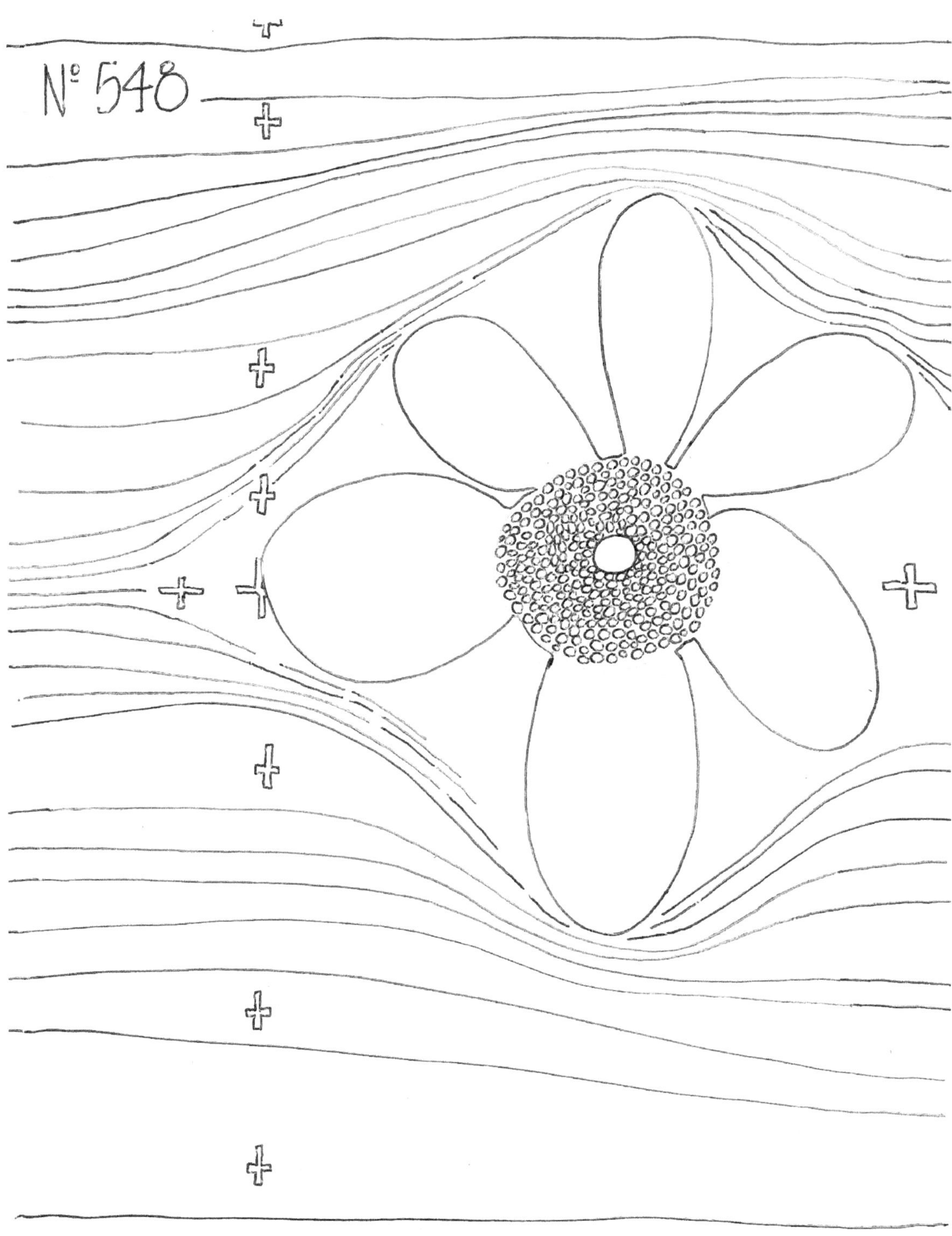
Nº 548

№549

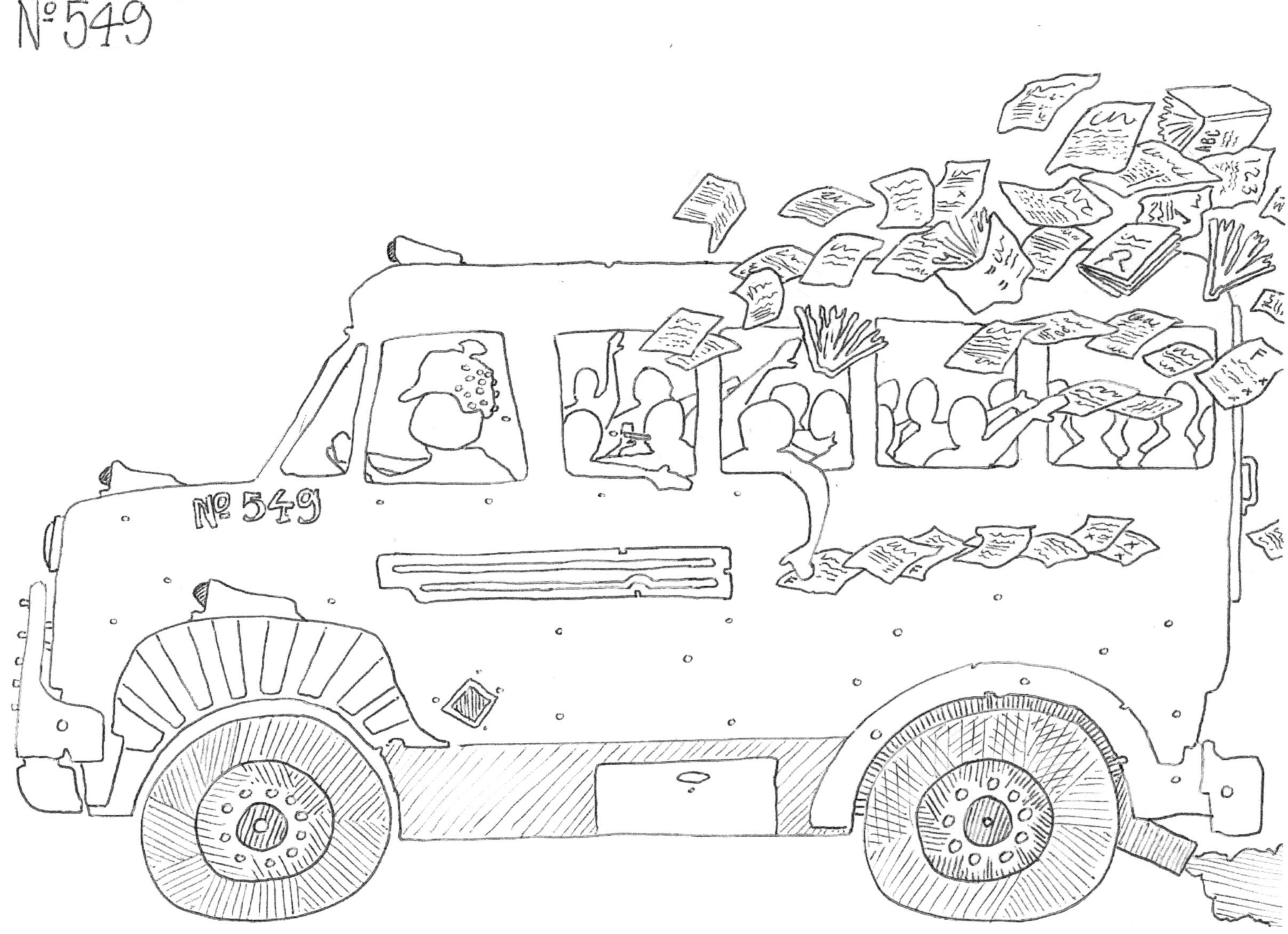

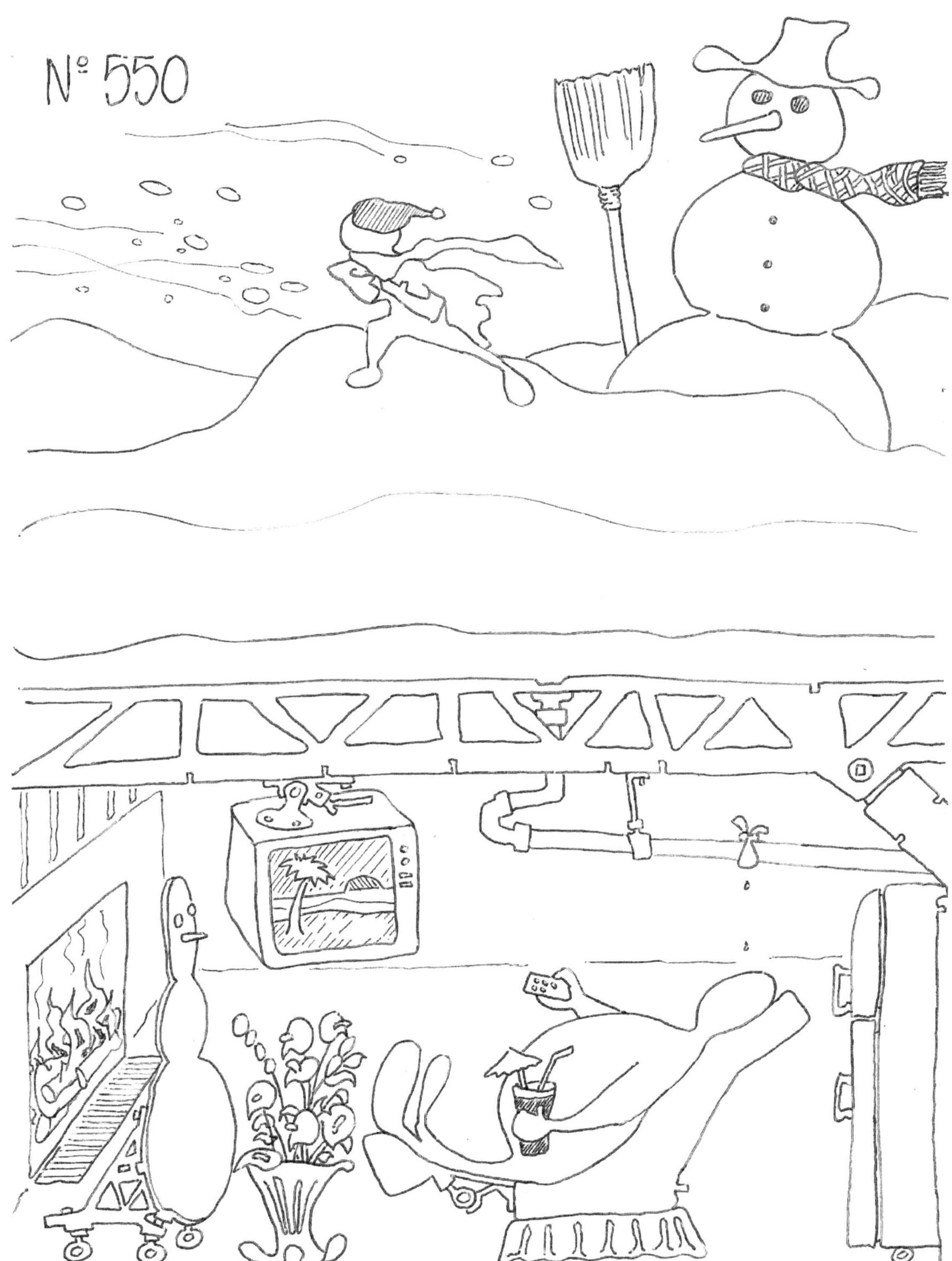
№ 550

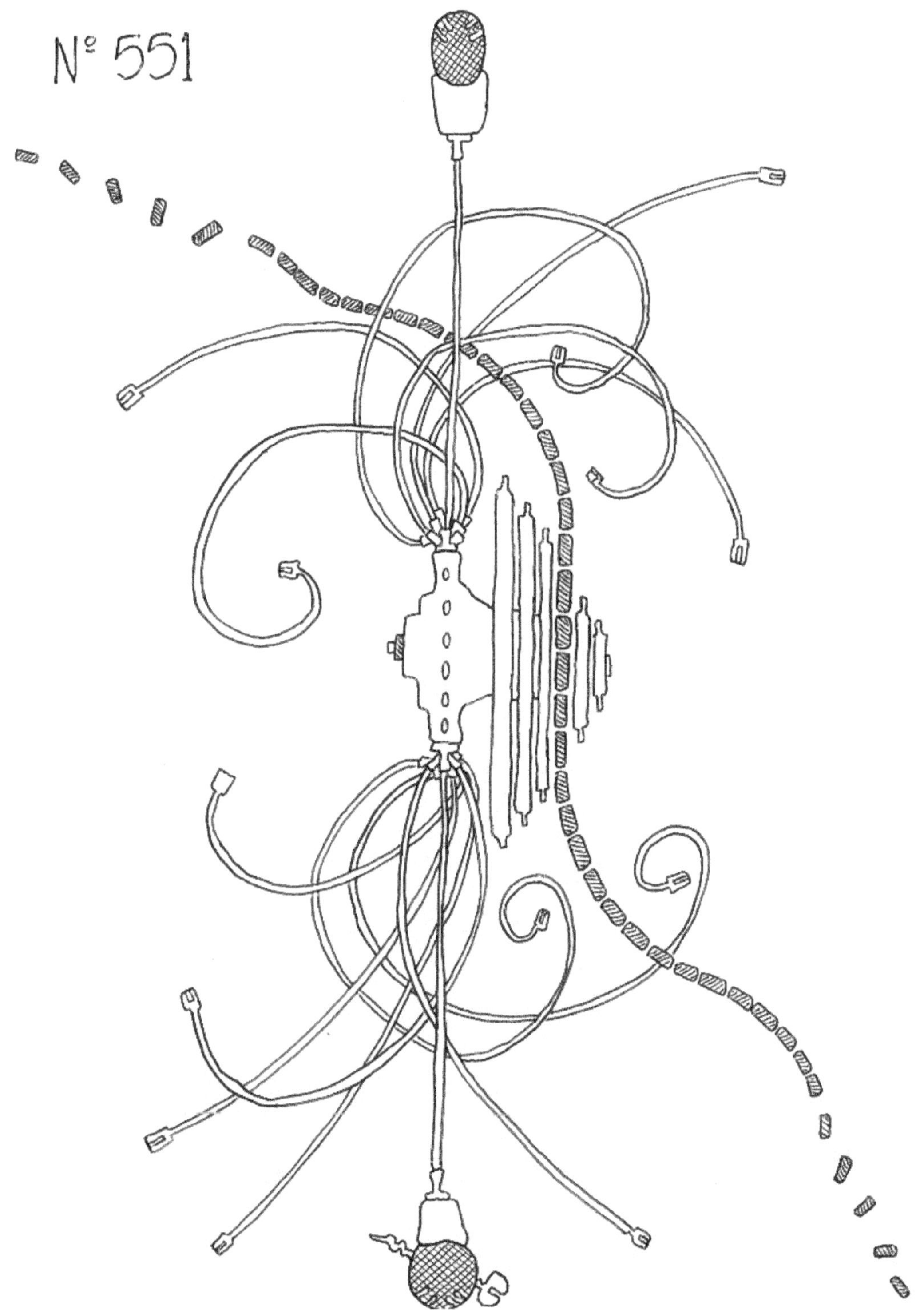
Nº 551

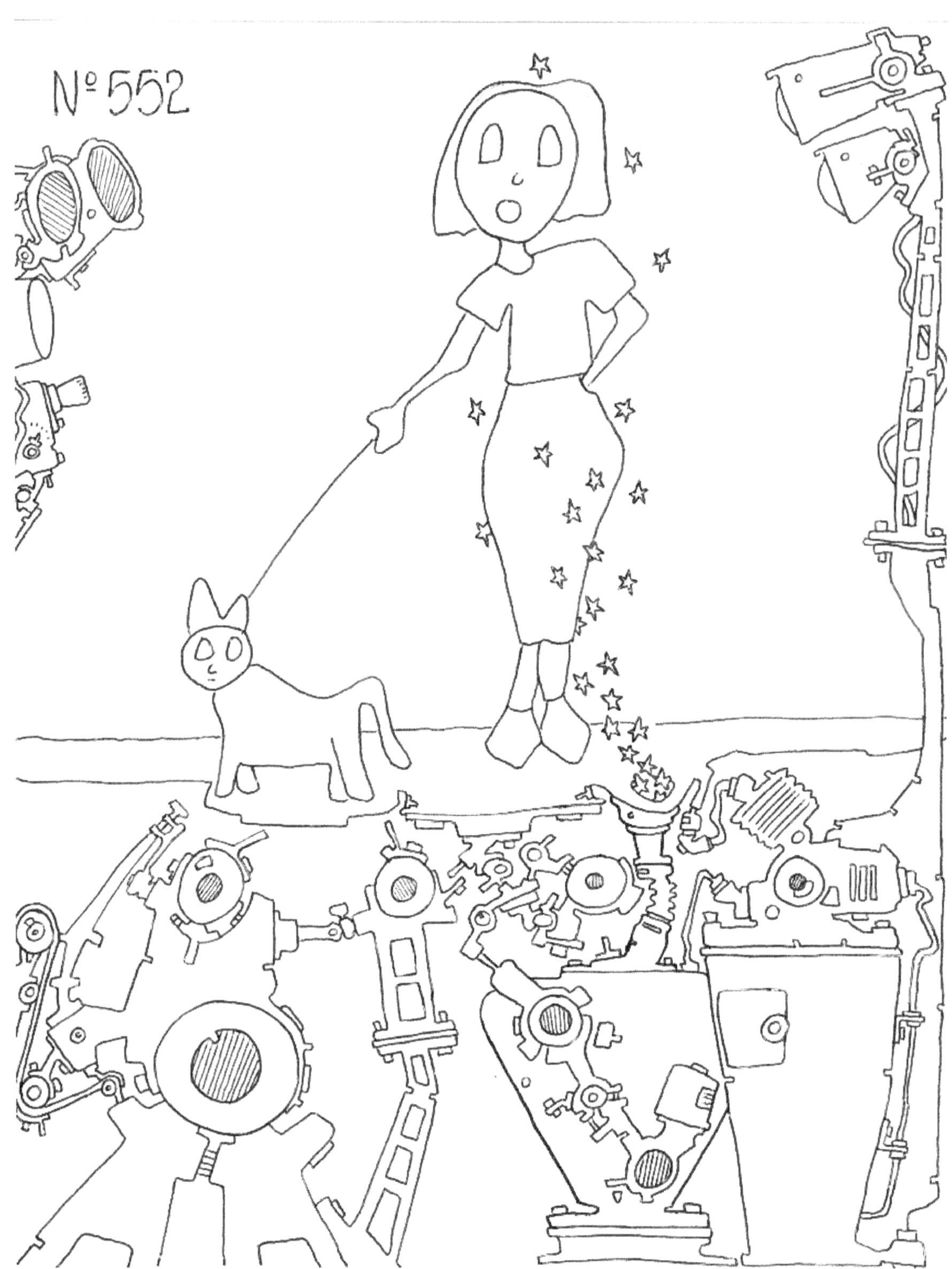
Nº552

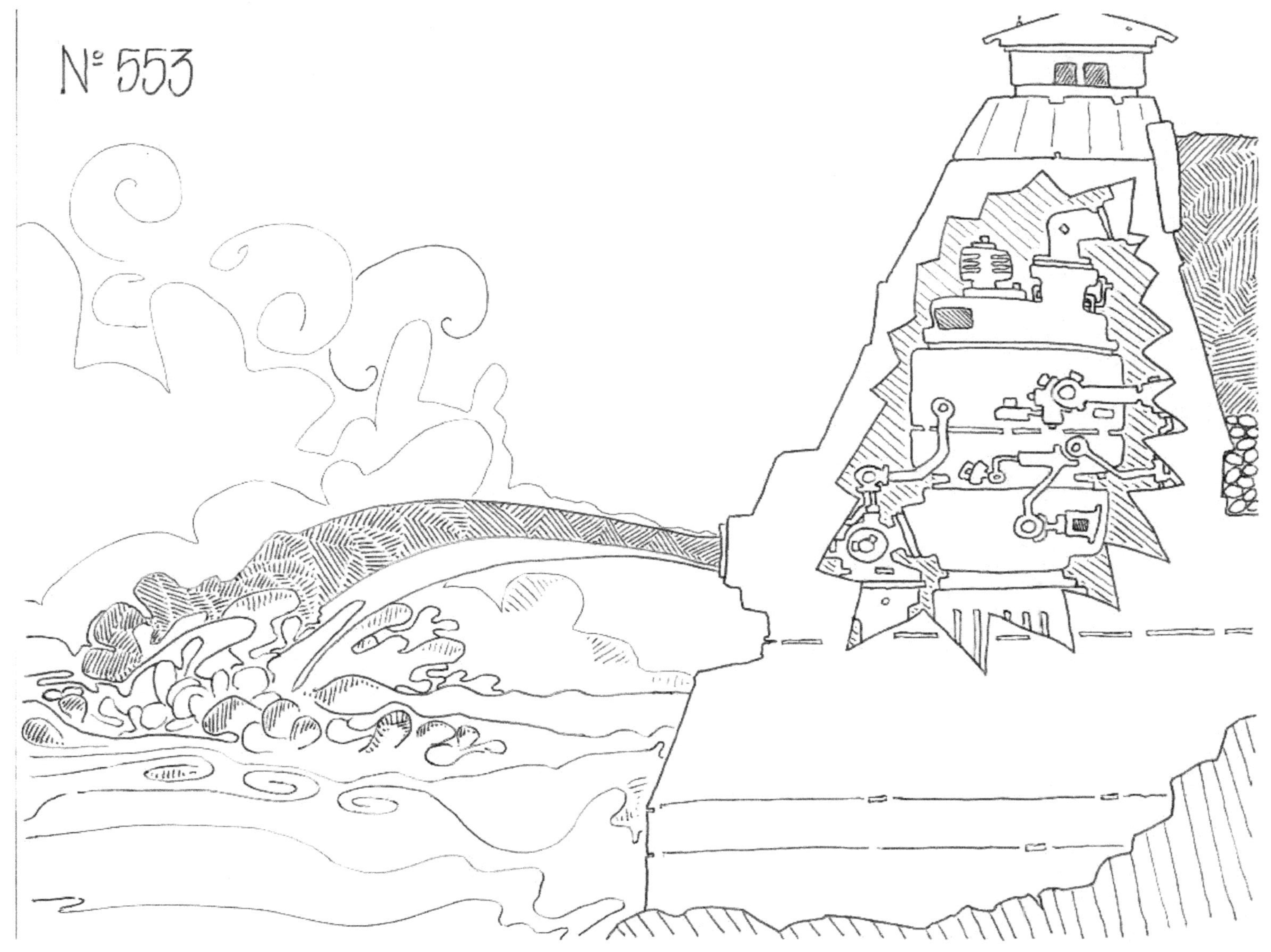
№ 553

№ 554

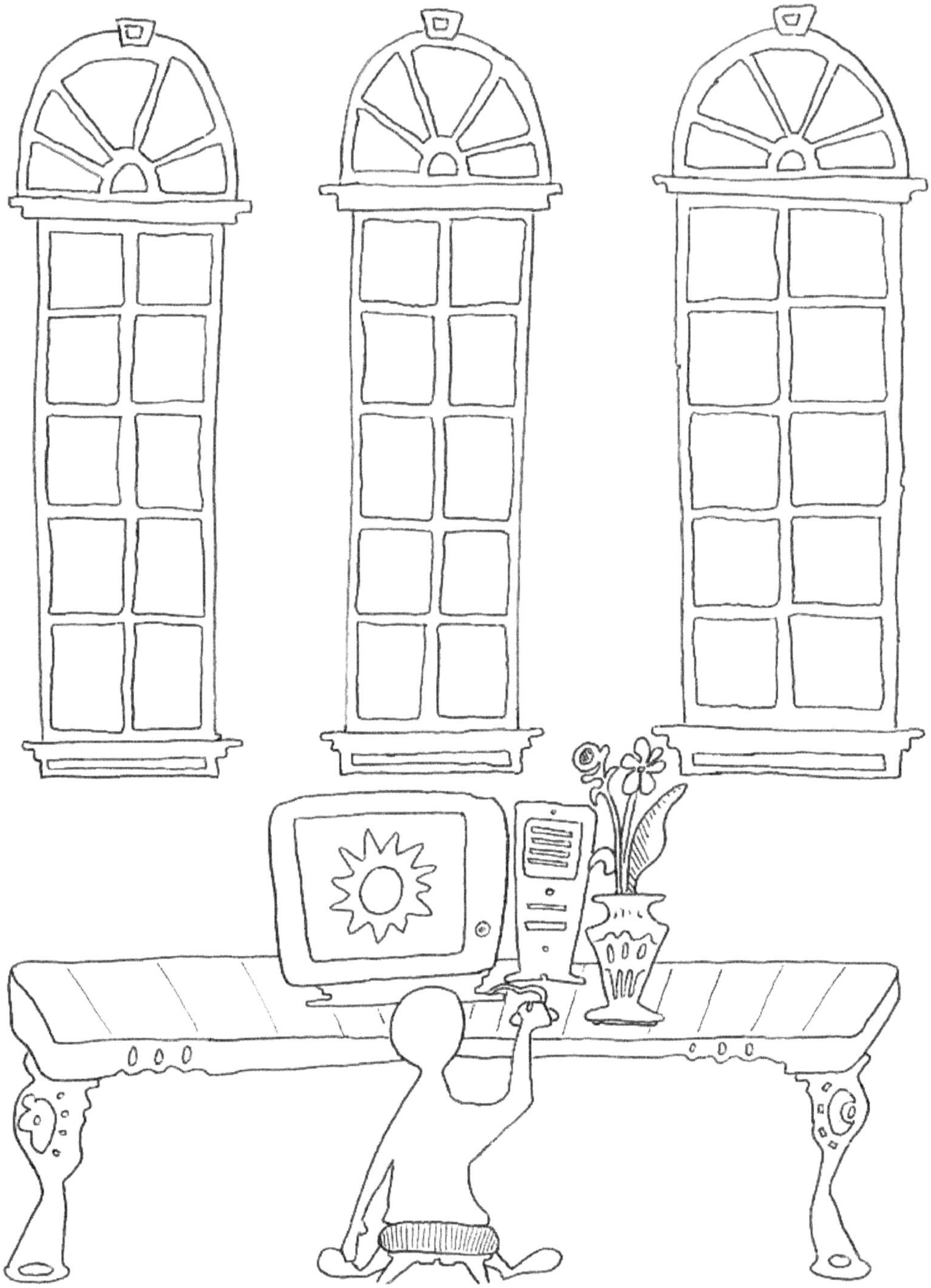

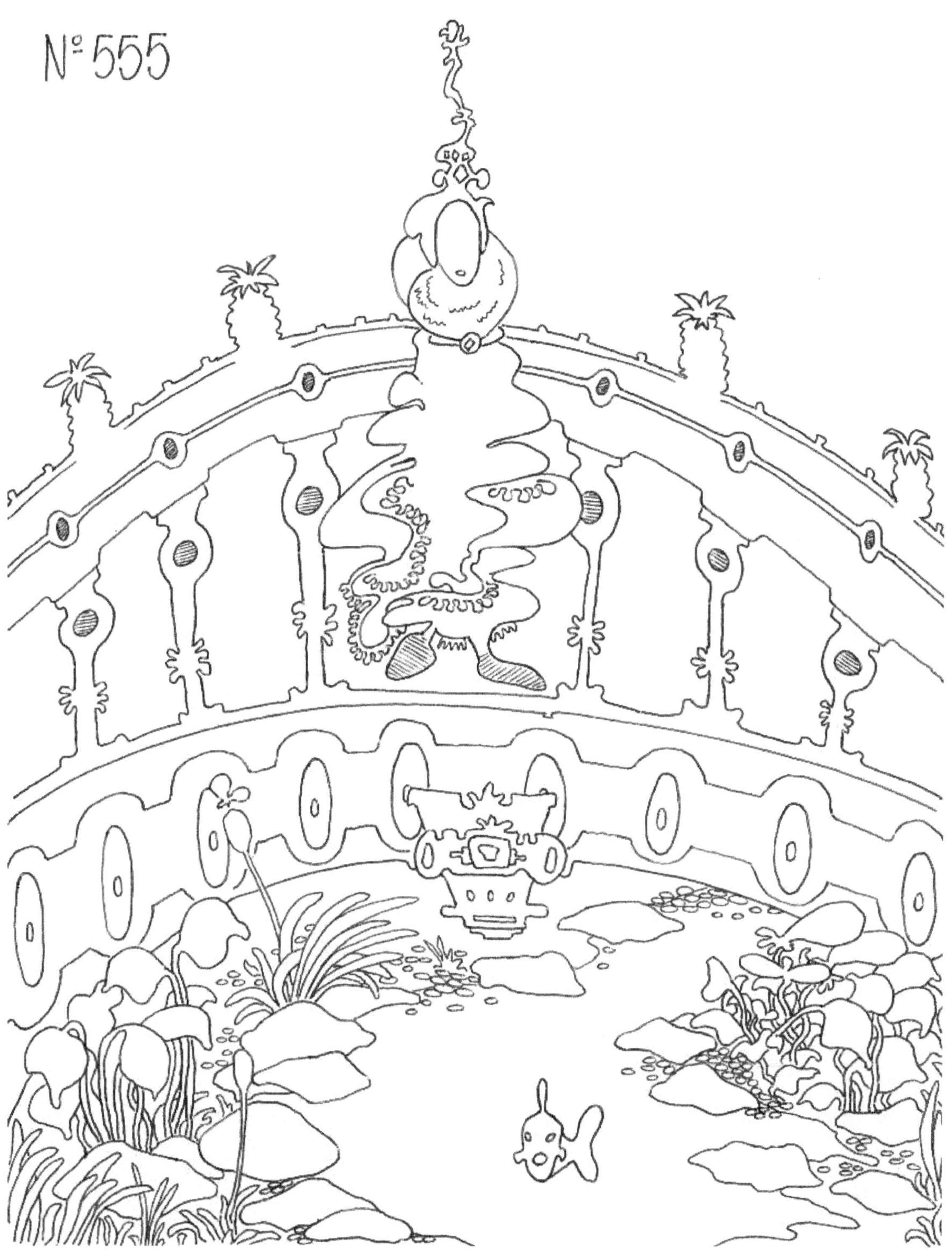
Nº 555

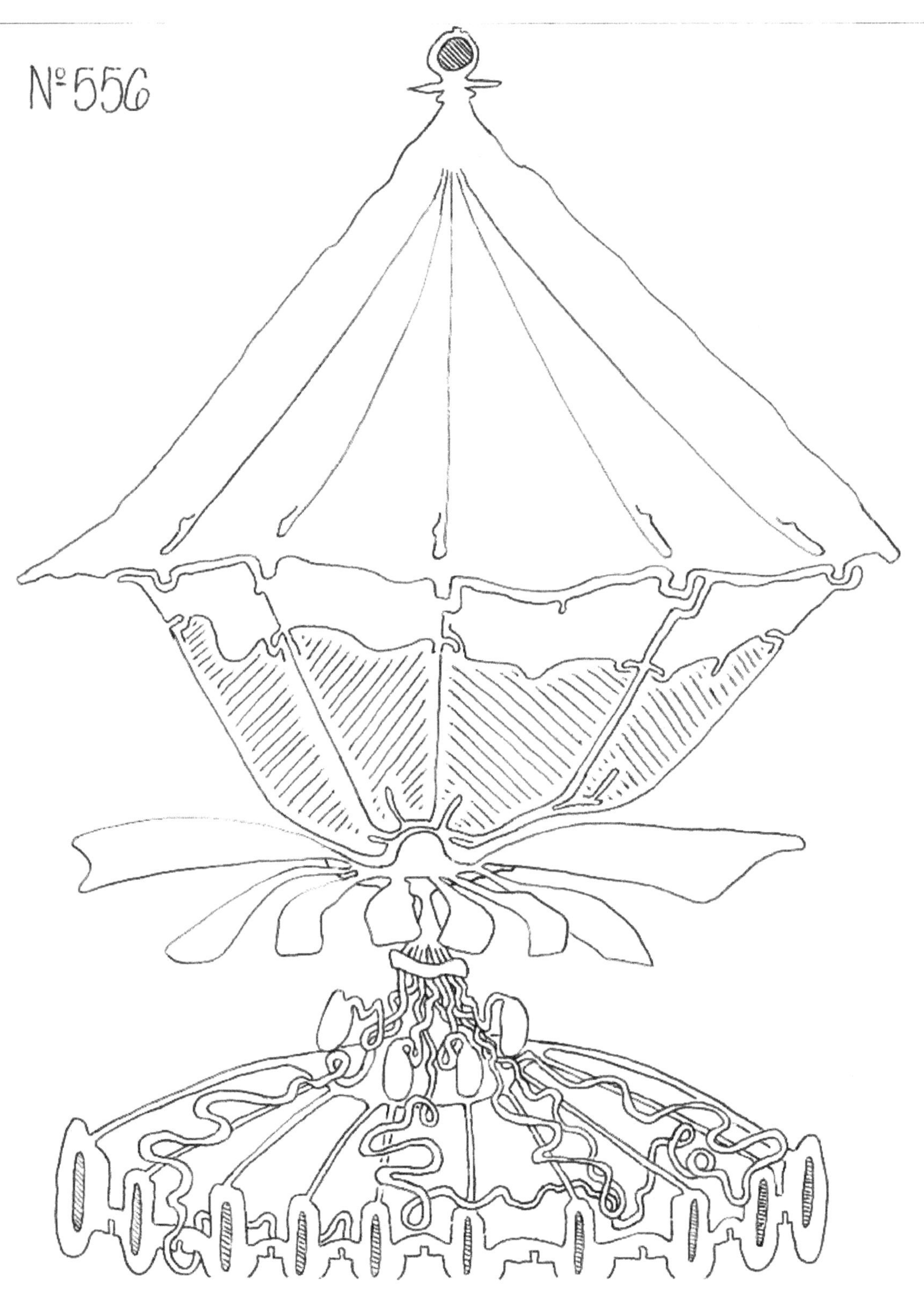
N° 556

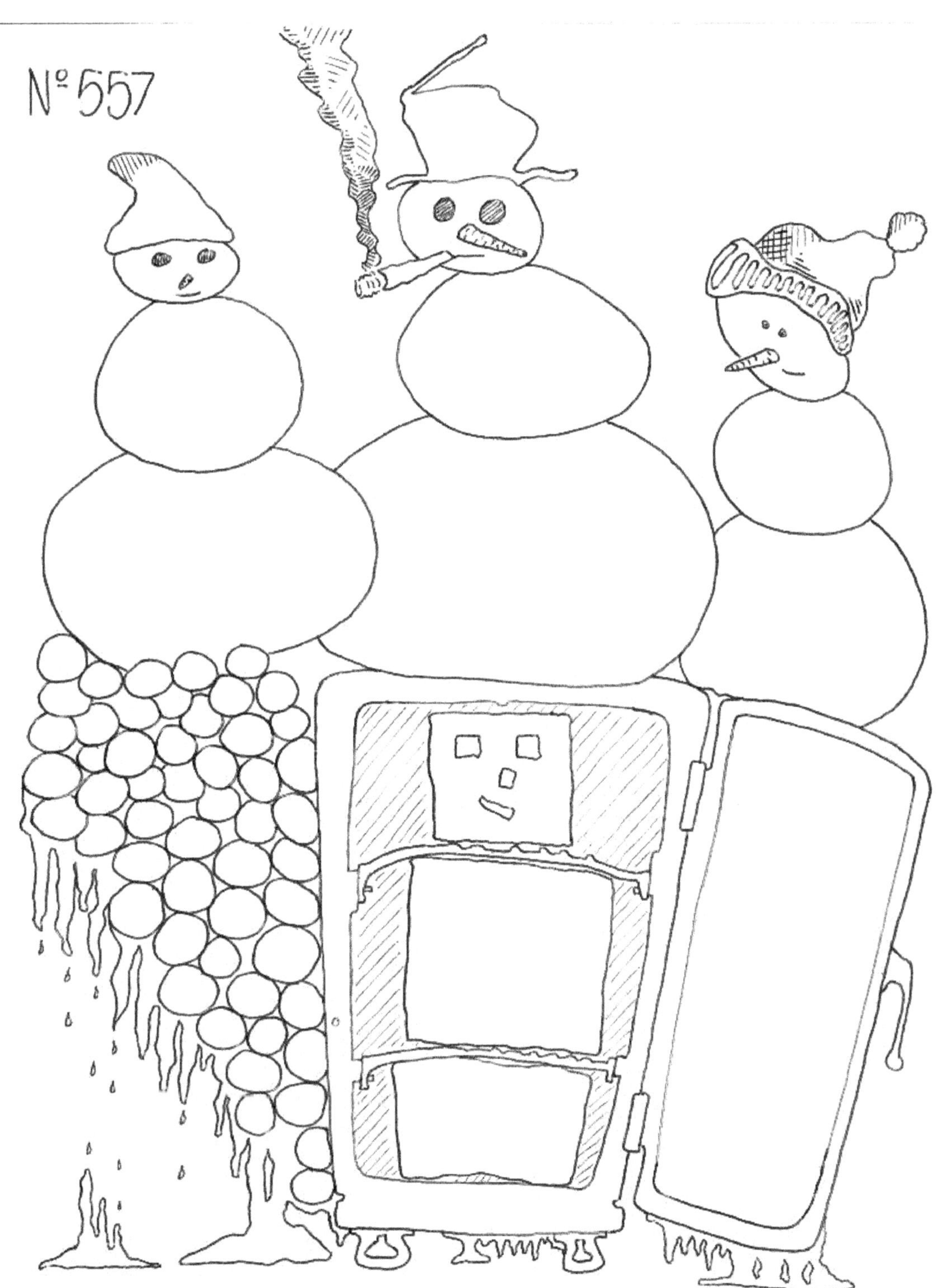
Nº 557

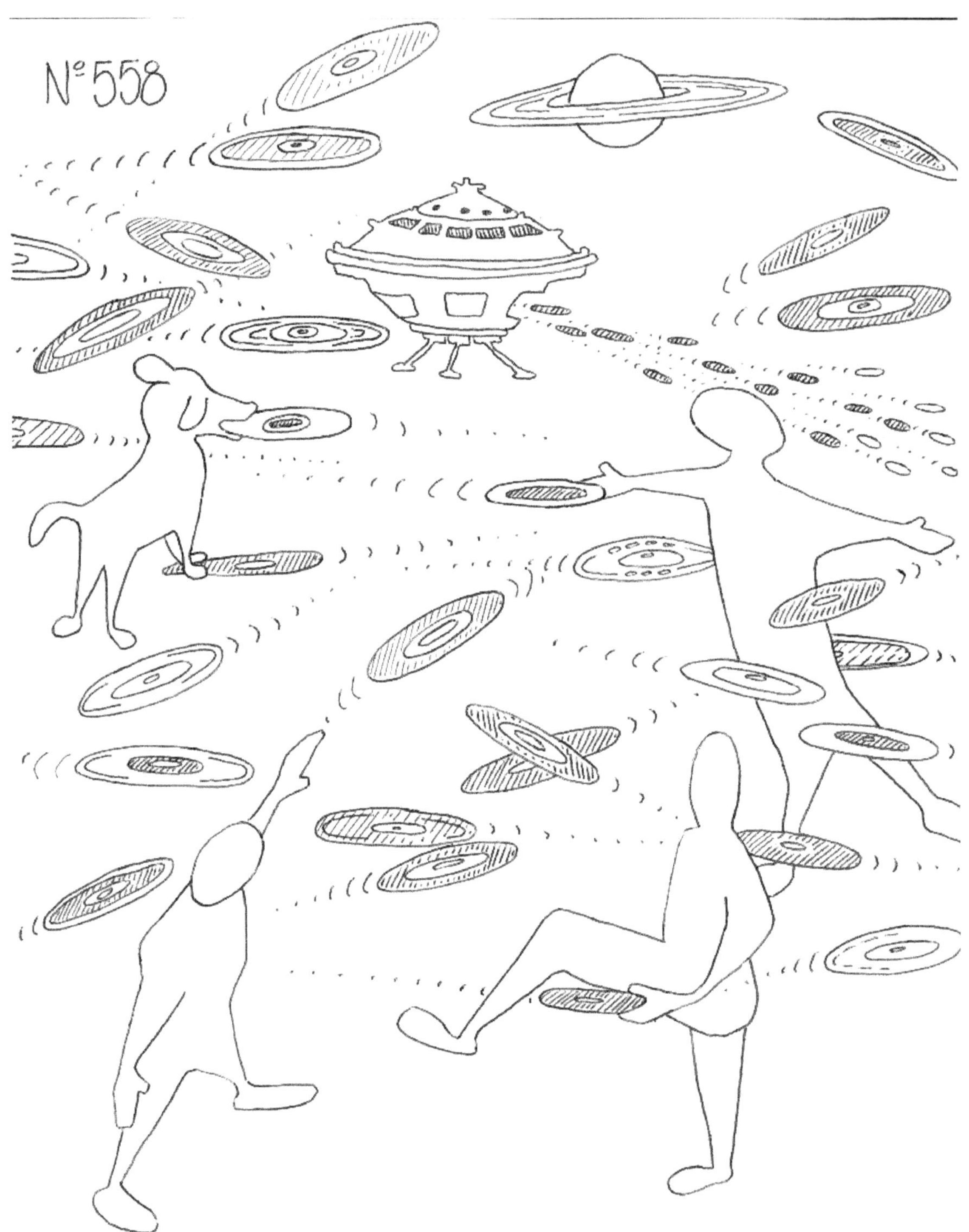
N°558

№559

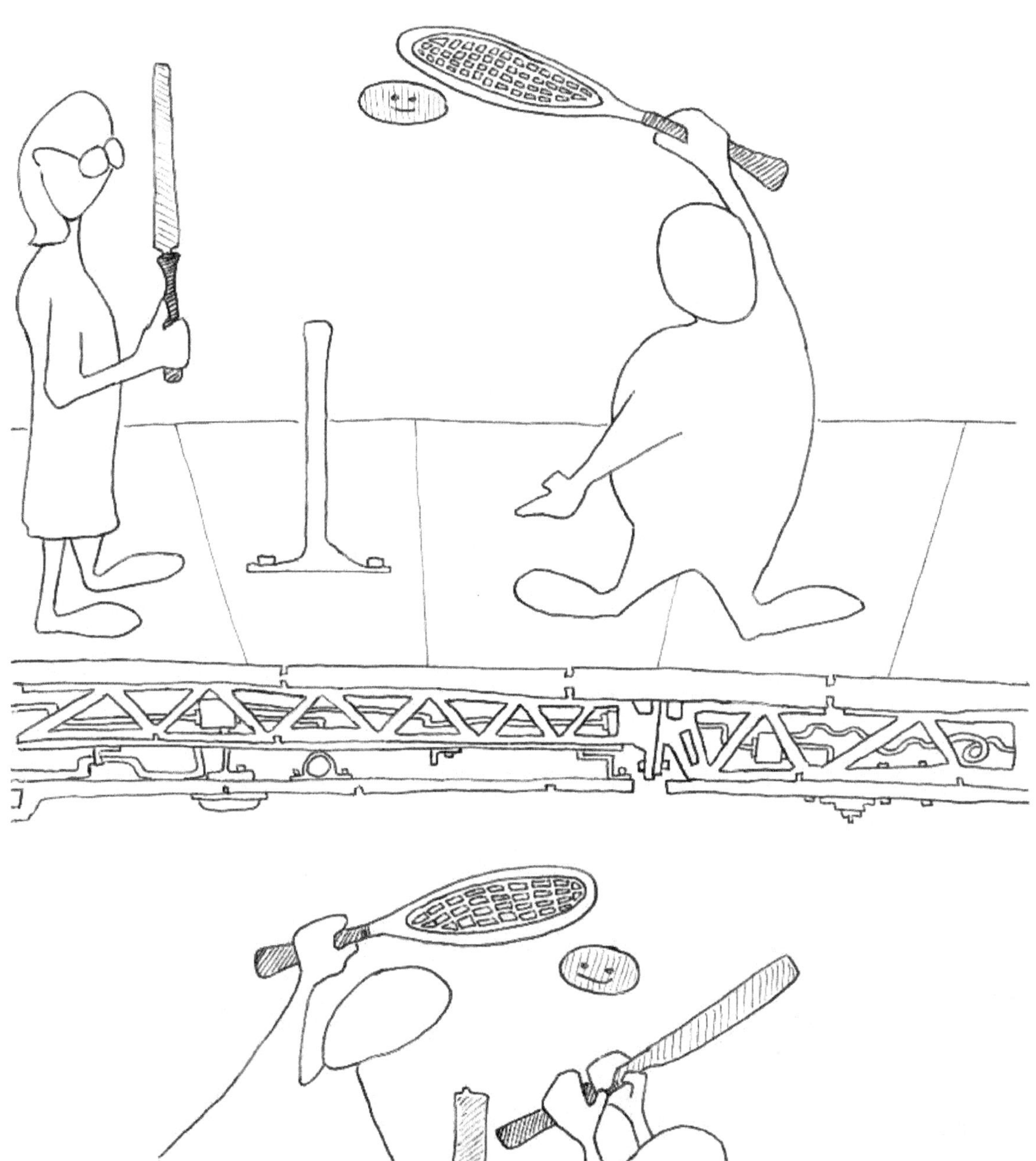

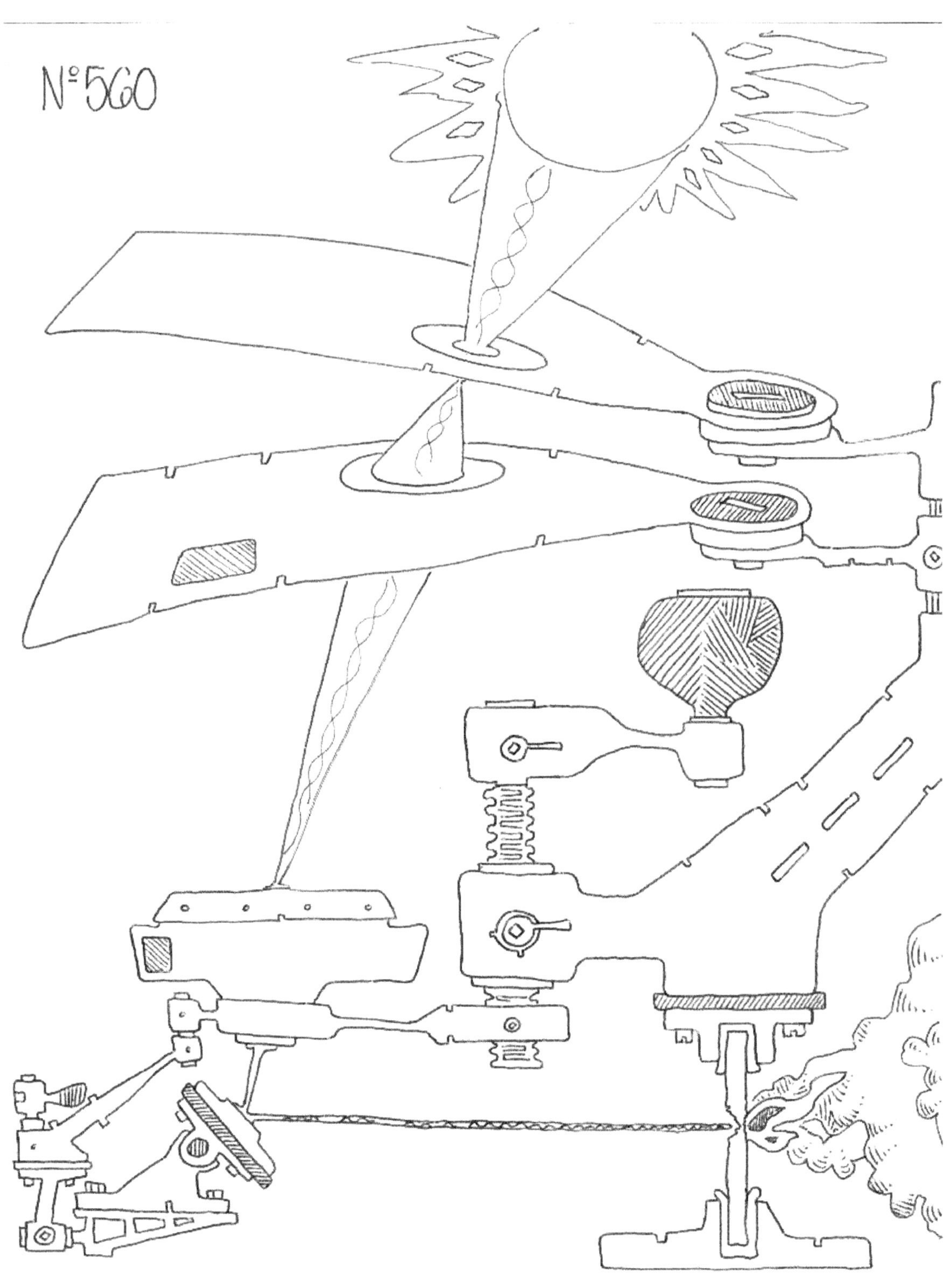
N°560

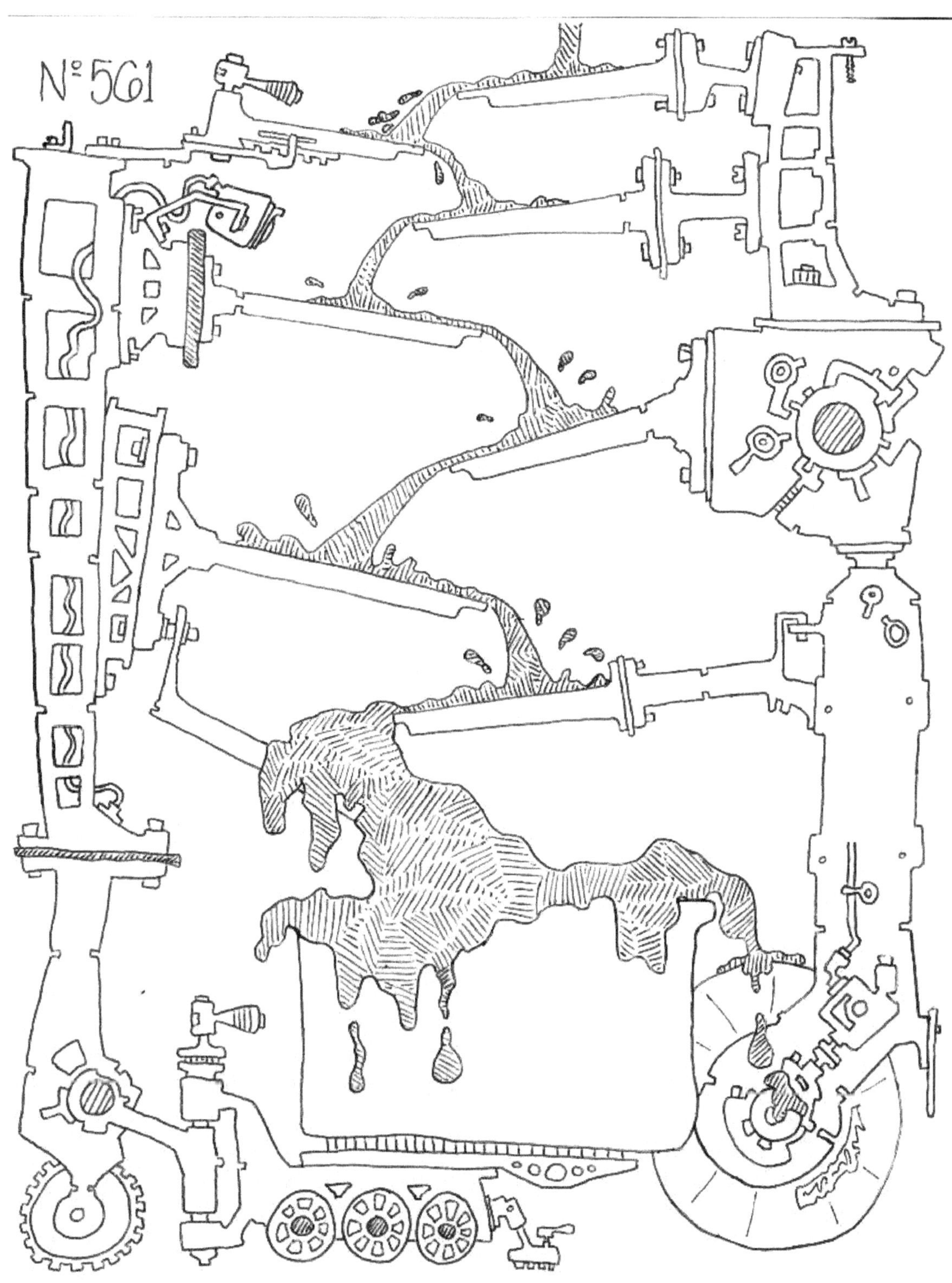
Nº 561

№ 562

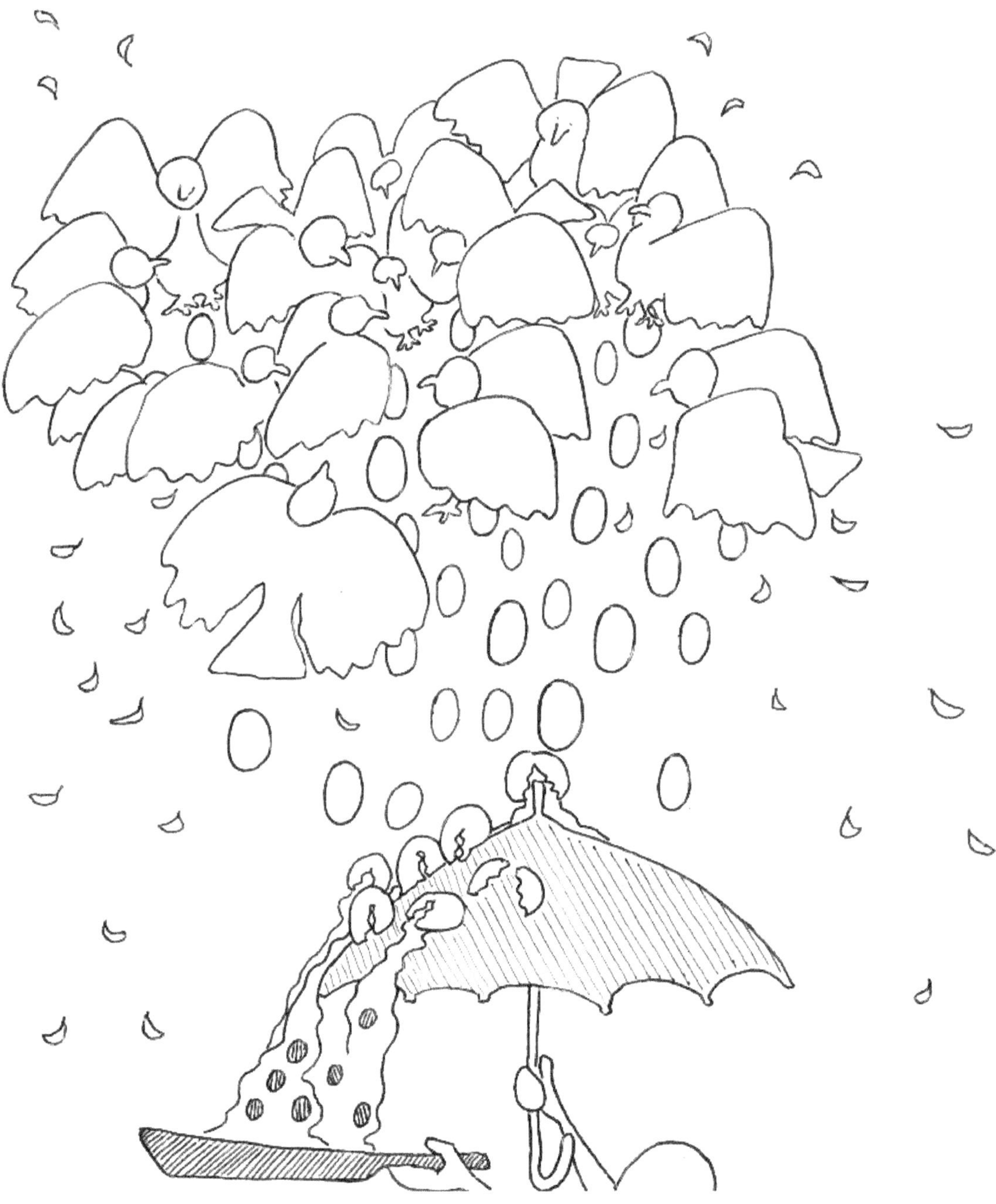

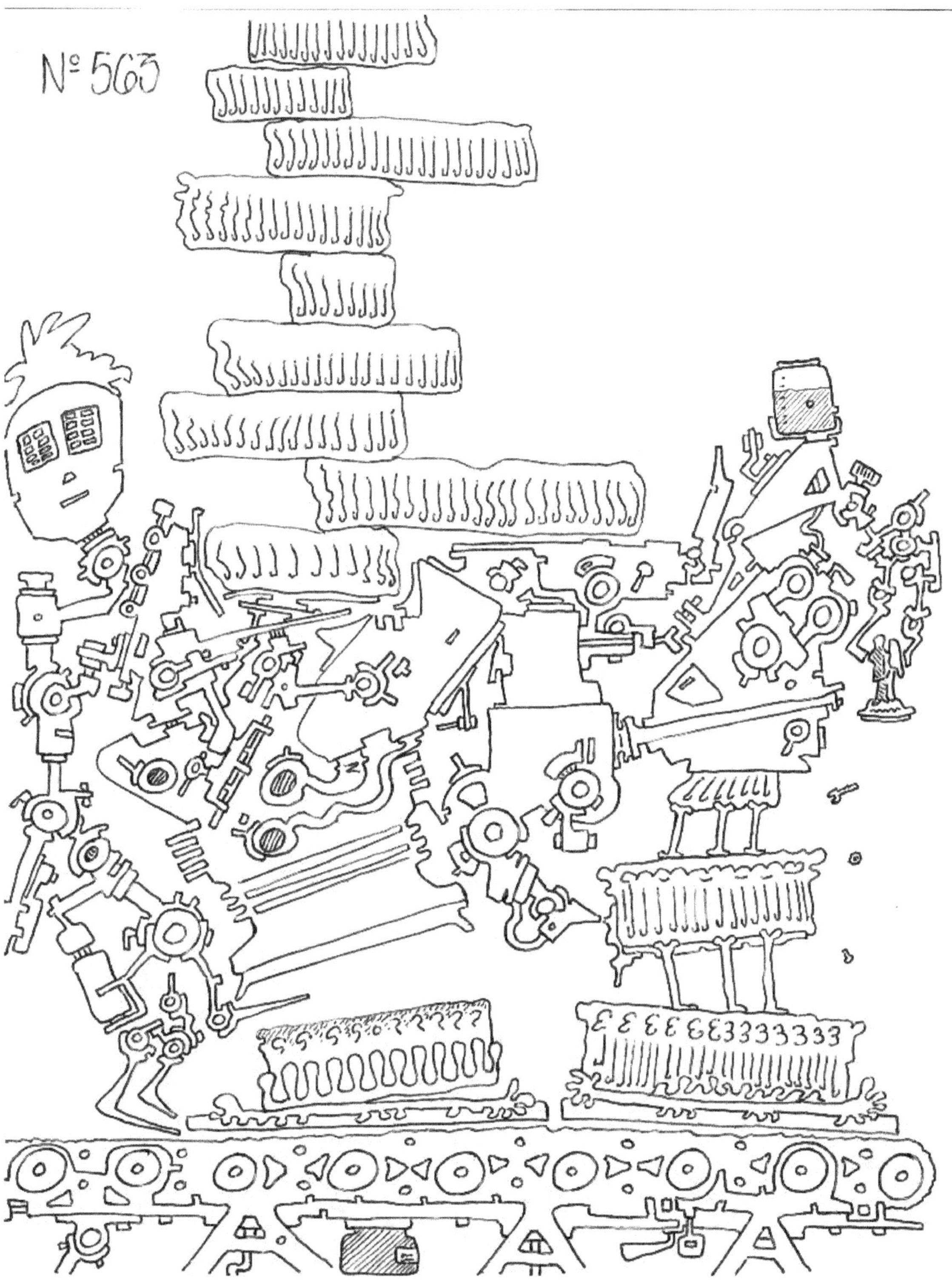
№ 565

Nº564

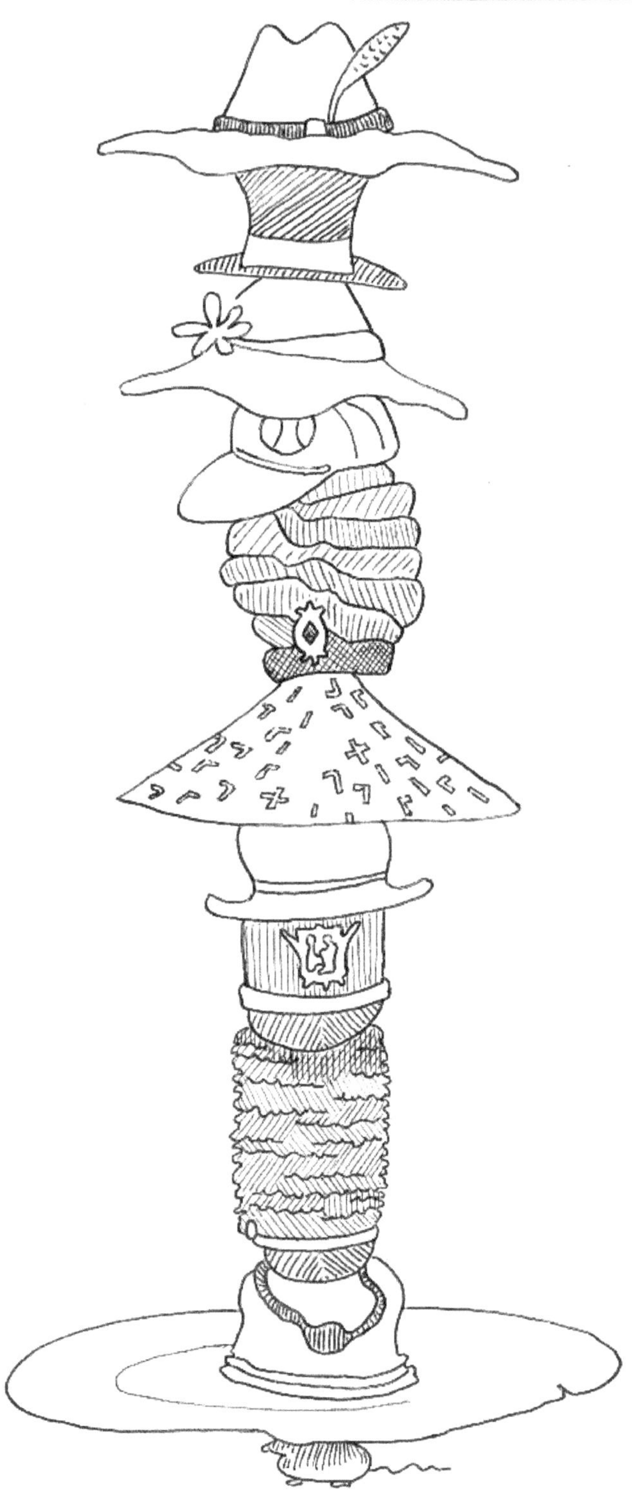

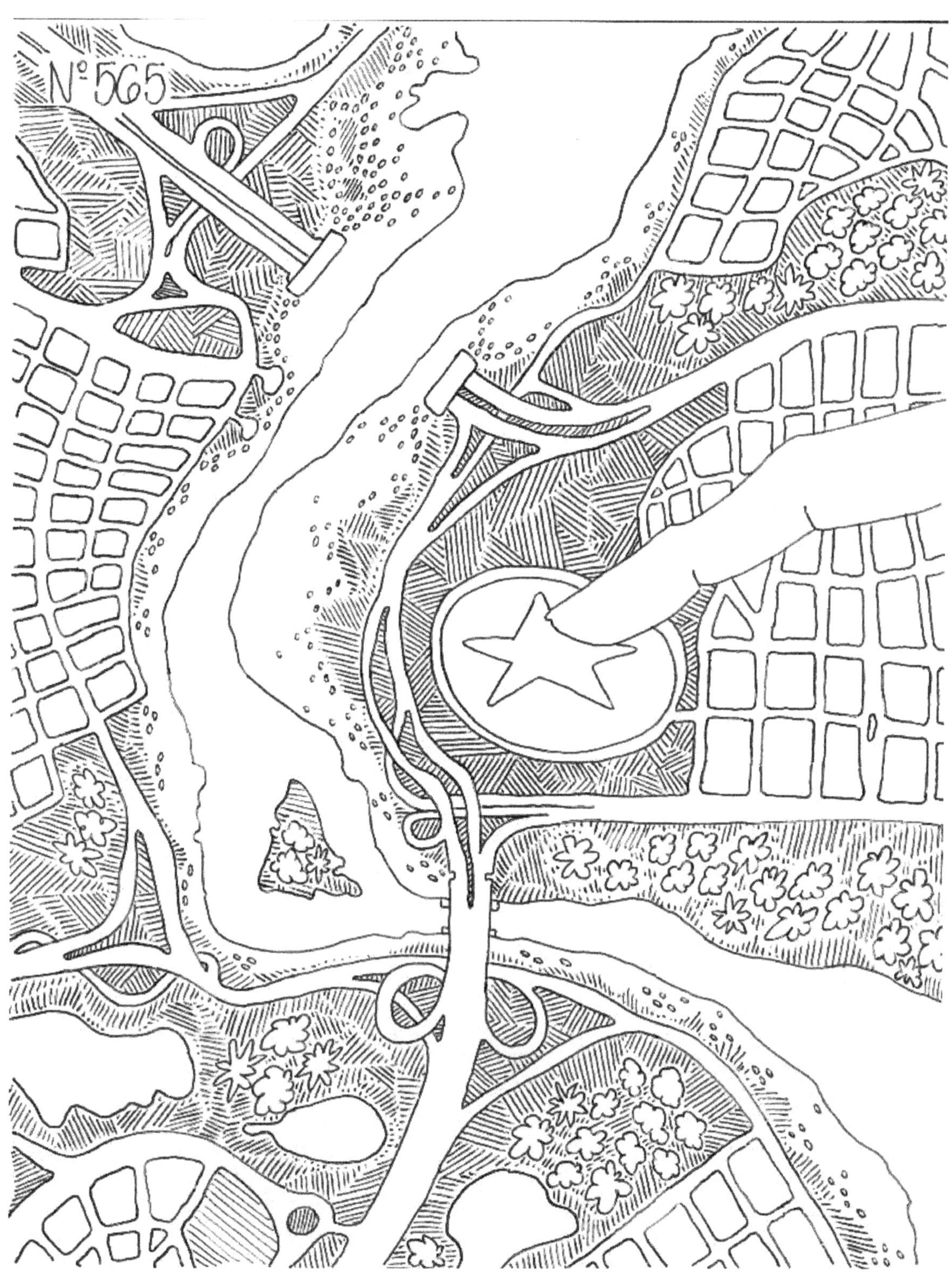

N° 565

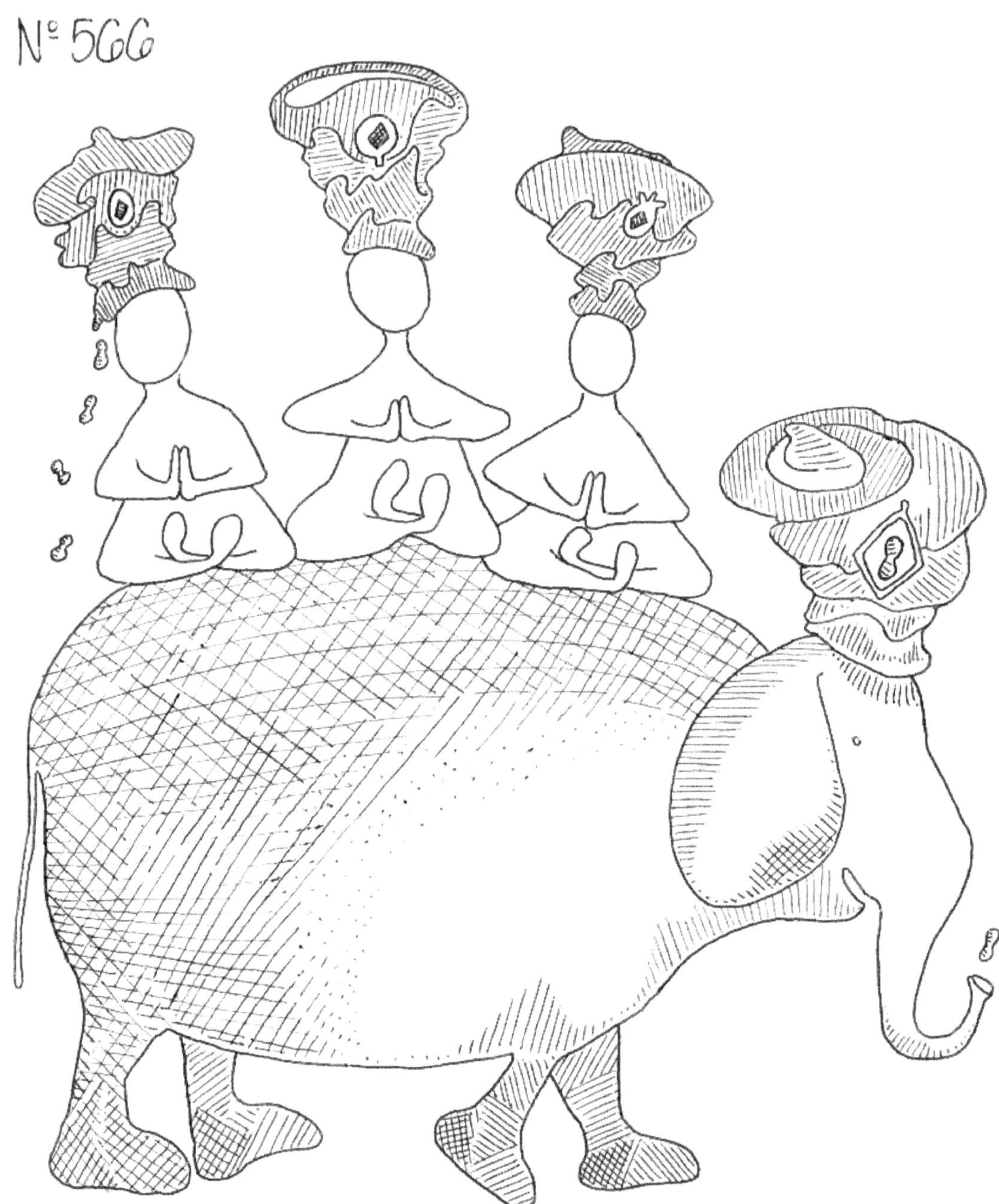
№ 566

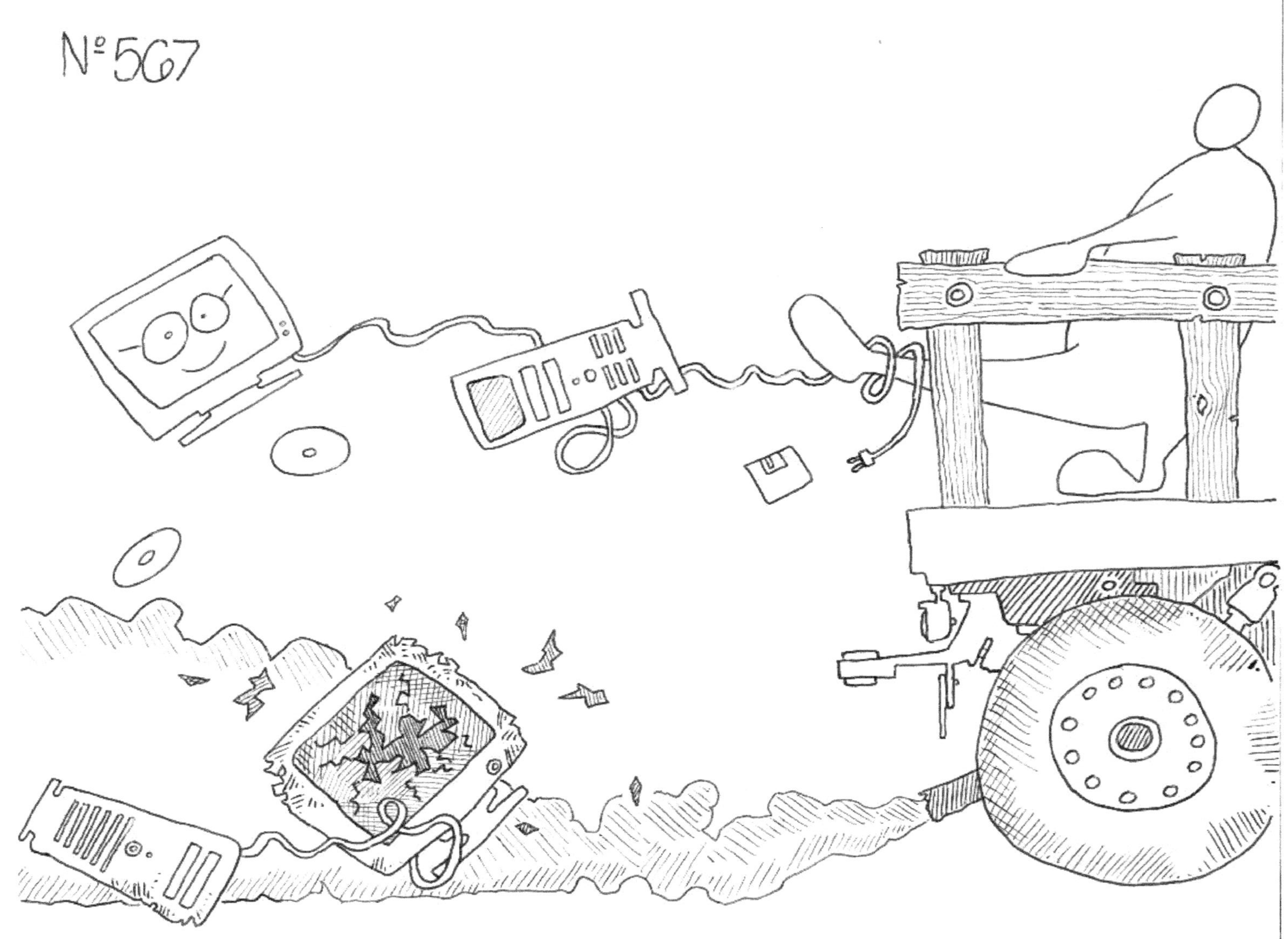
№567

№ 568

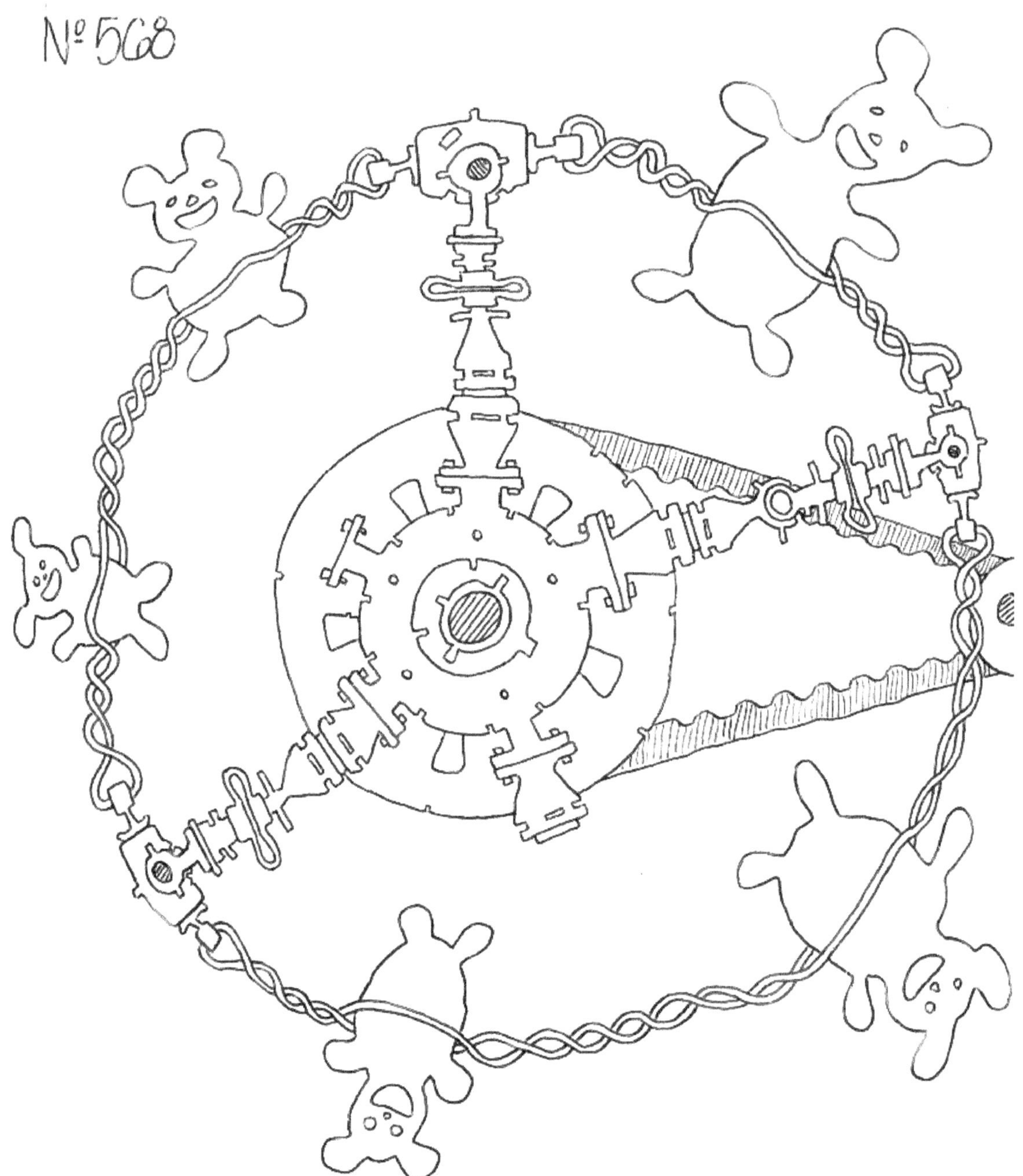

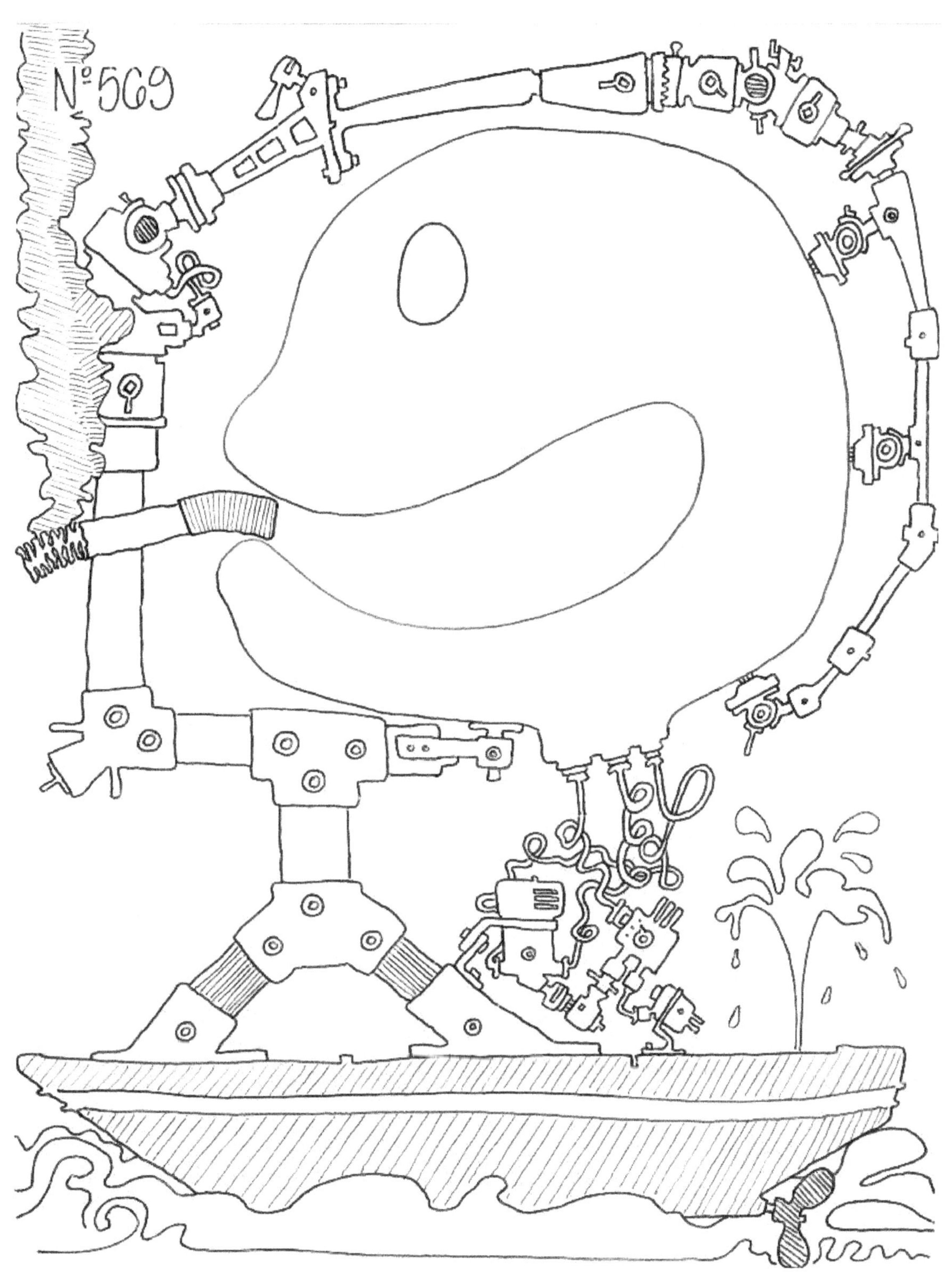
Nº569

Nº570

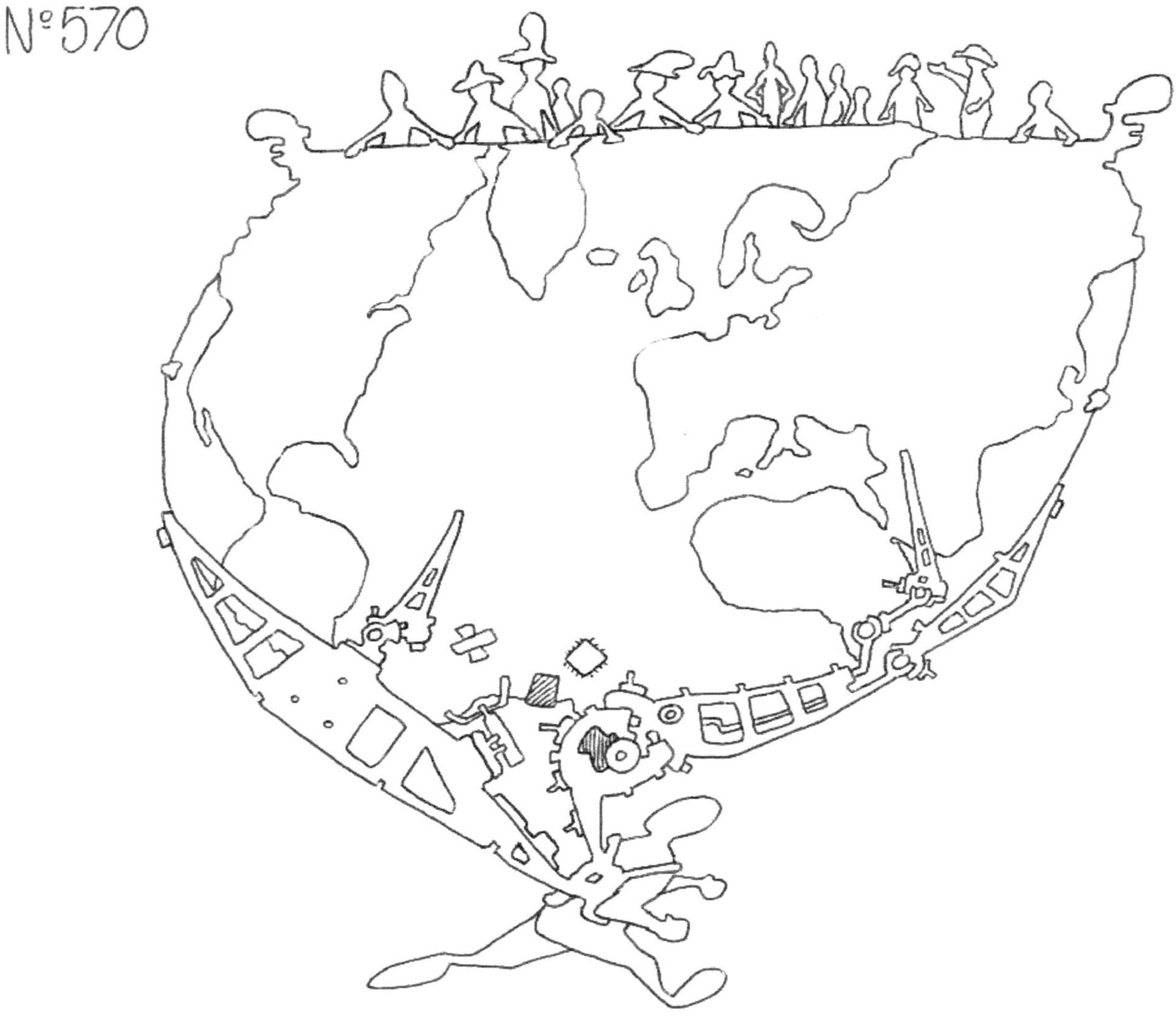

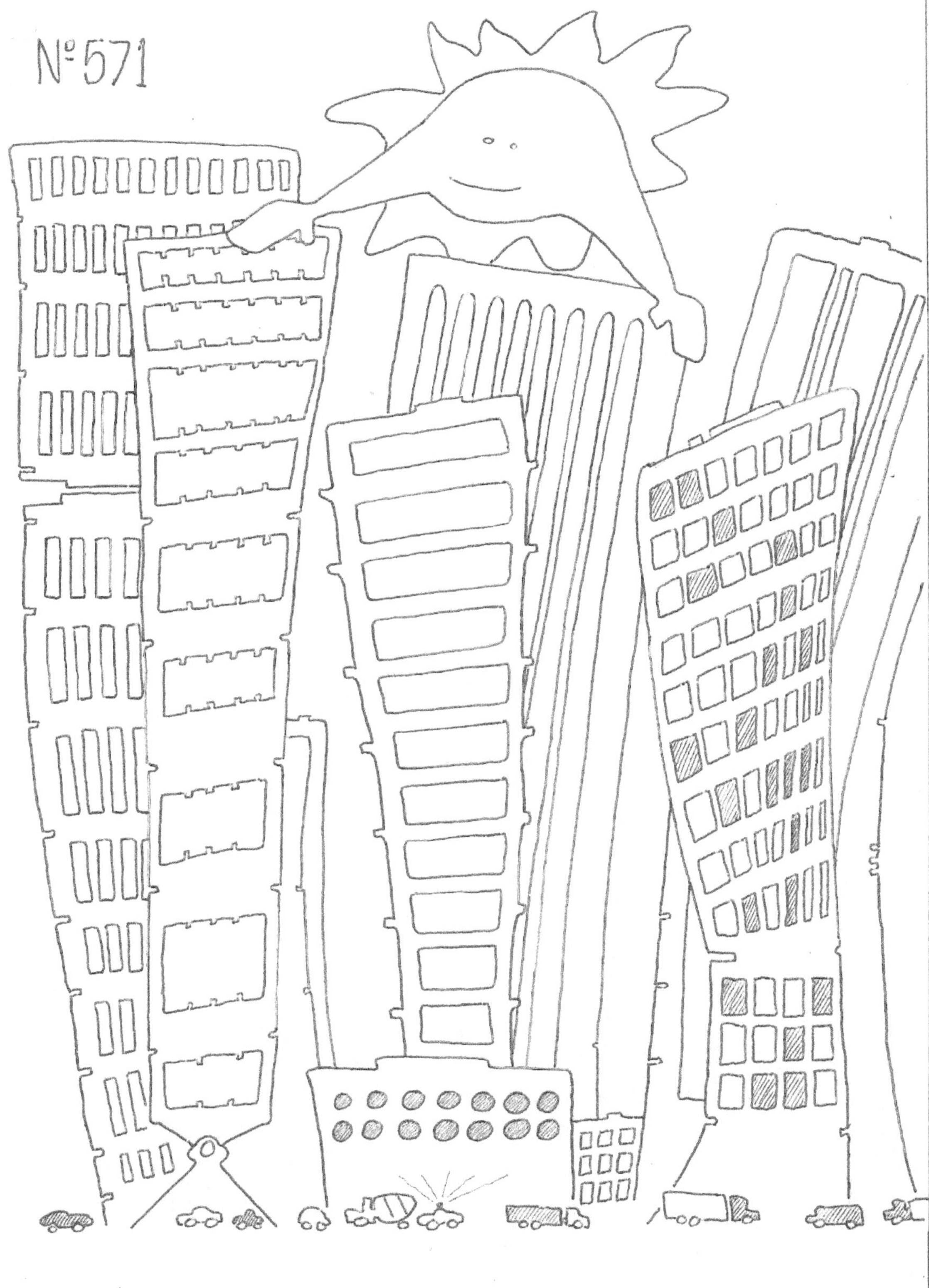
№ 571

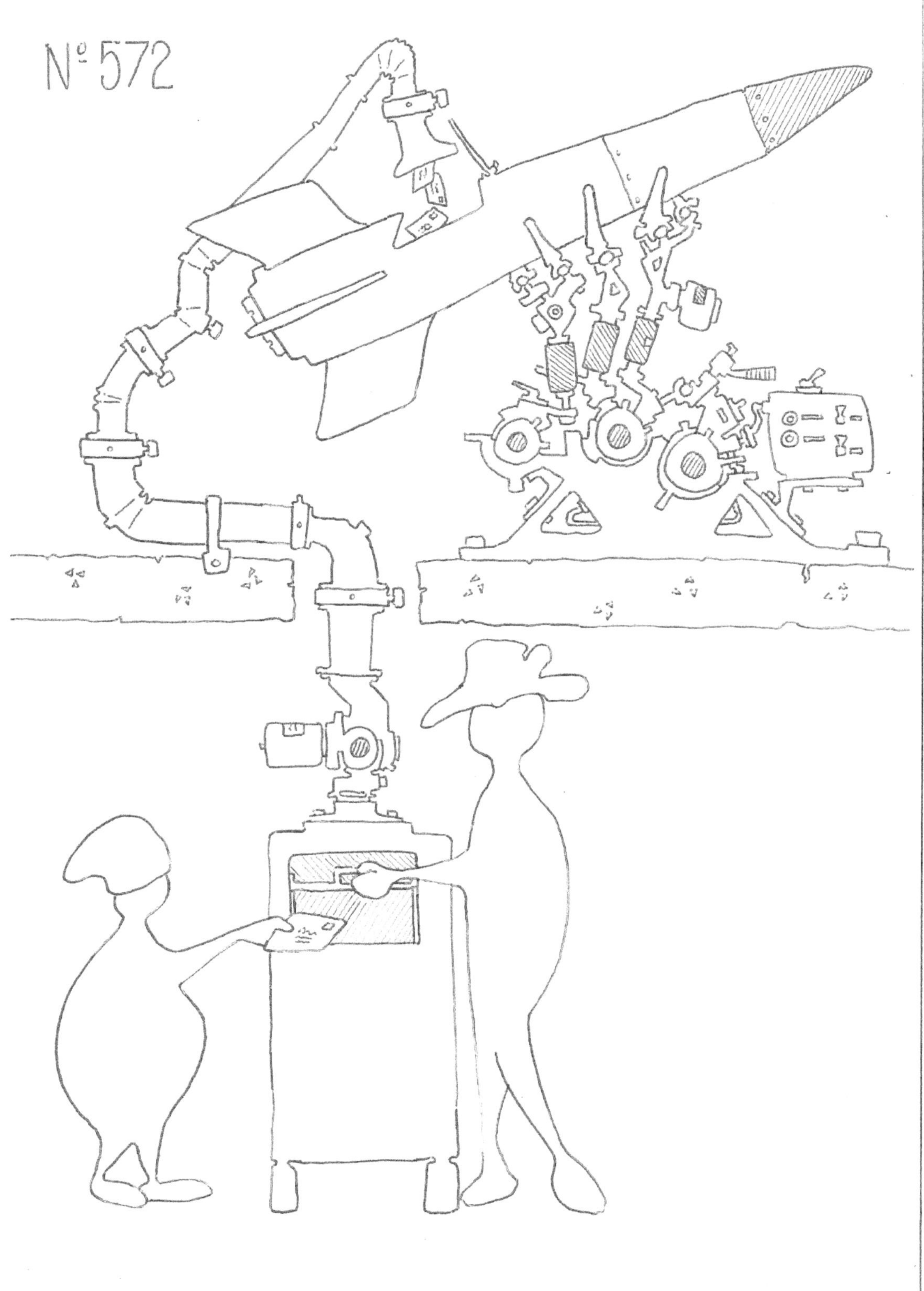
Nº 572

№ 573

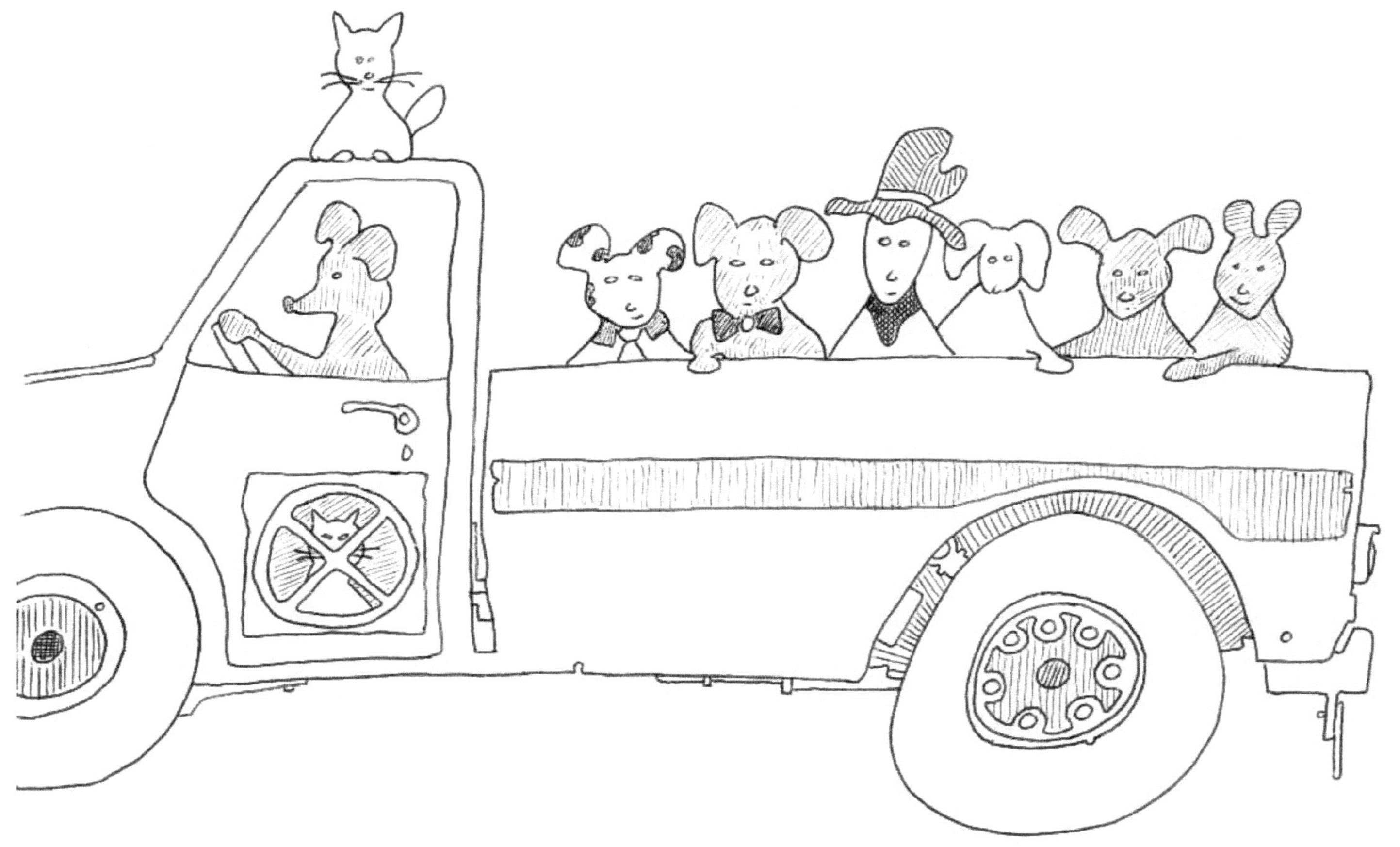

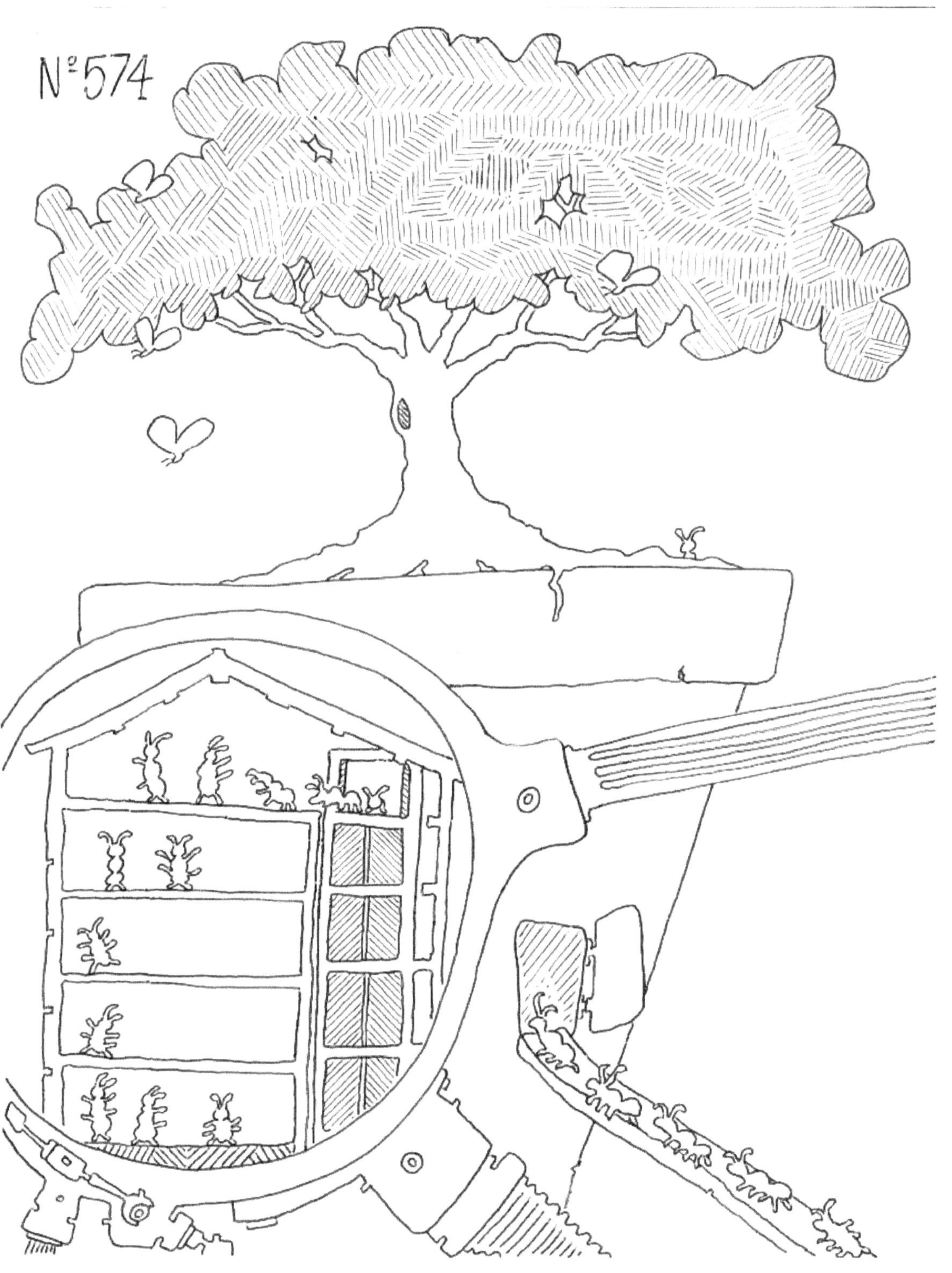
Nº574

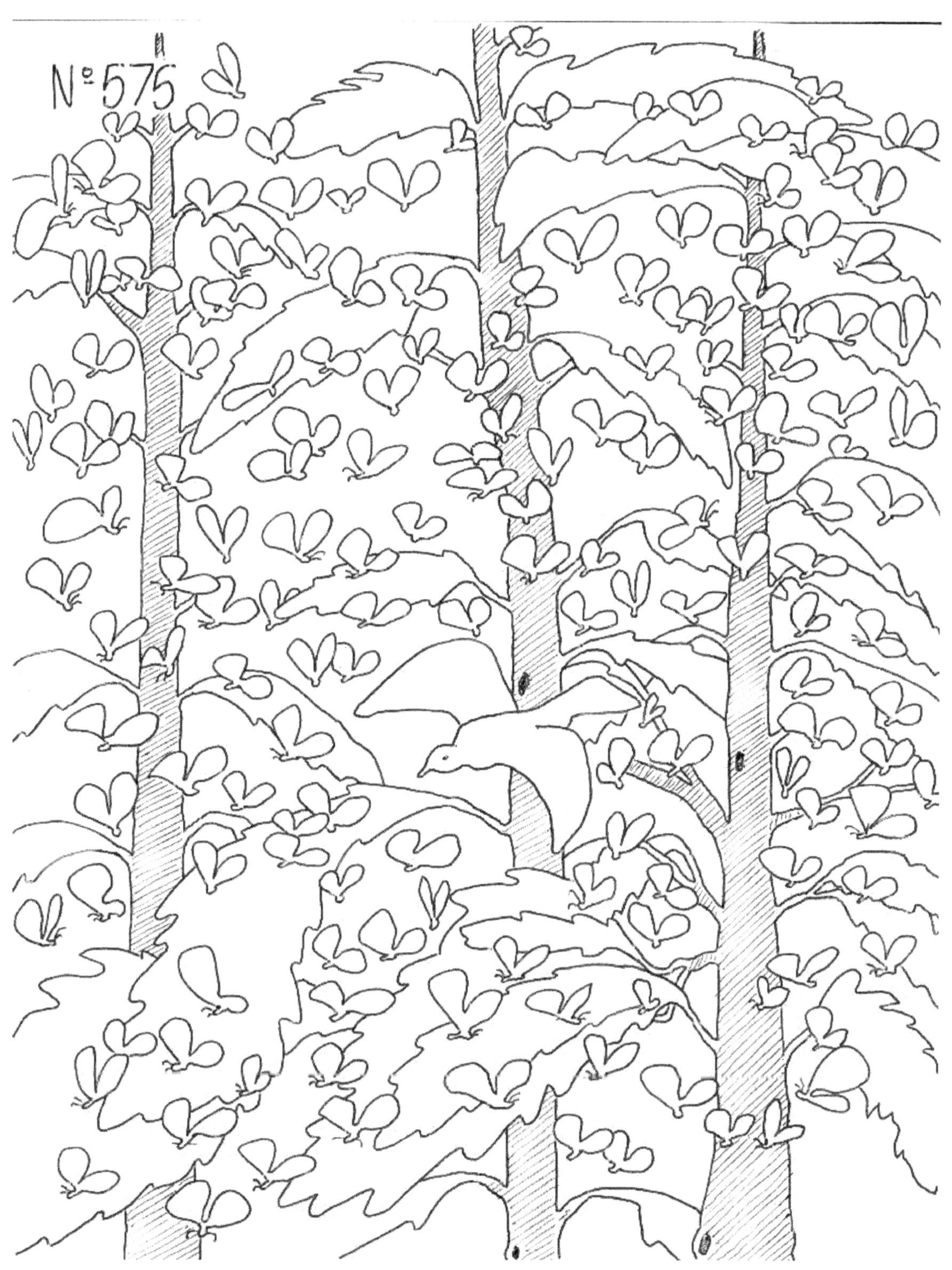
N° 575

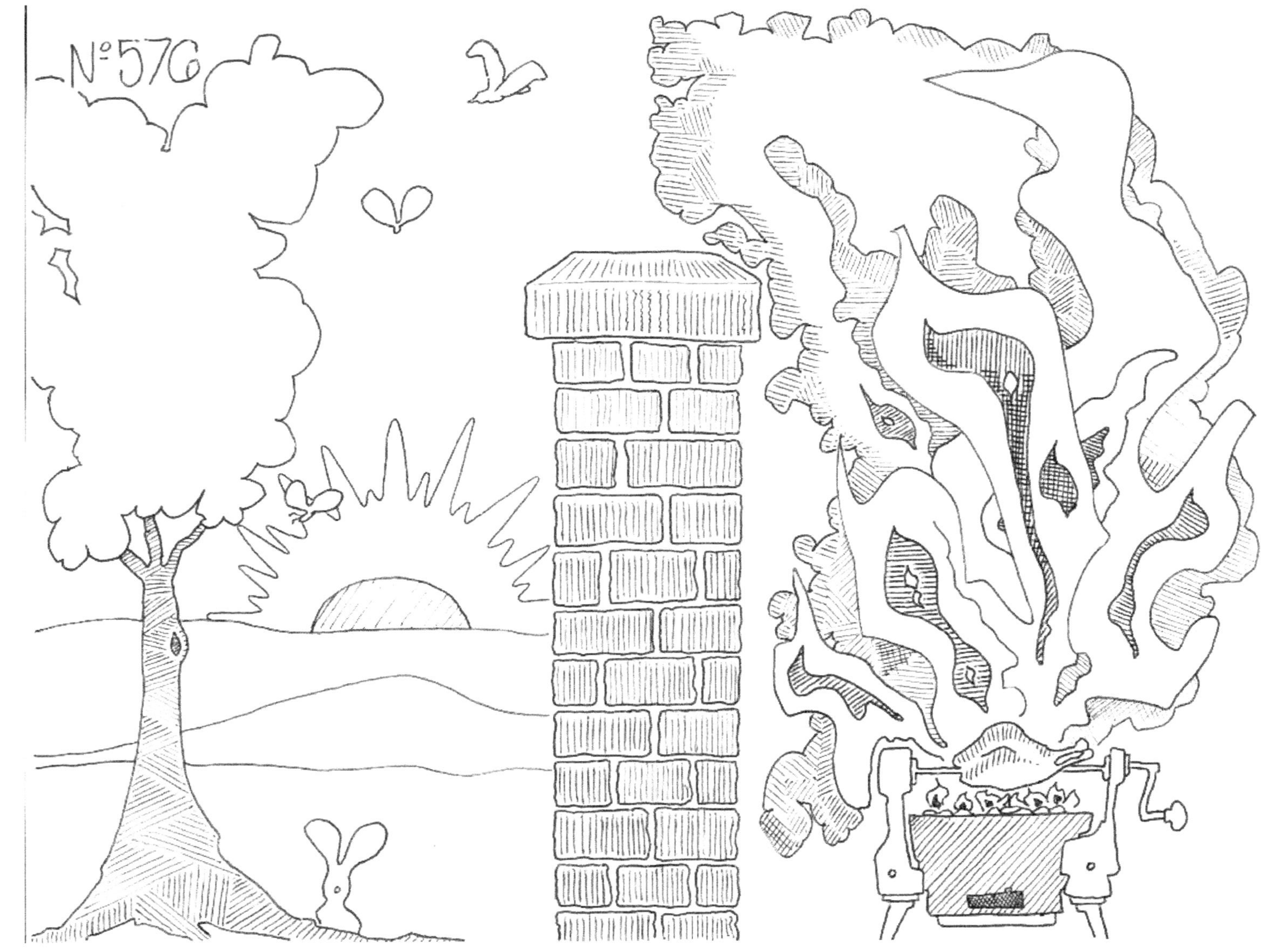
№576

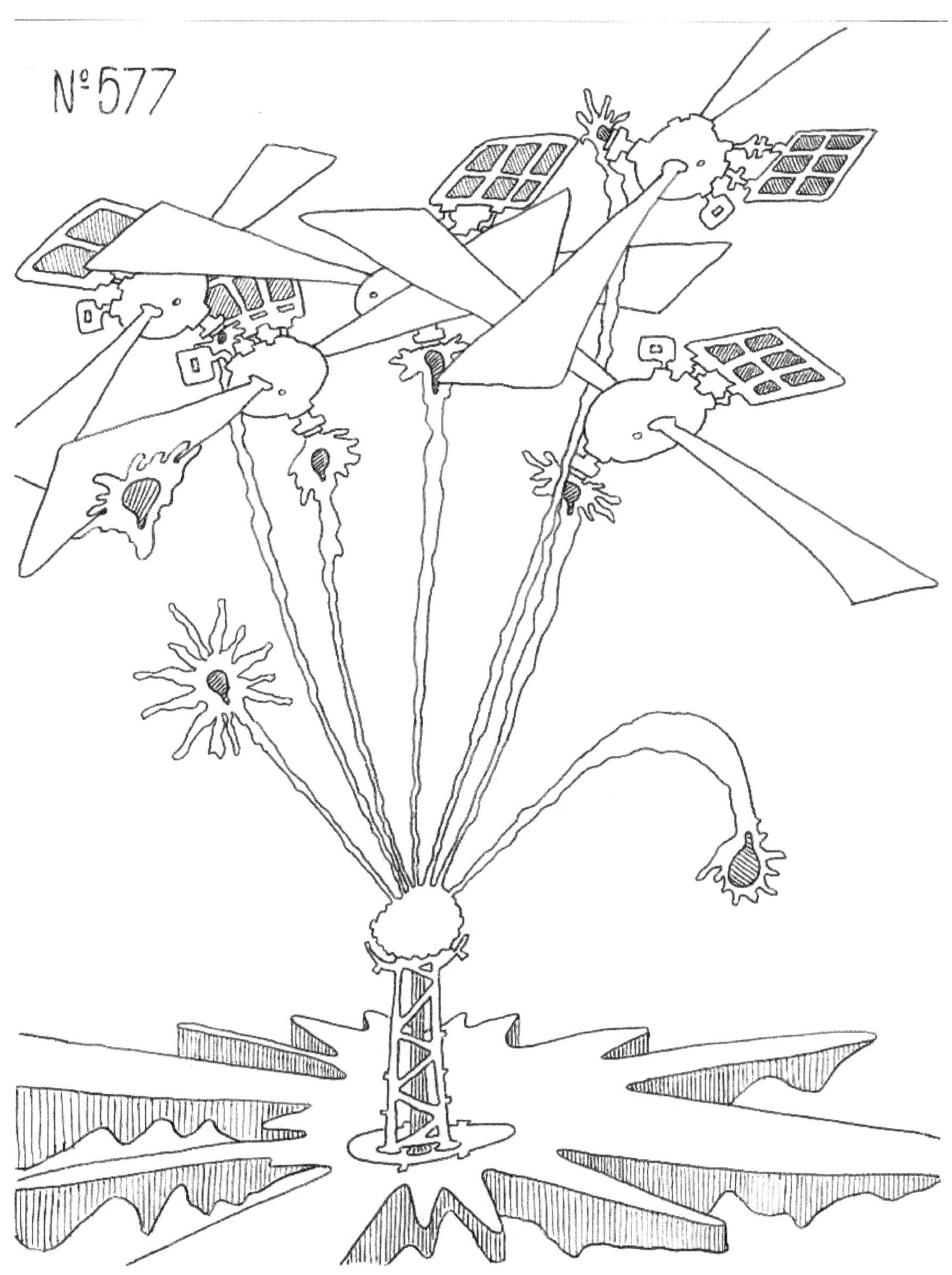
№577

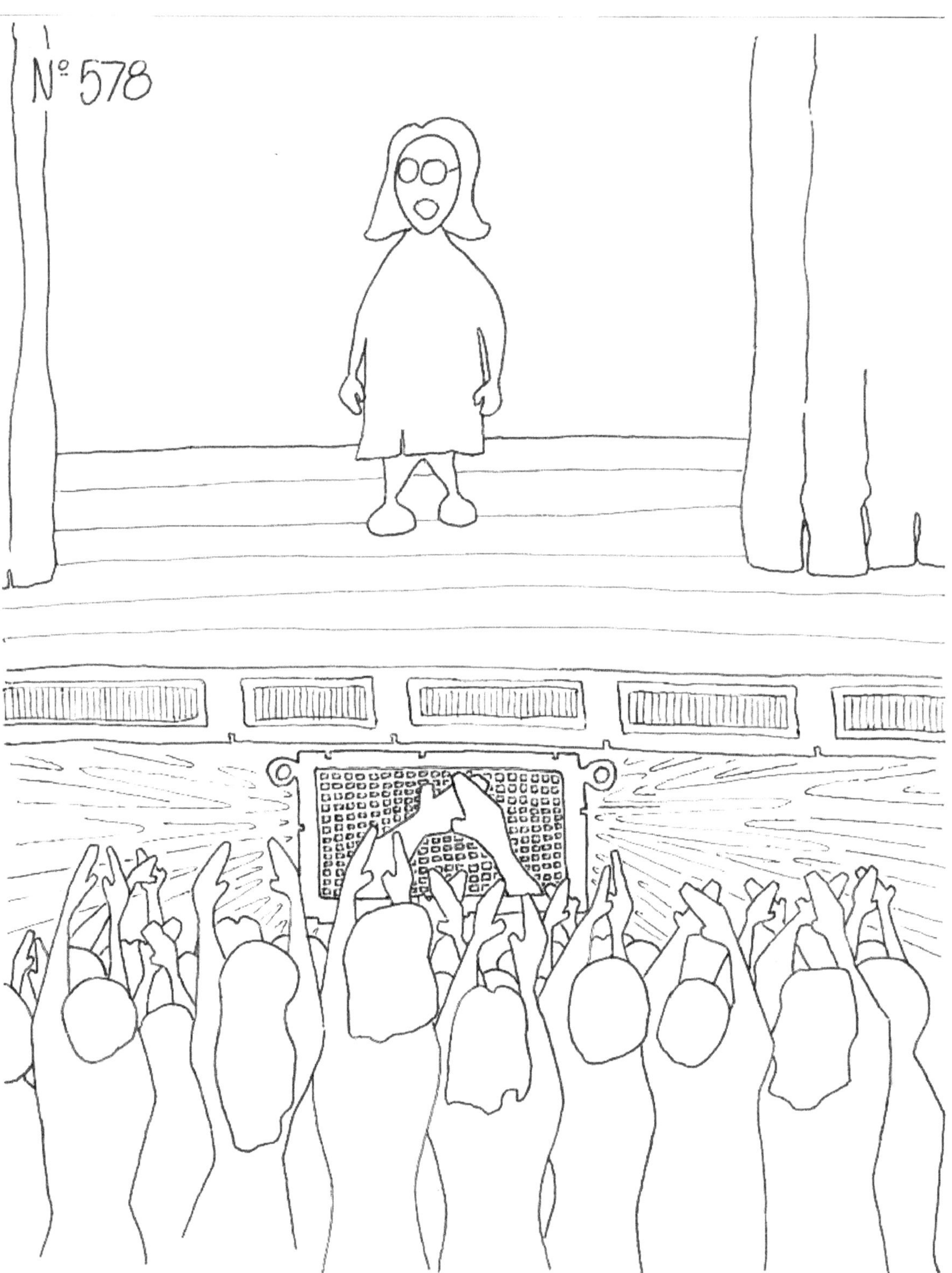
Nº 578

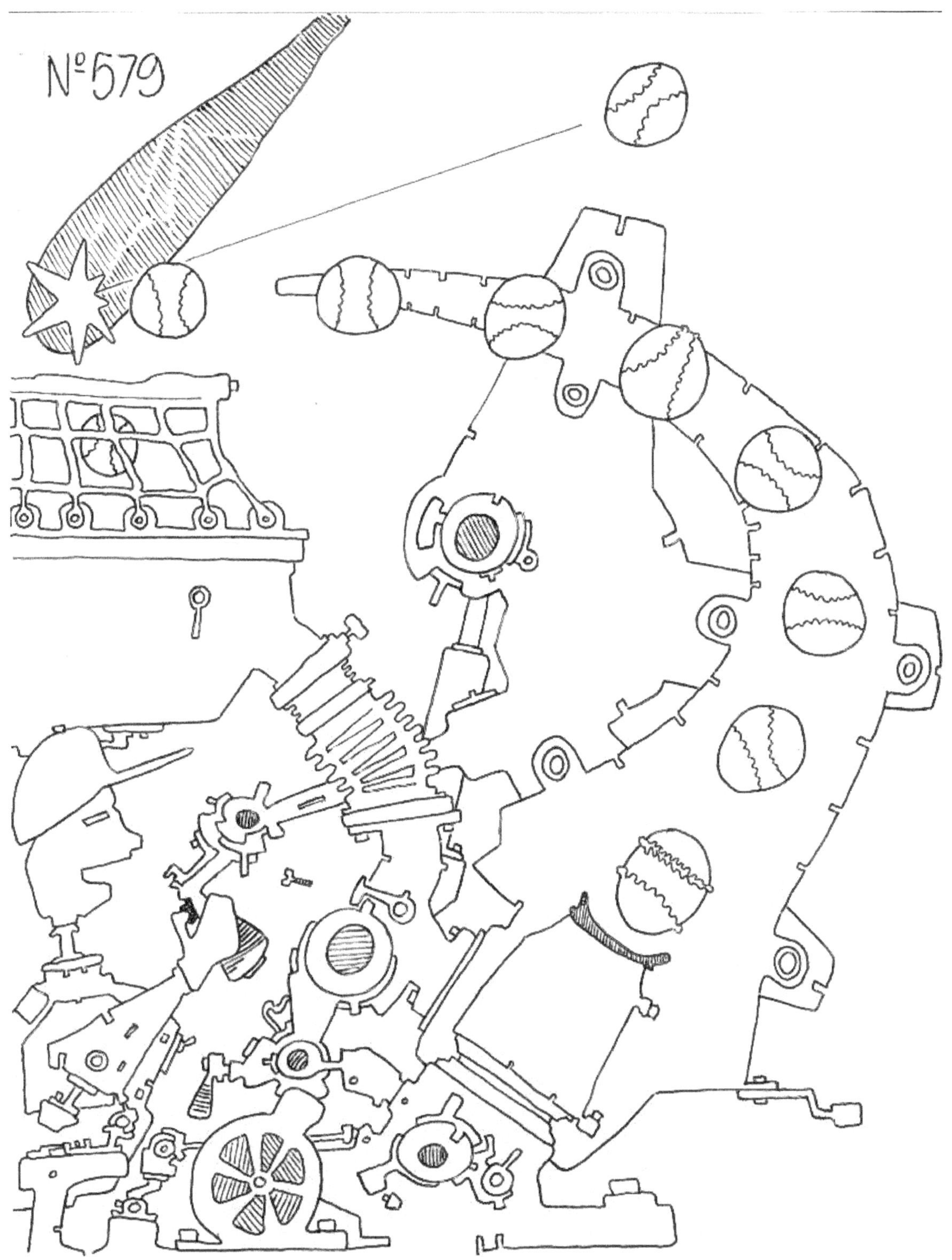
№579

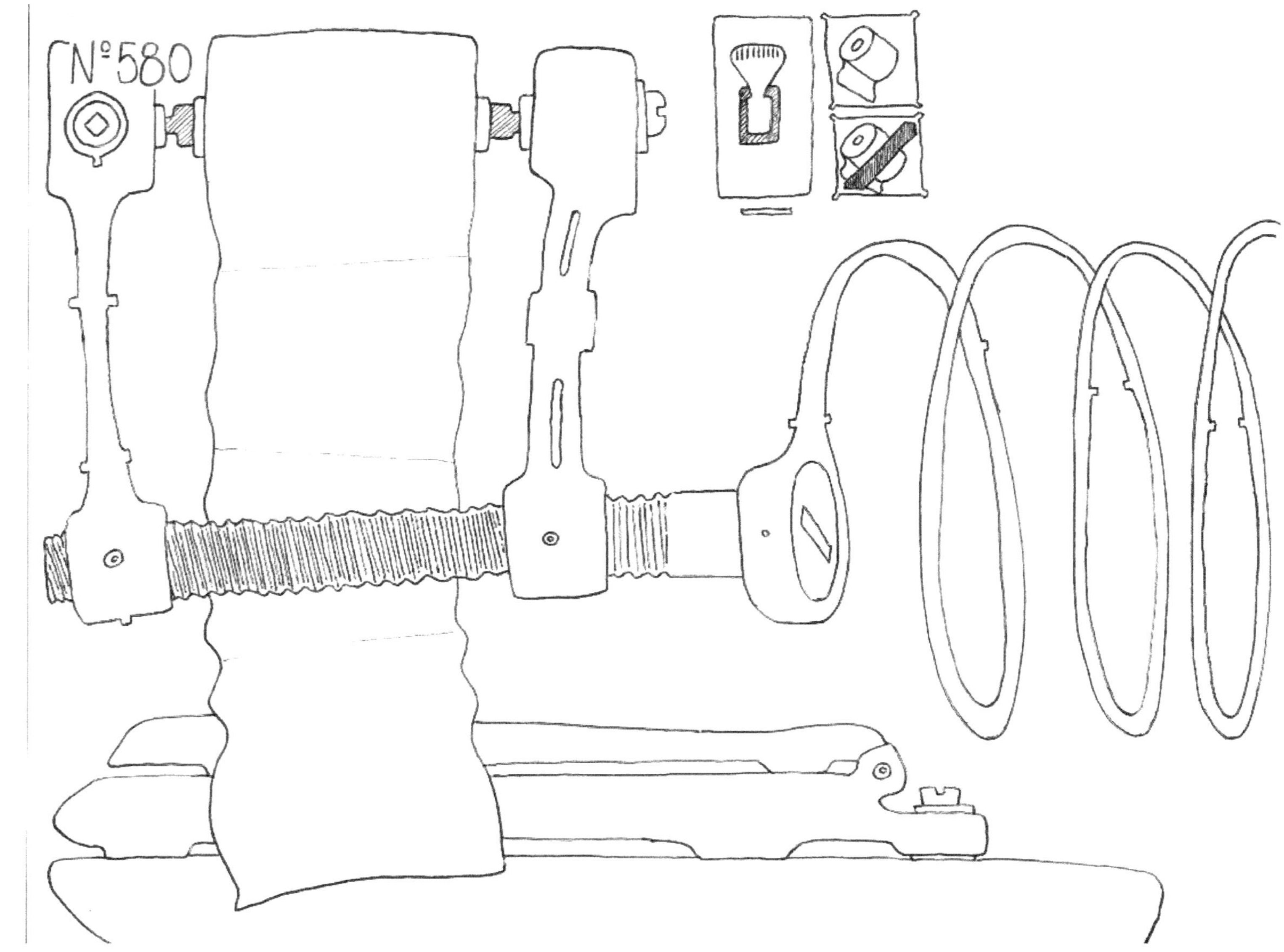
Nº580

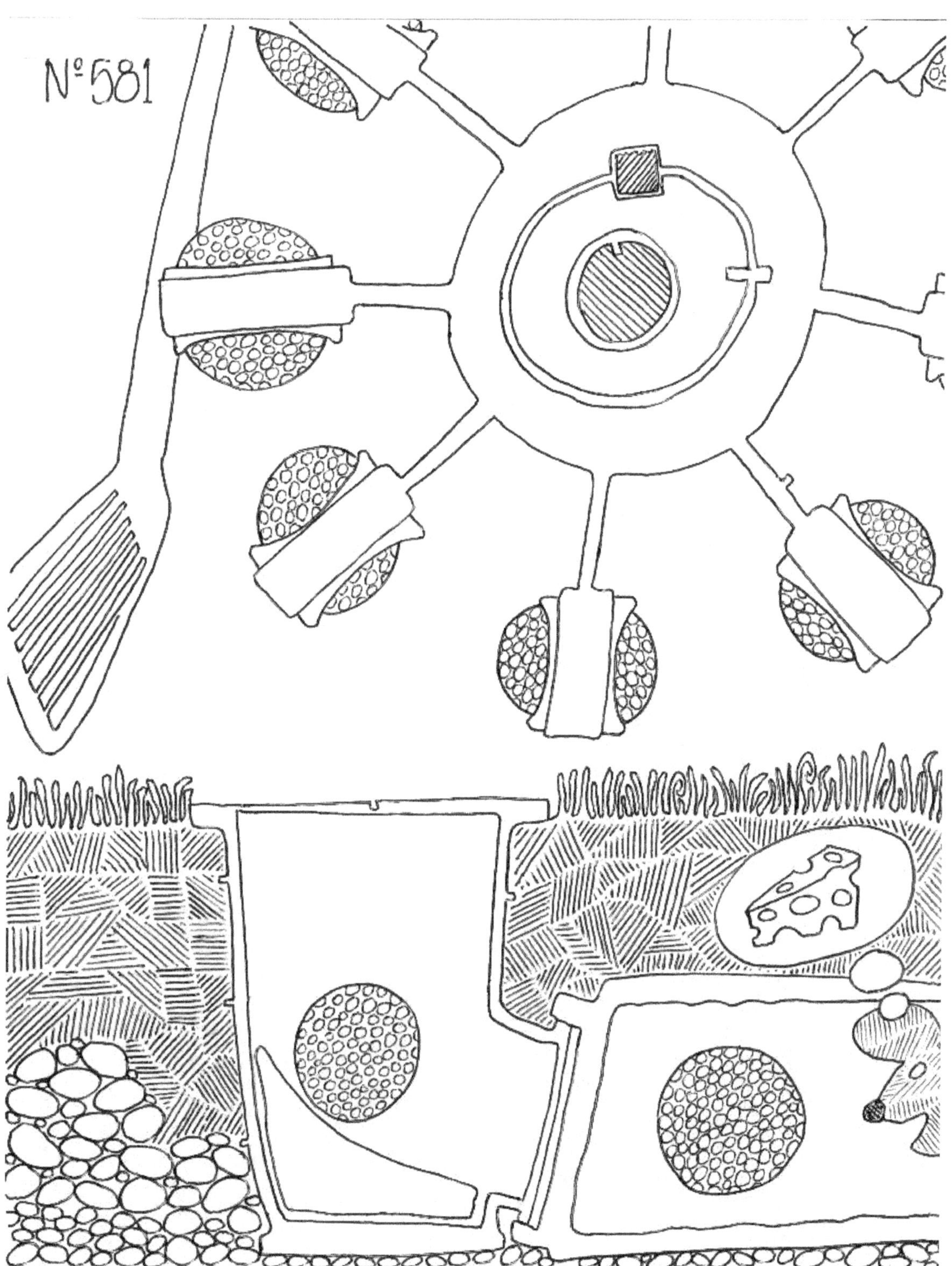
Nº581

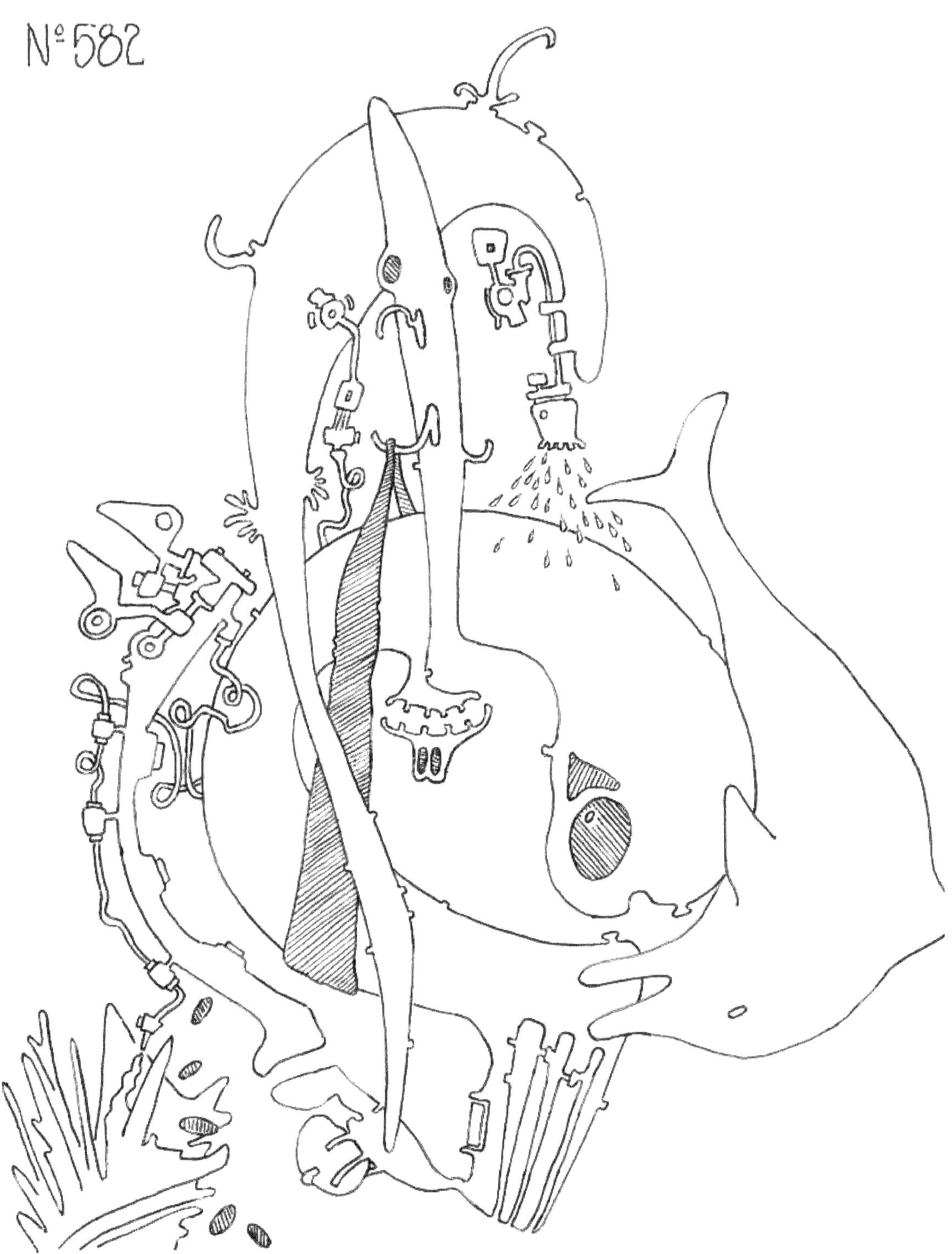
Nº 582

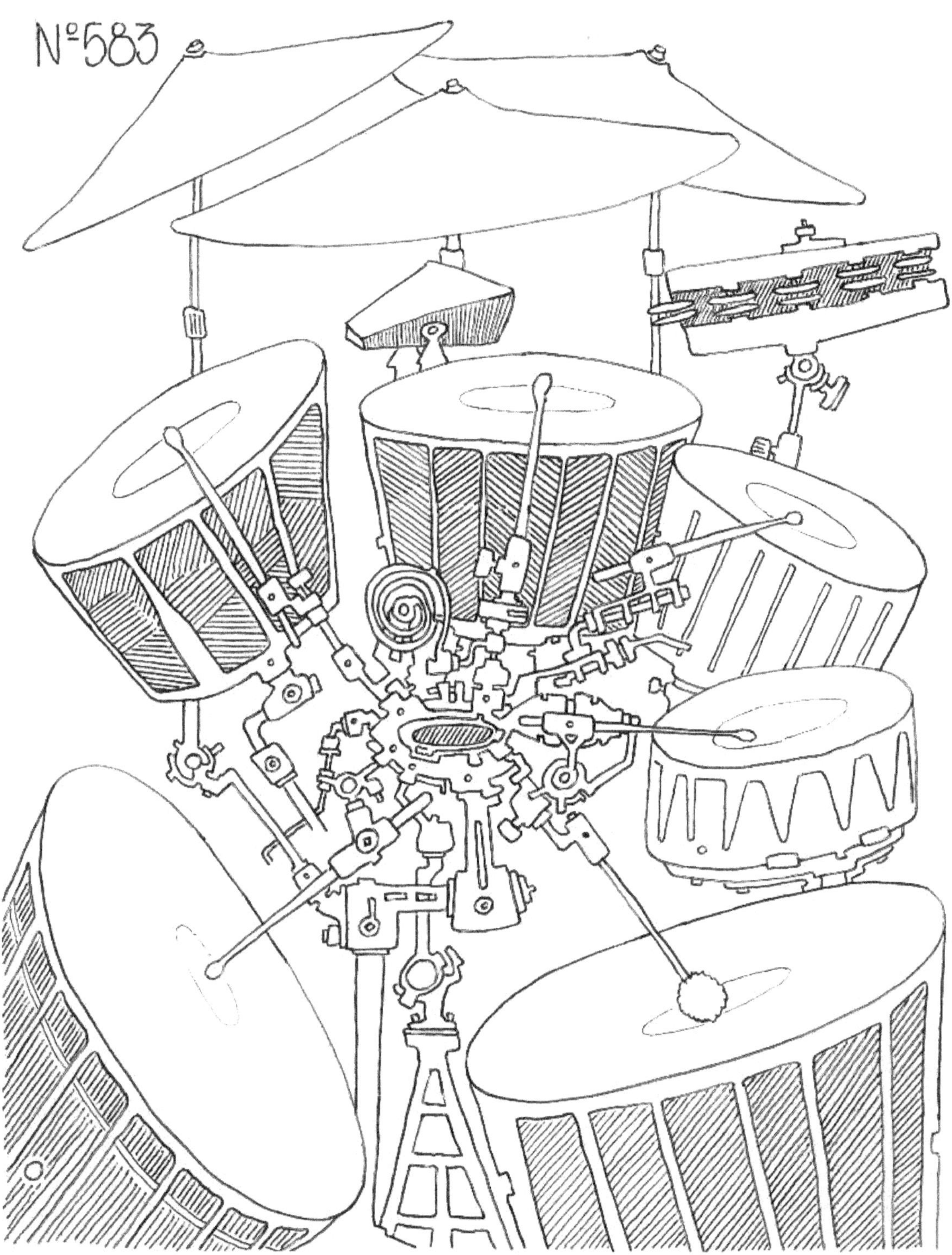
№583

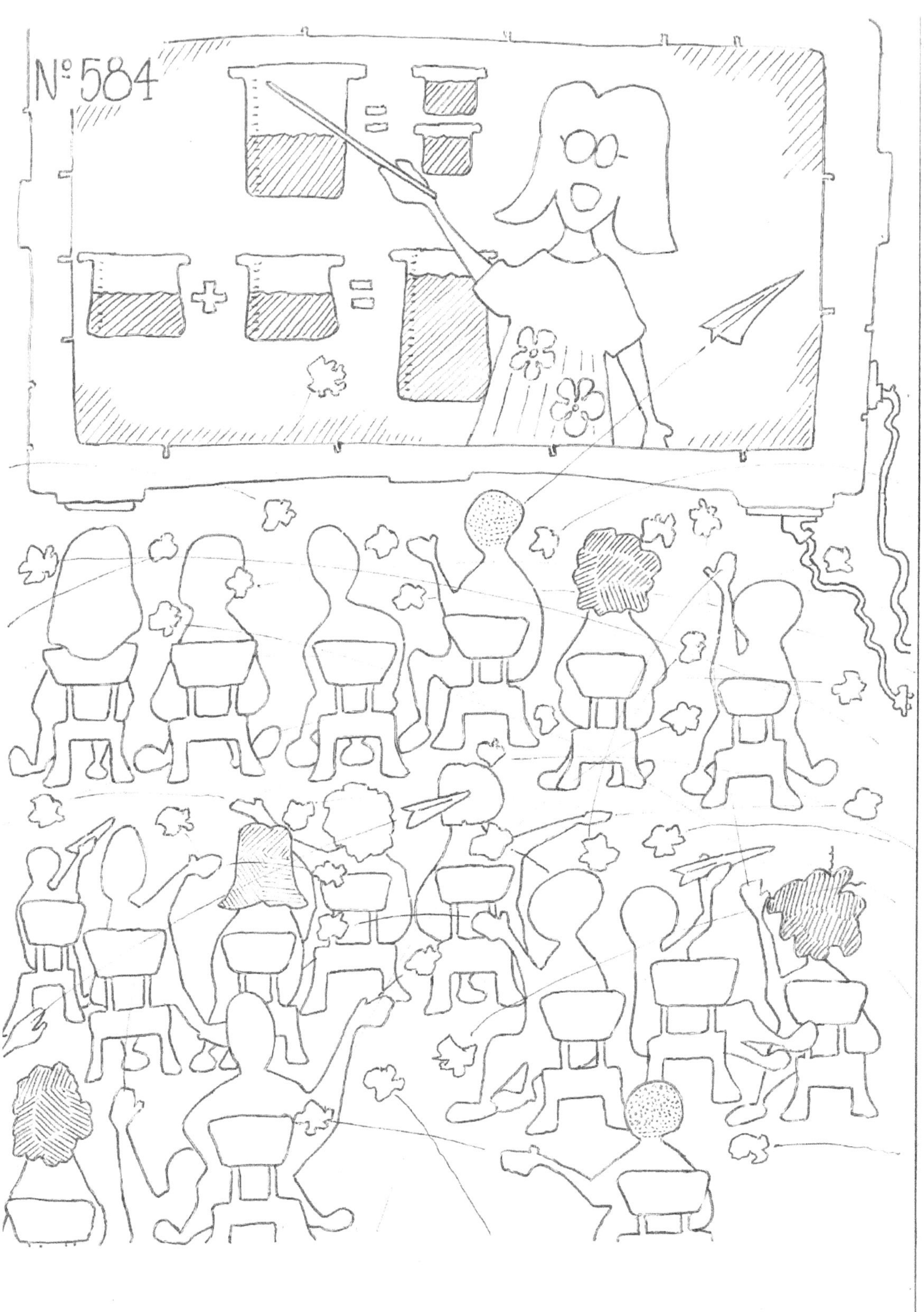
№584

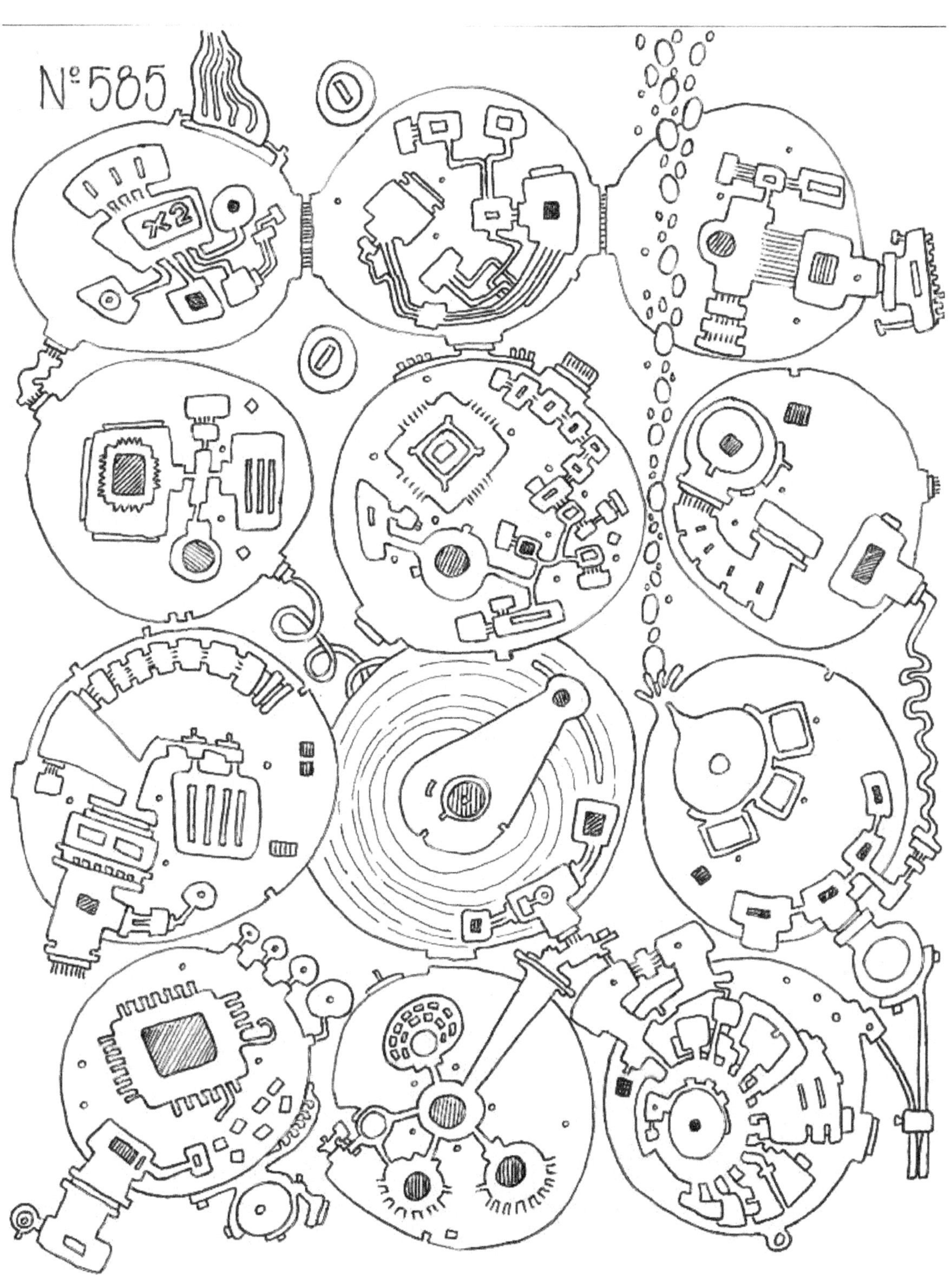
Nº 585
x2

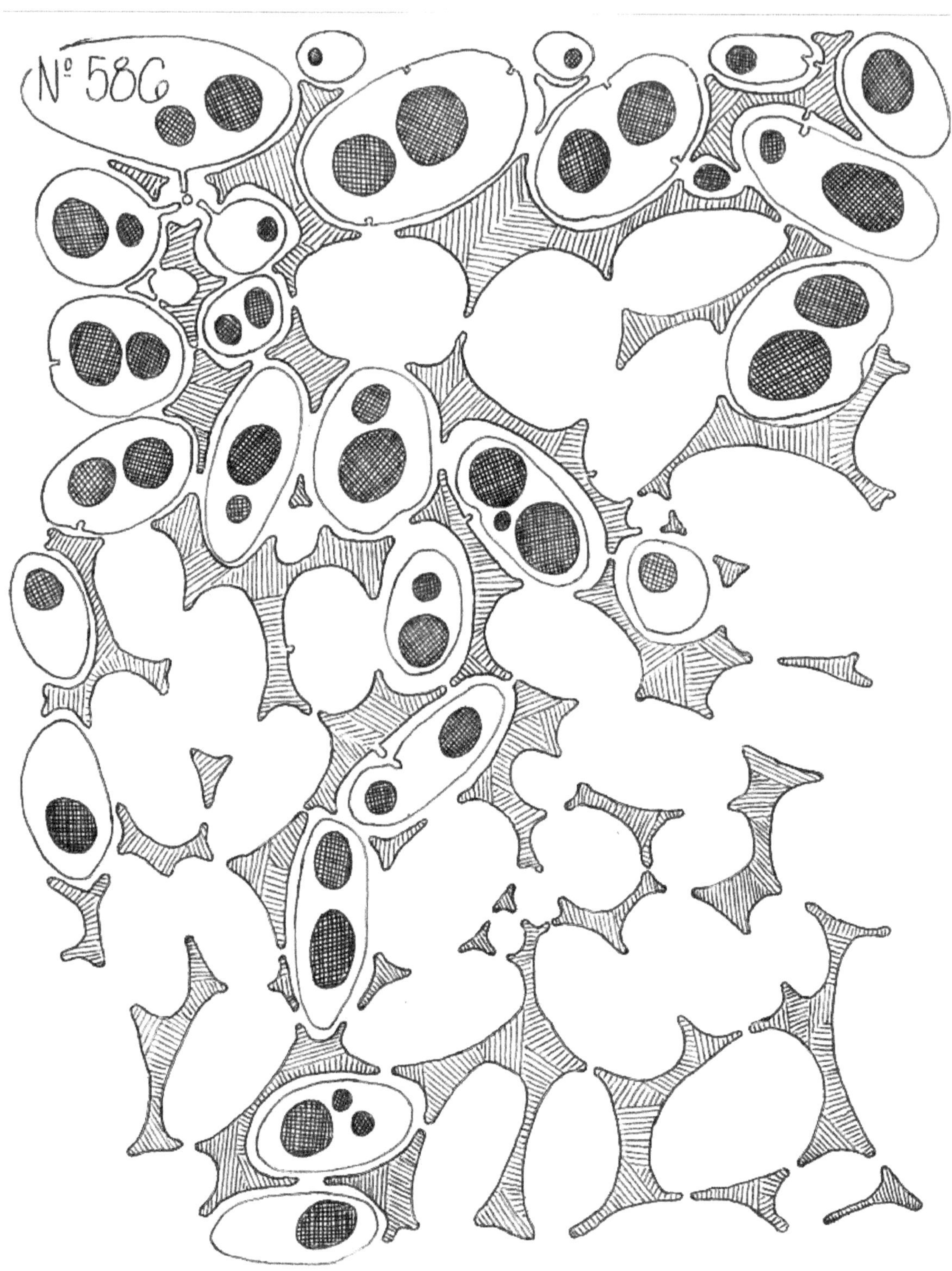

N° 586

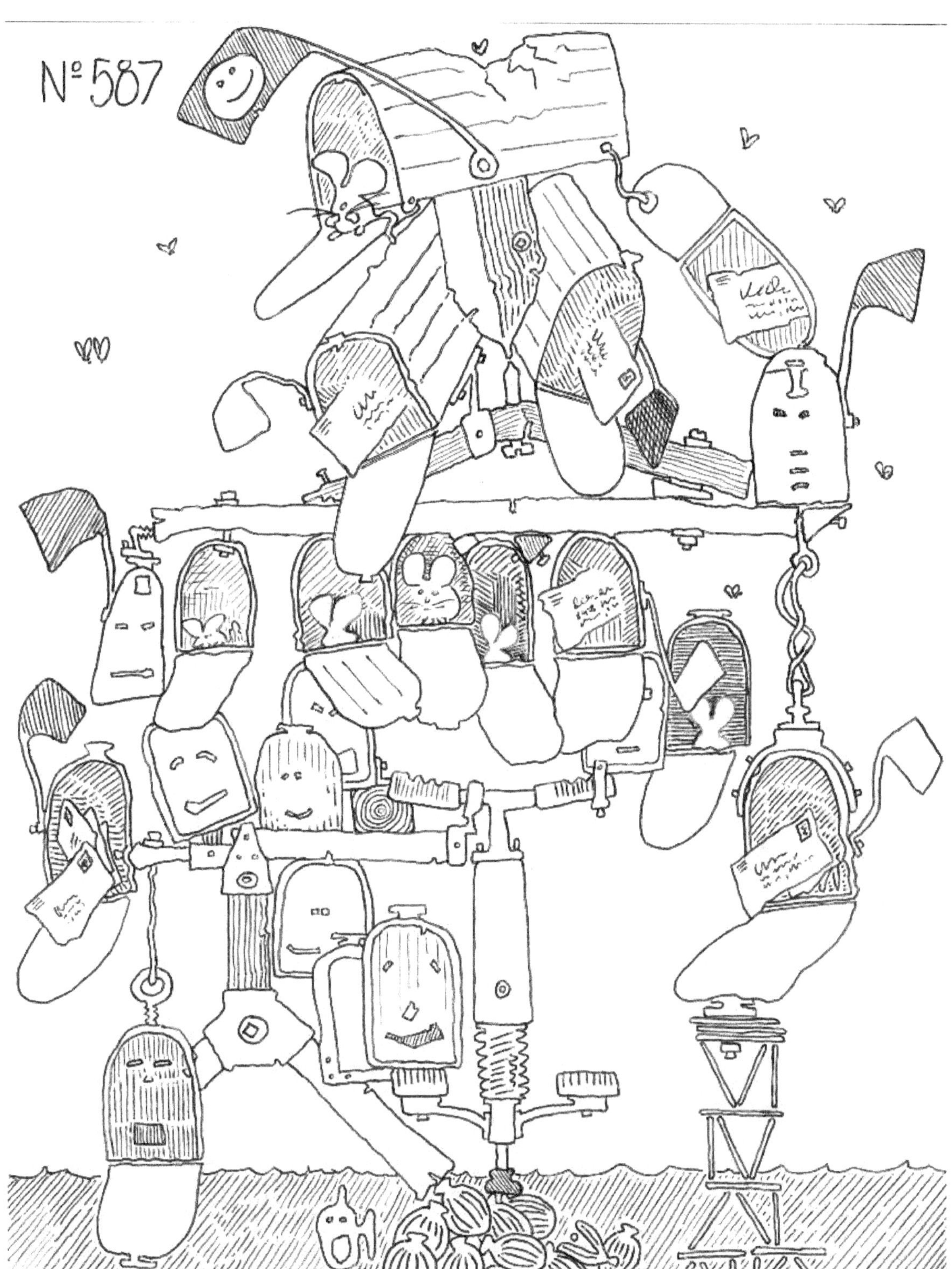
Nº 587

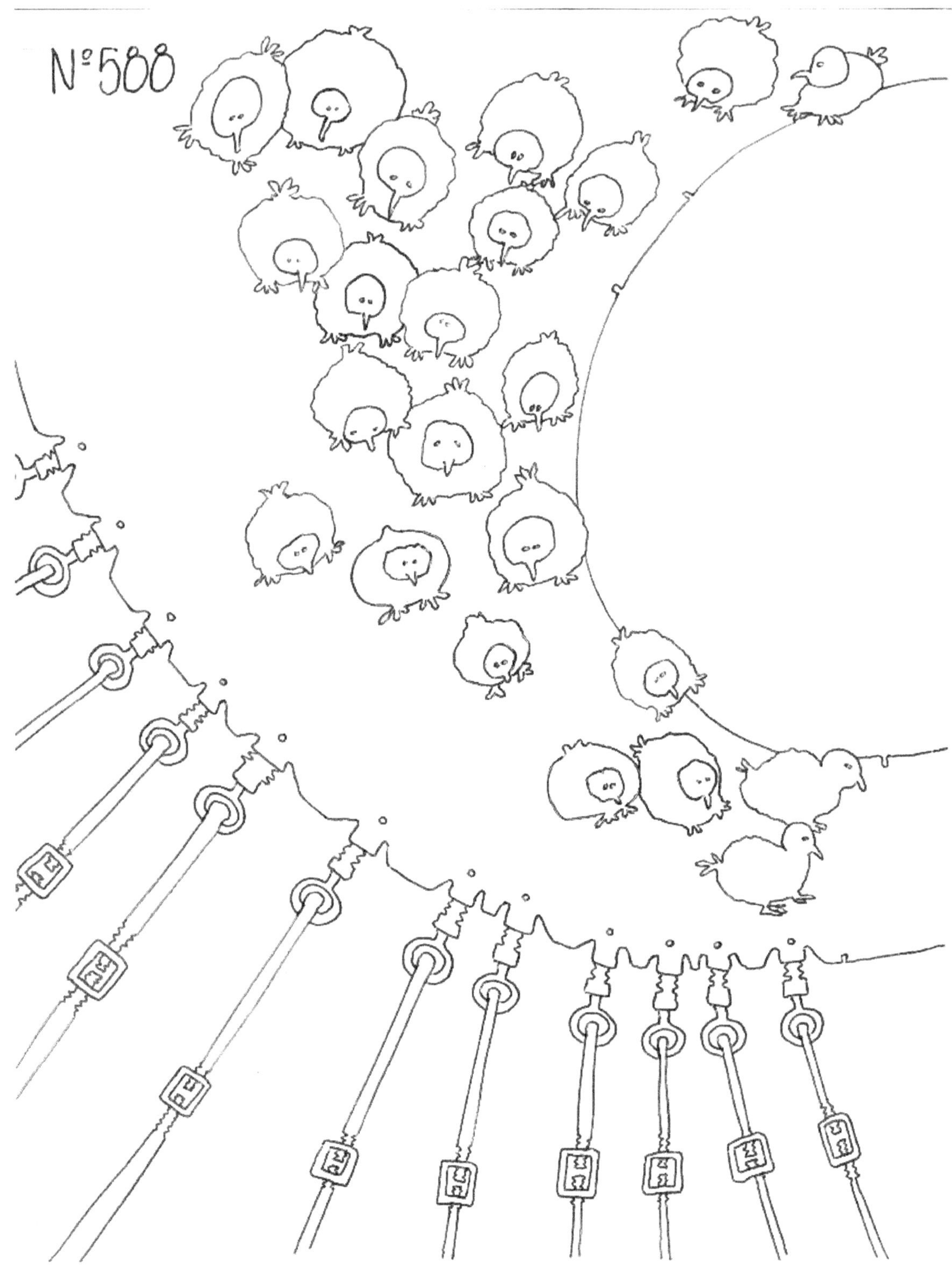
Nº588

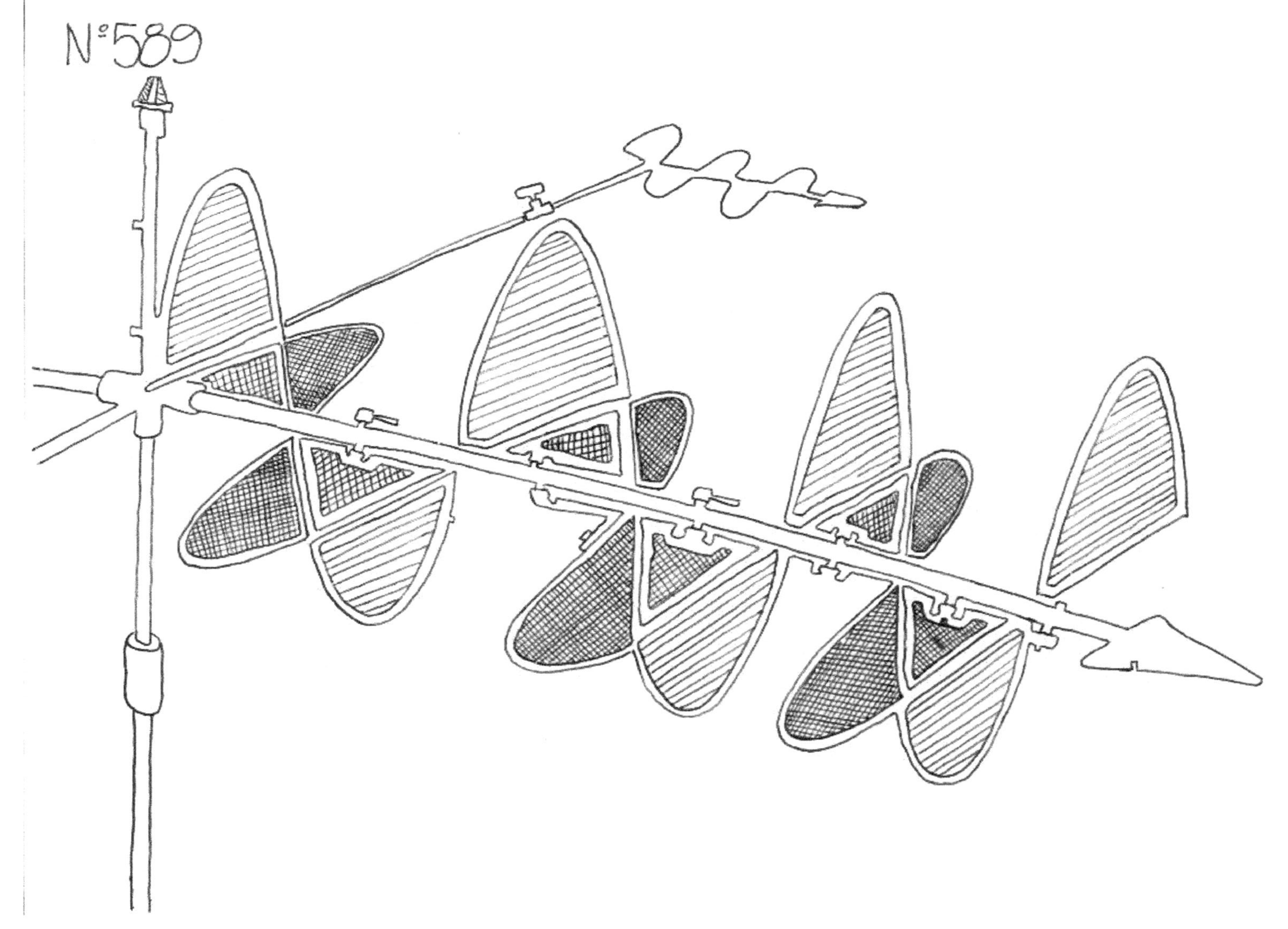
N° 589

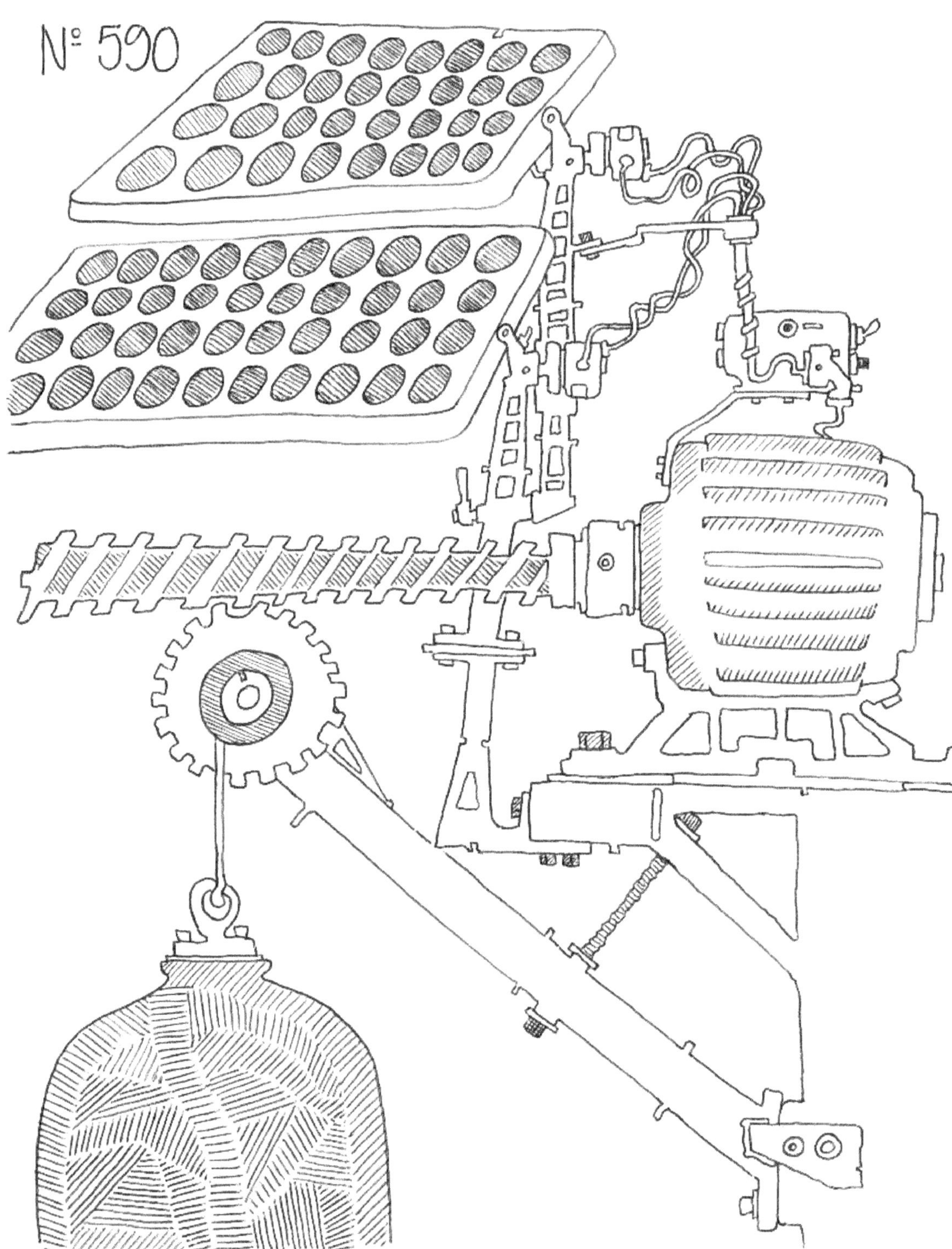
№ 590

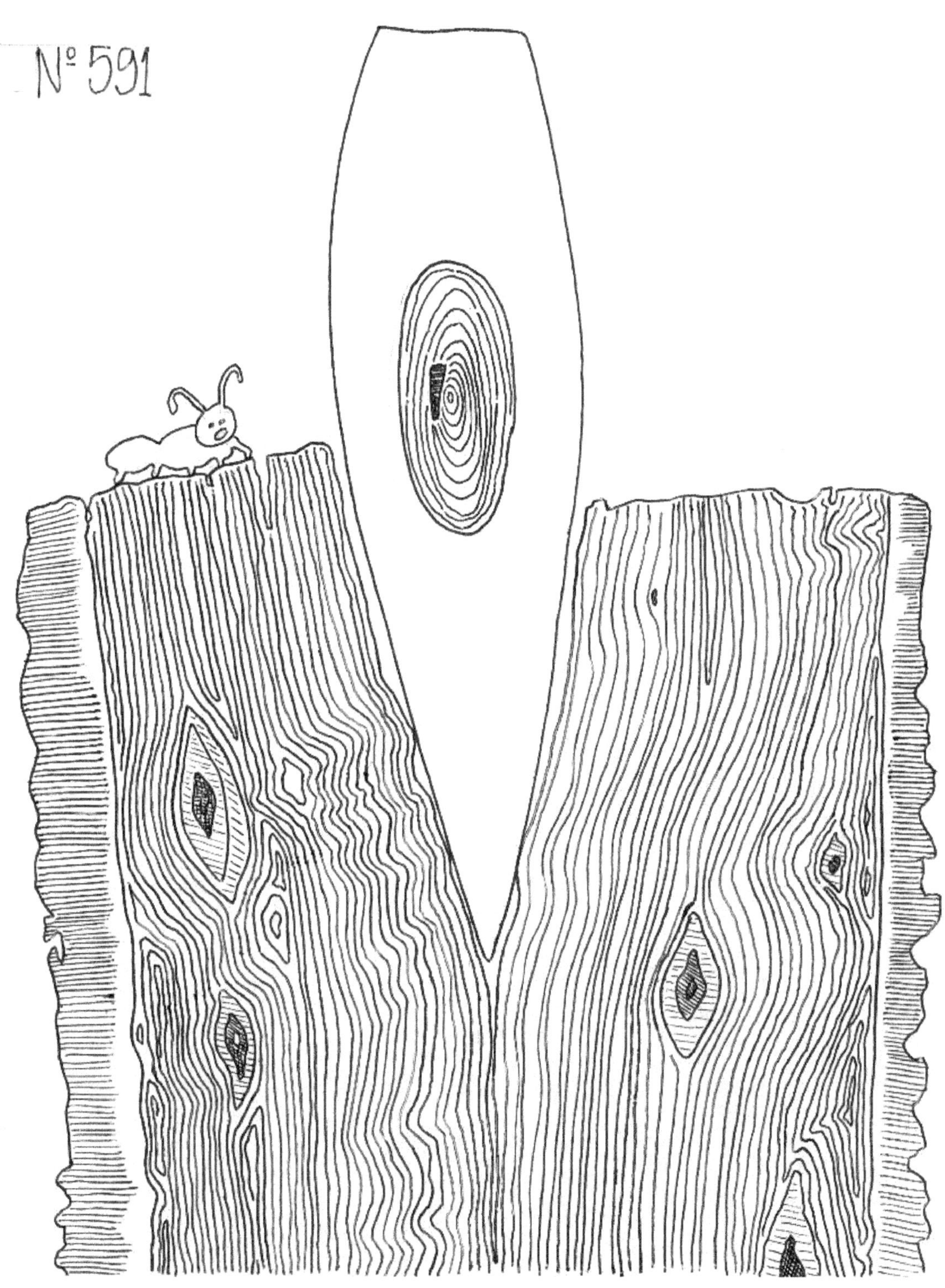
№ 591

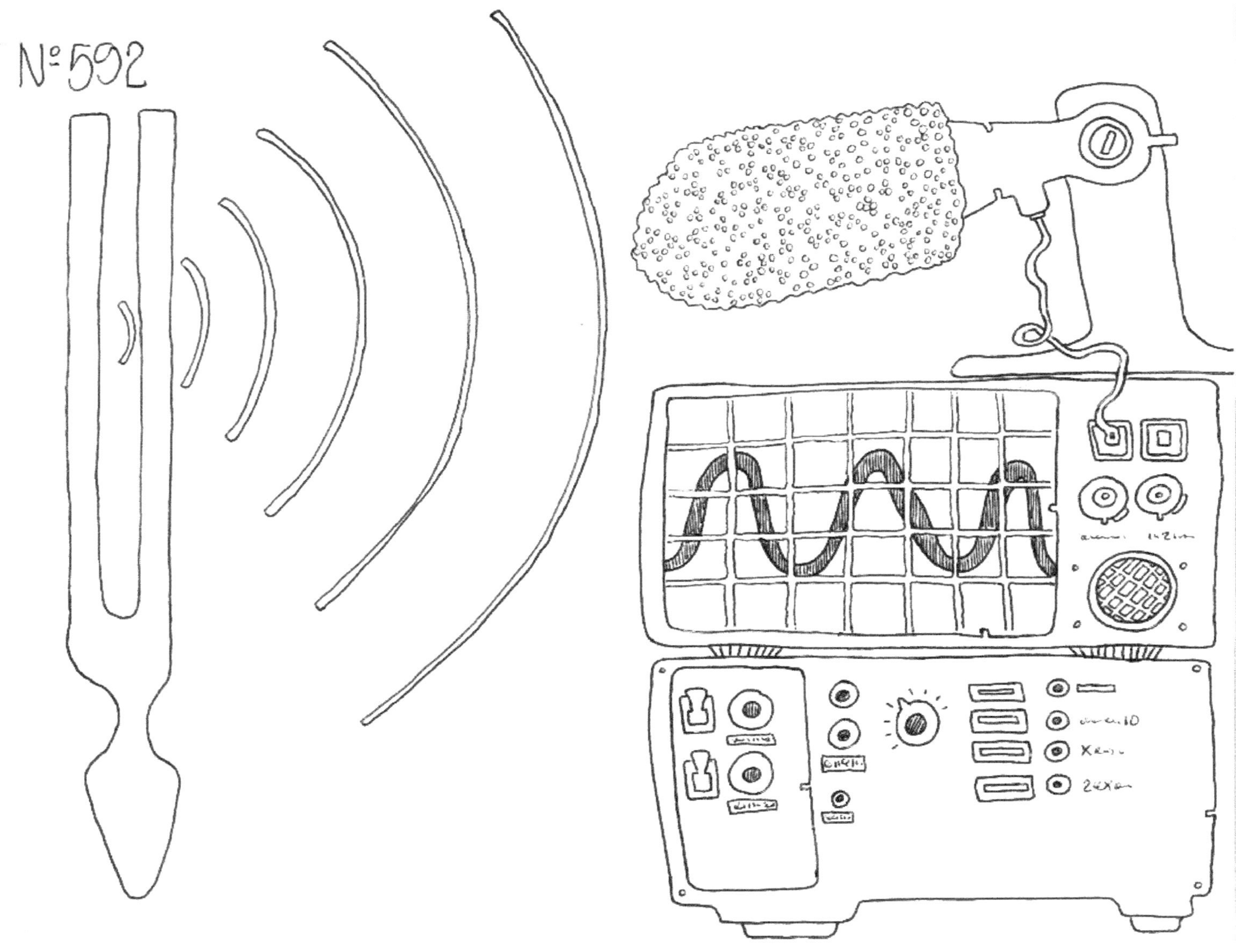
Nº592

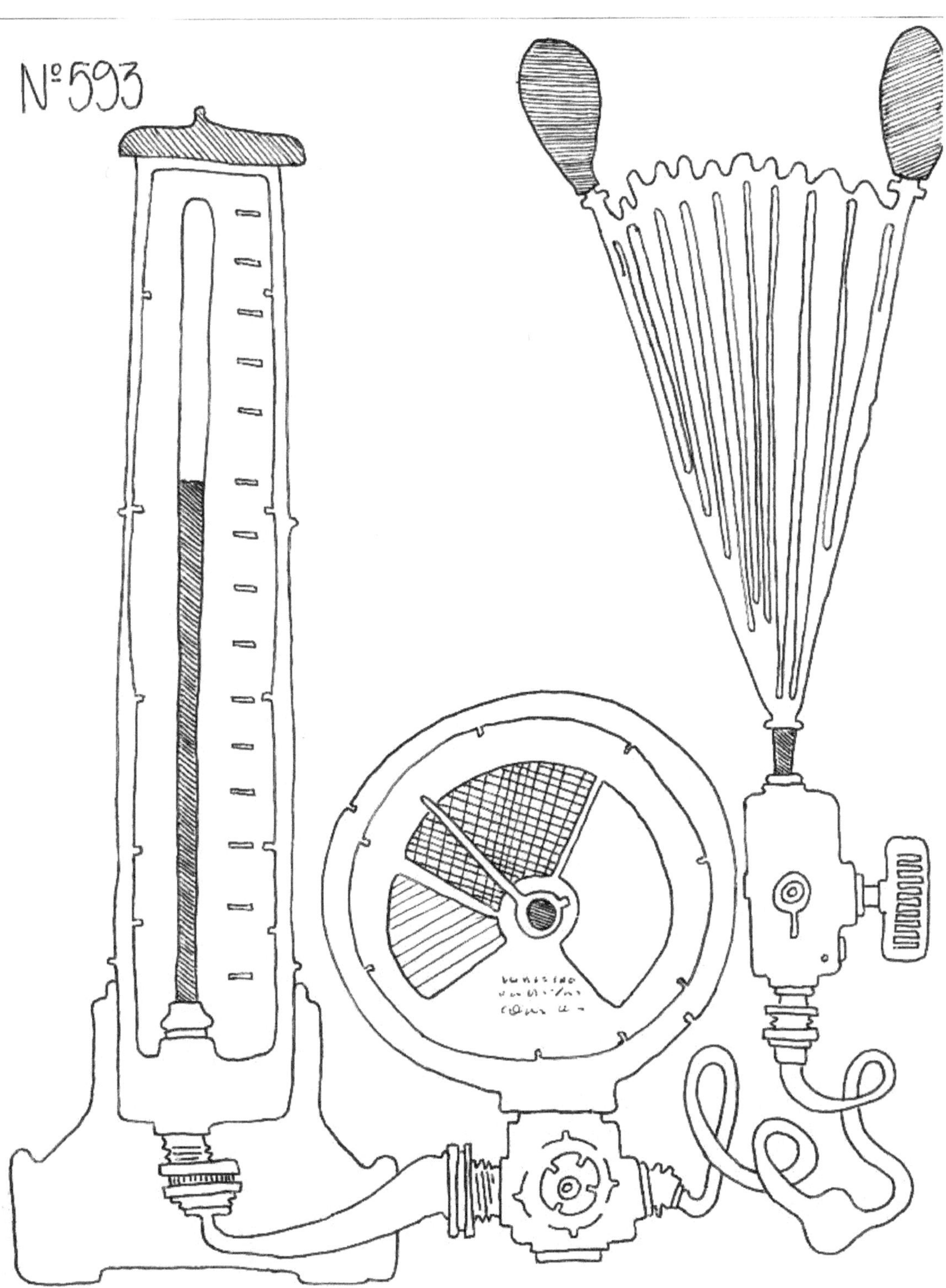
Nº593

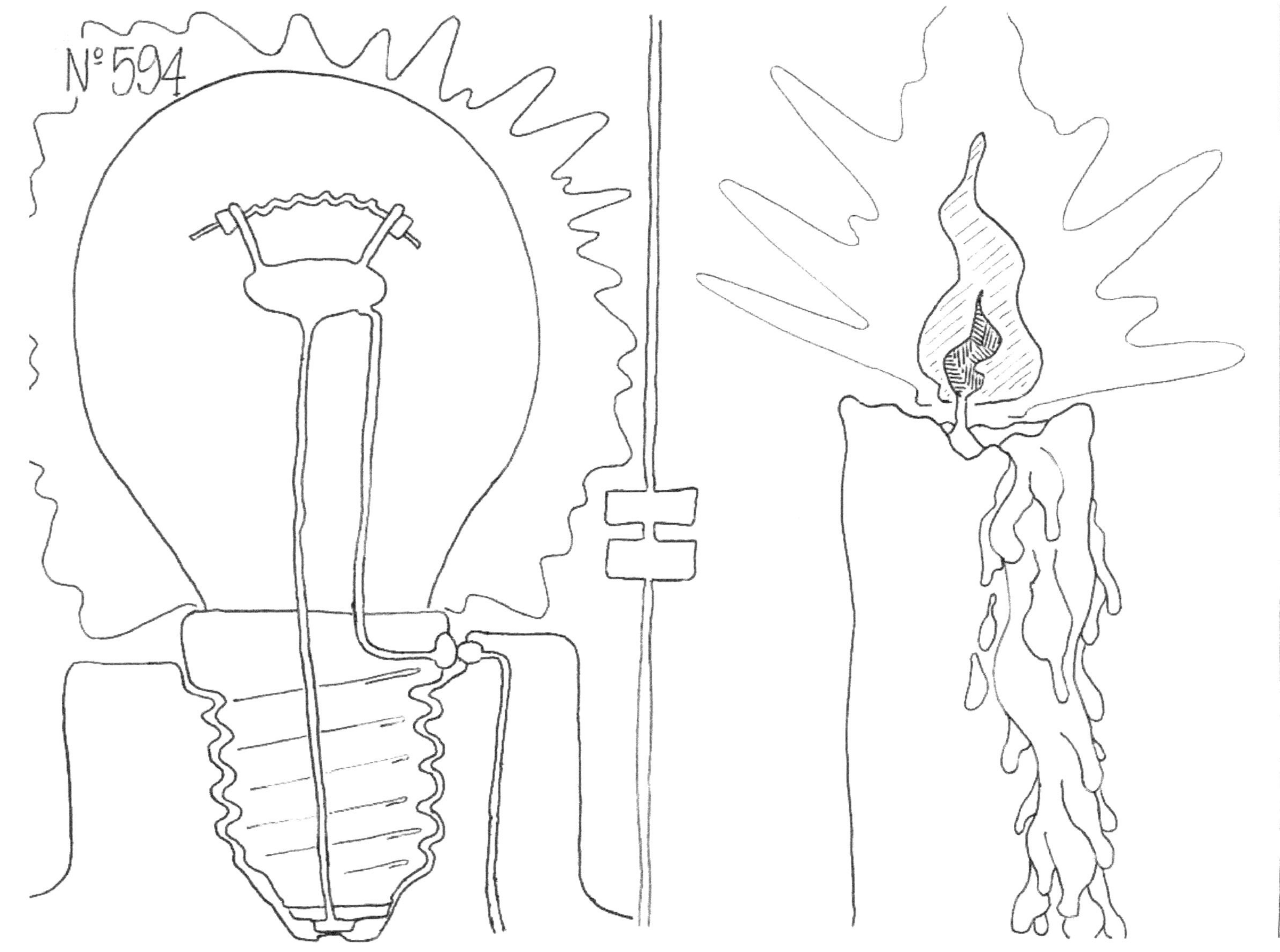
№ 594

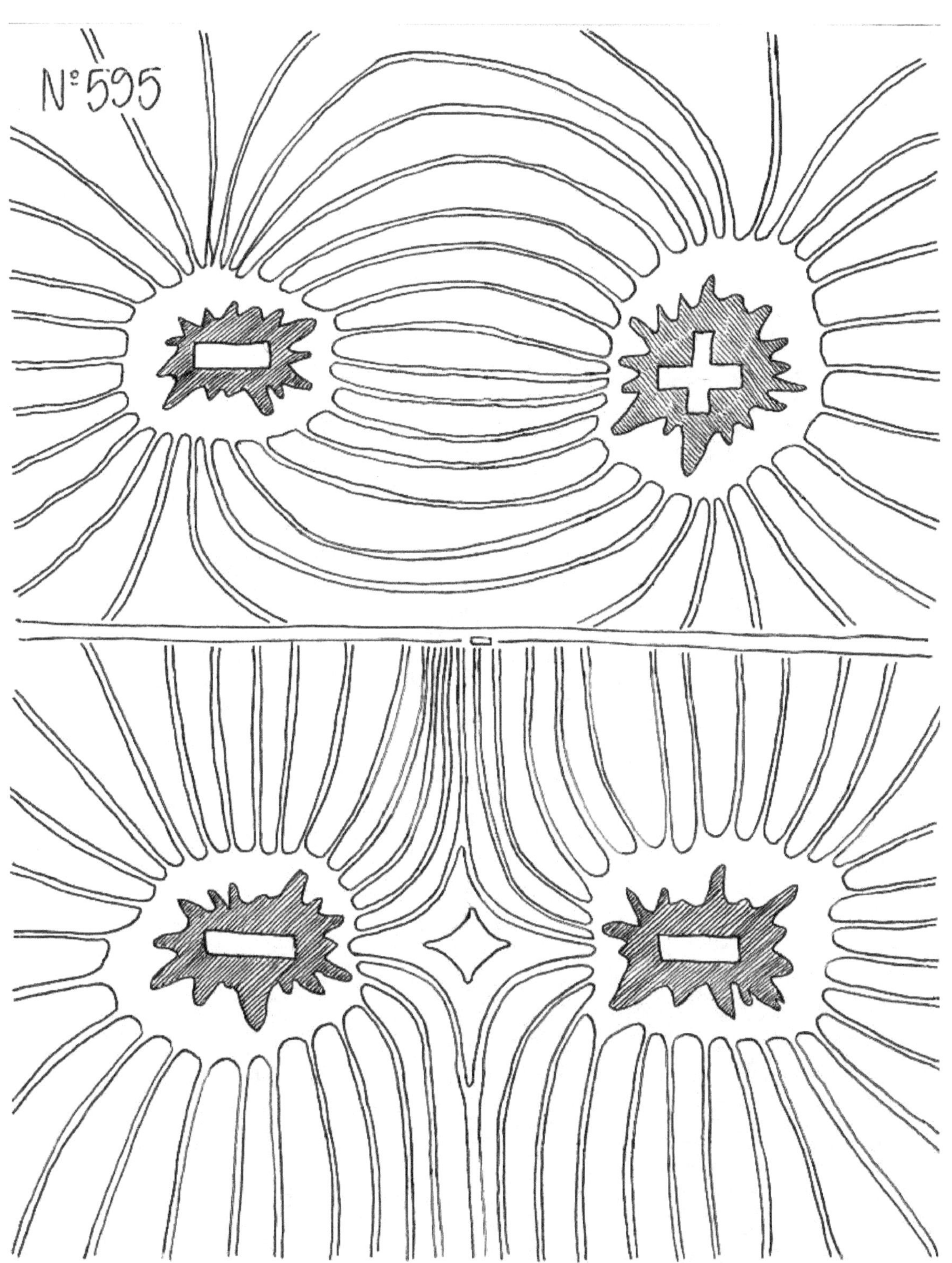
N° 595

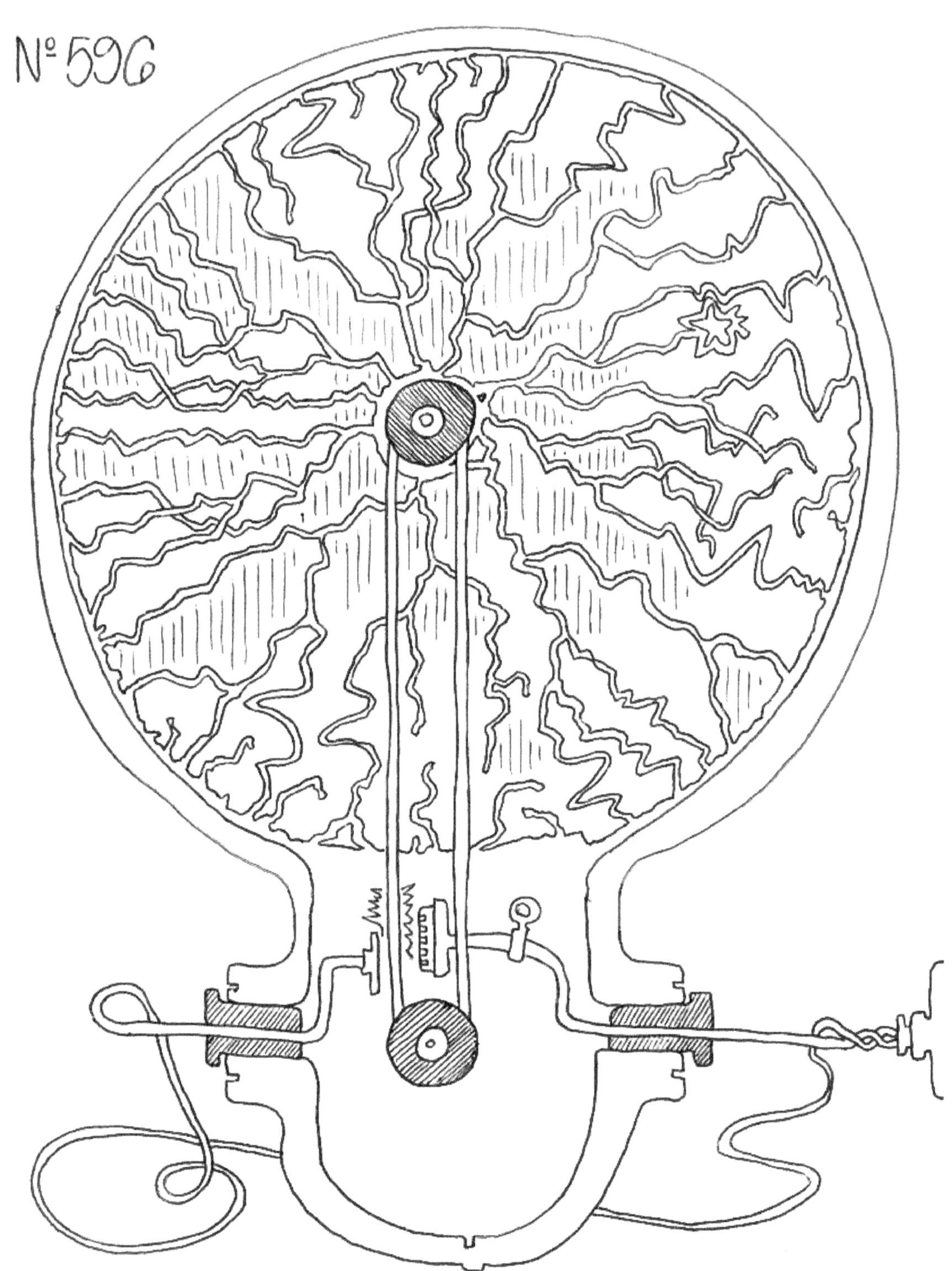
№ 596

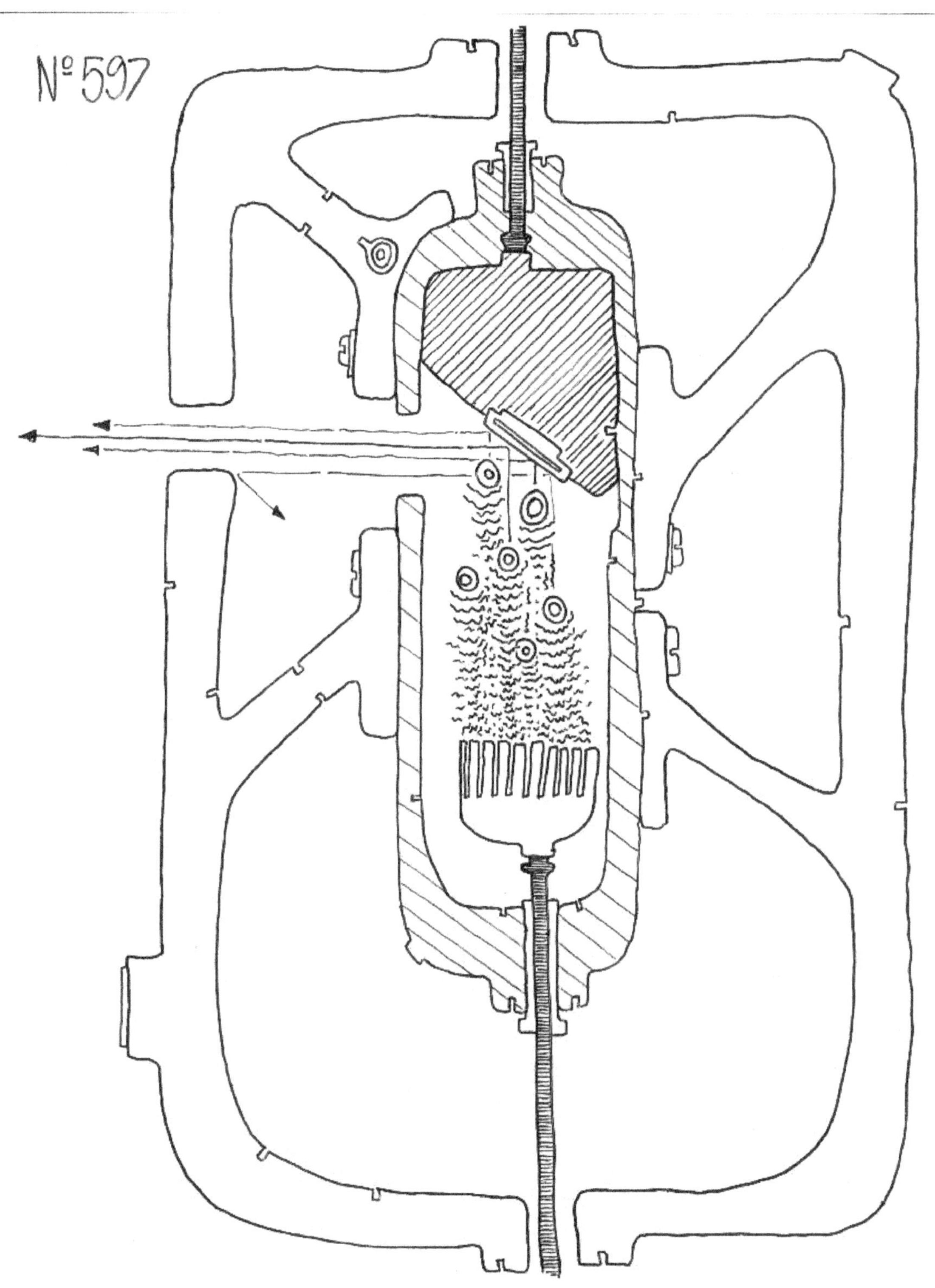
Nº 597

Nº 598

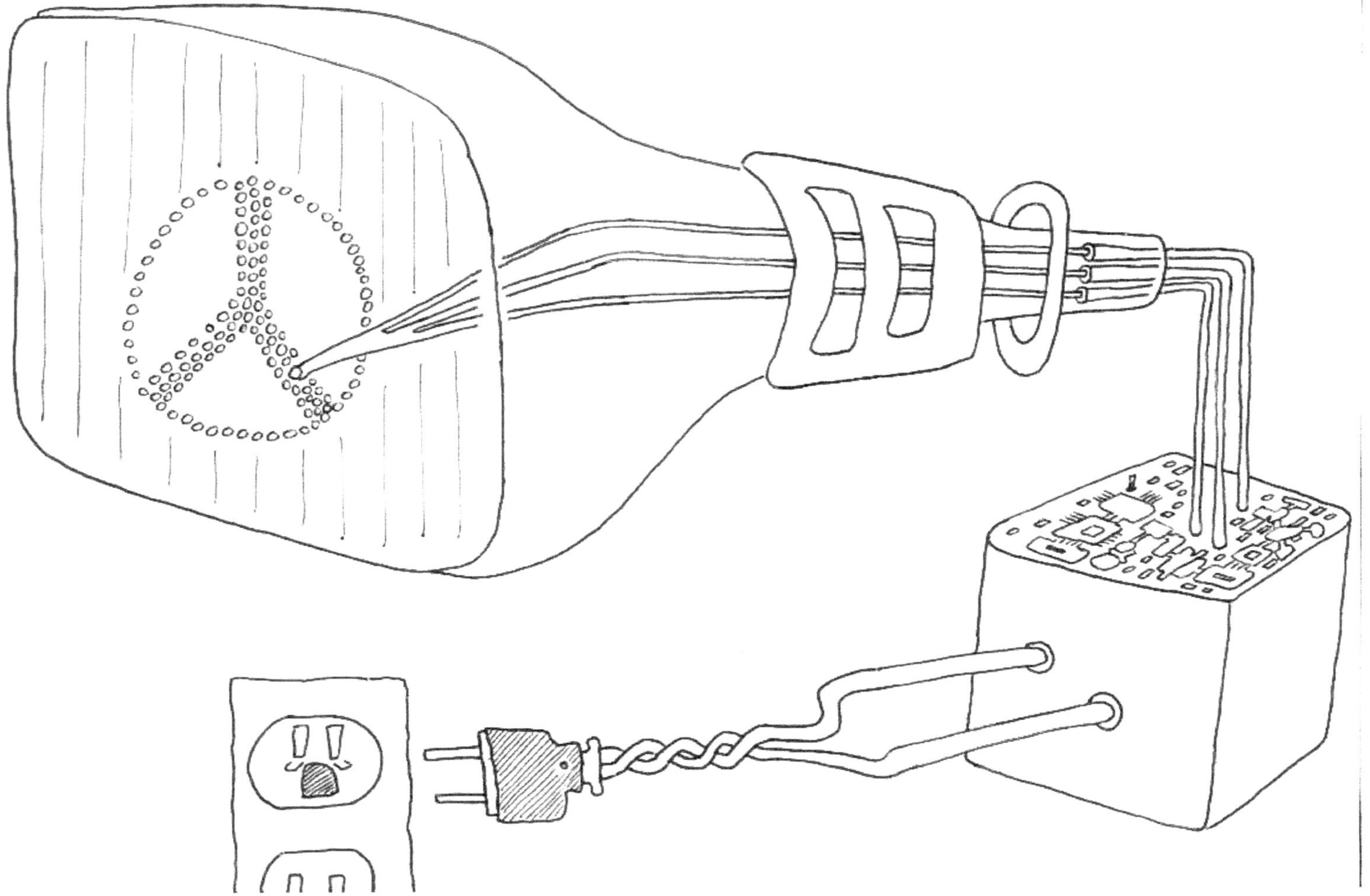

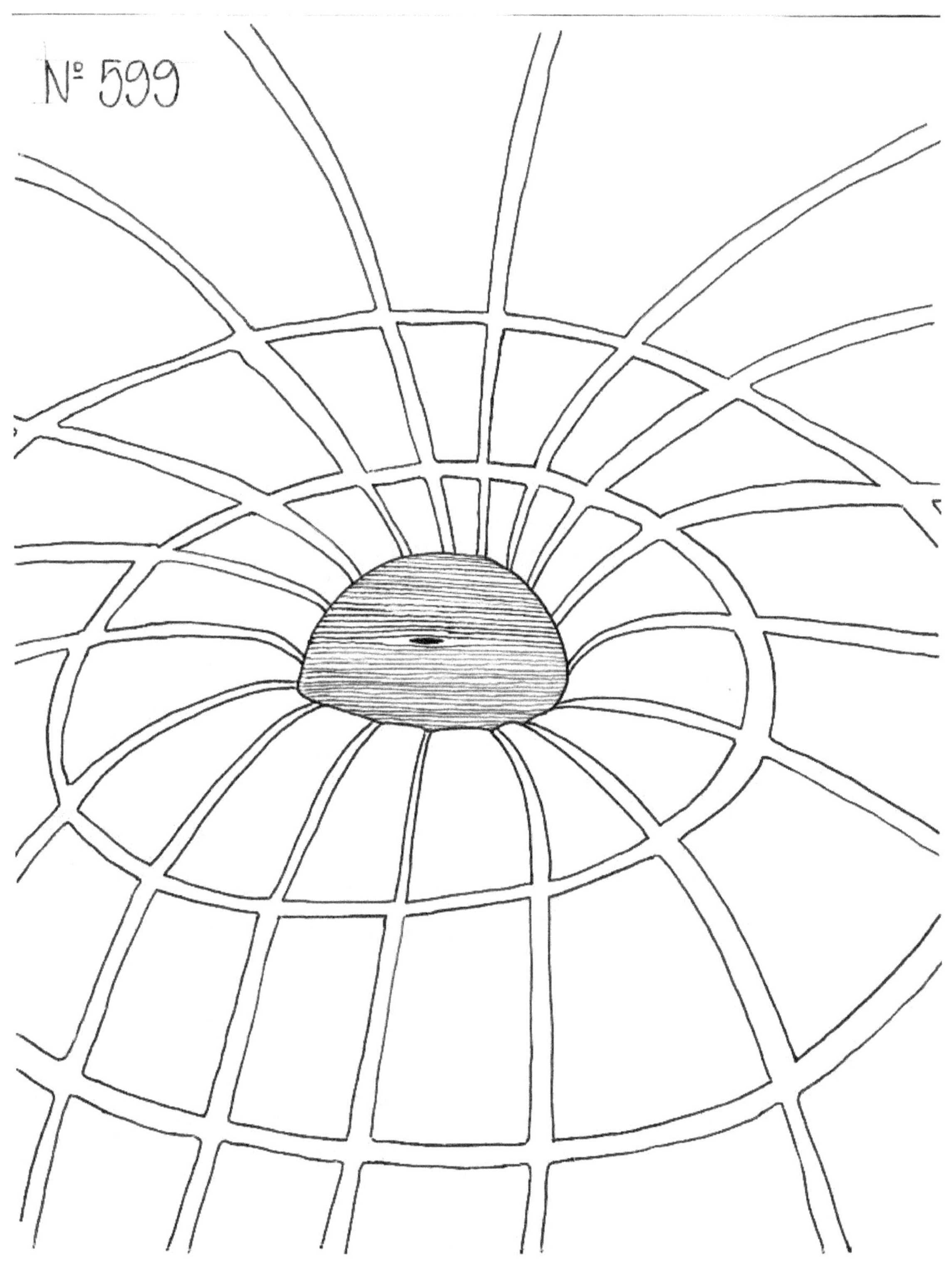
№ 599

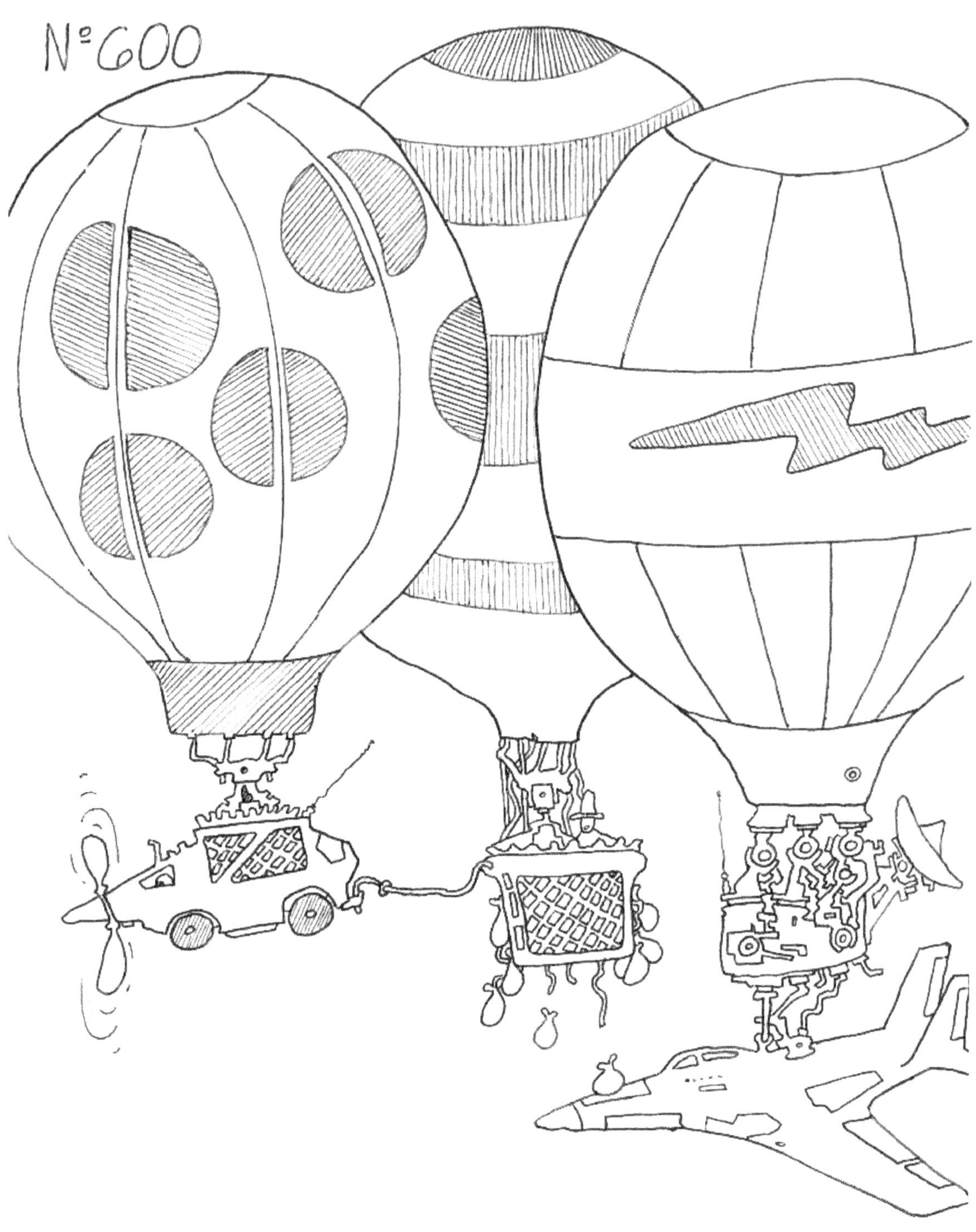
N°600

N°601

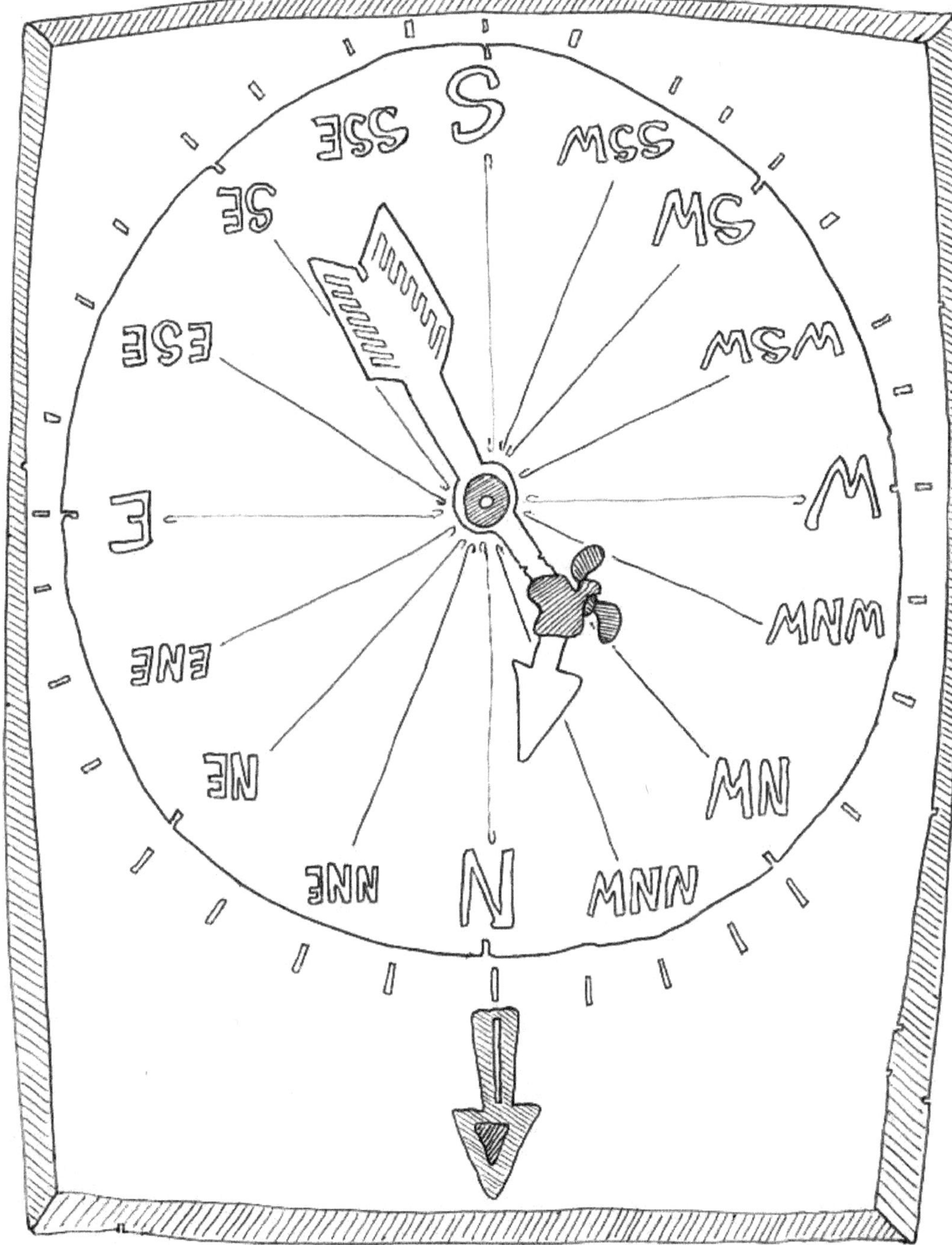

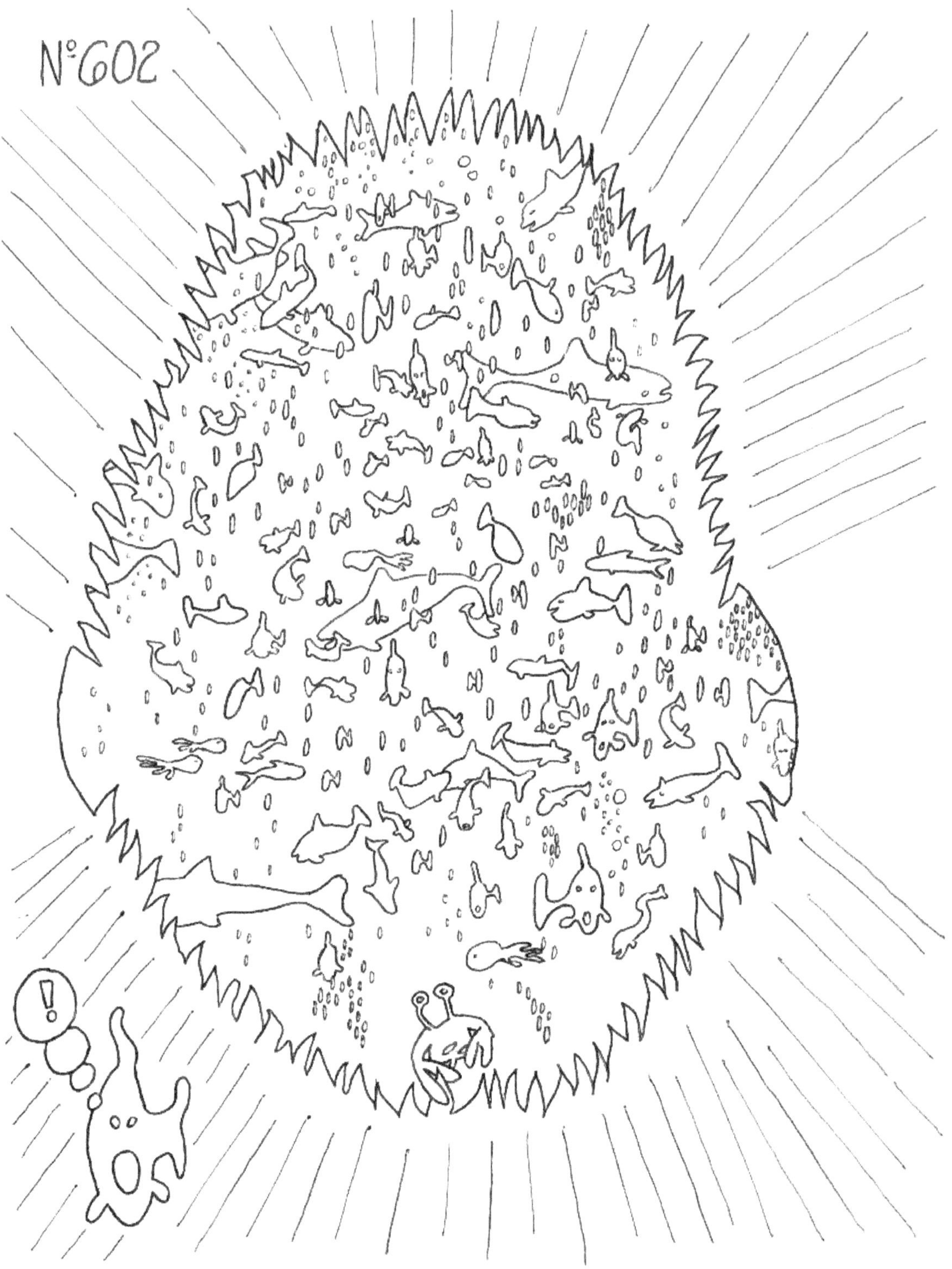
№602
!

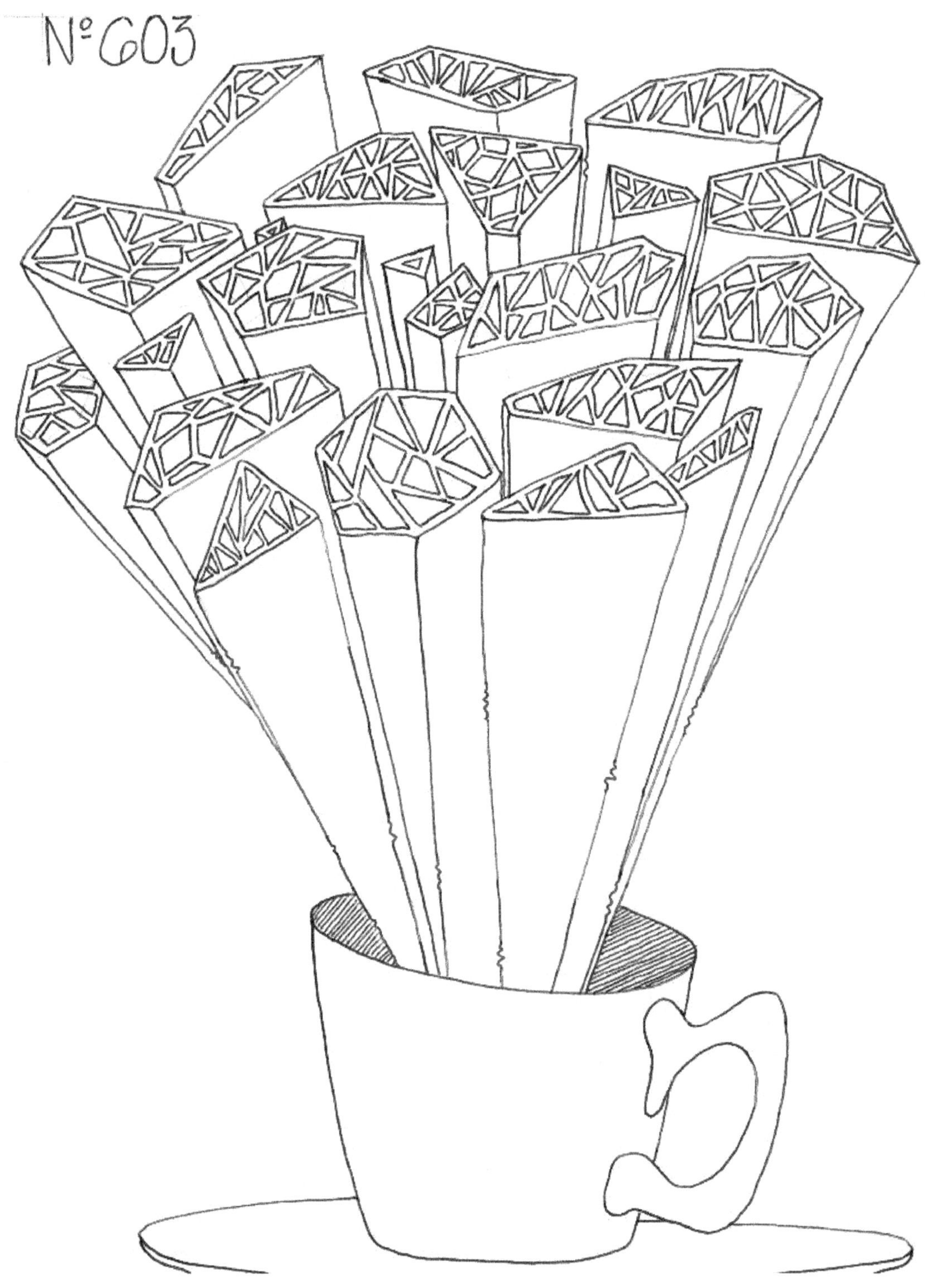
№603

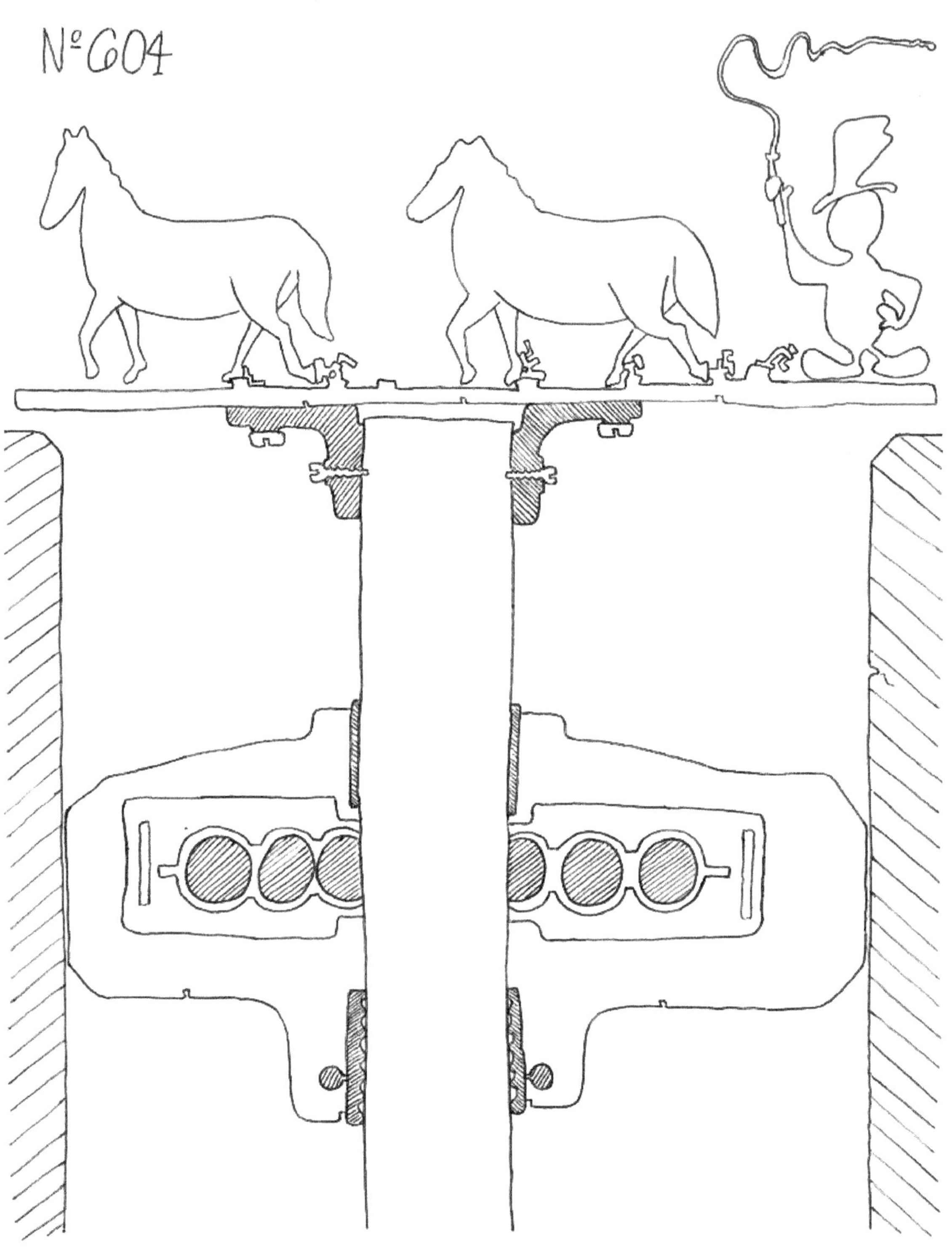
№604

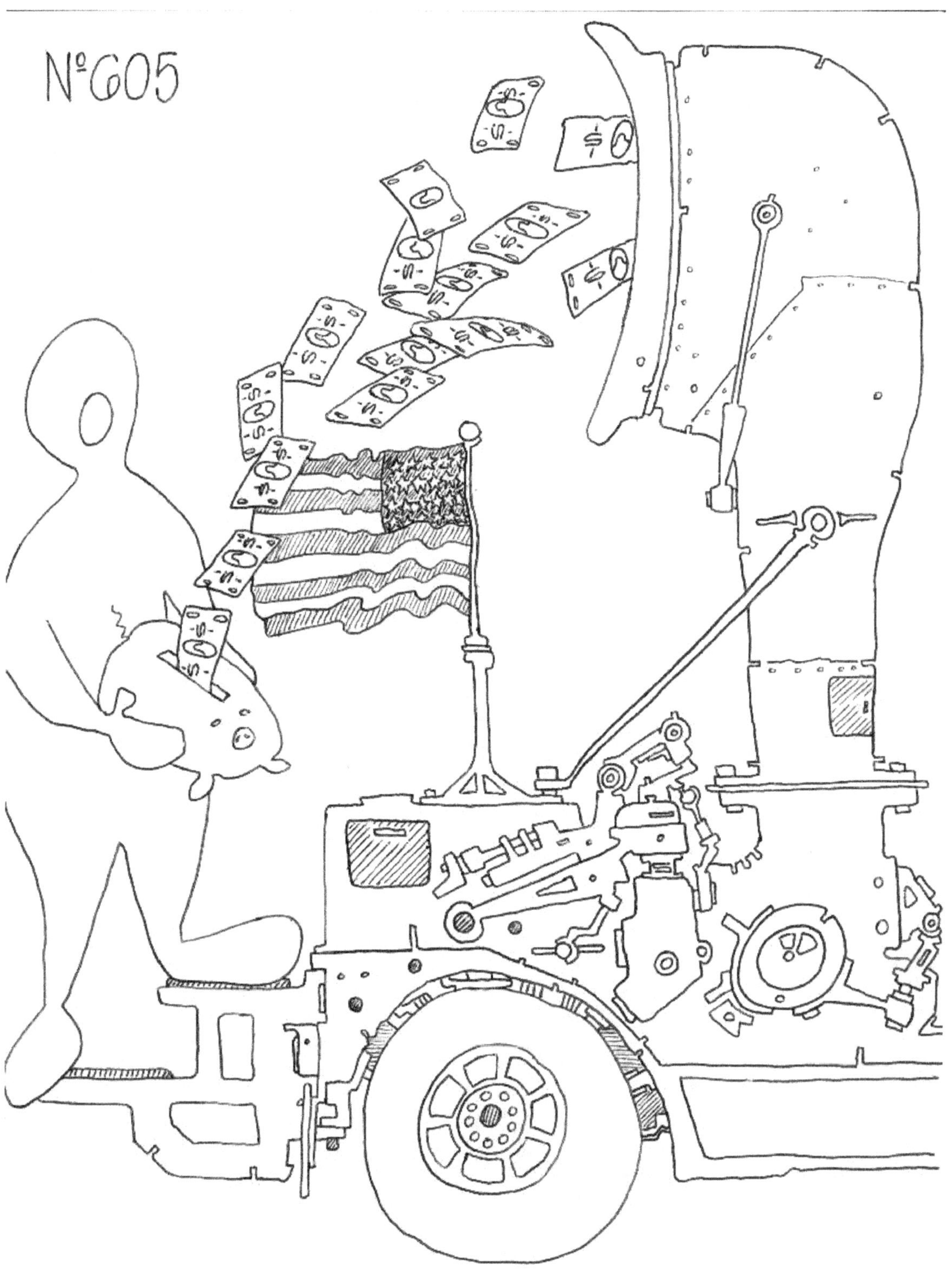
№605

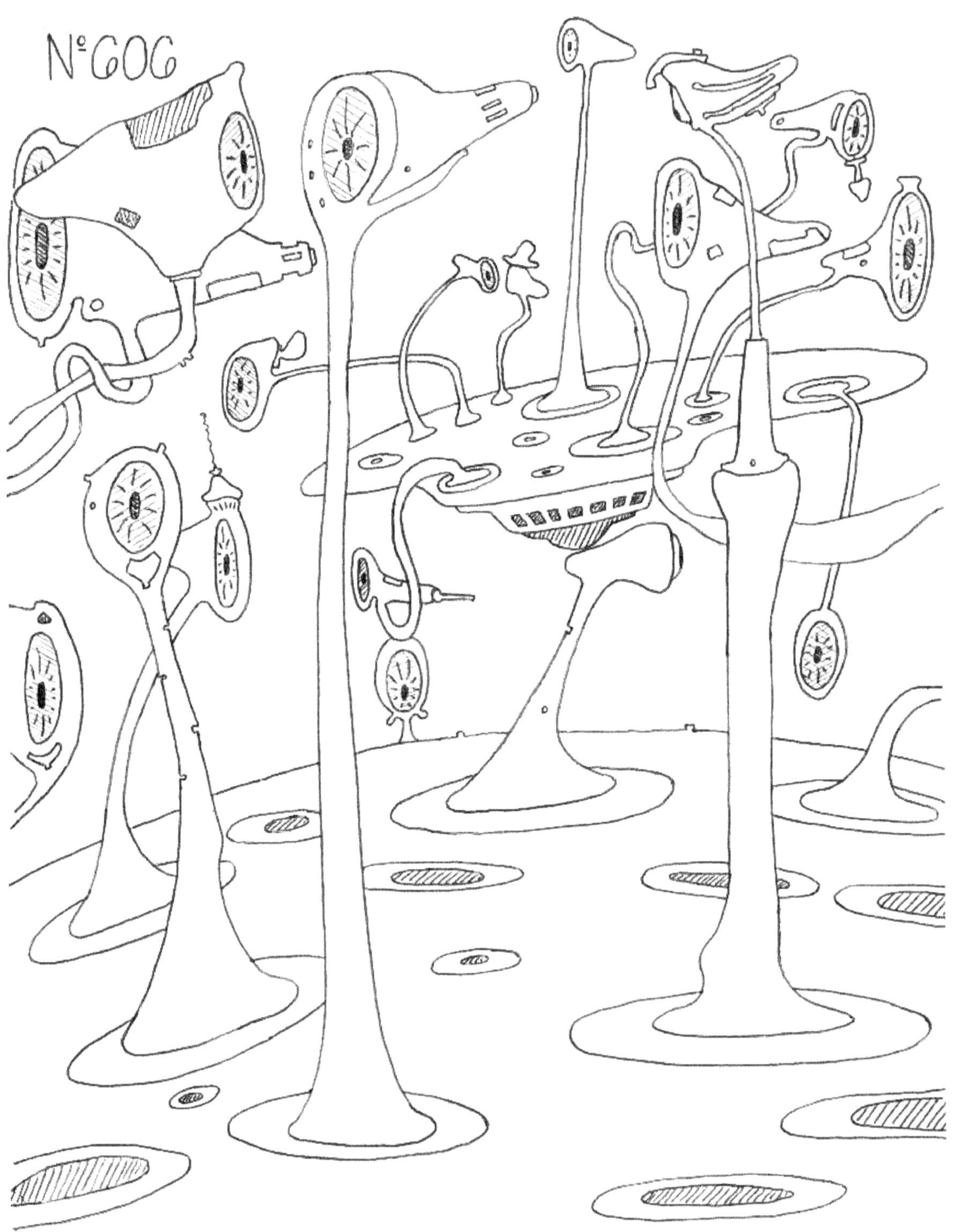
№606

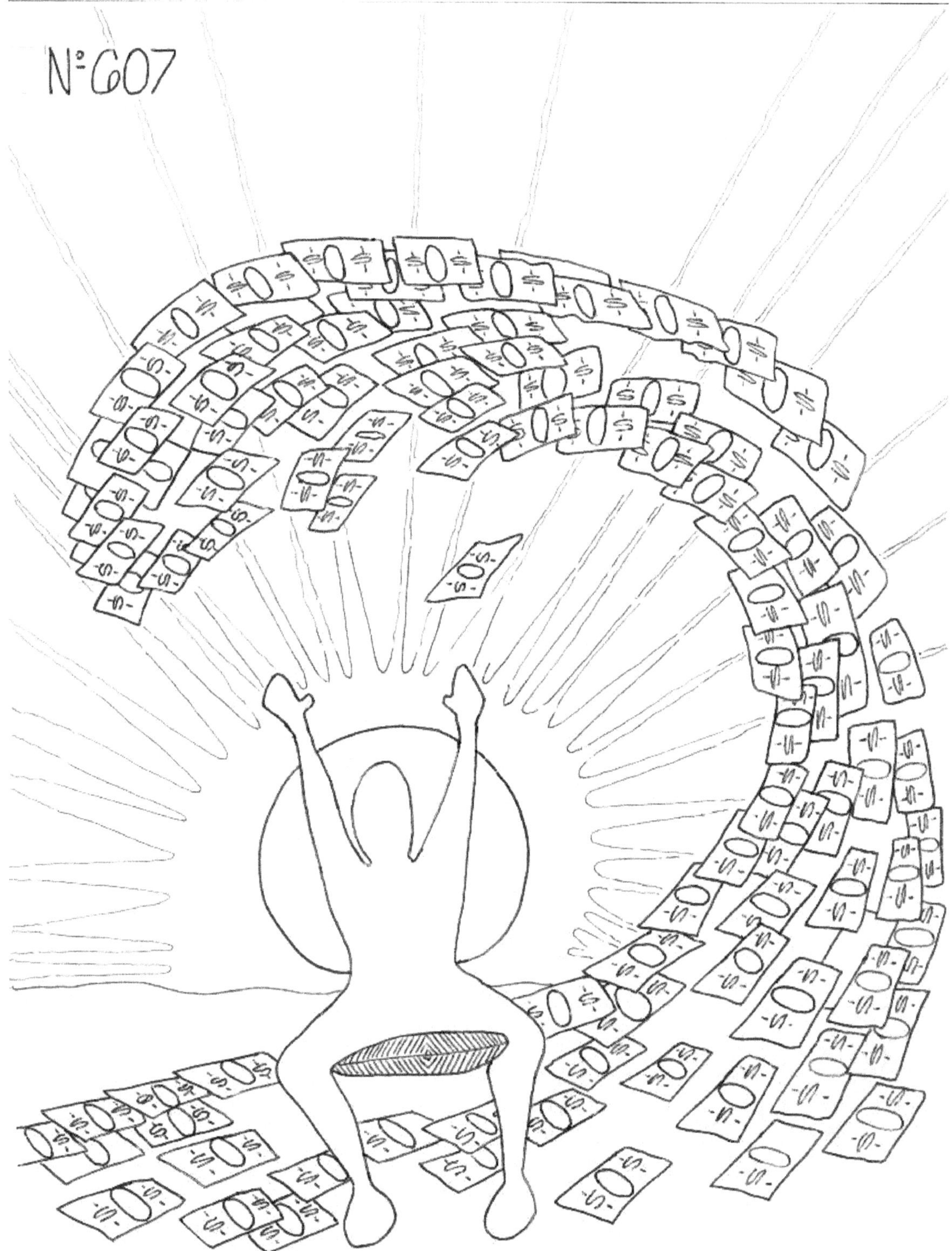
N°607

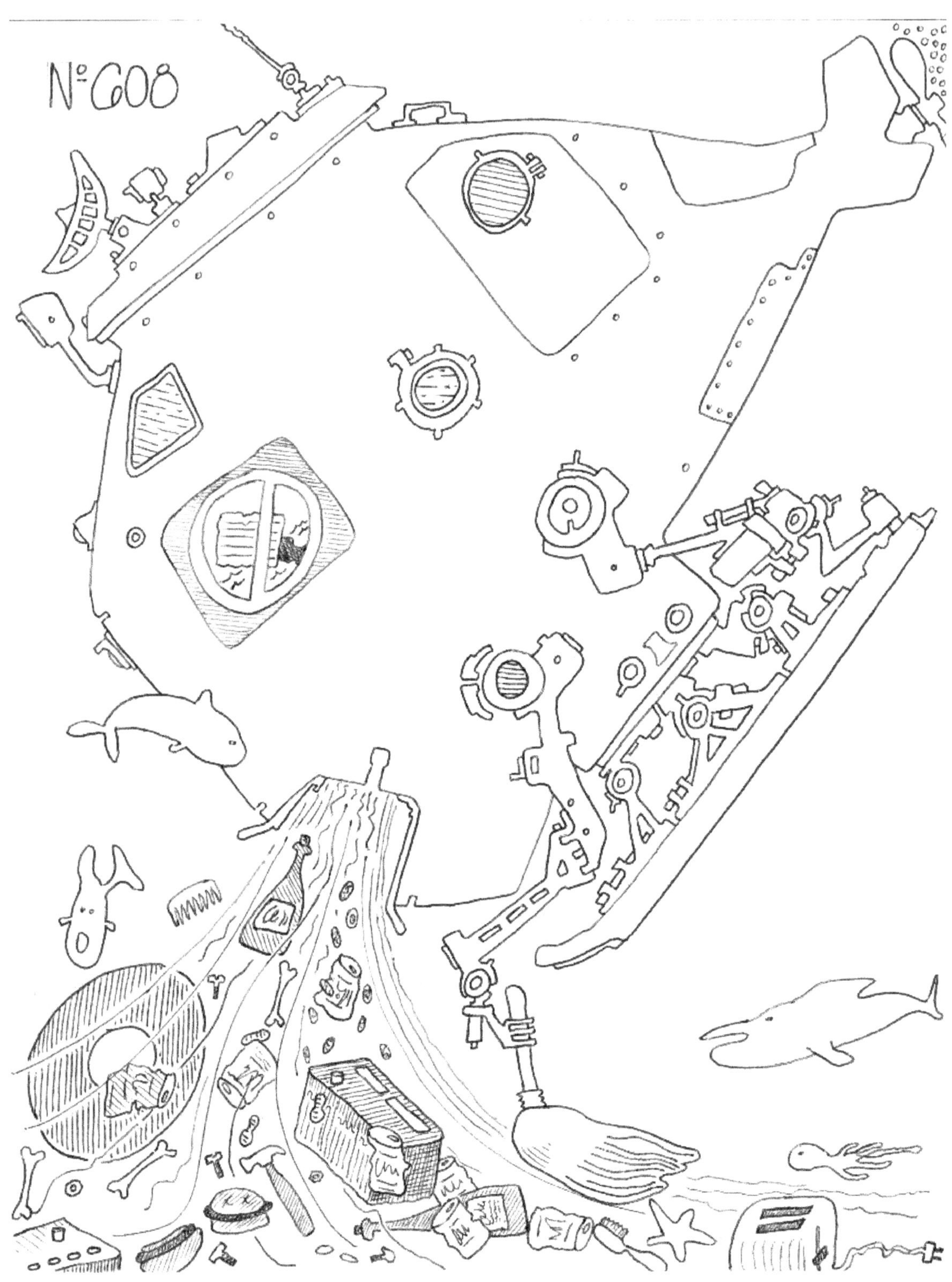
№608

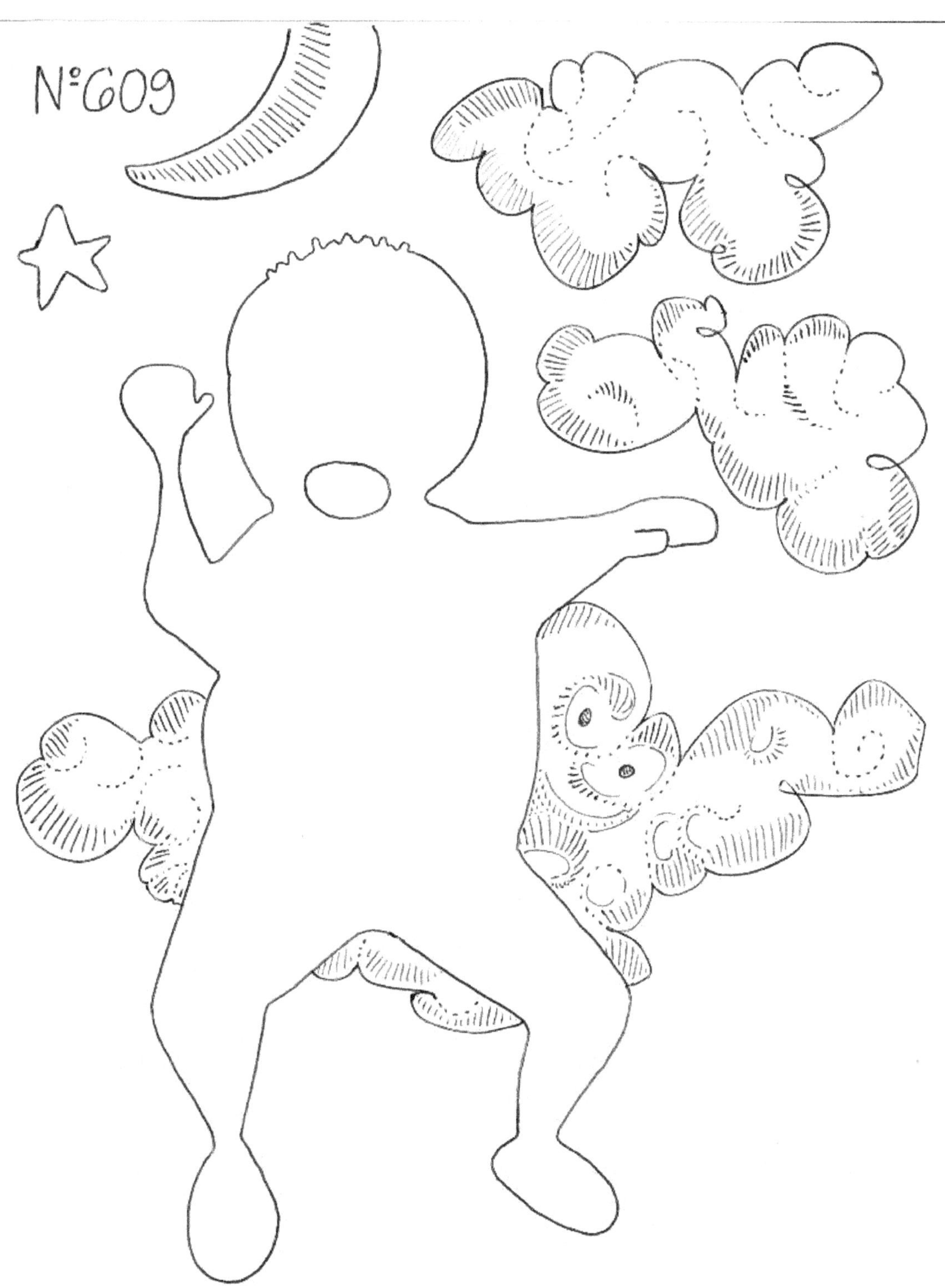
N°609

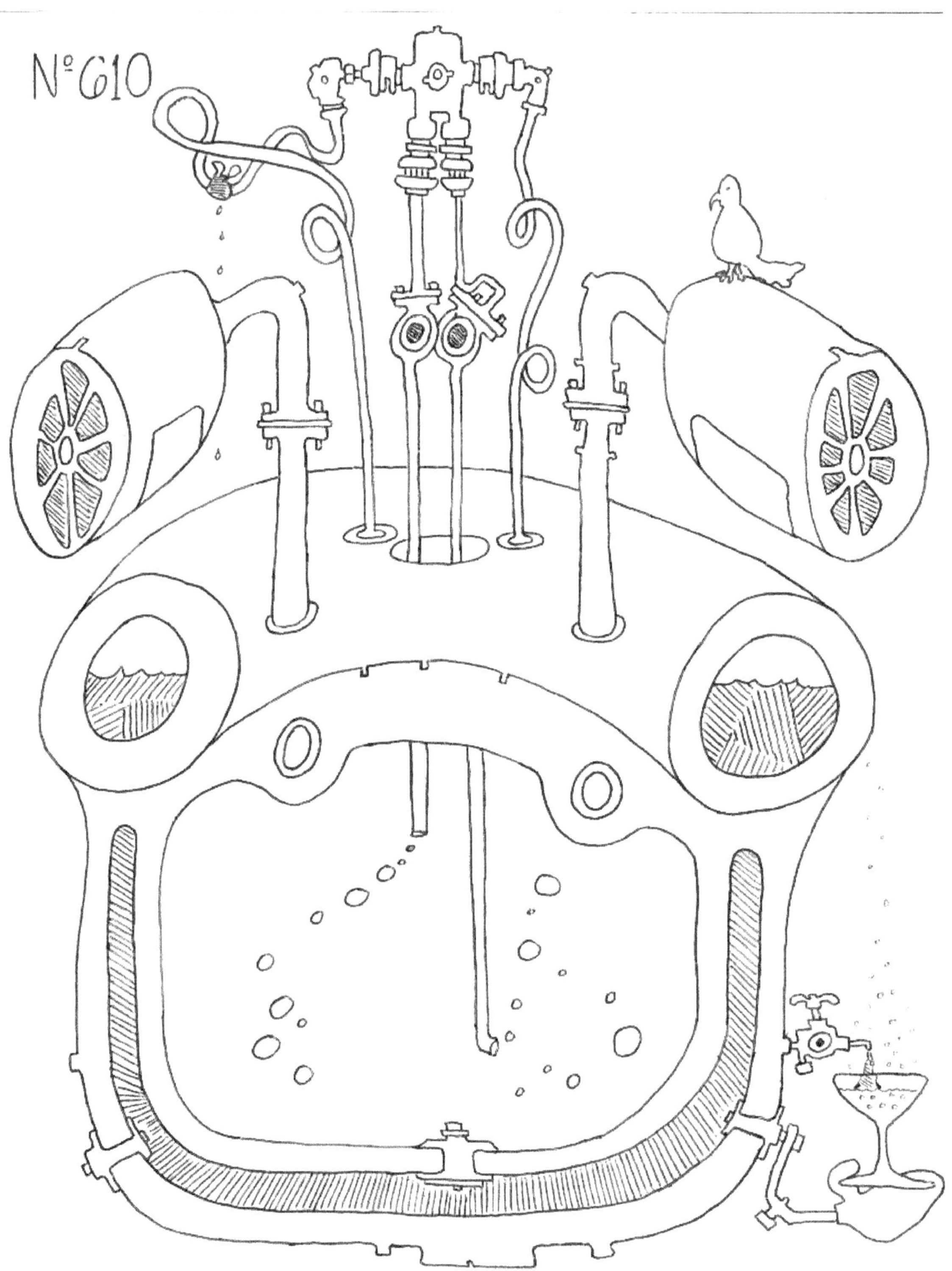
Nº610

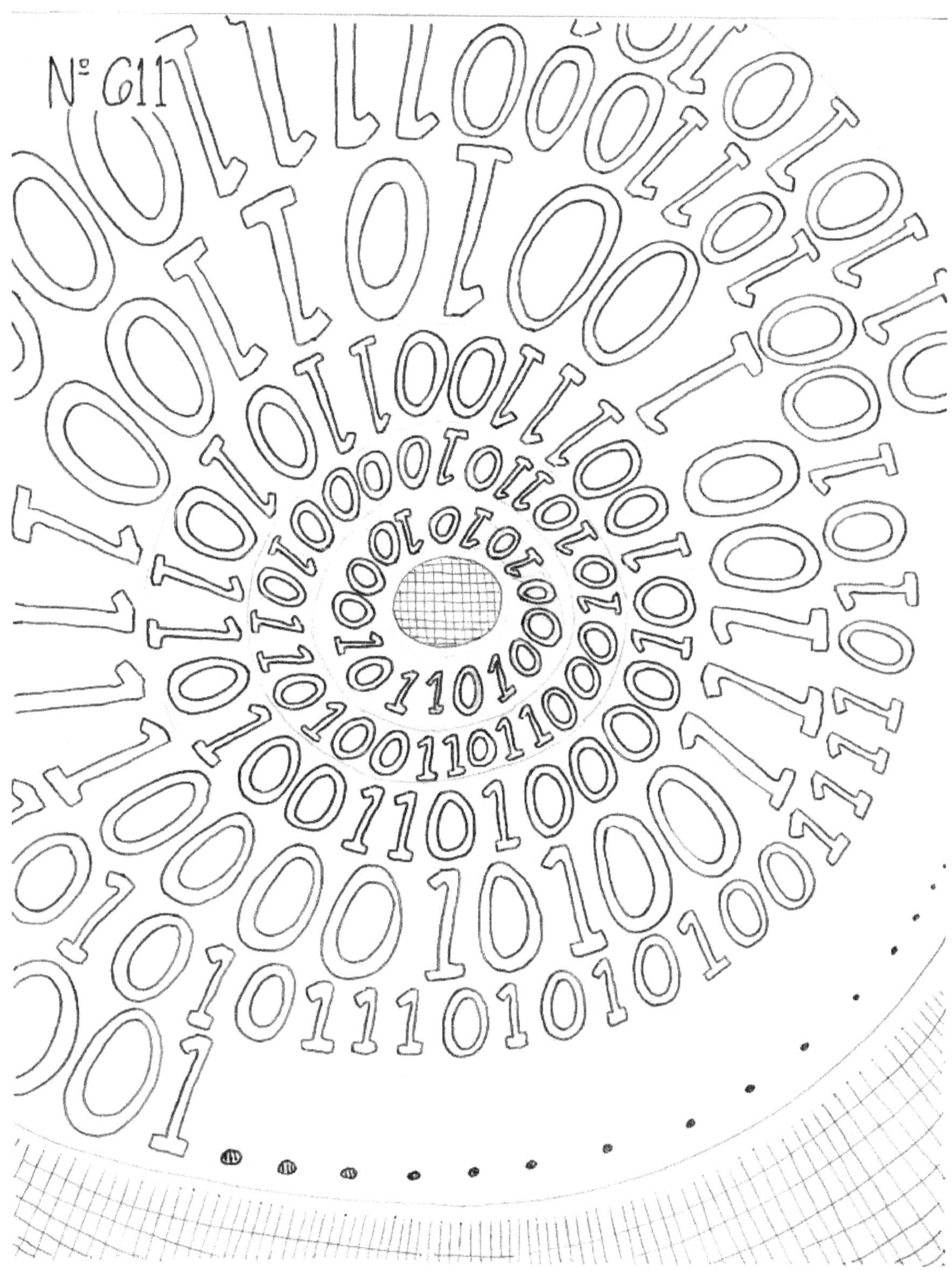
№ 611

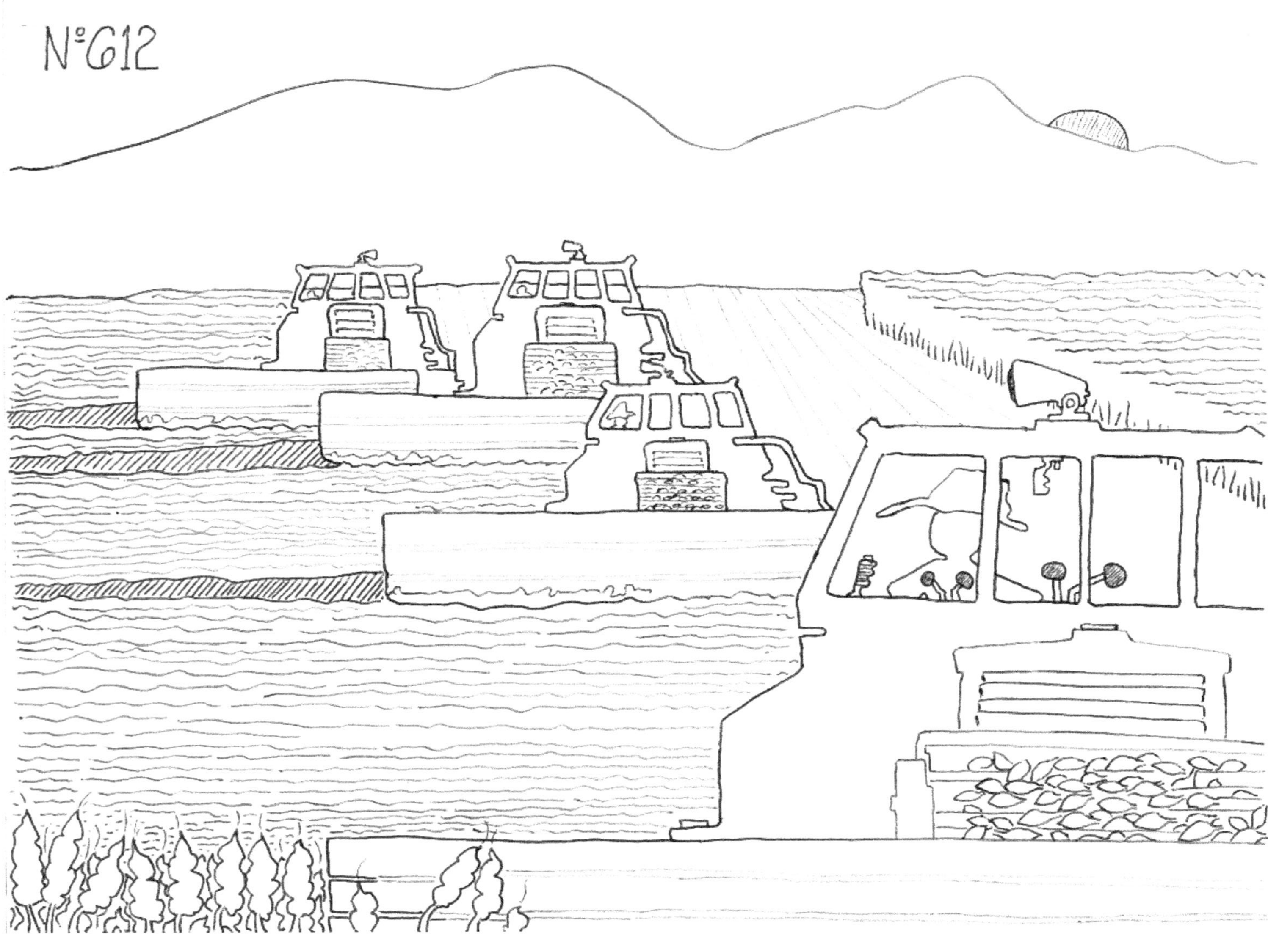
N°612

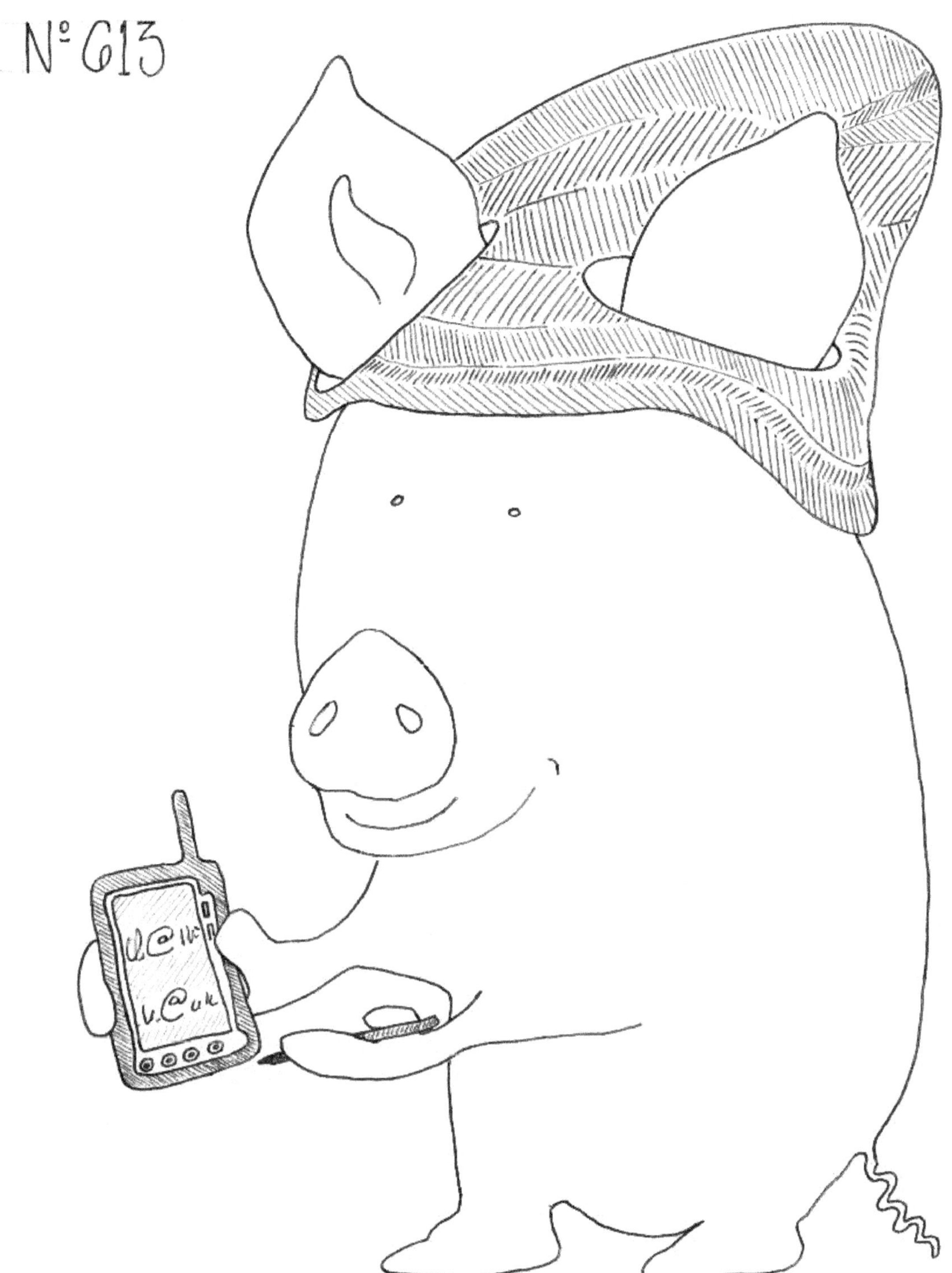

№ 613

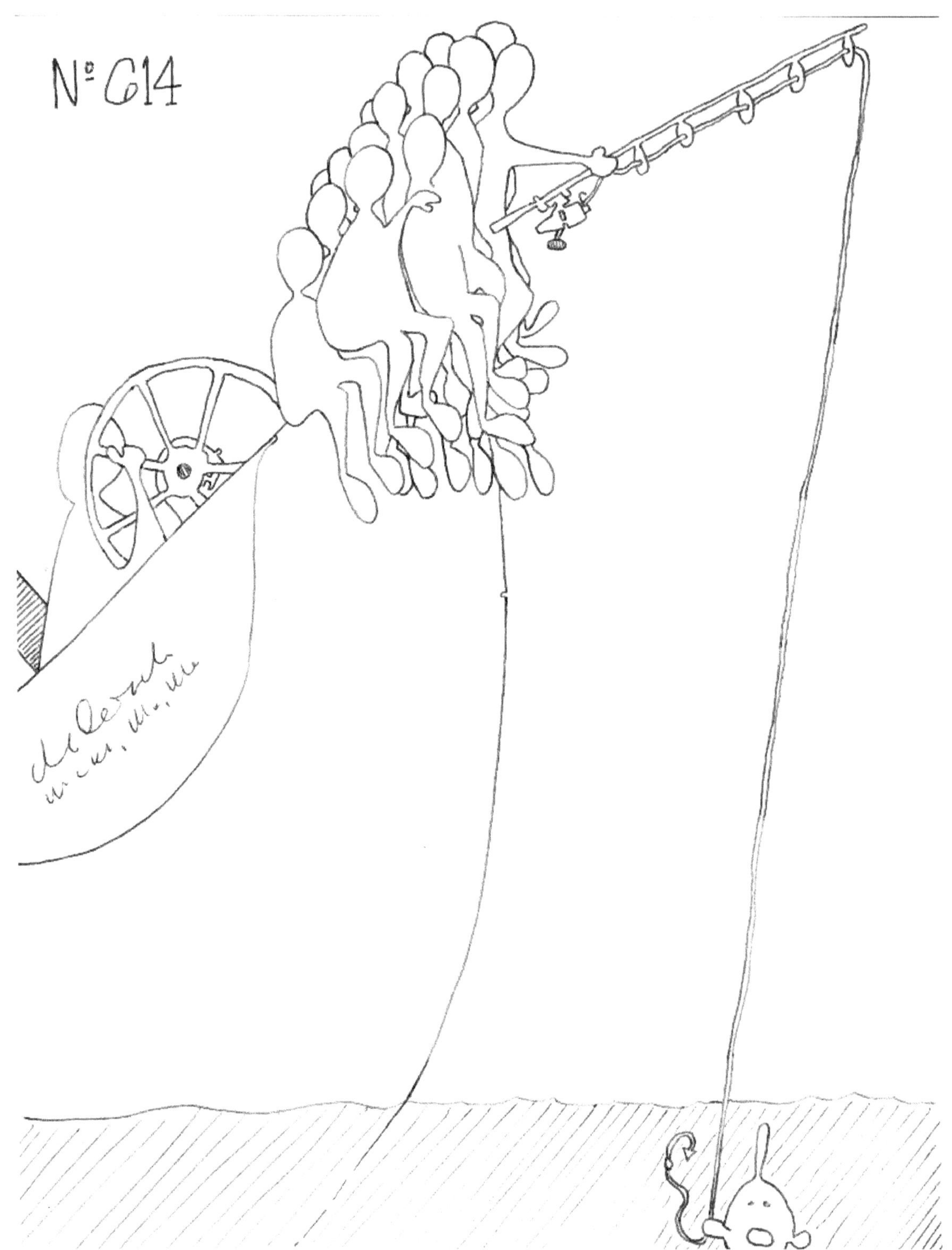
N° 614

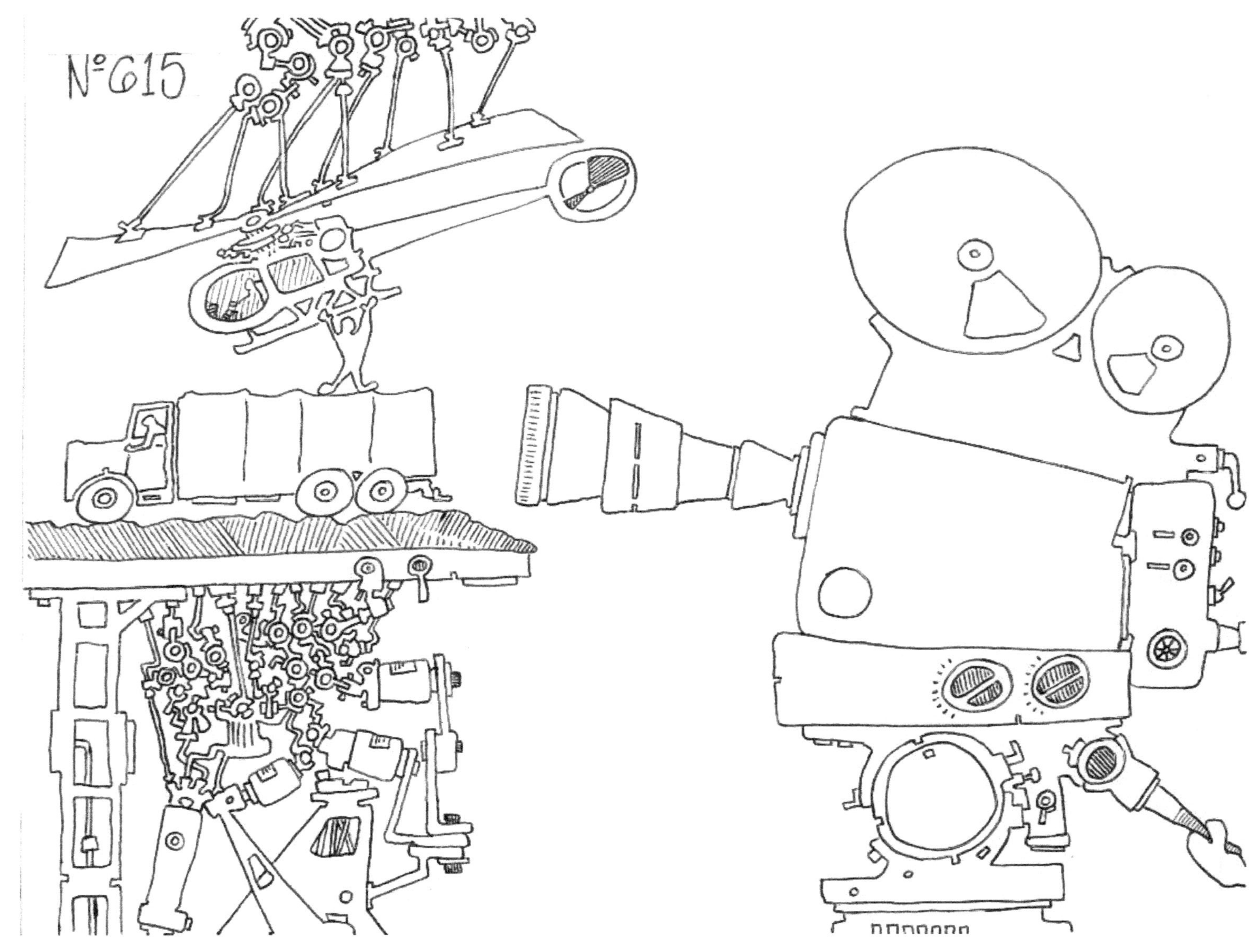
№615

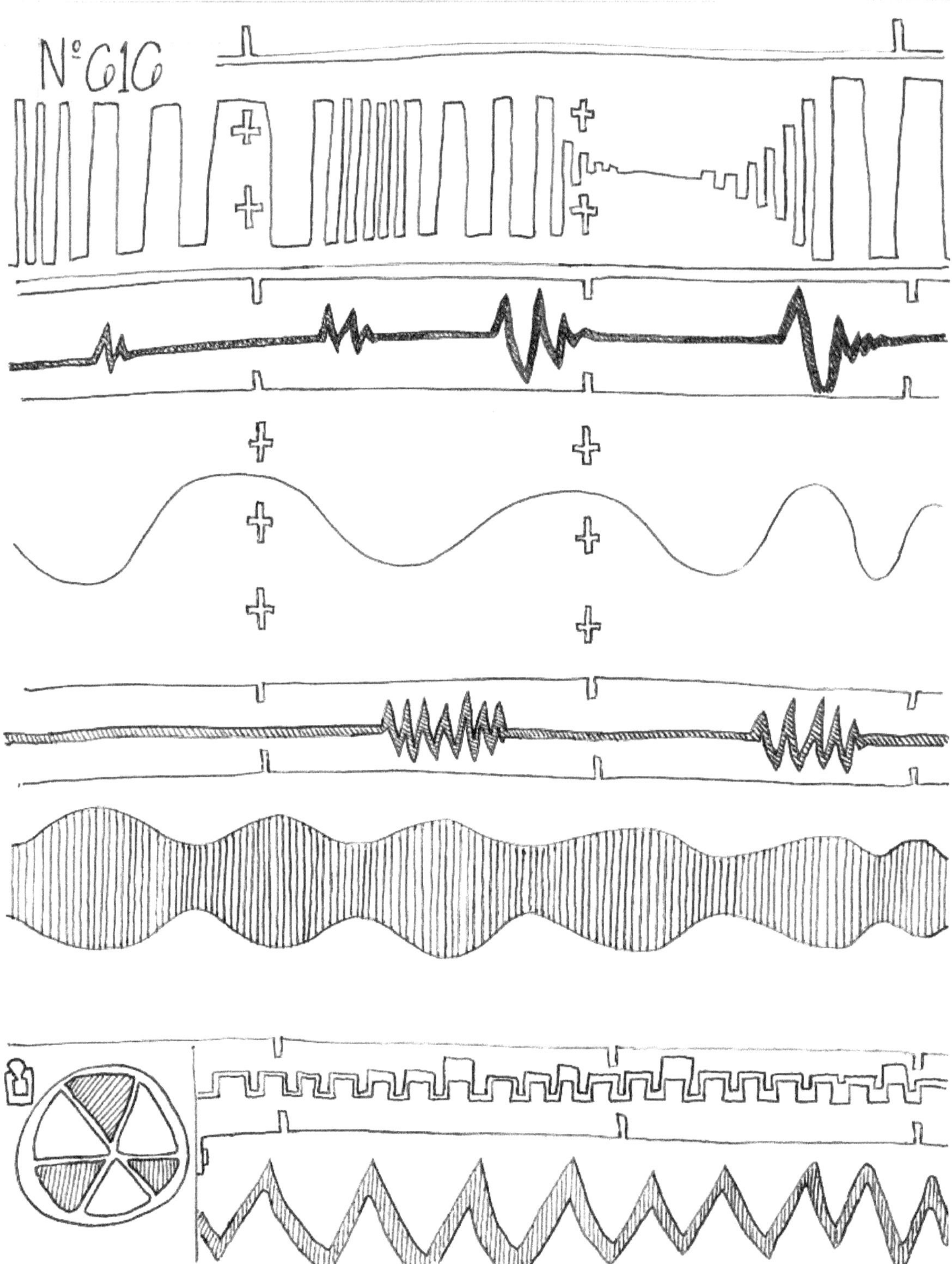
№616

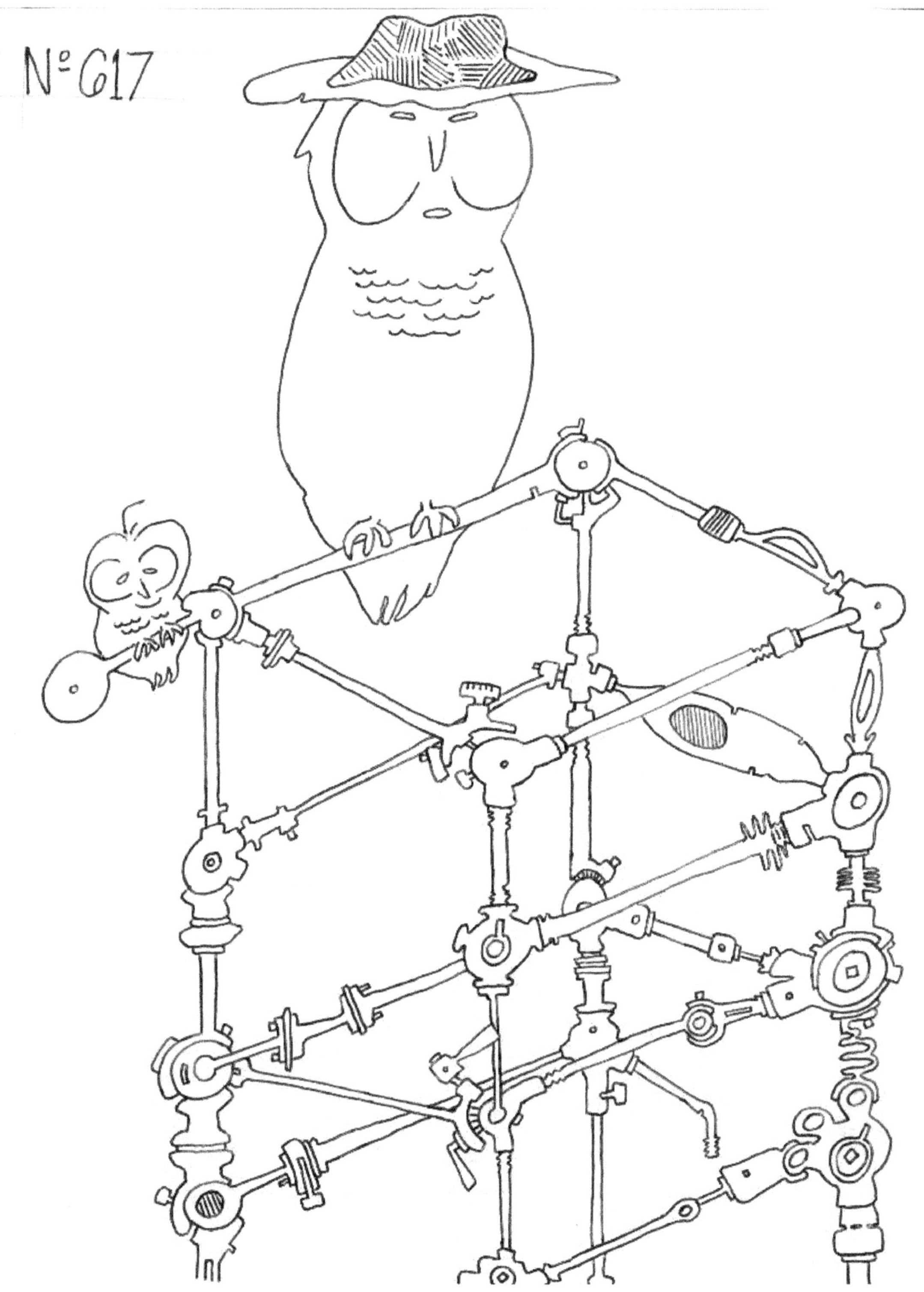
Nº 617

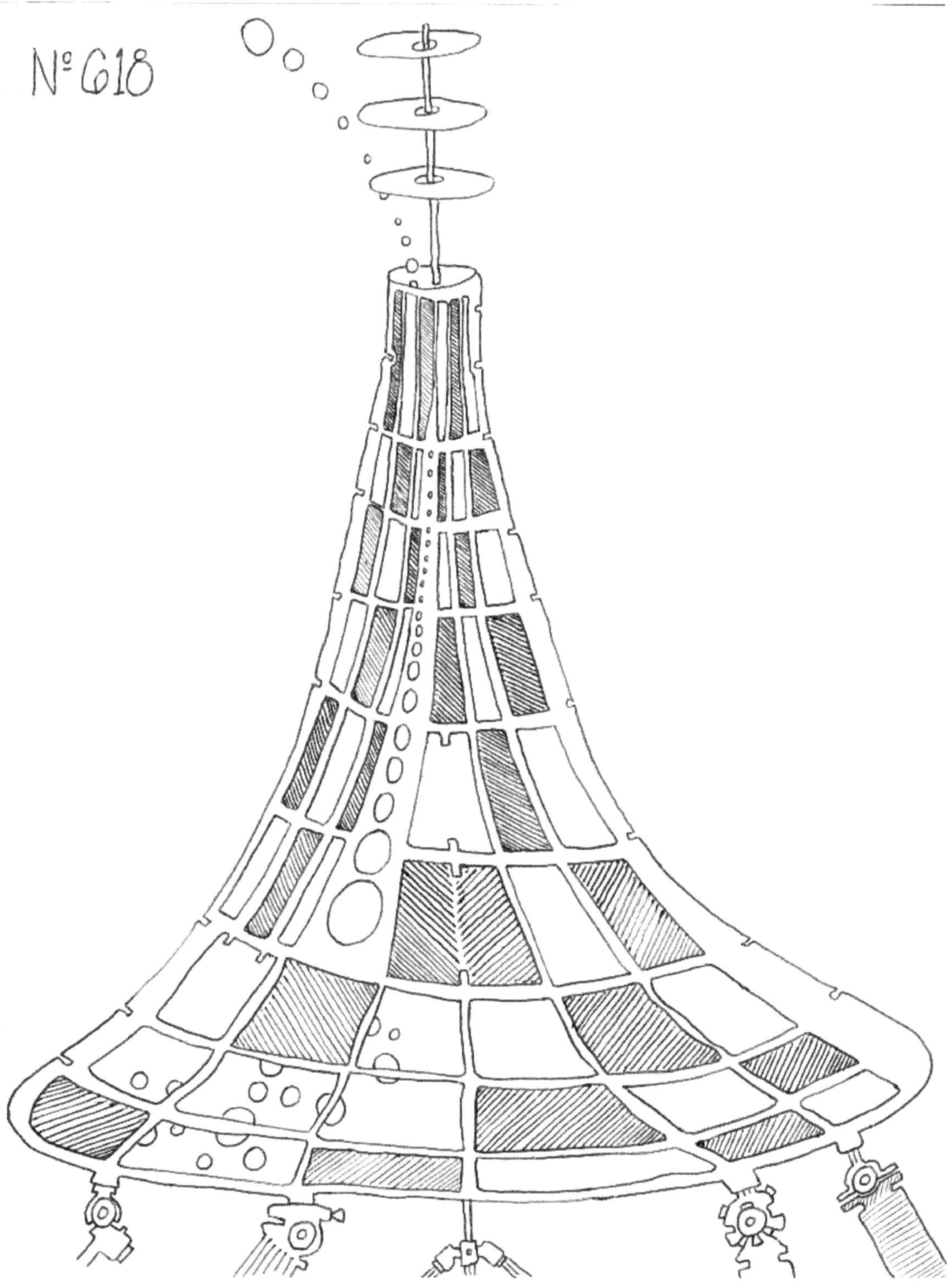
Nº618

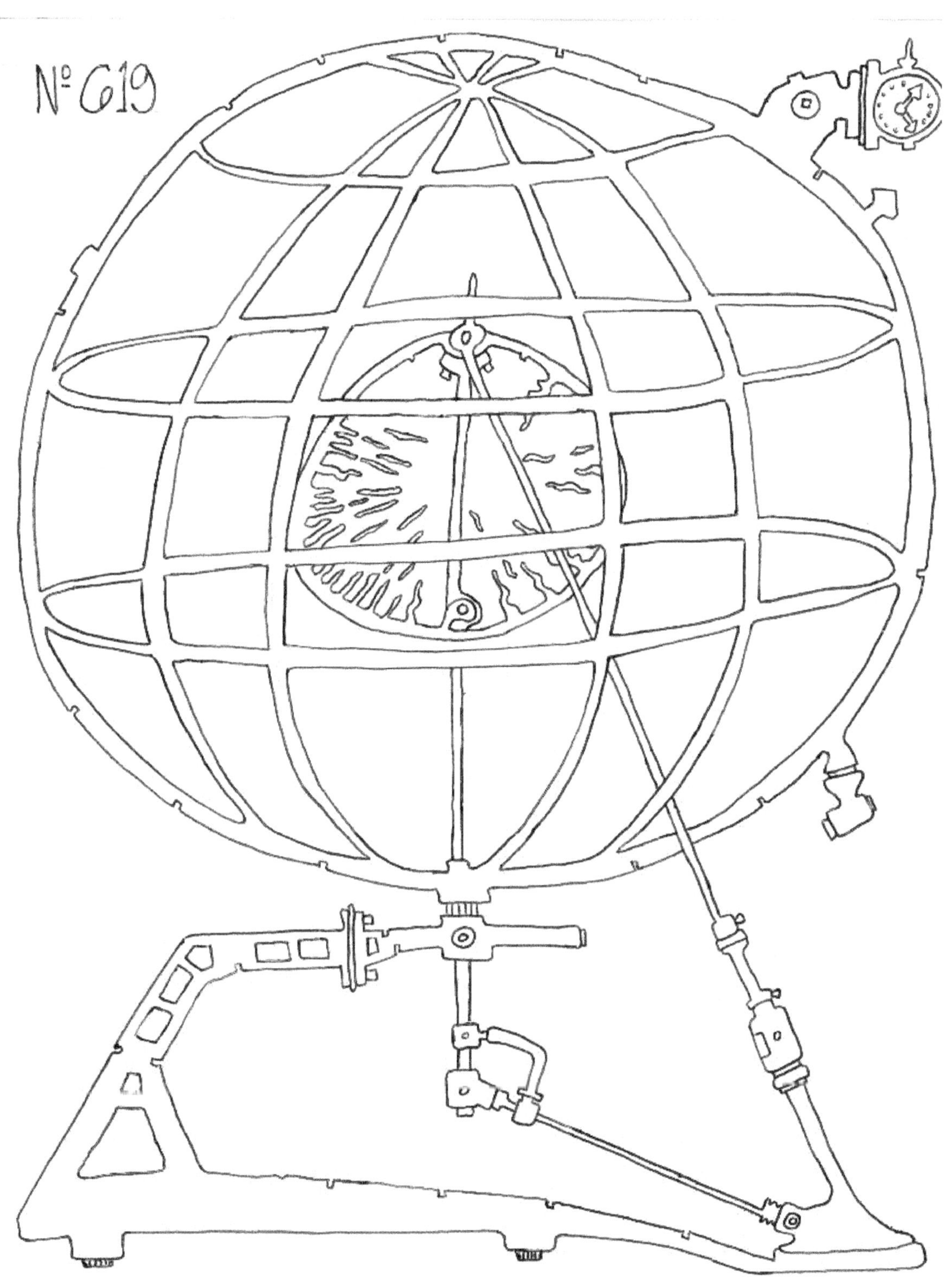
№ 619

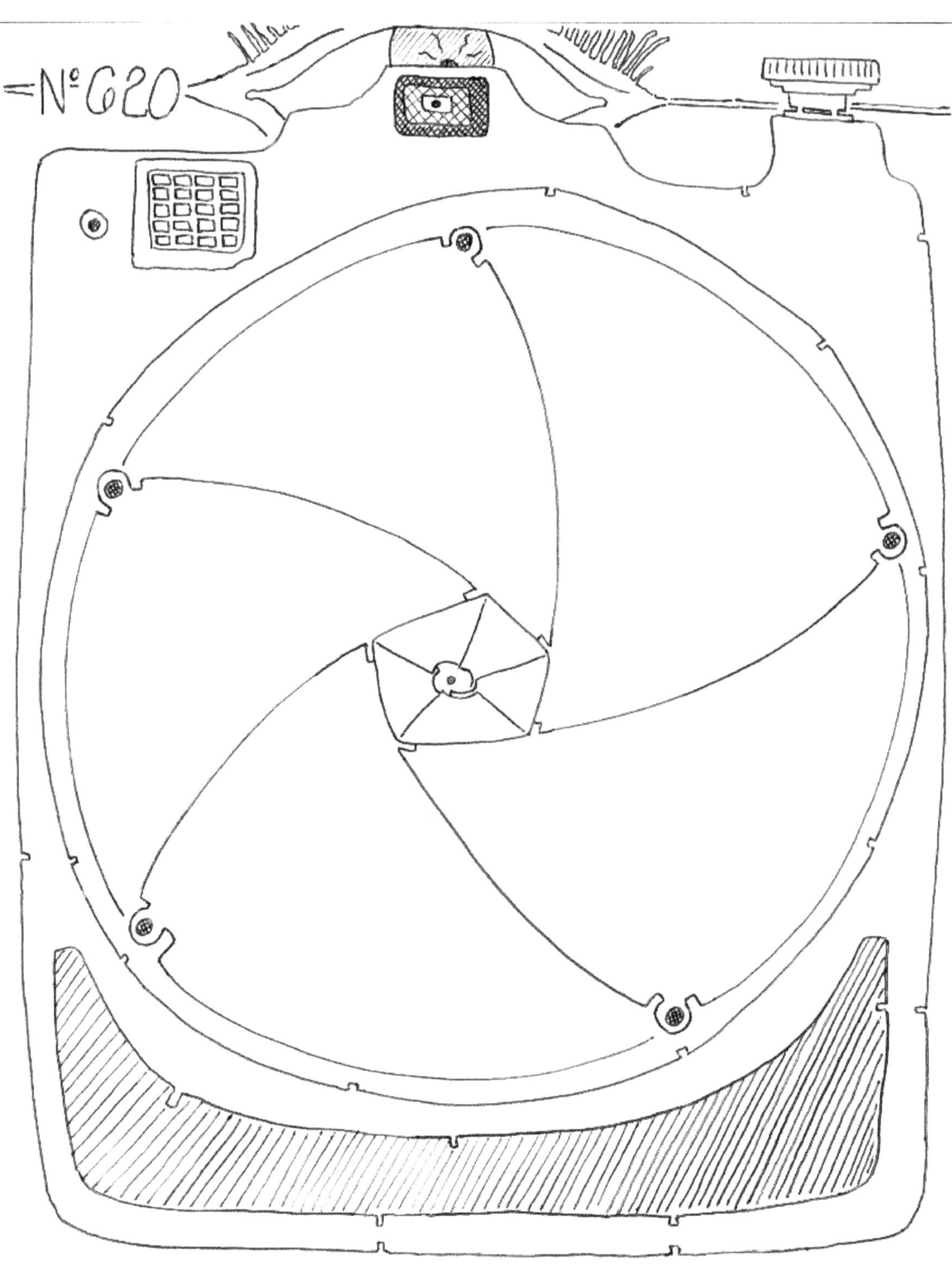
№620

№ 621

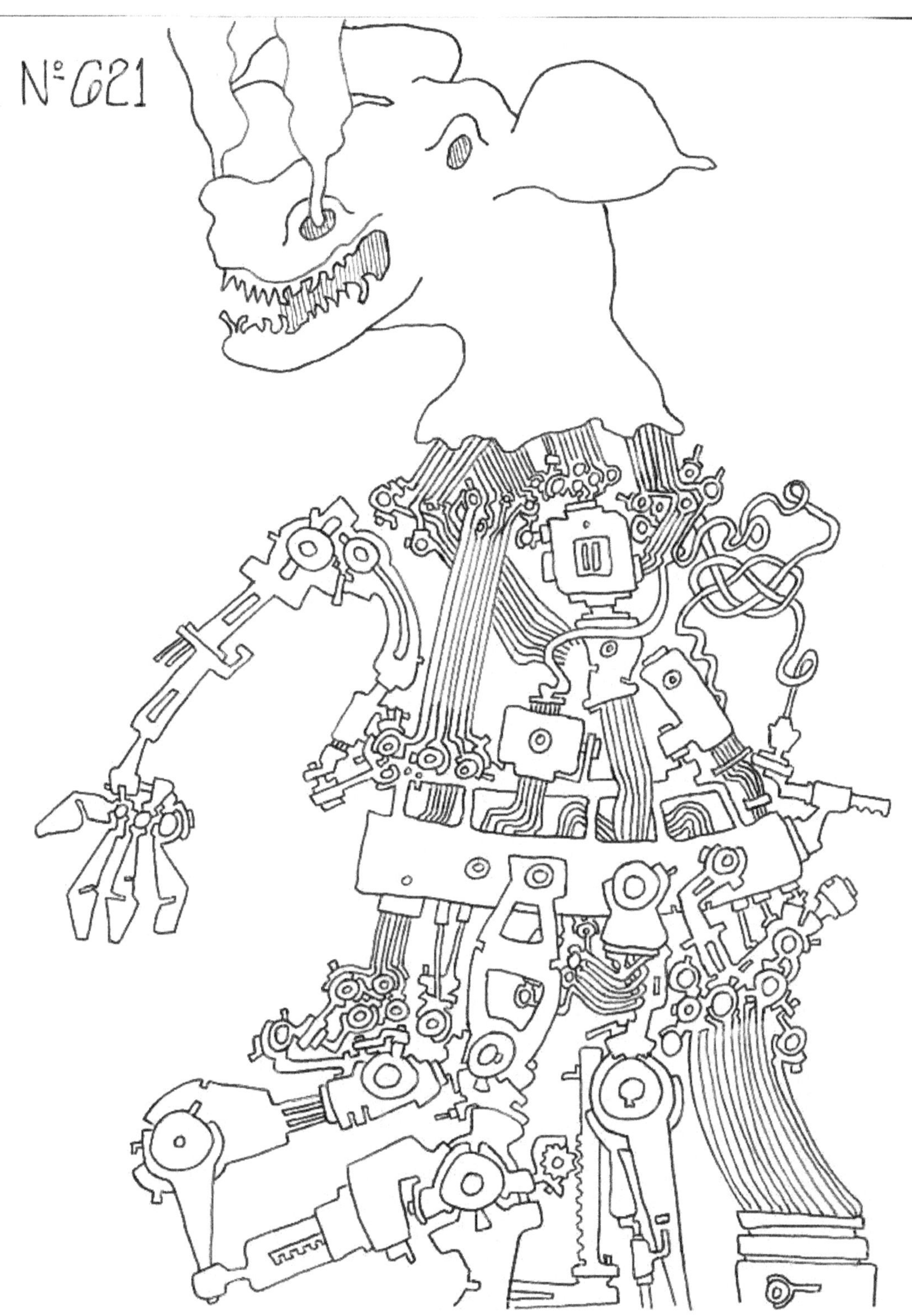

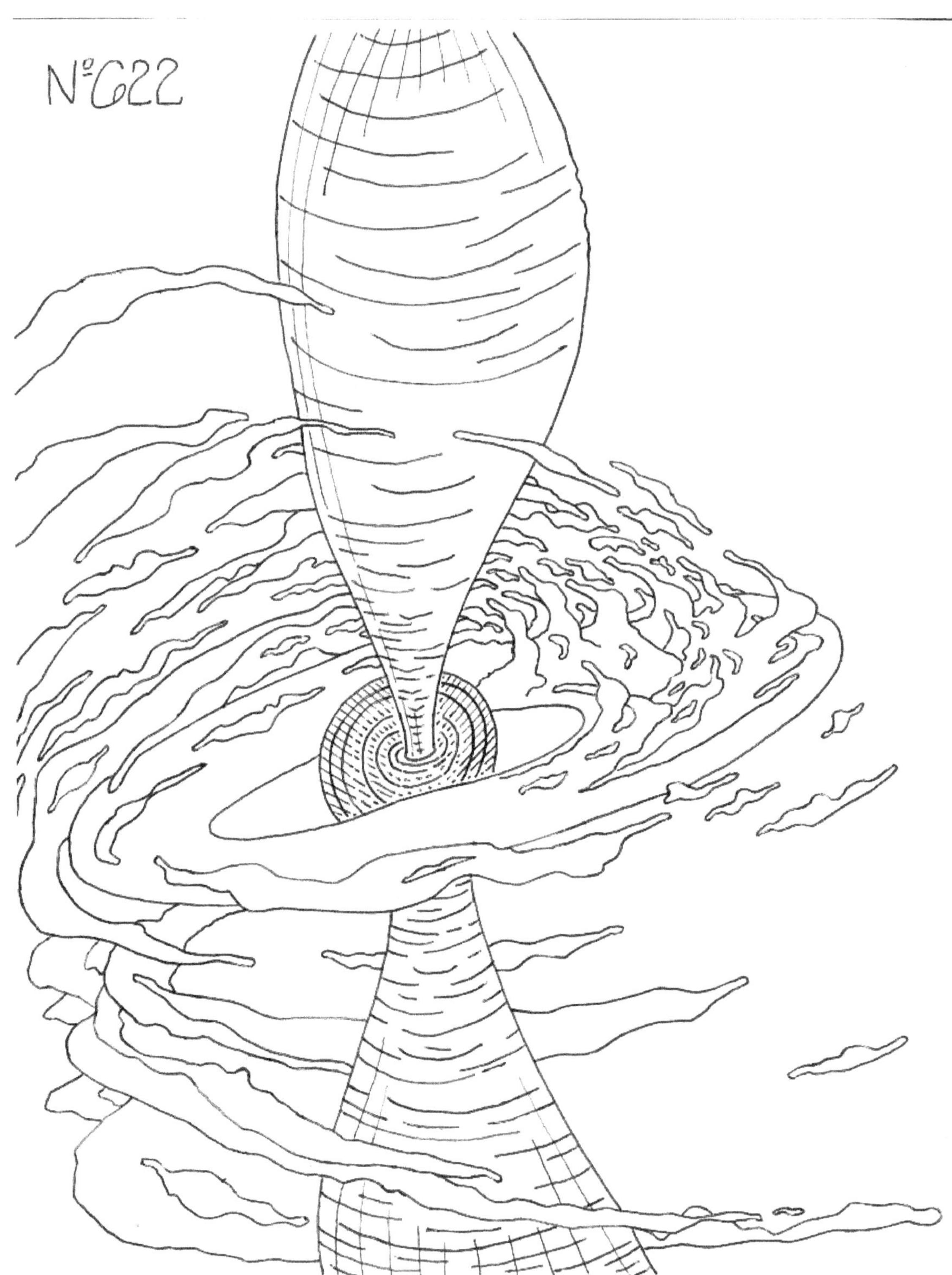
Nº622

N°623

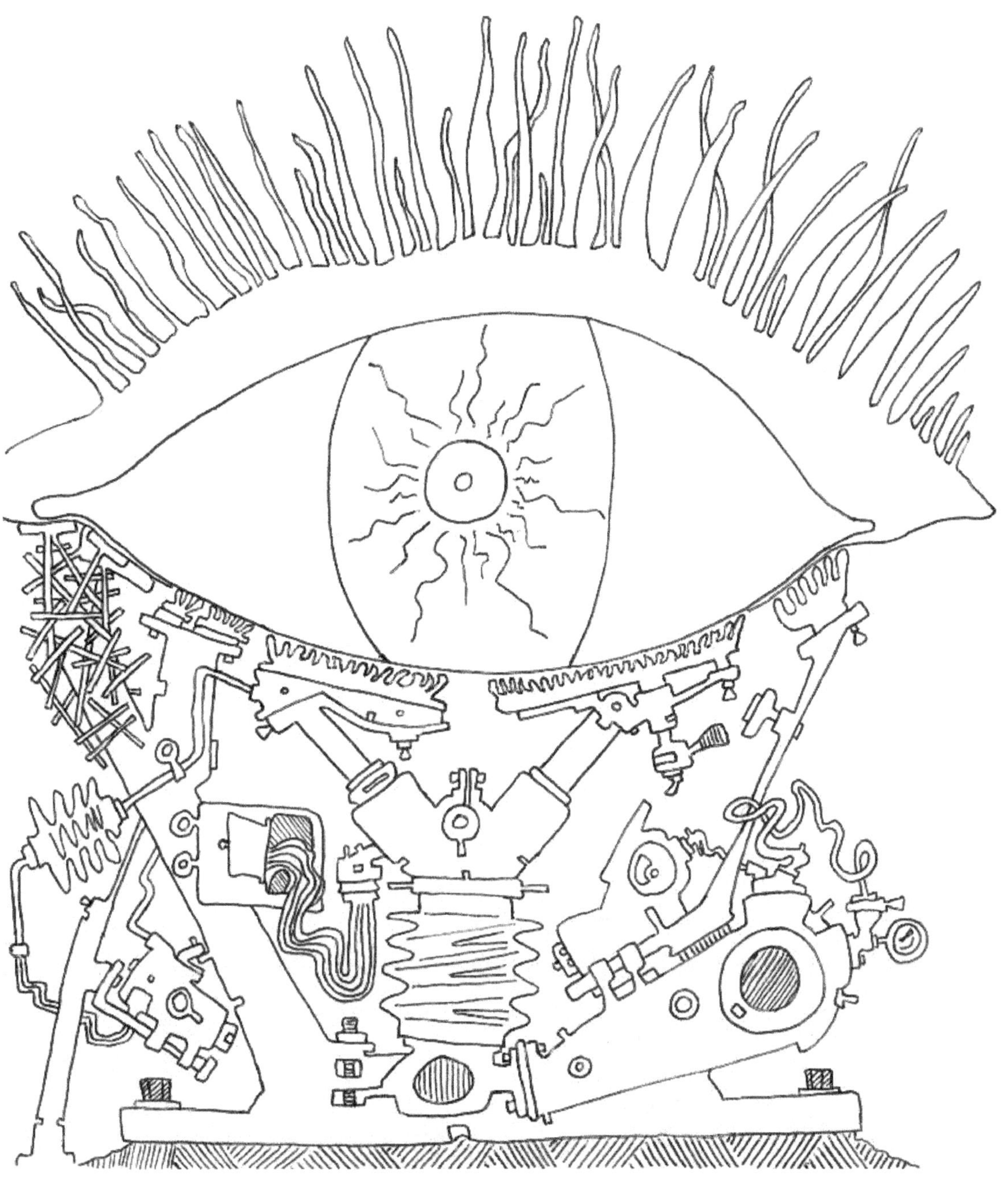

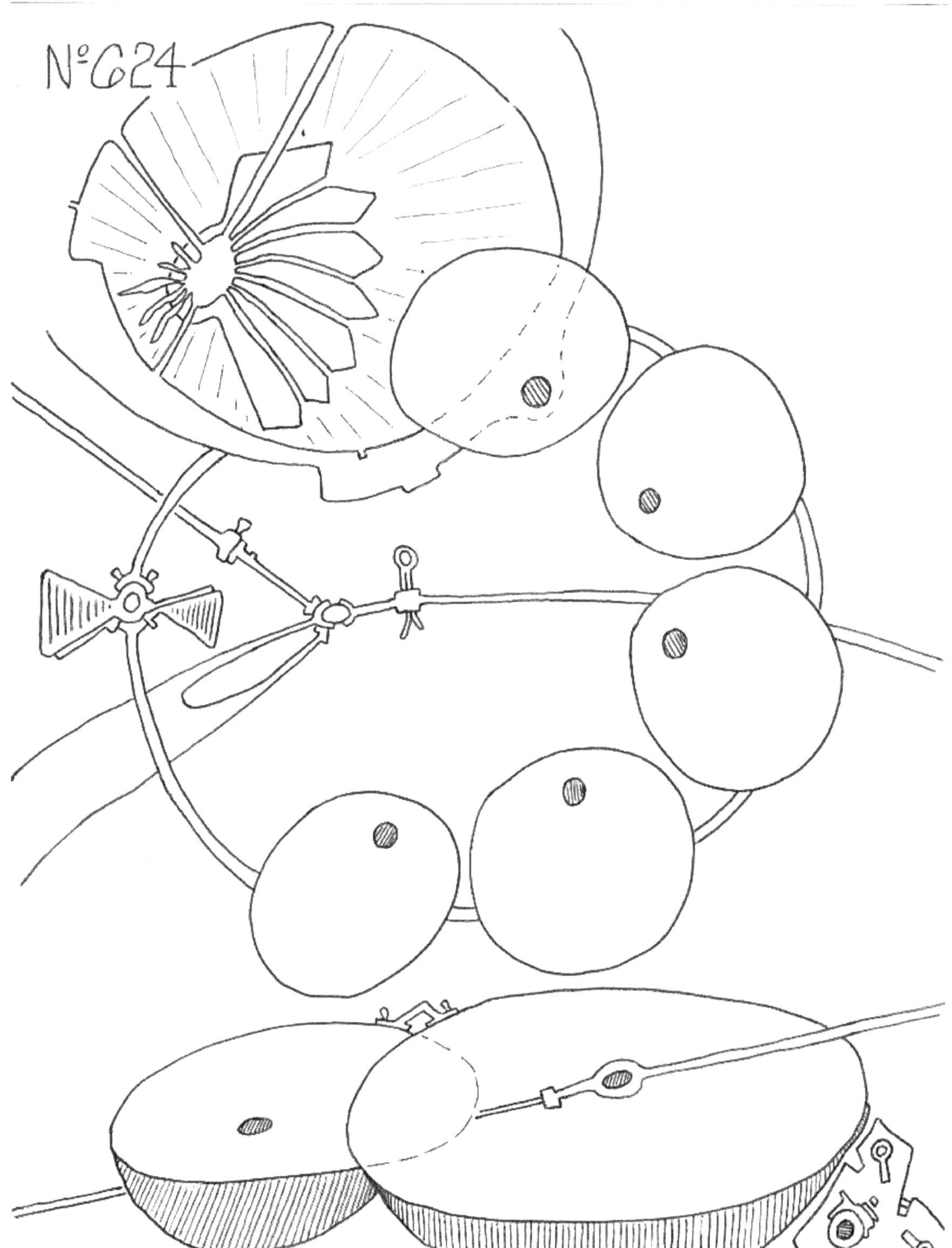
N°624

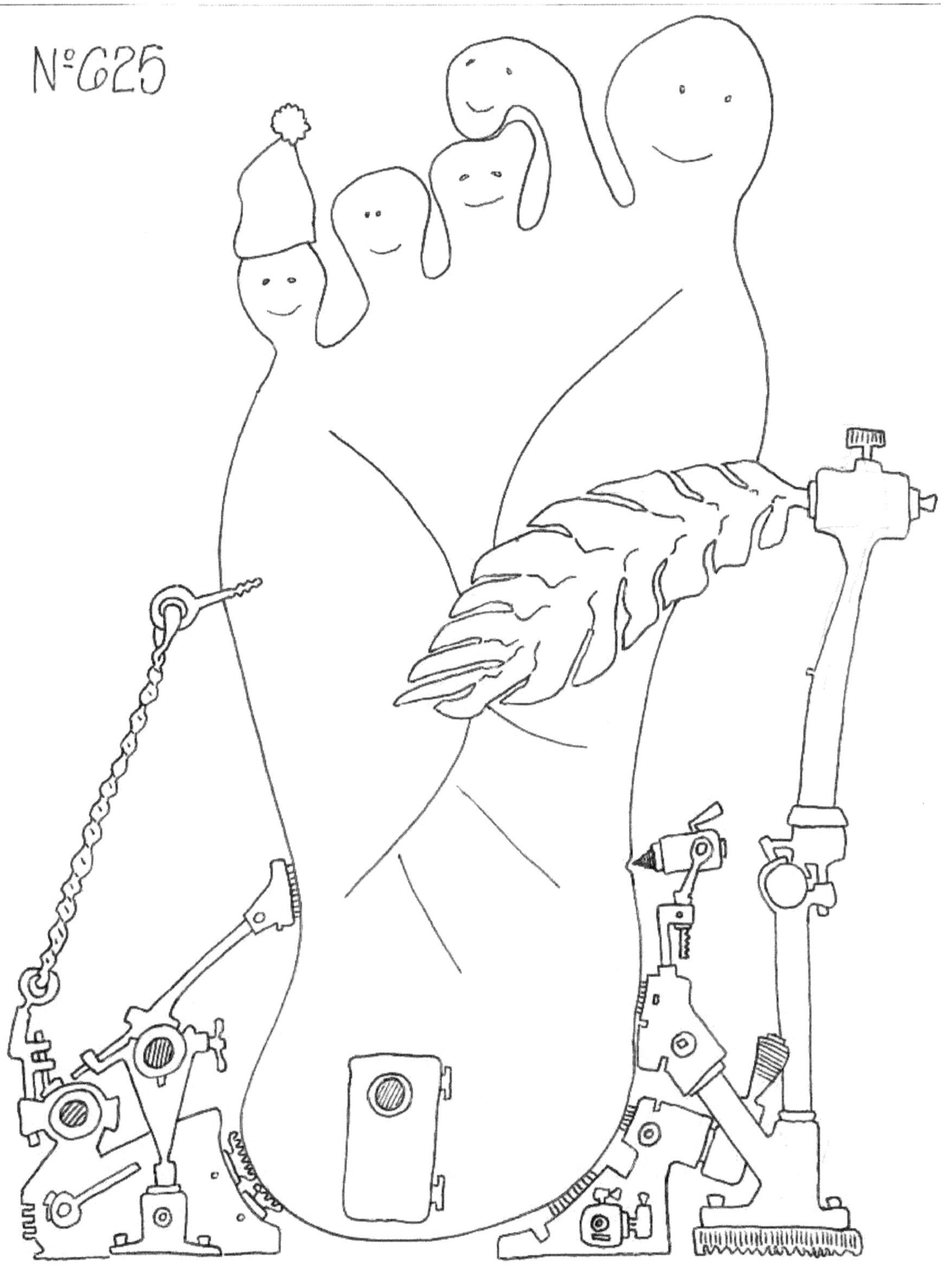
№625

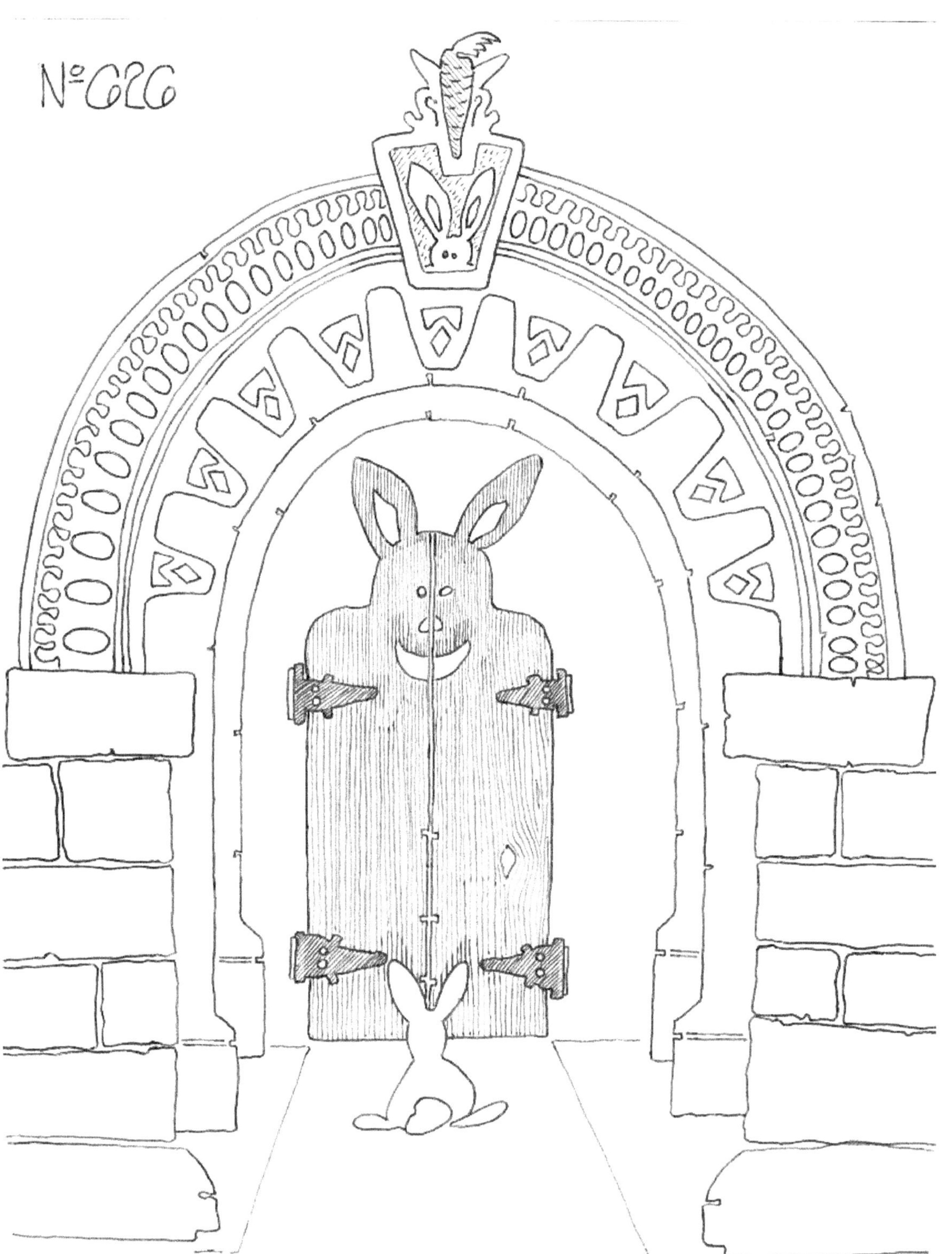
№626

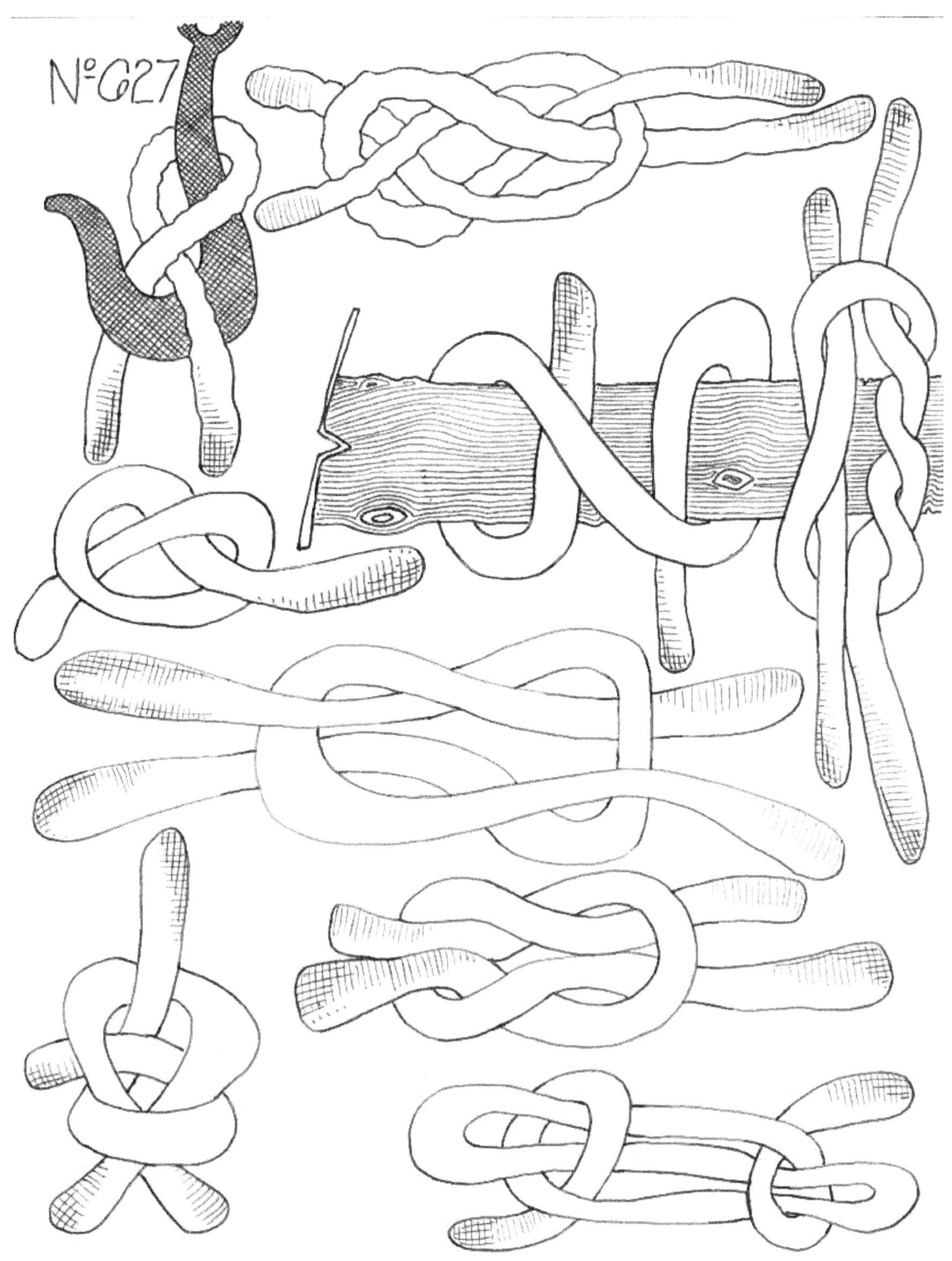
№ 627

№628

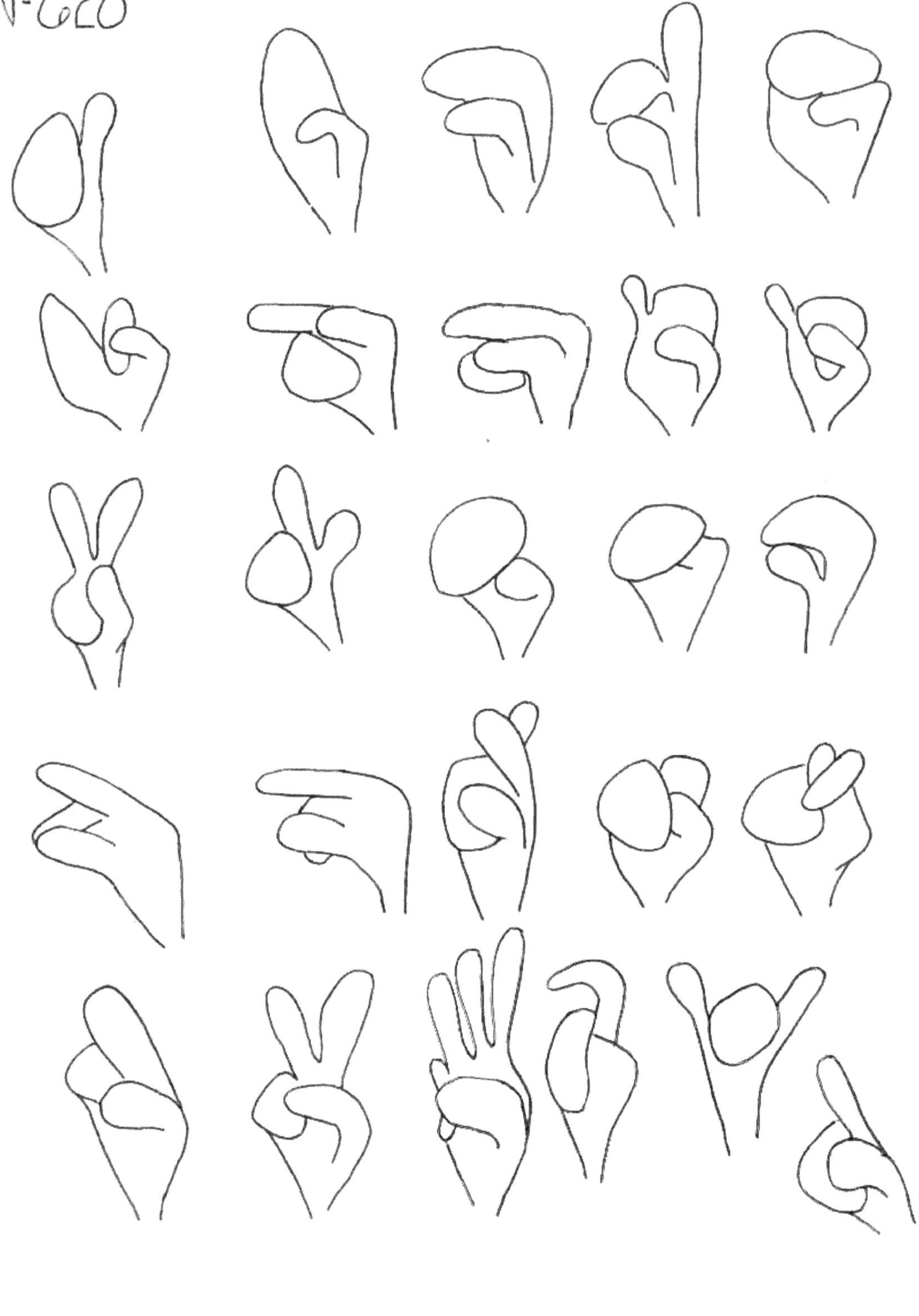

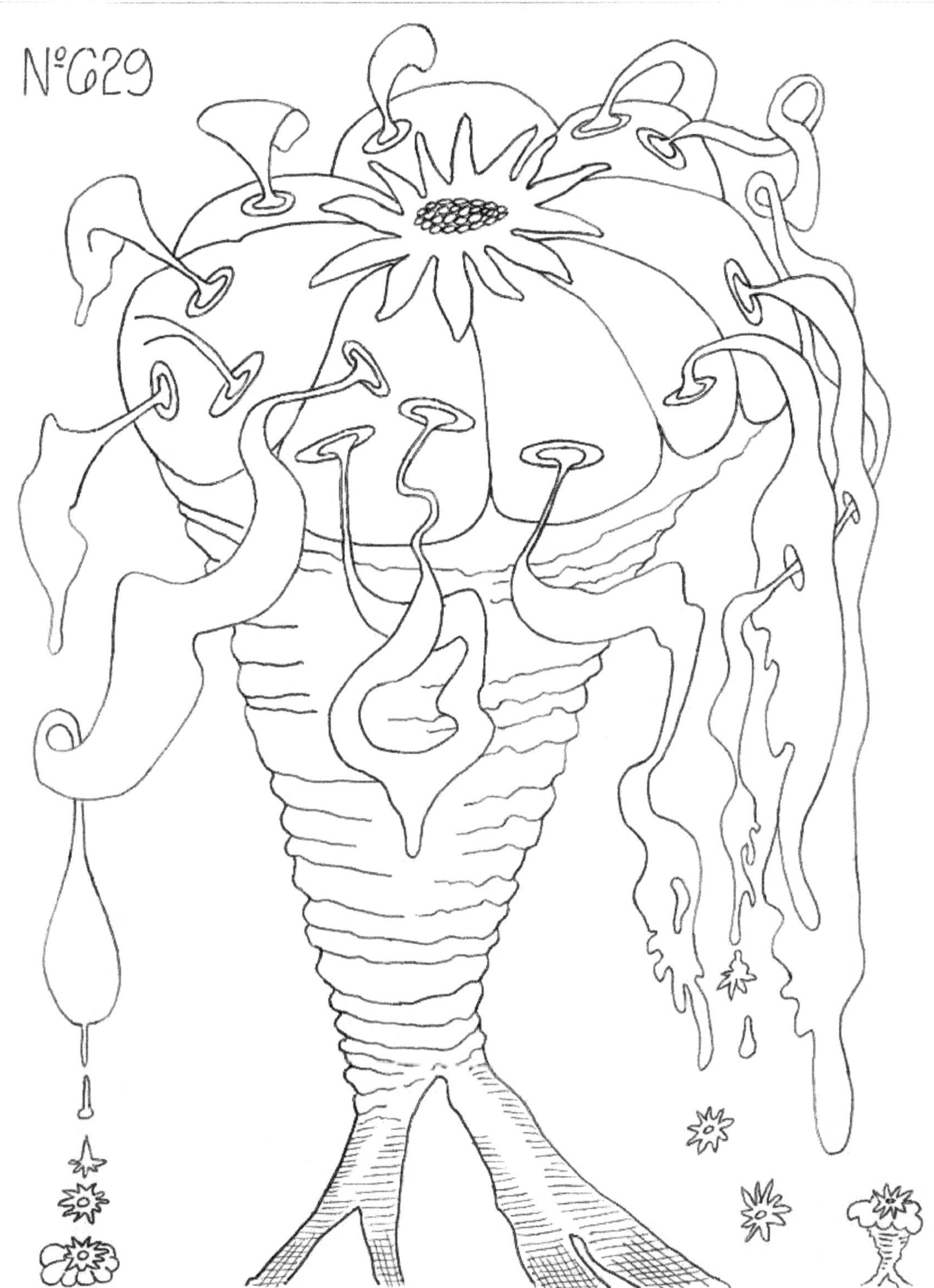
Nº629

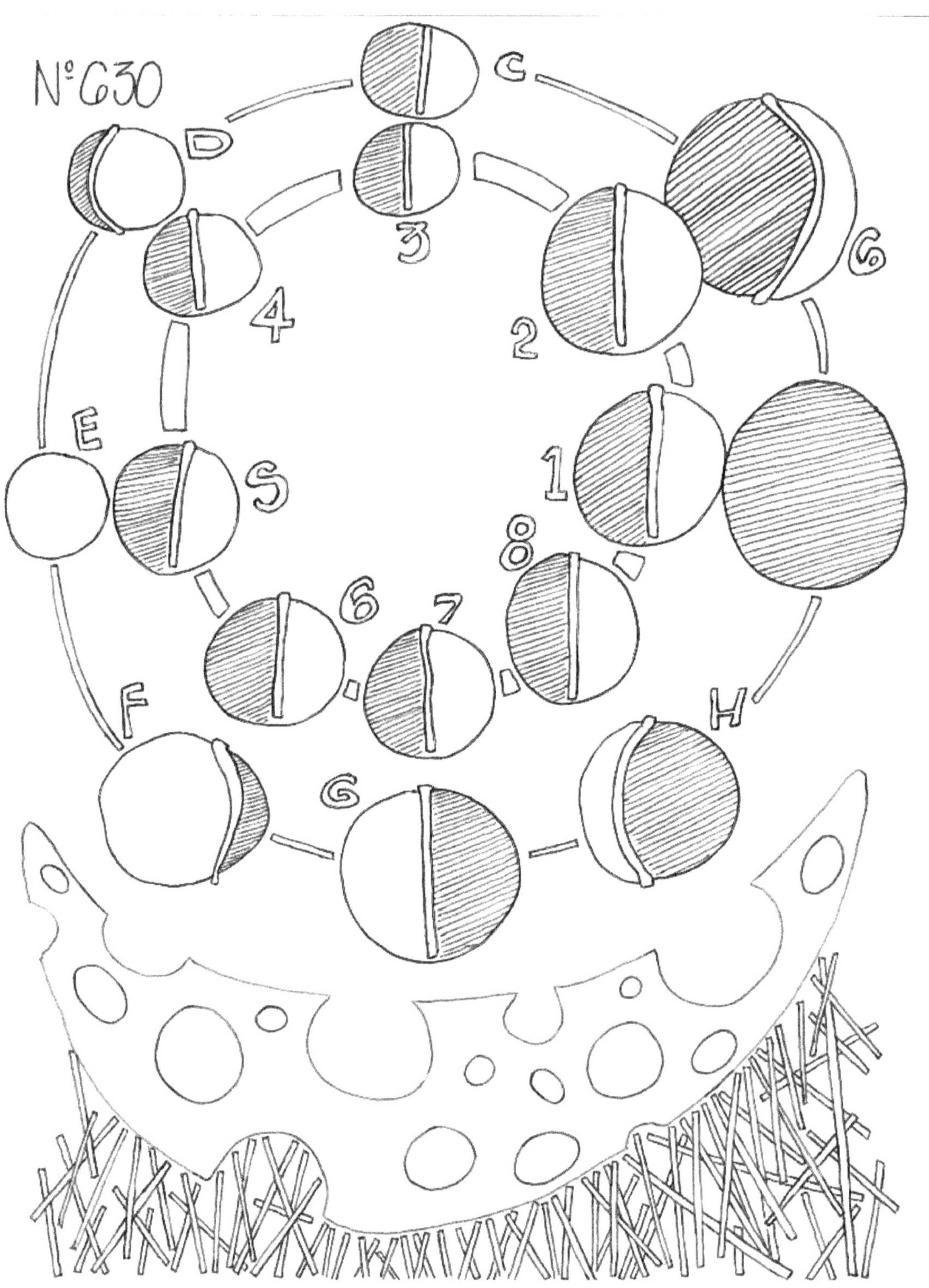

Nº630
C
D
3
4
2
G
E
S
1
8
6
7
F
G
H

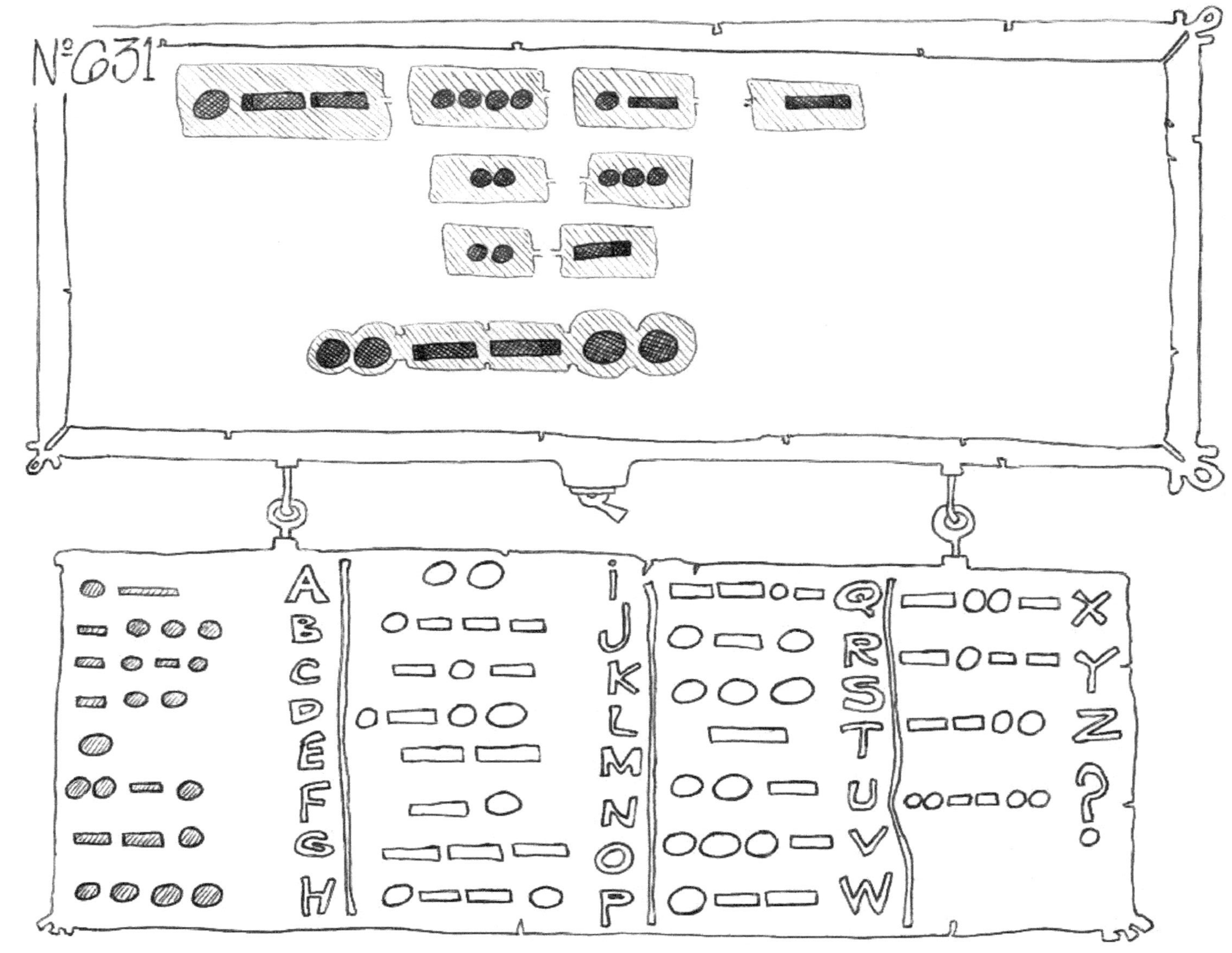
№ 631
A
B
C
D
E
F
G
H
I
J
K
L
M
N
O
P
Q
R
S
T
U
V
W
X
Y
Z
?

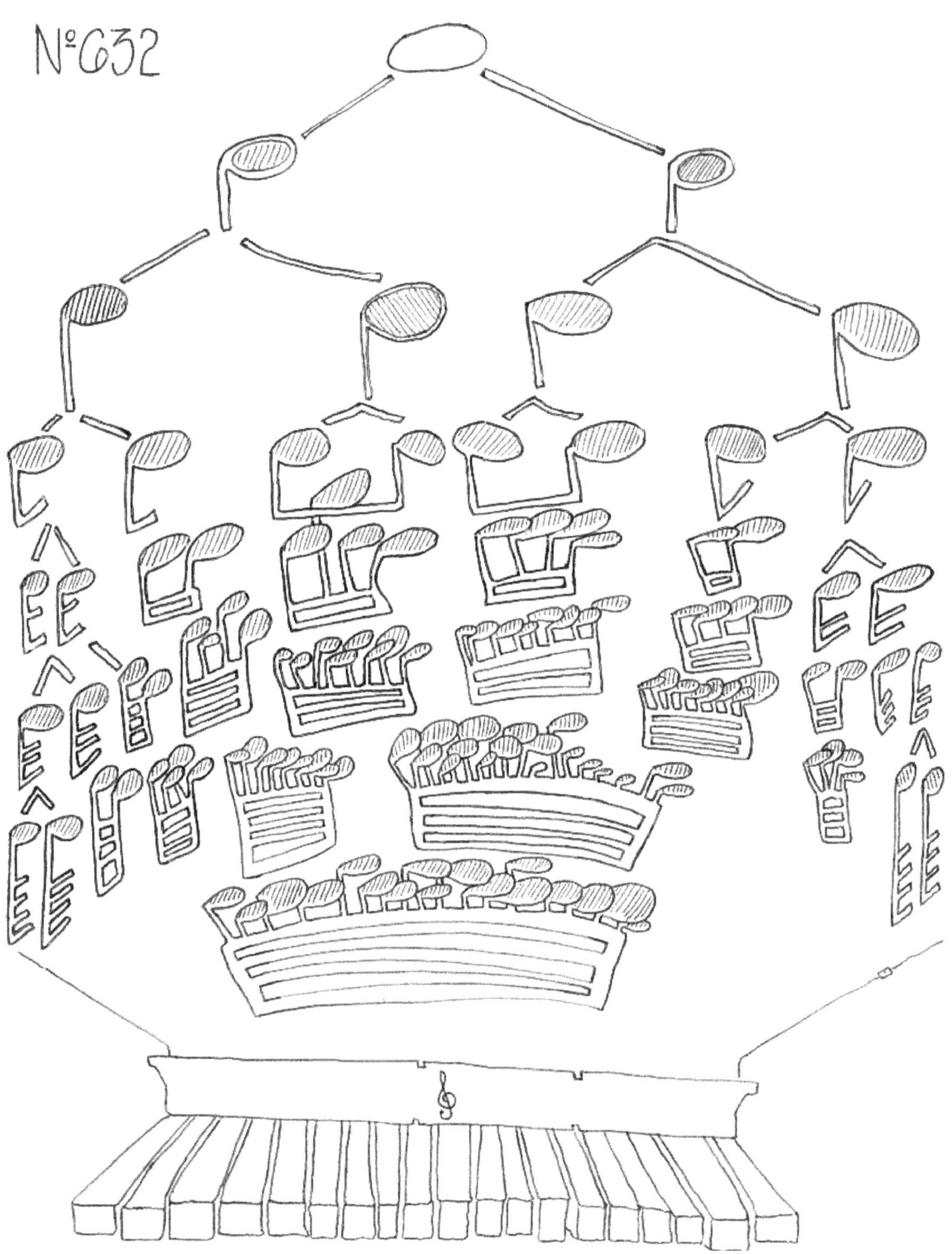
№632

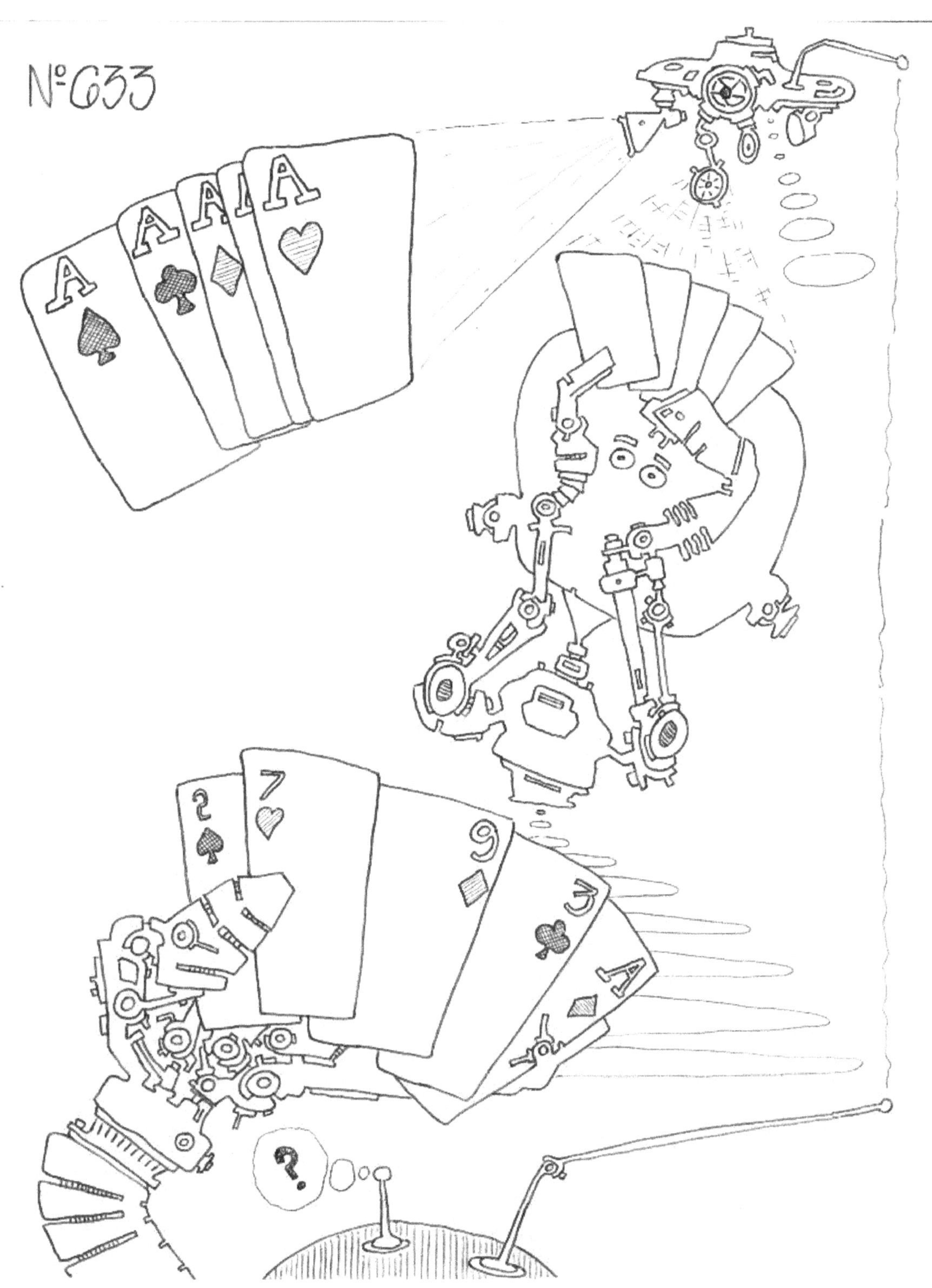
№633

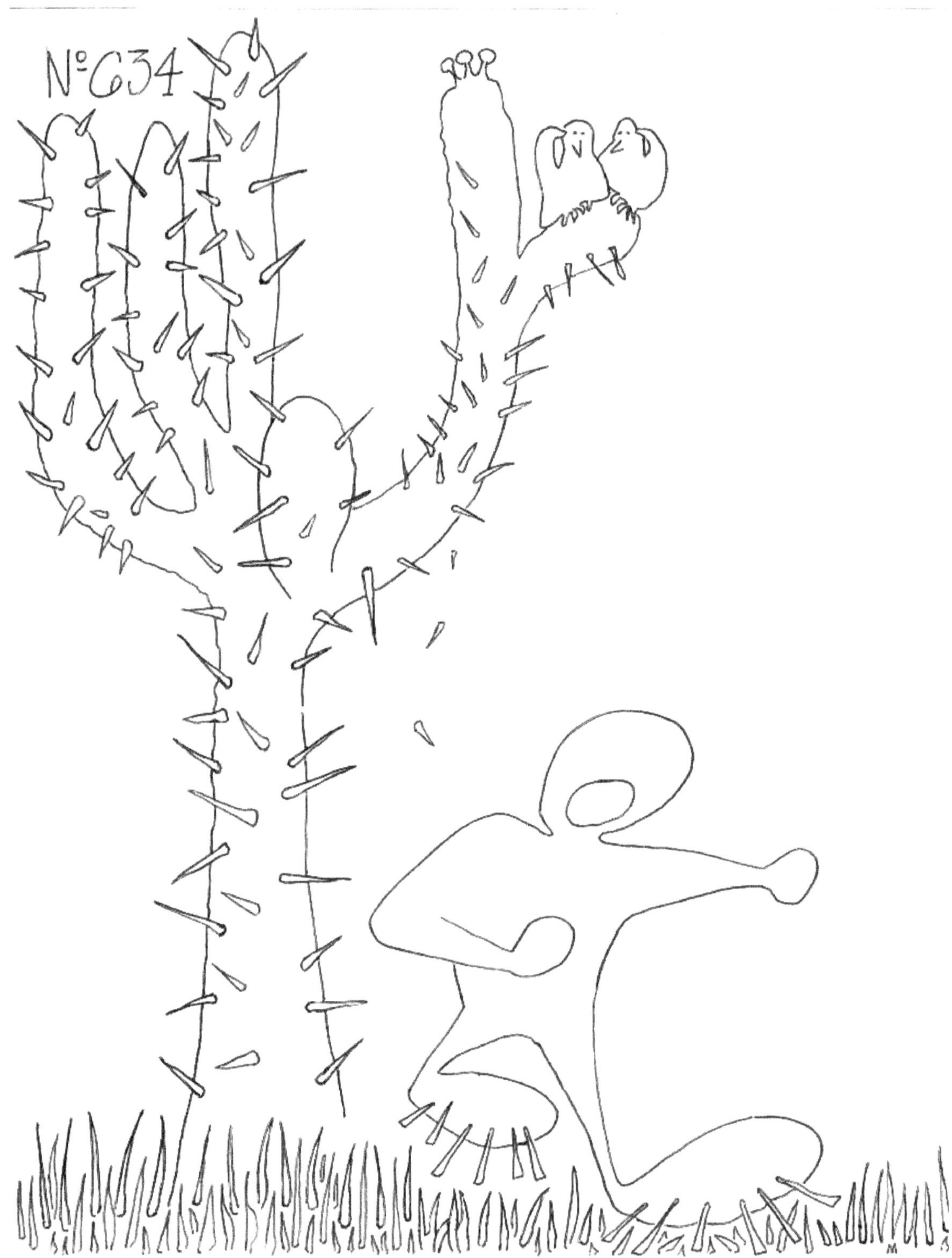
Nº634

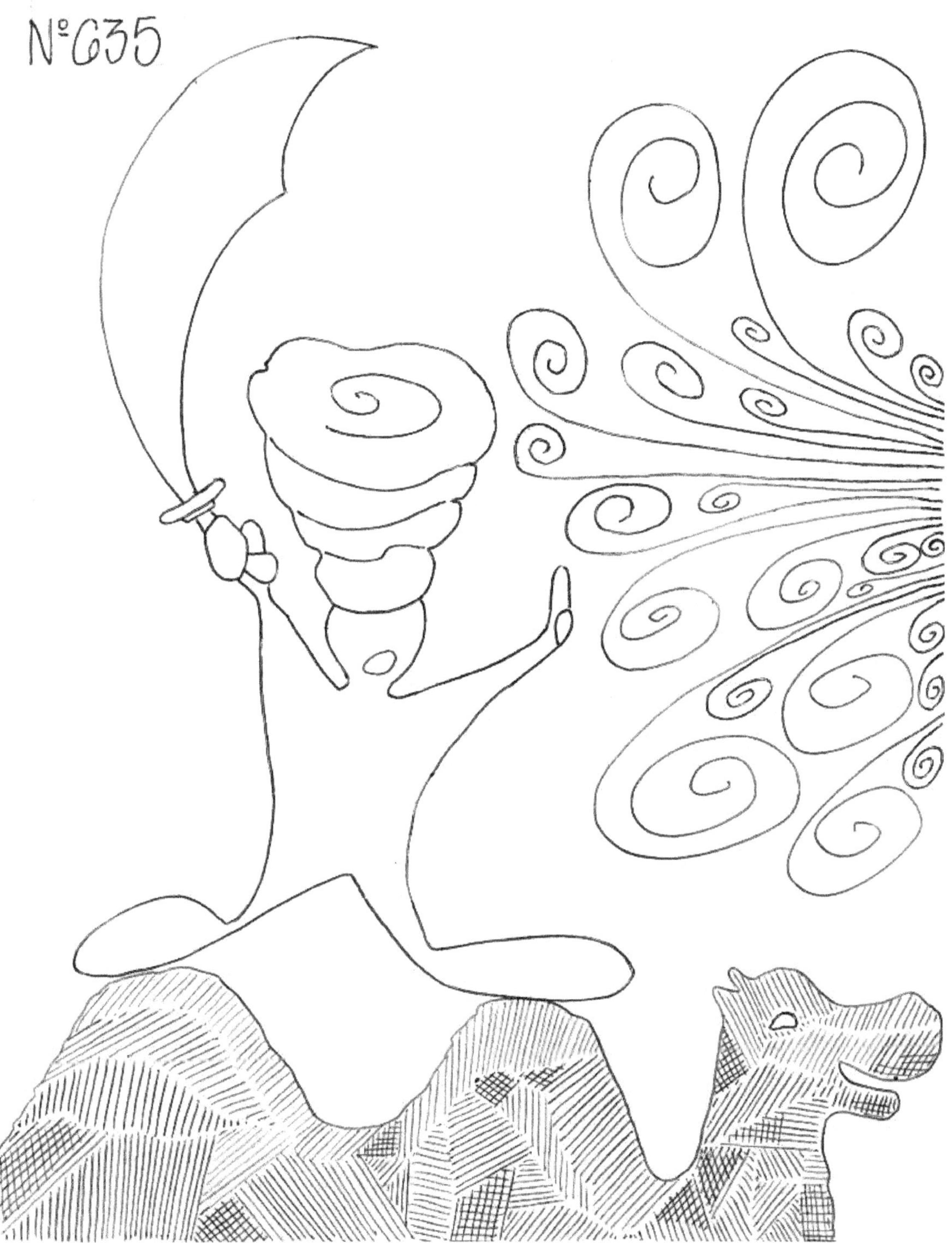
№635

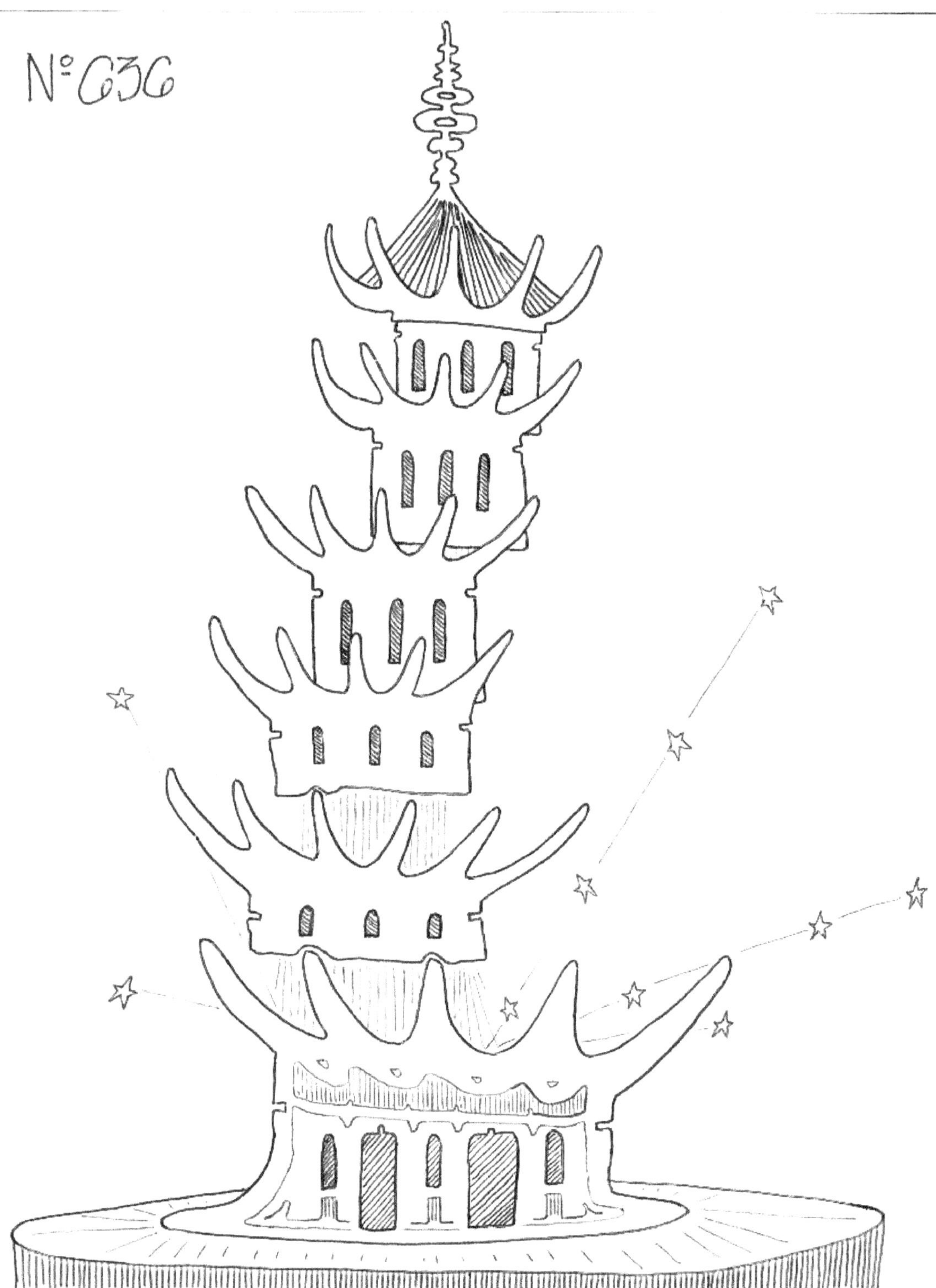

Nº036

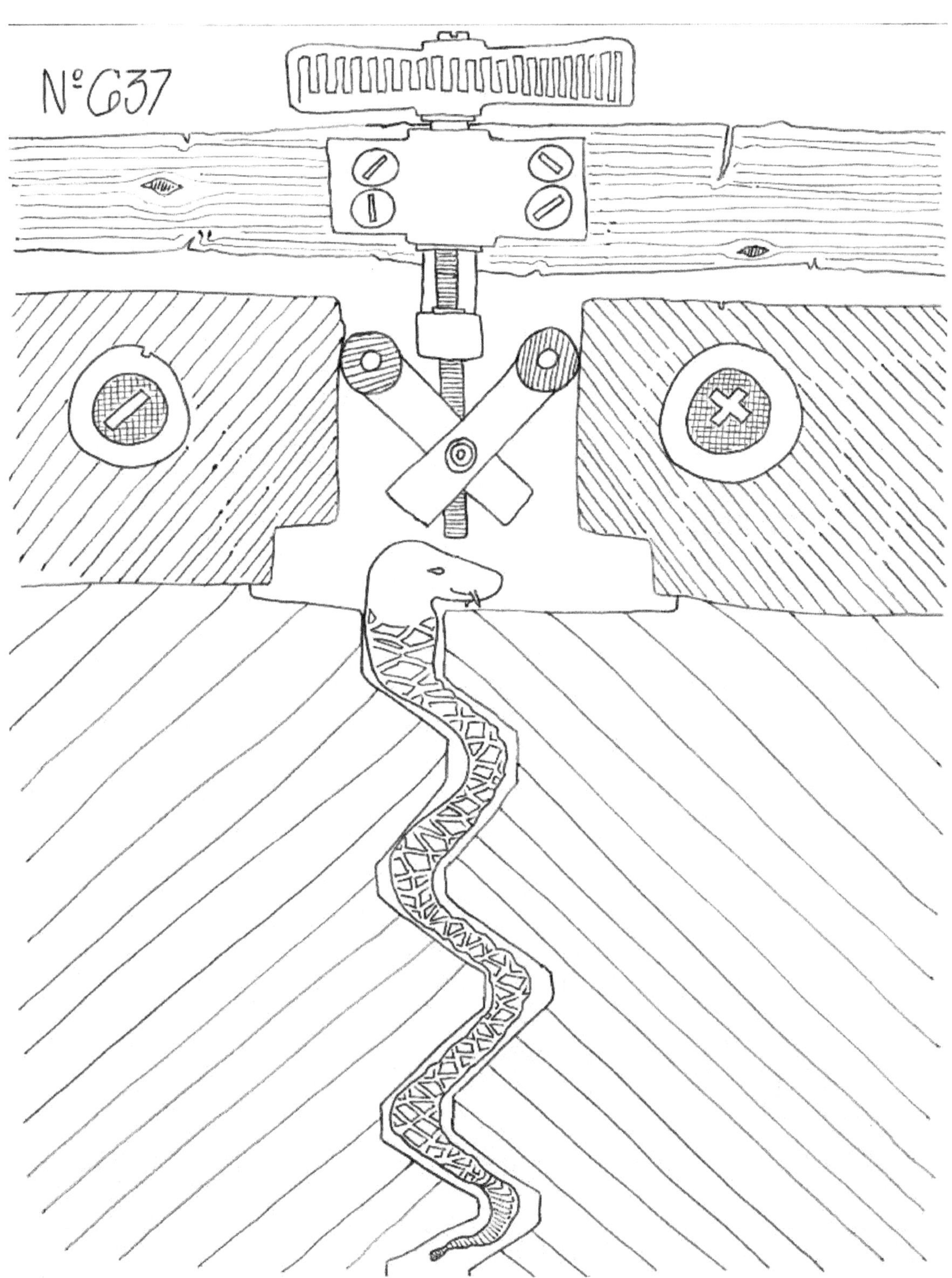
Nº G37

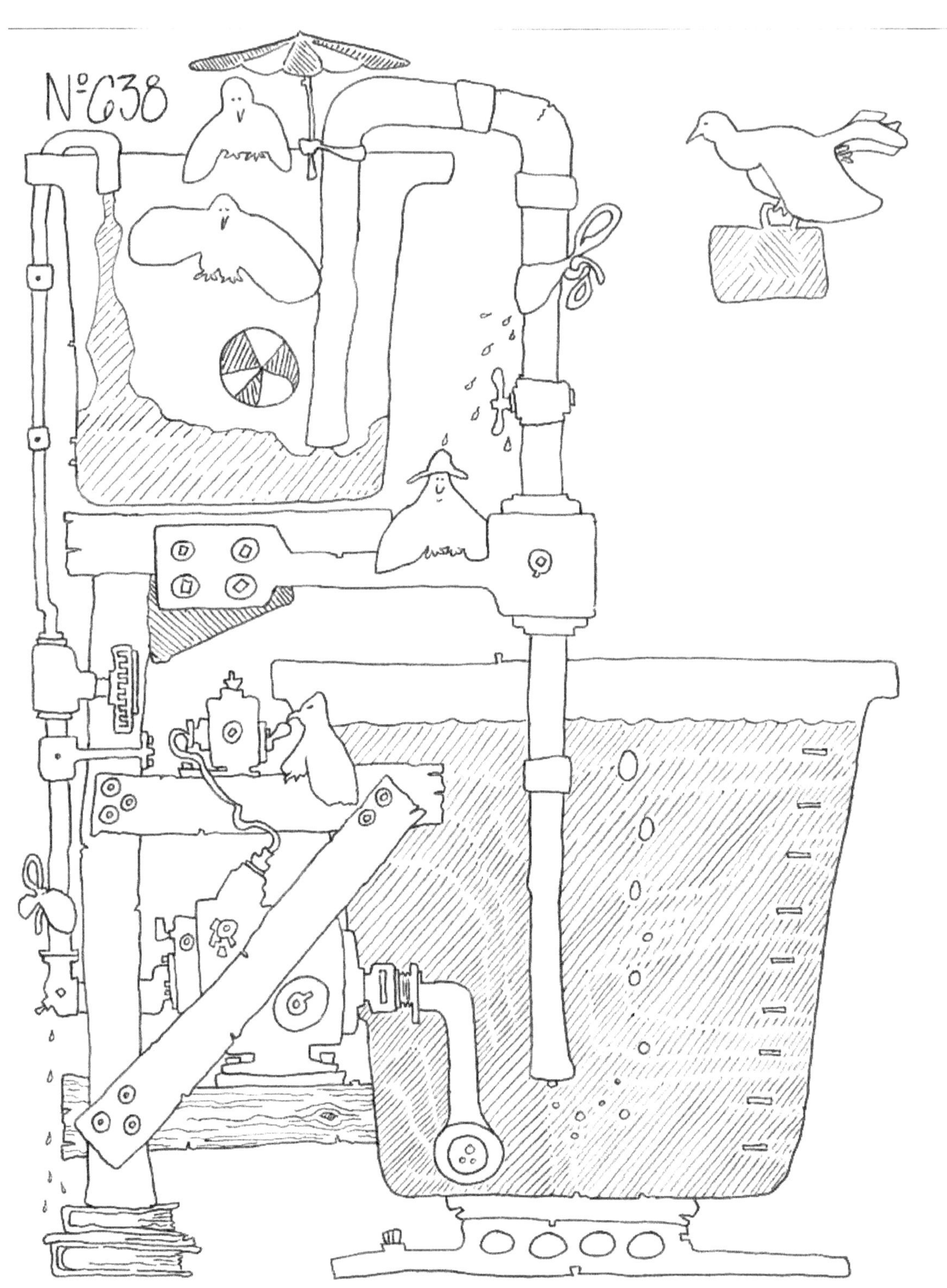
Nº638

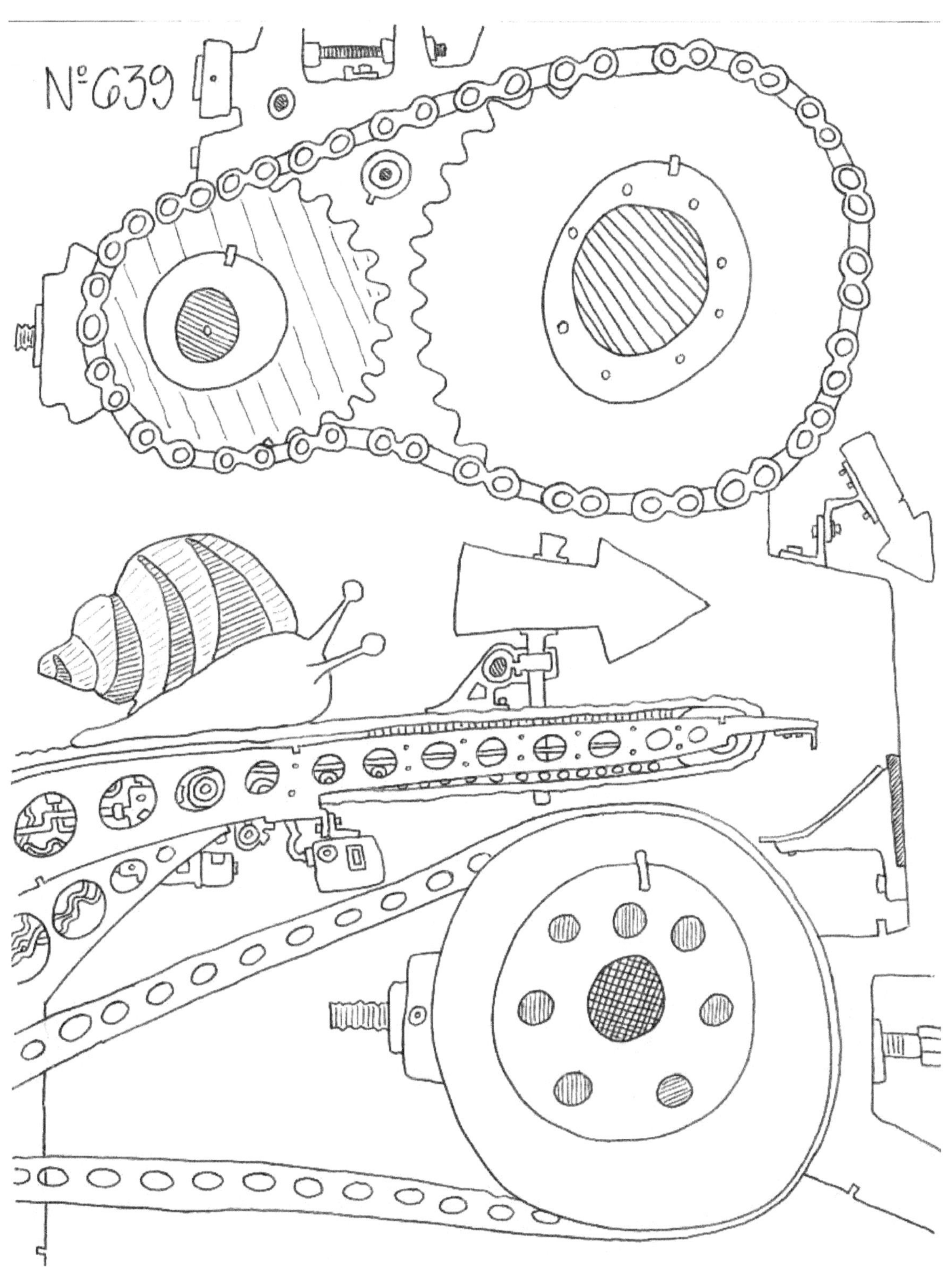
N°639

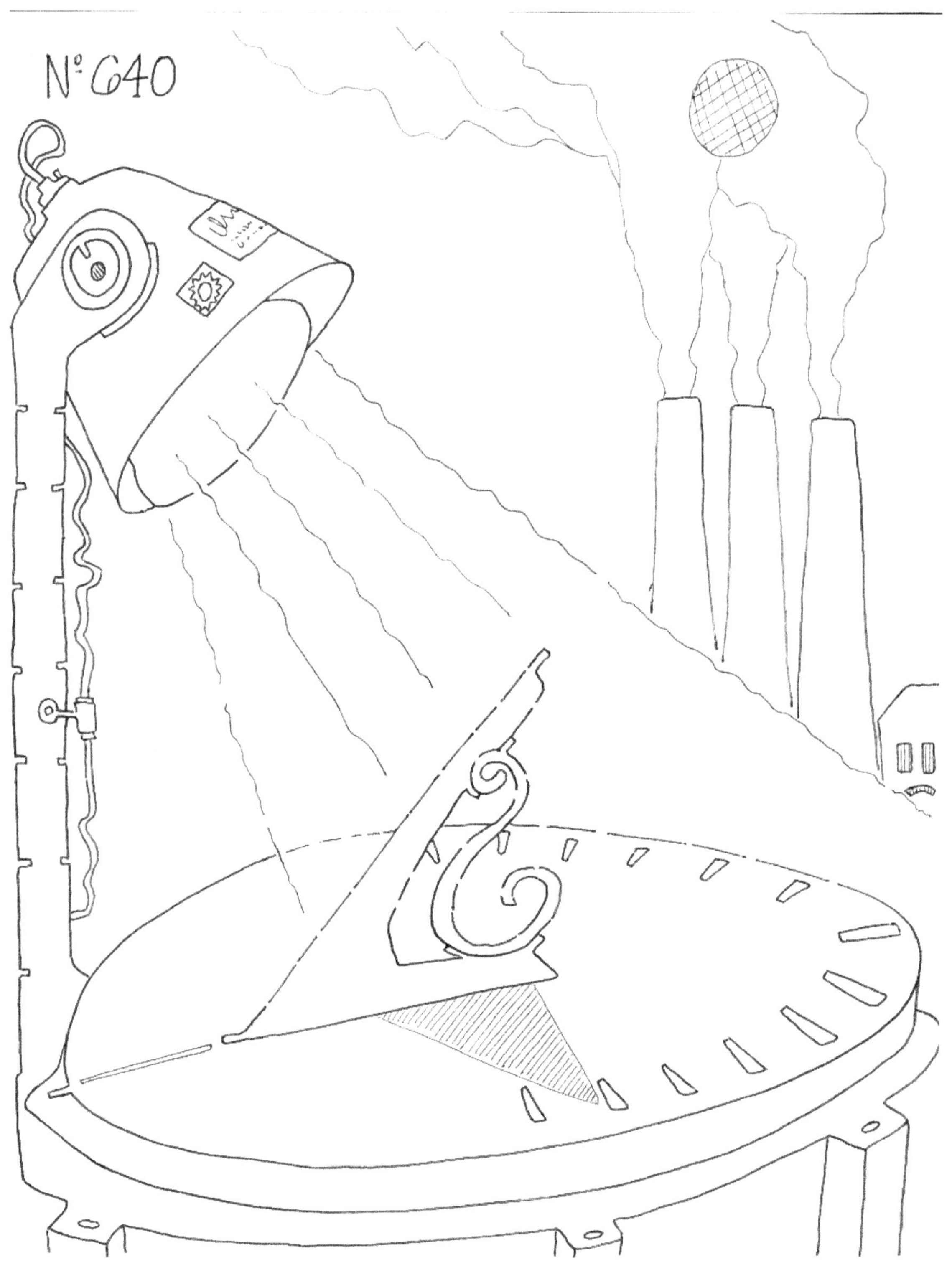
N° 640

№641

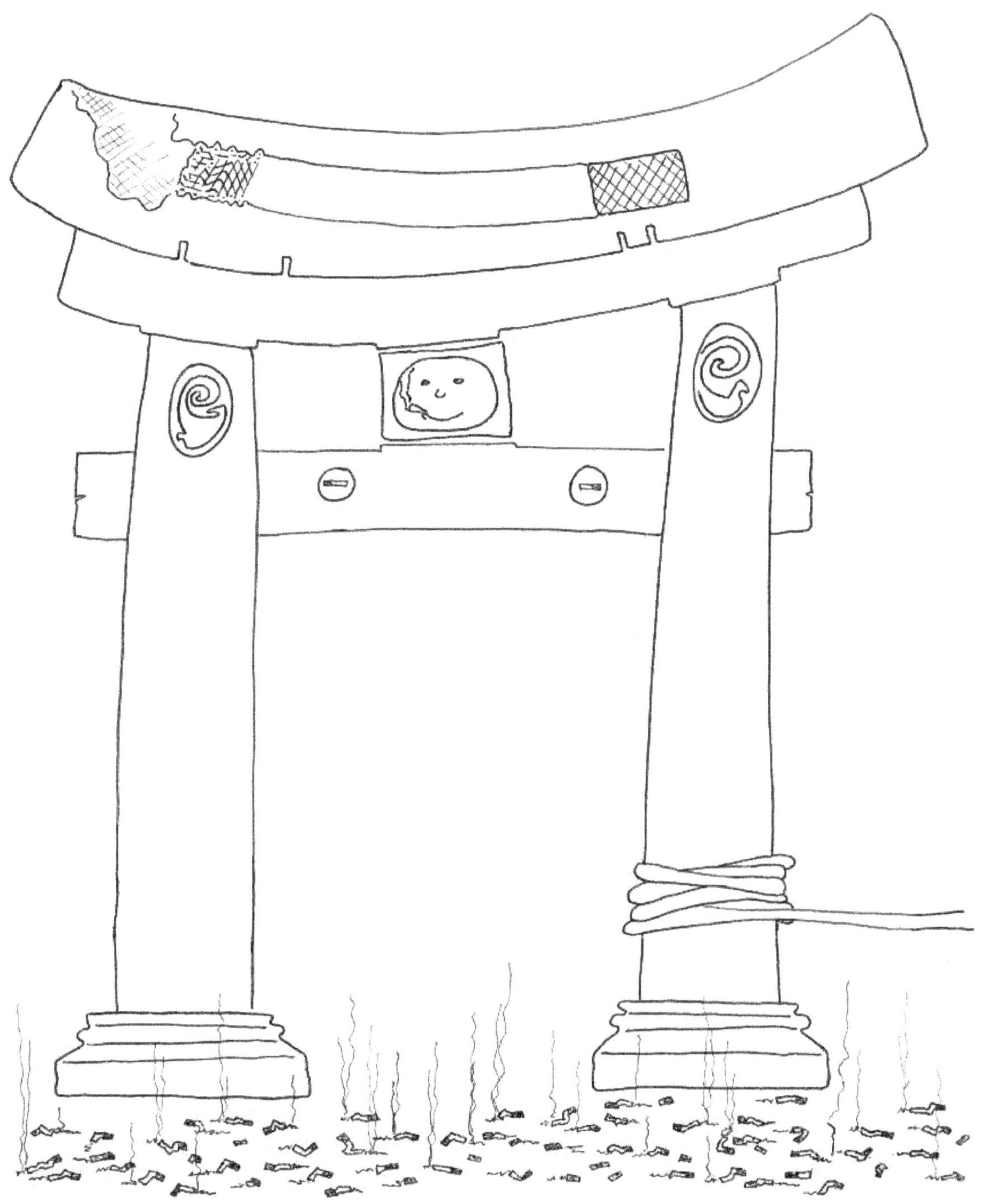

№642

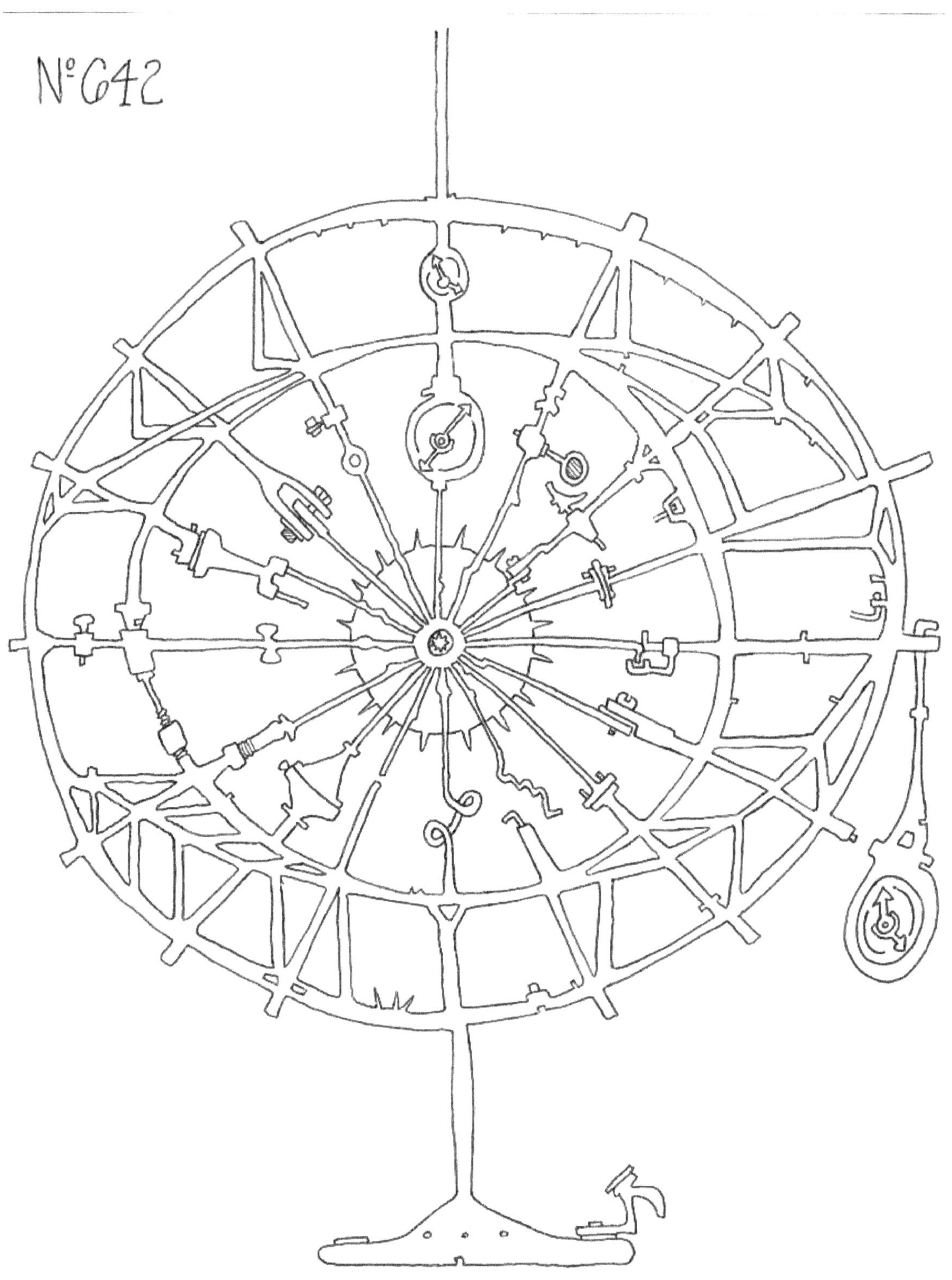

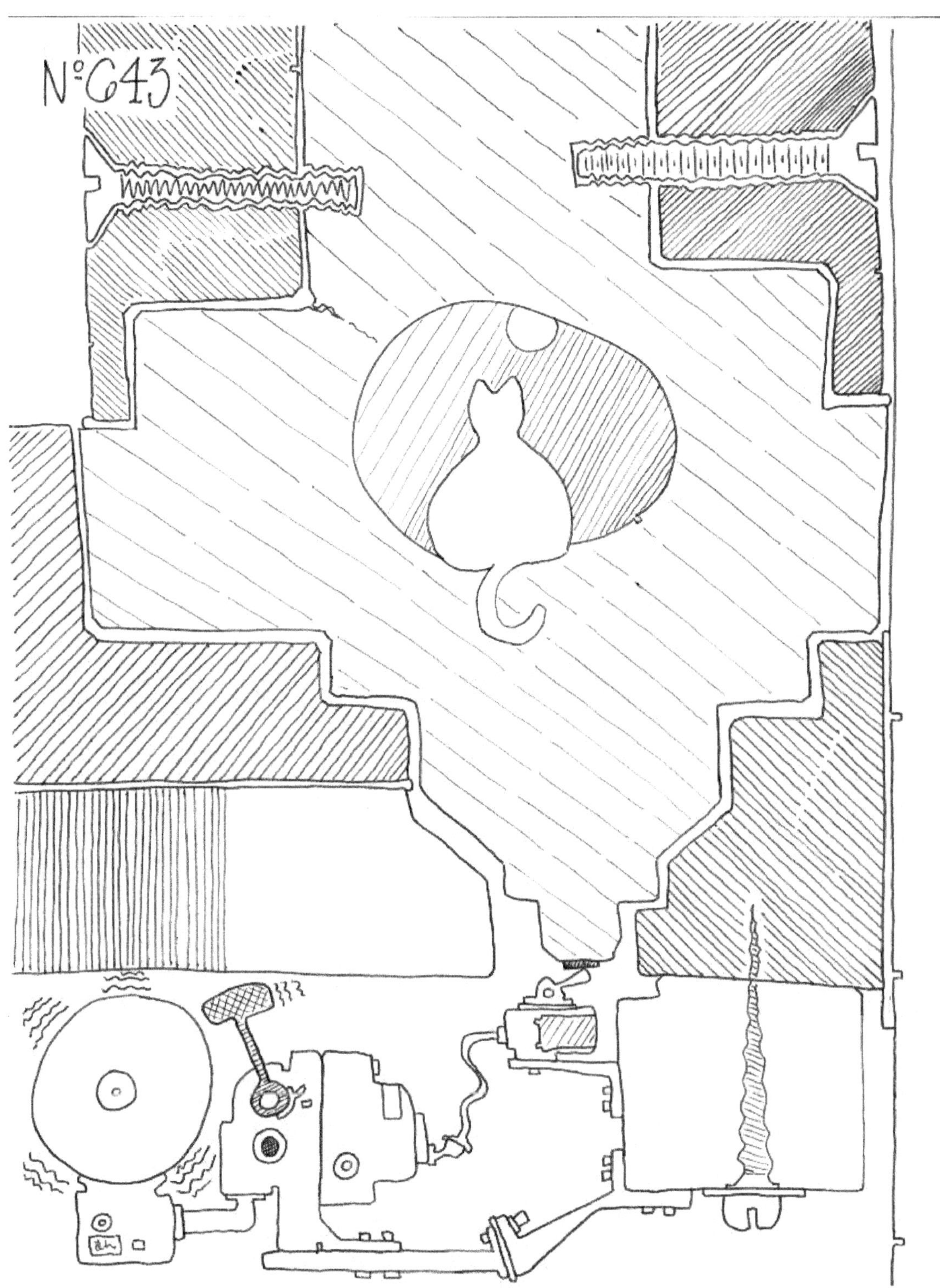
Nº643

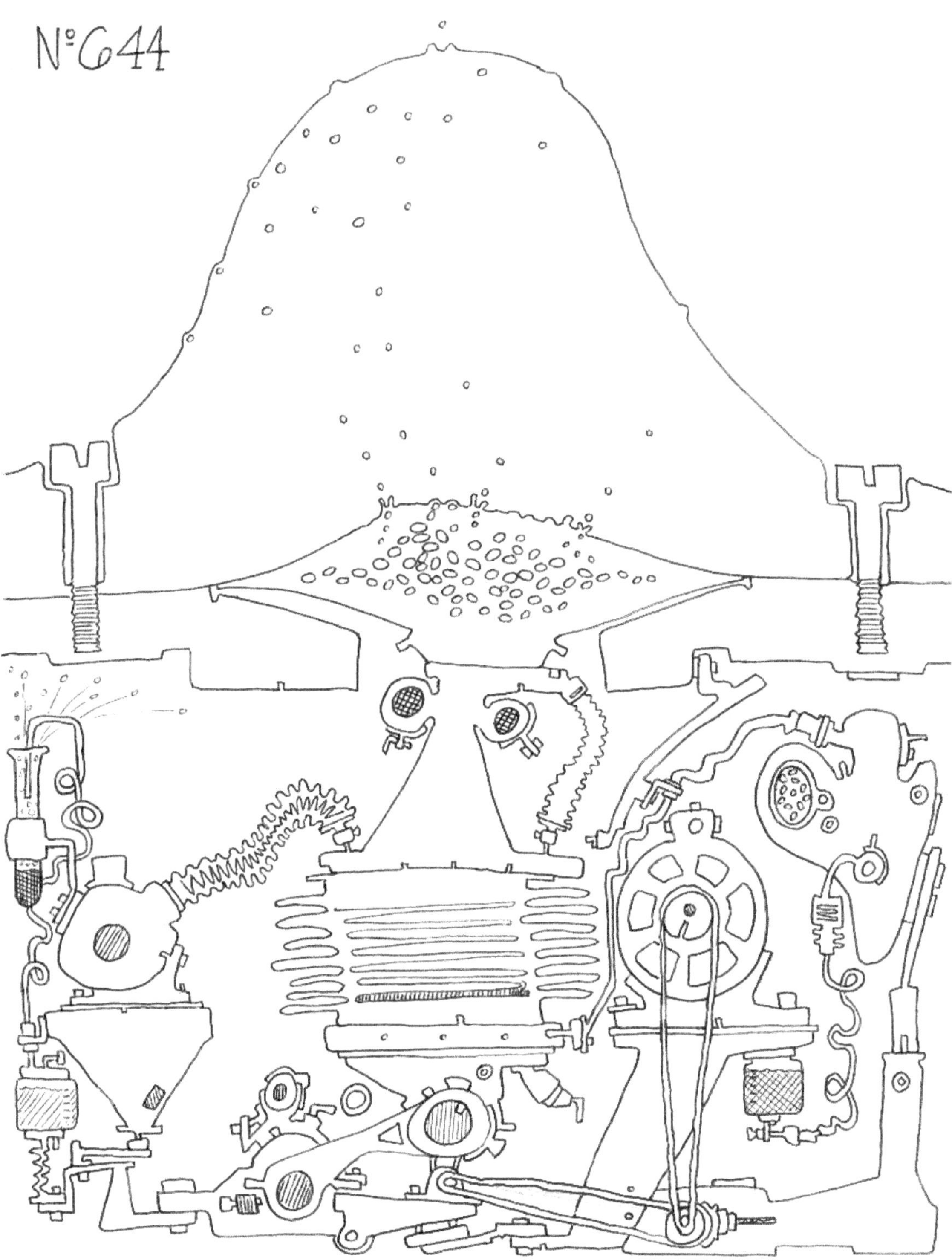
N°644

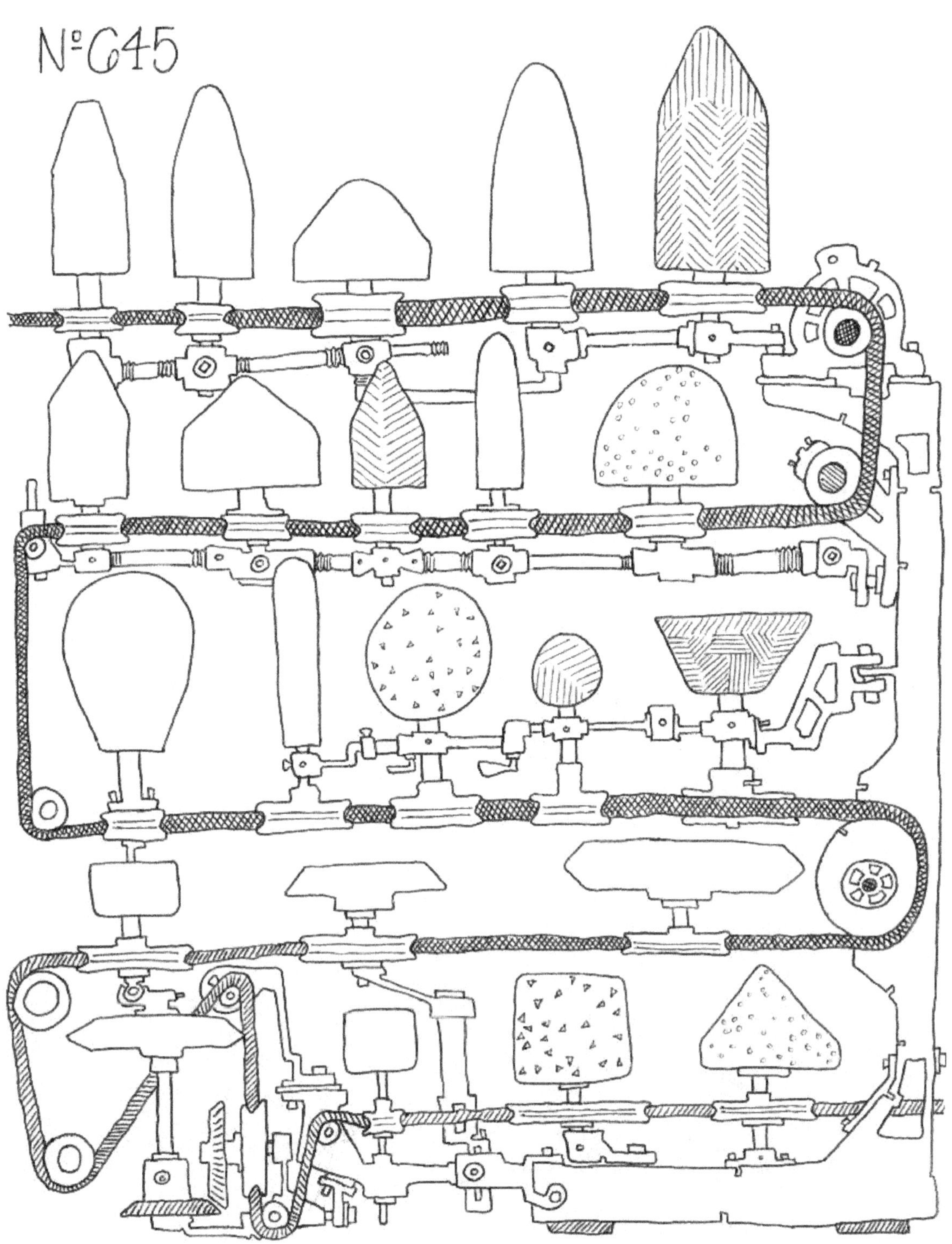
Nº645

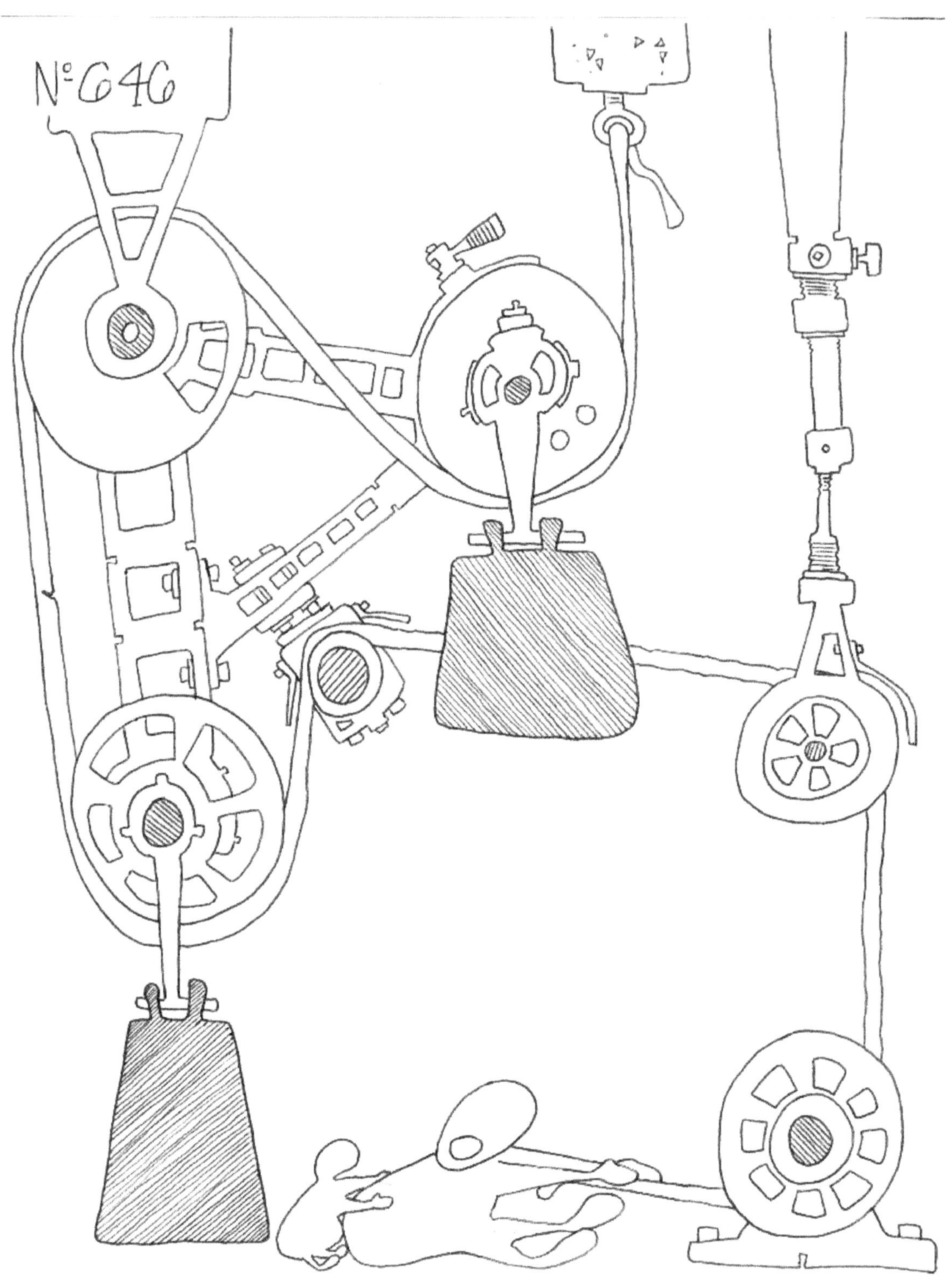
№ 646

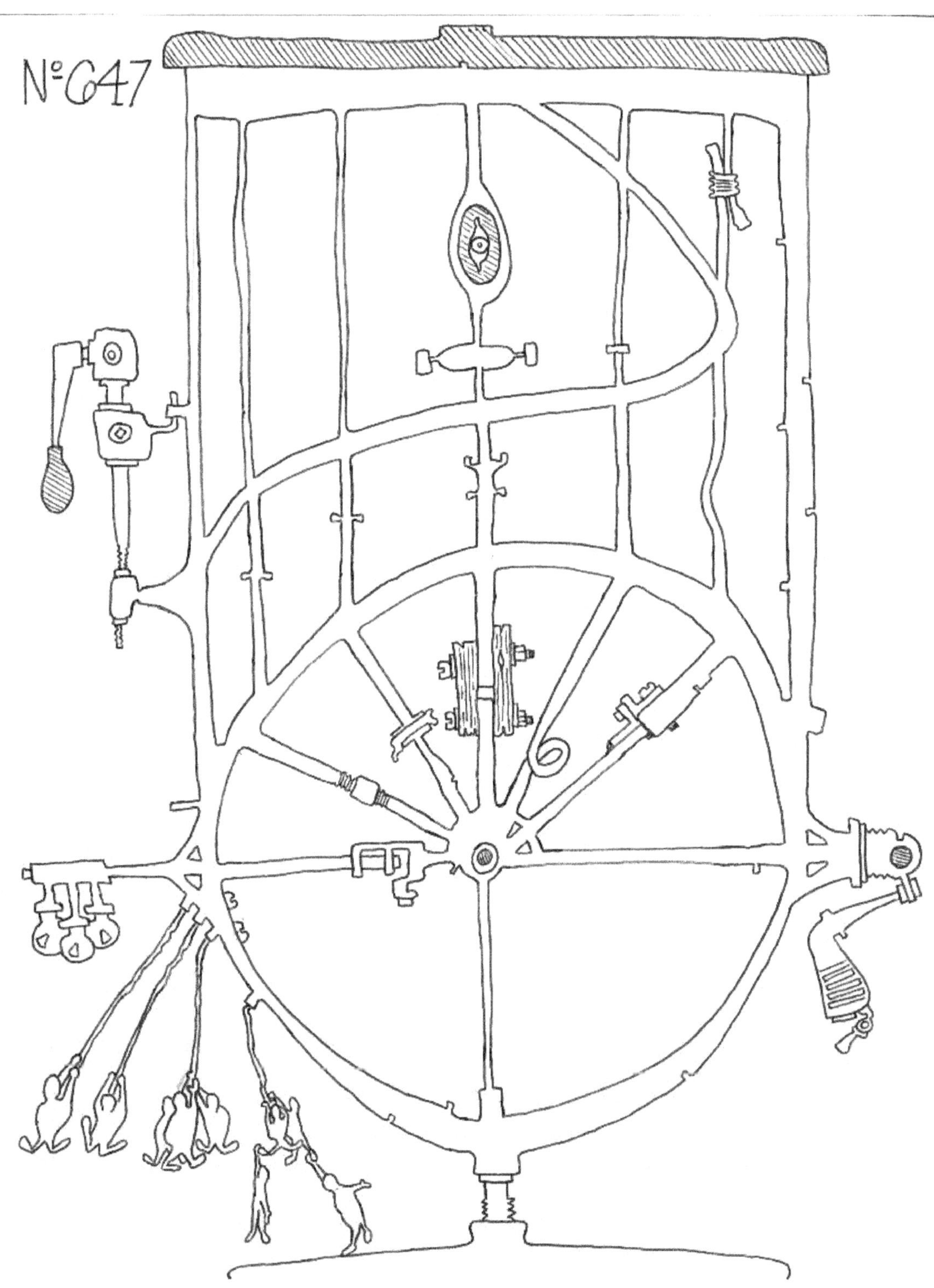
N°647

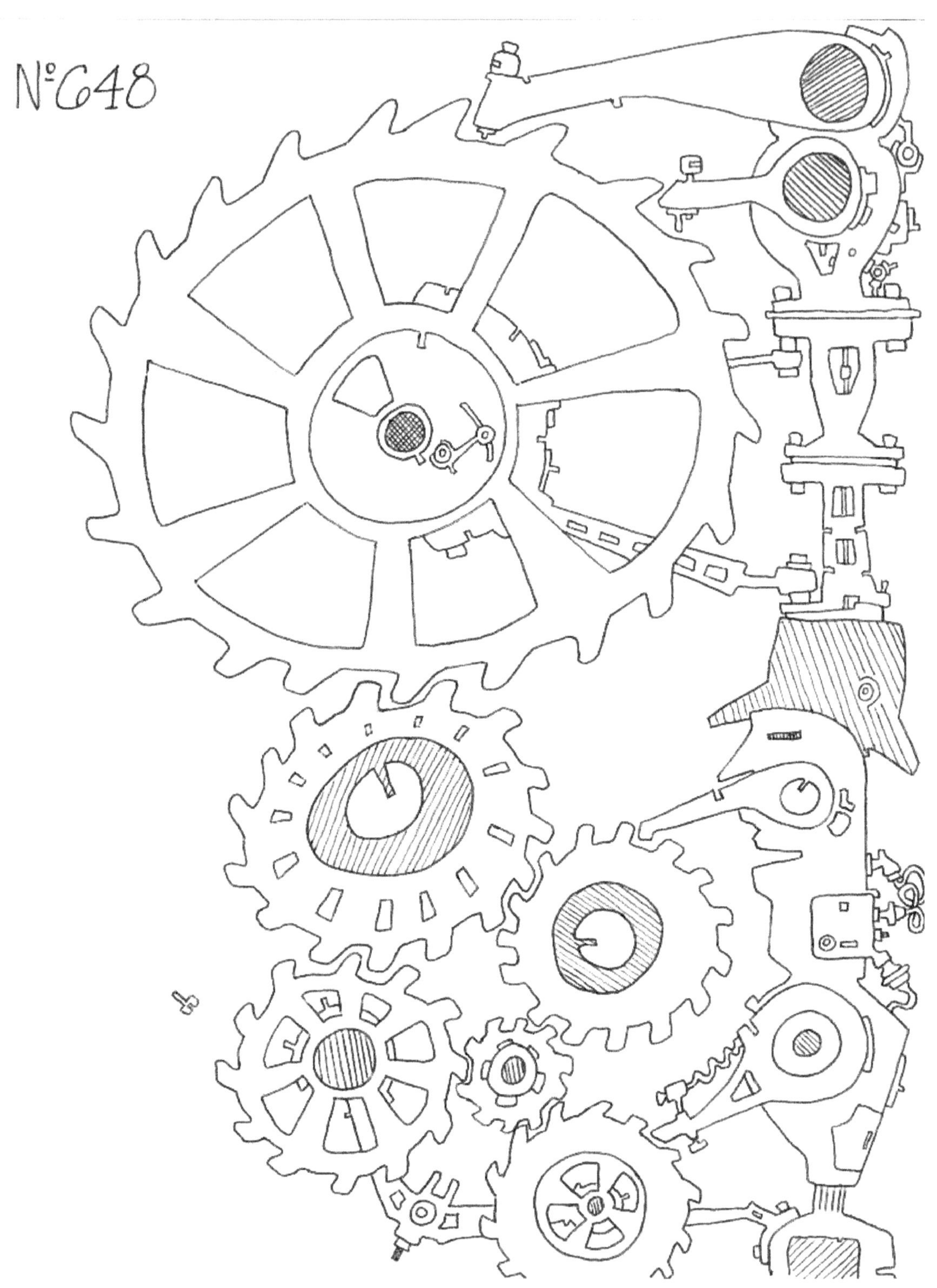
N°648

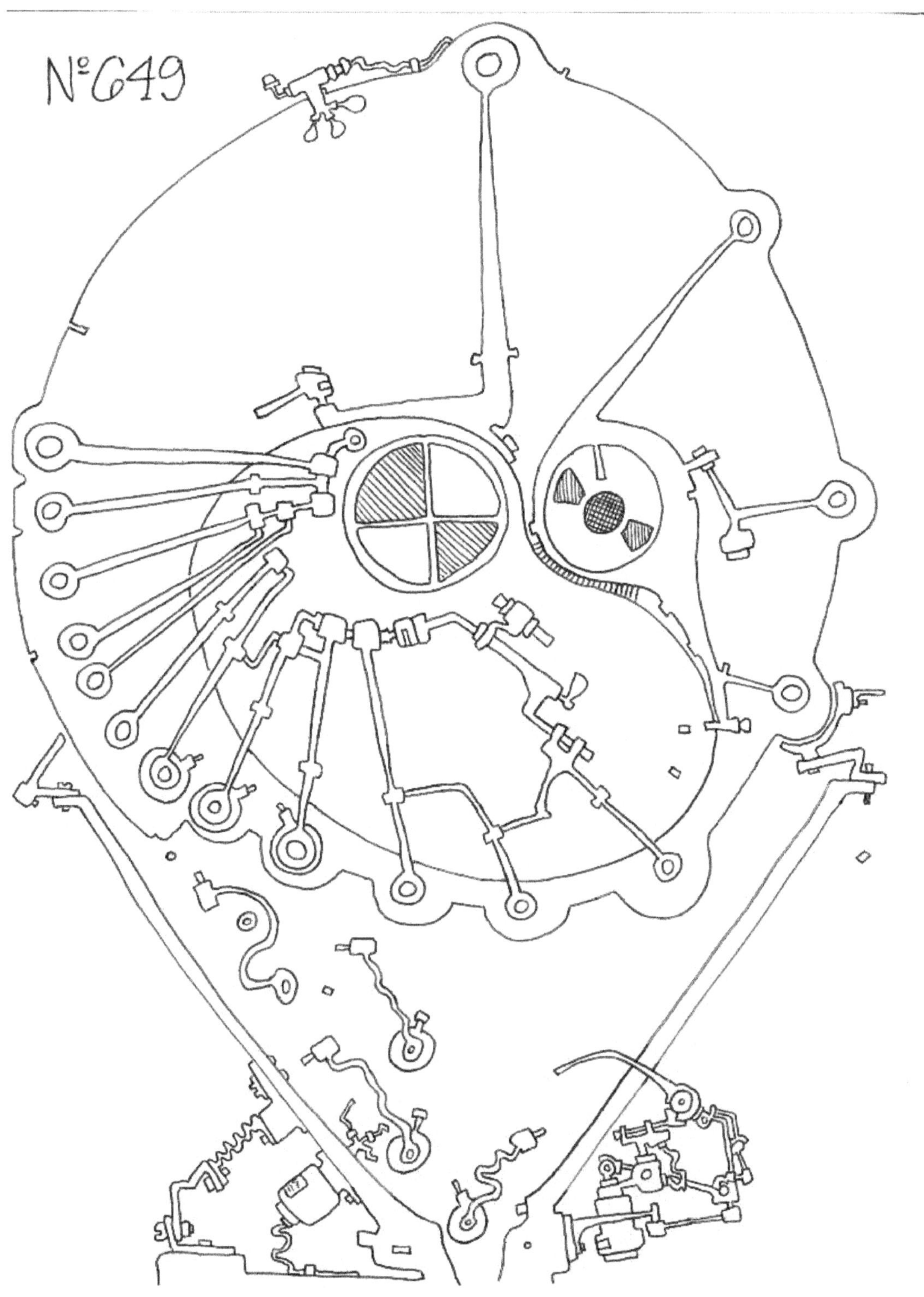
№649

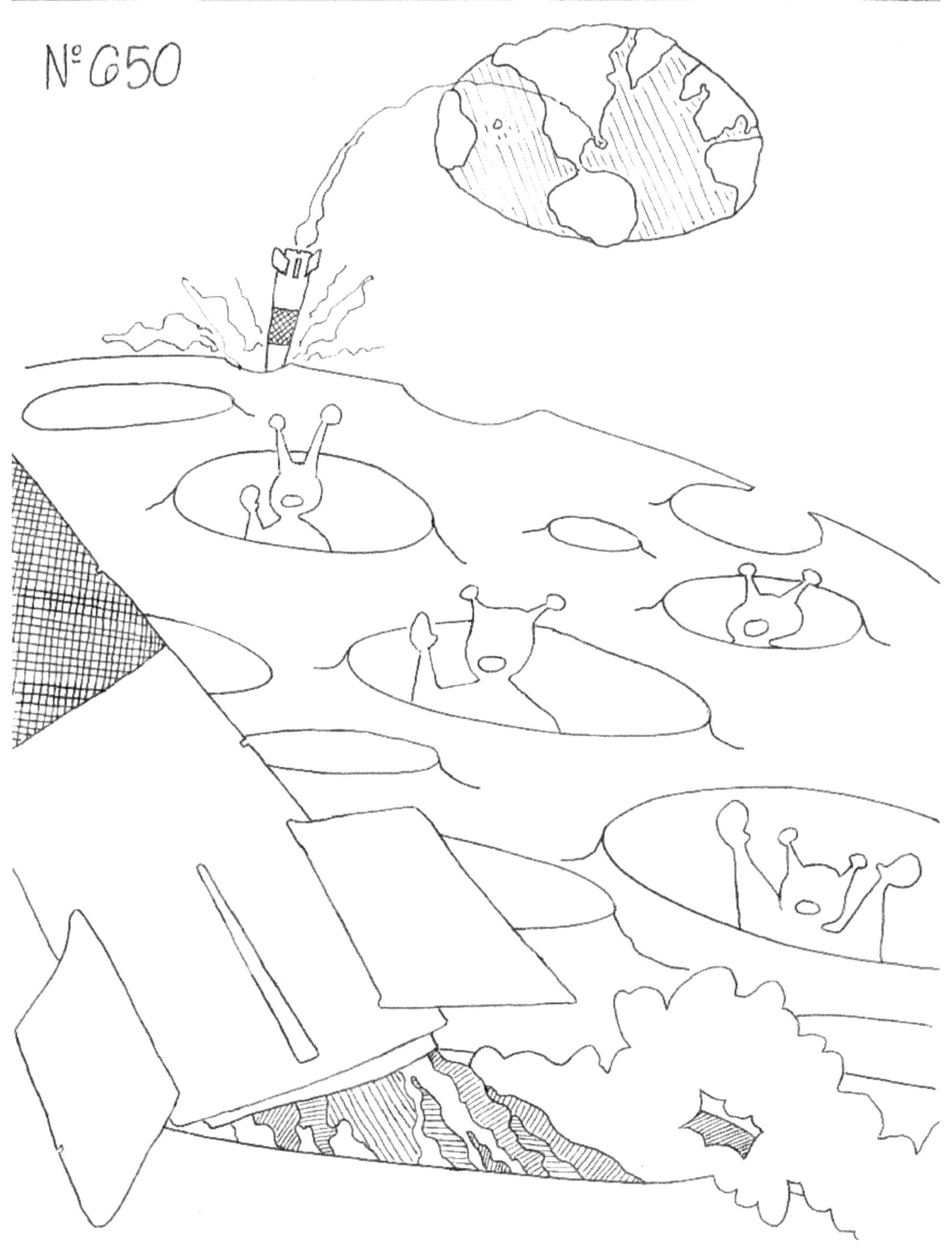
№650

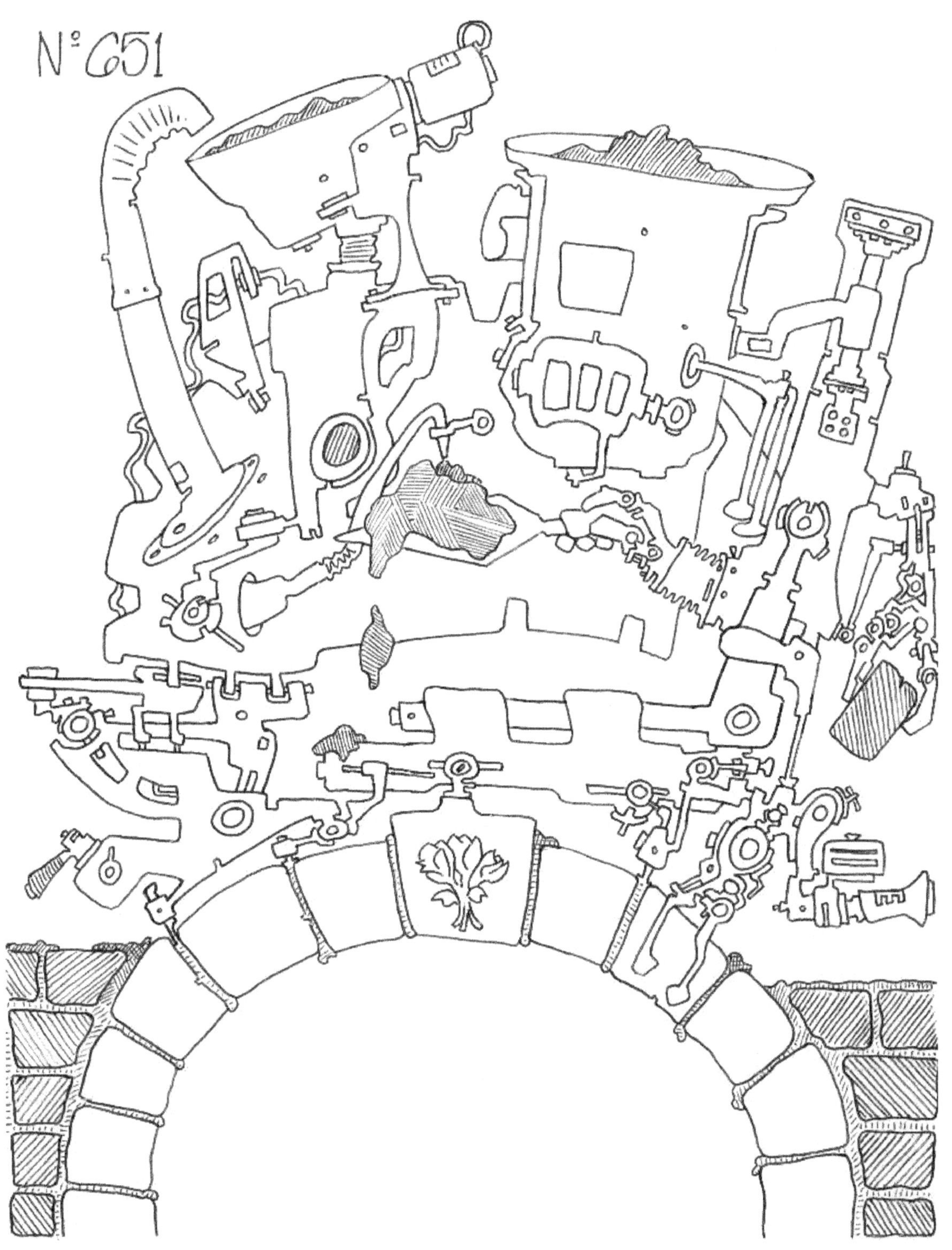
N°651

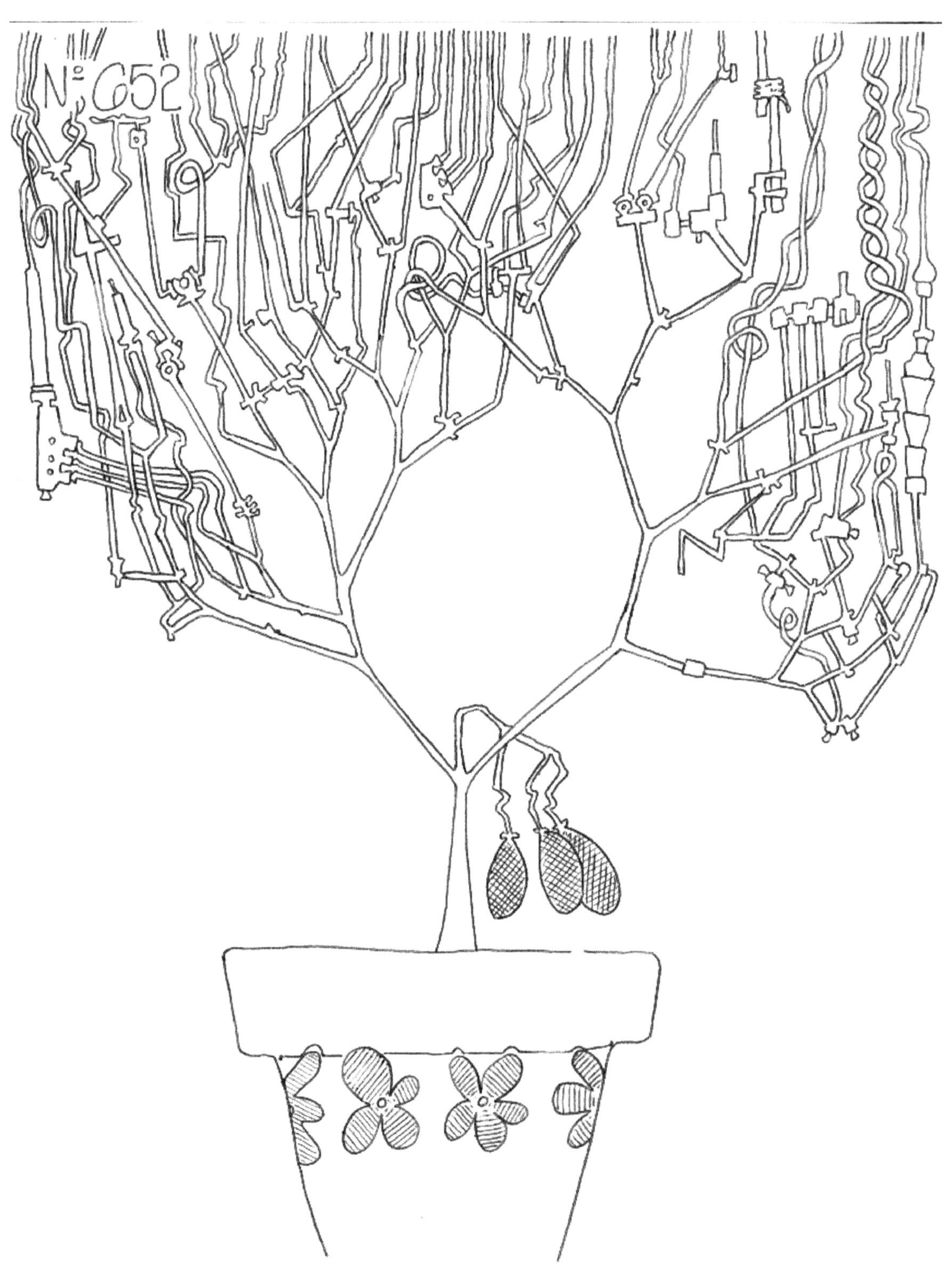
Nº G52

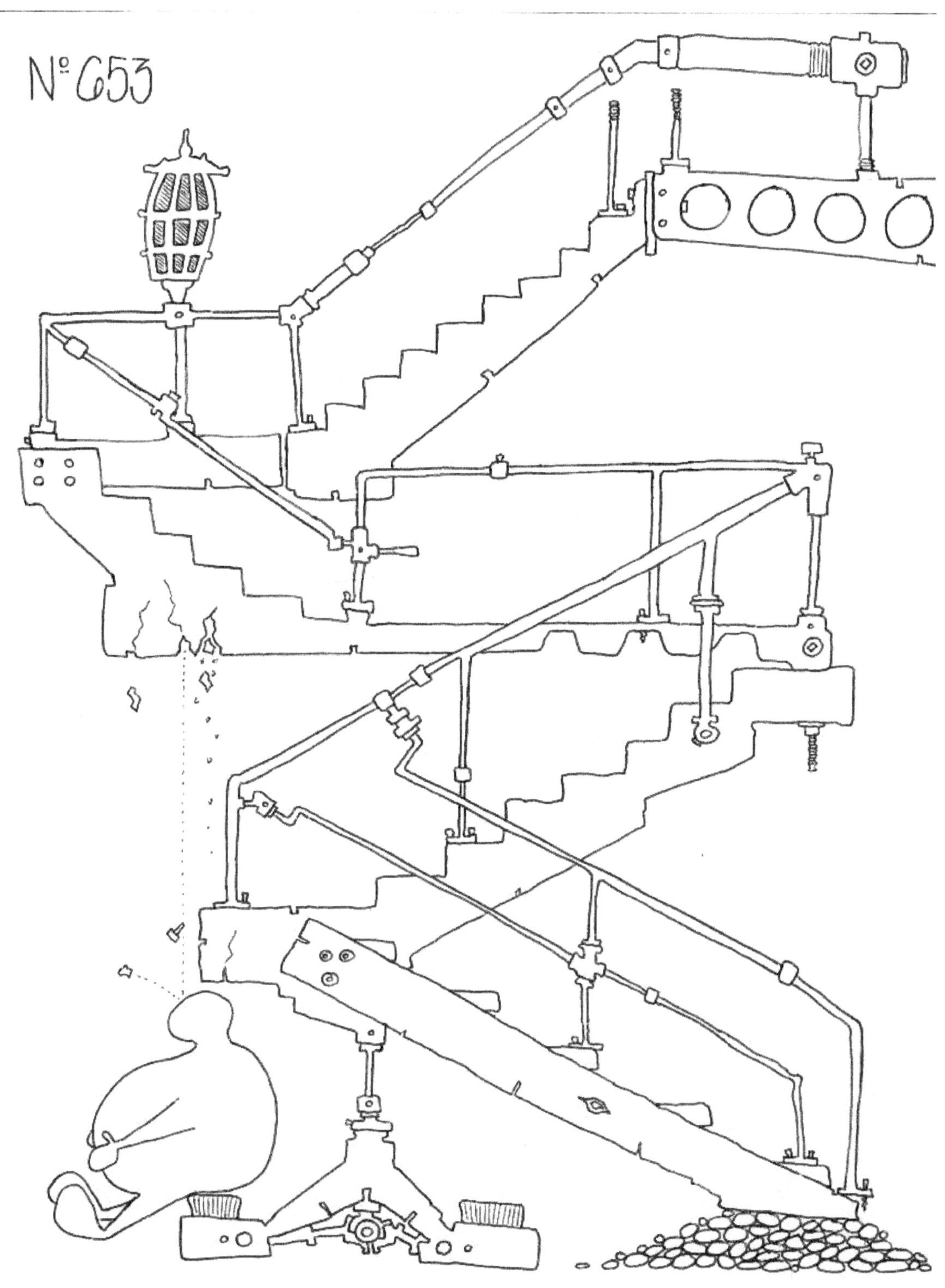
N°653

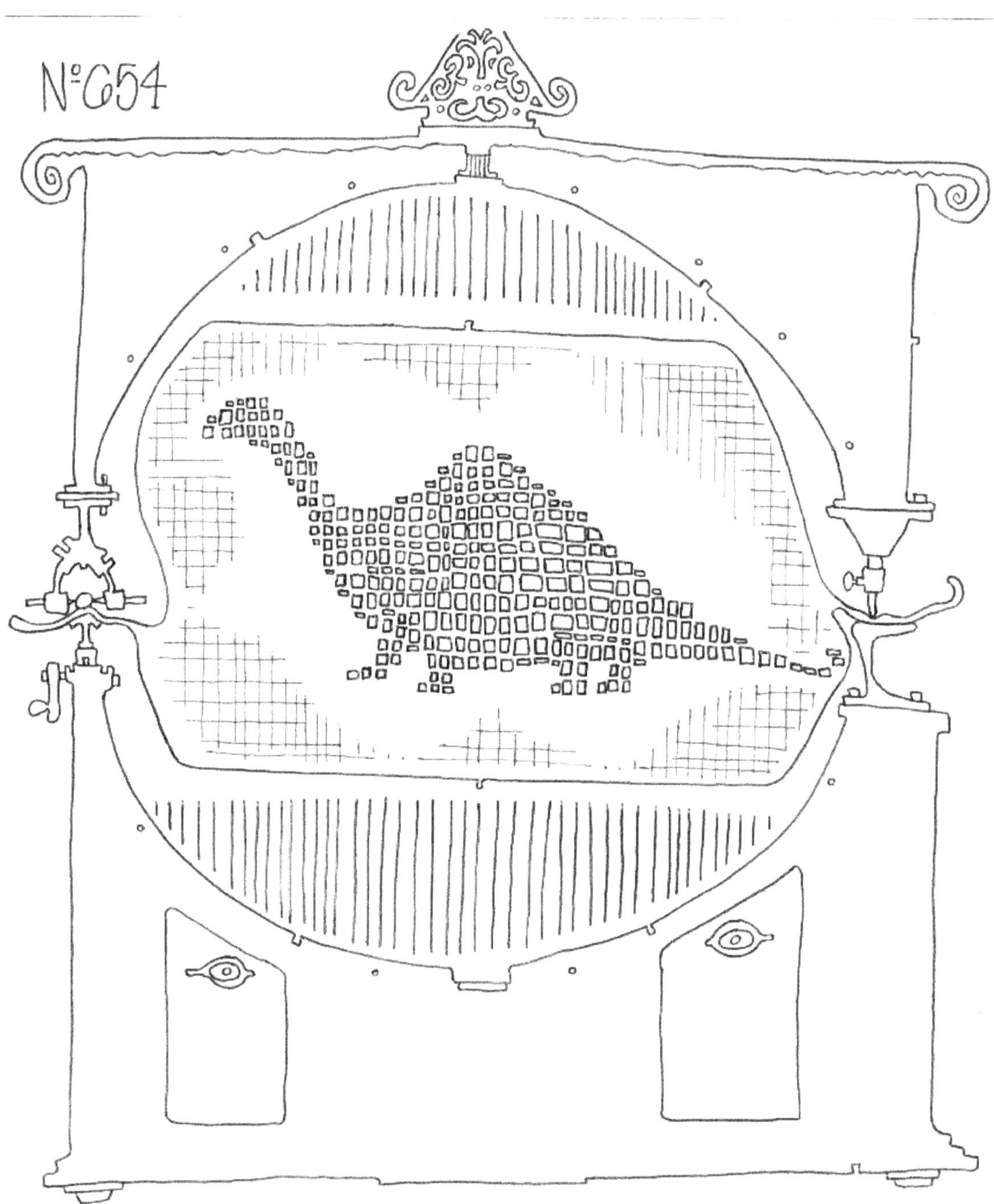
№654

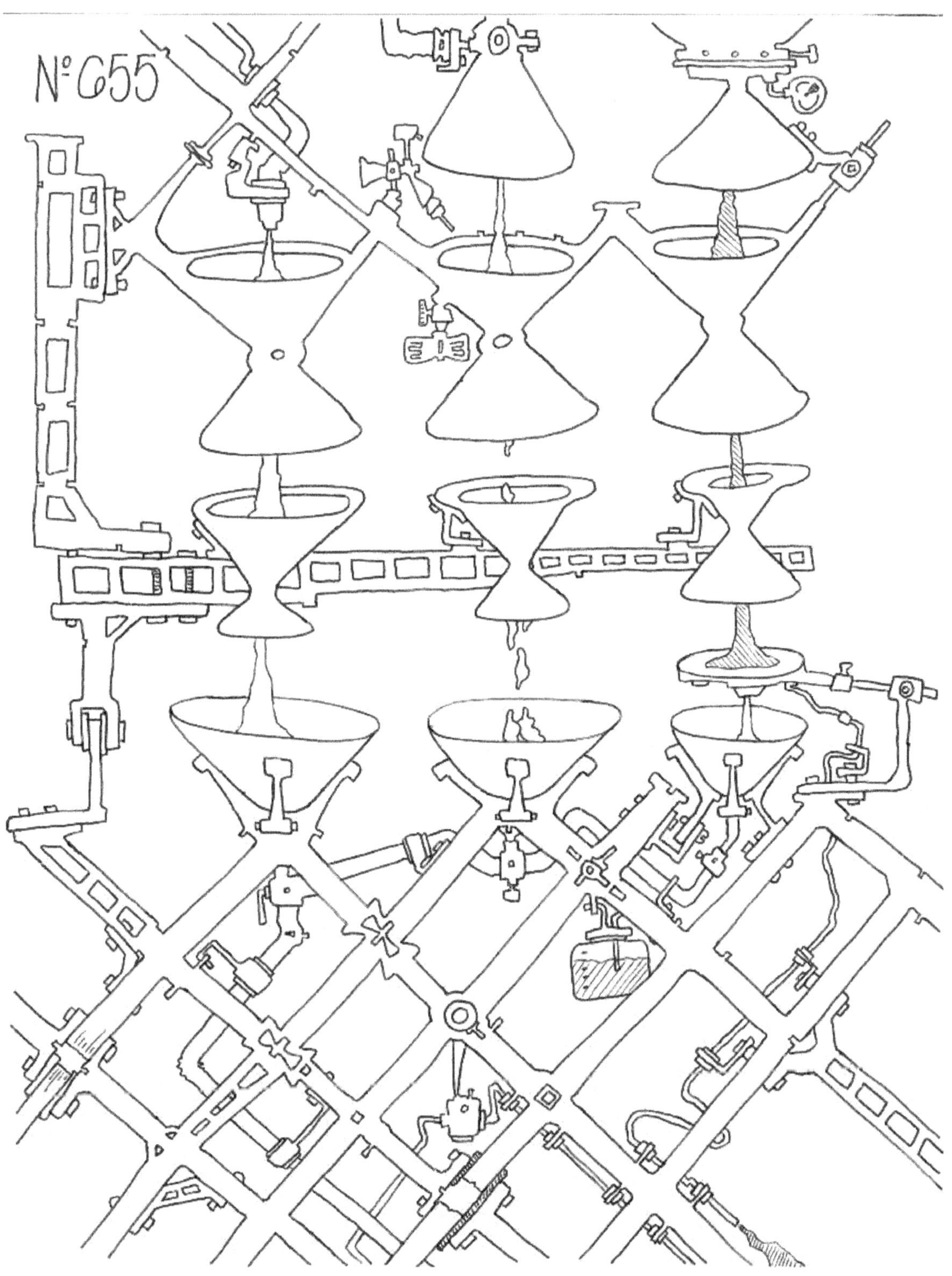
№655

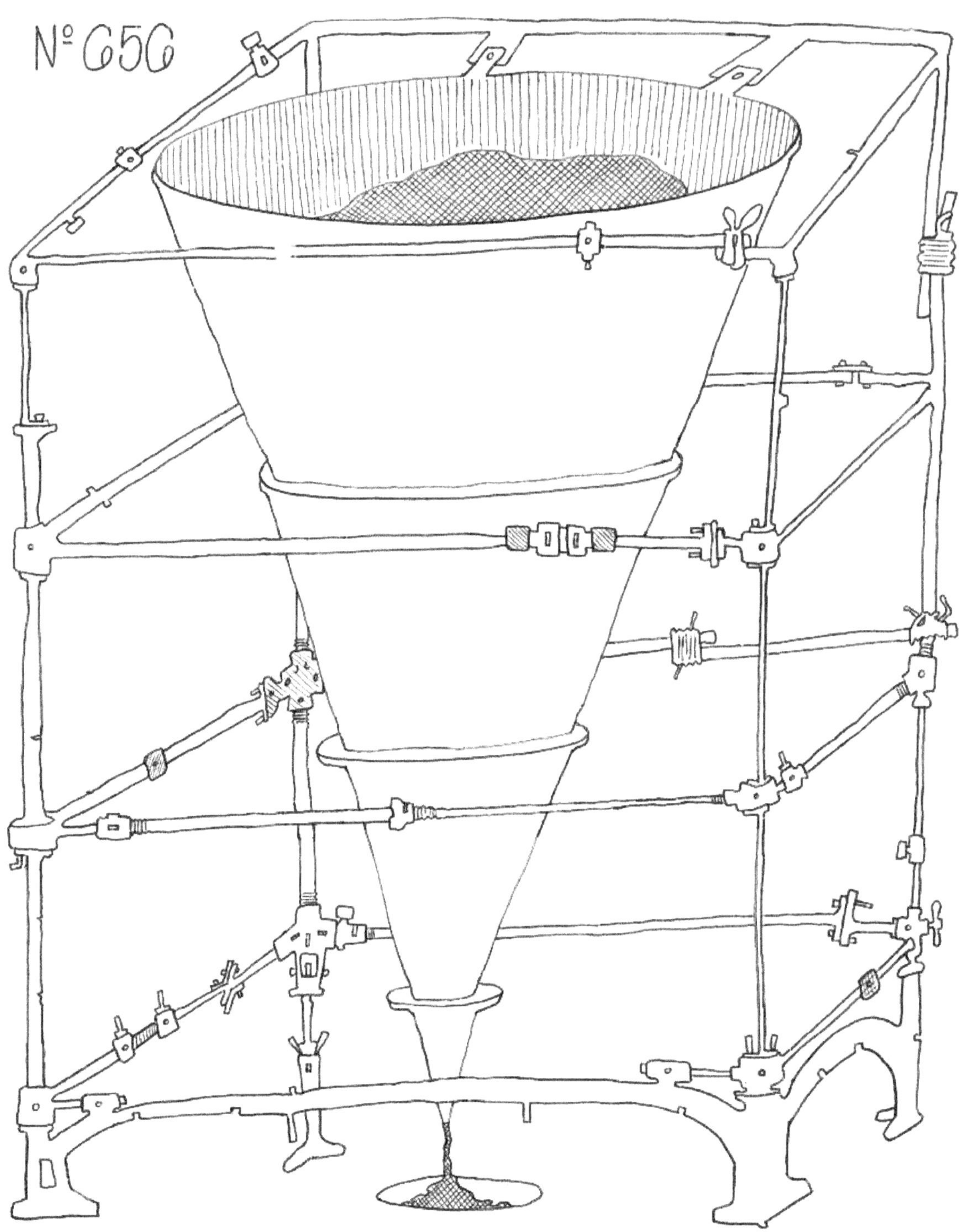
N° 656

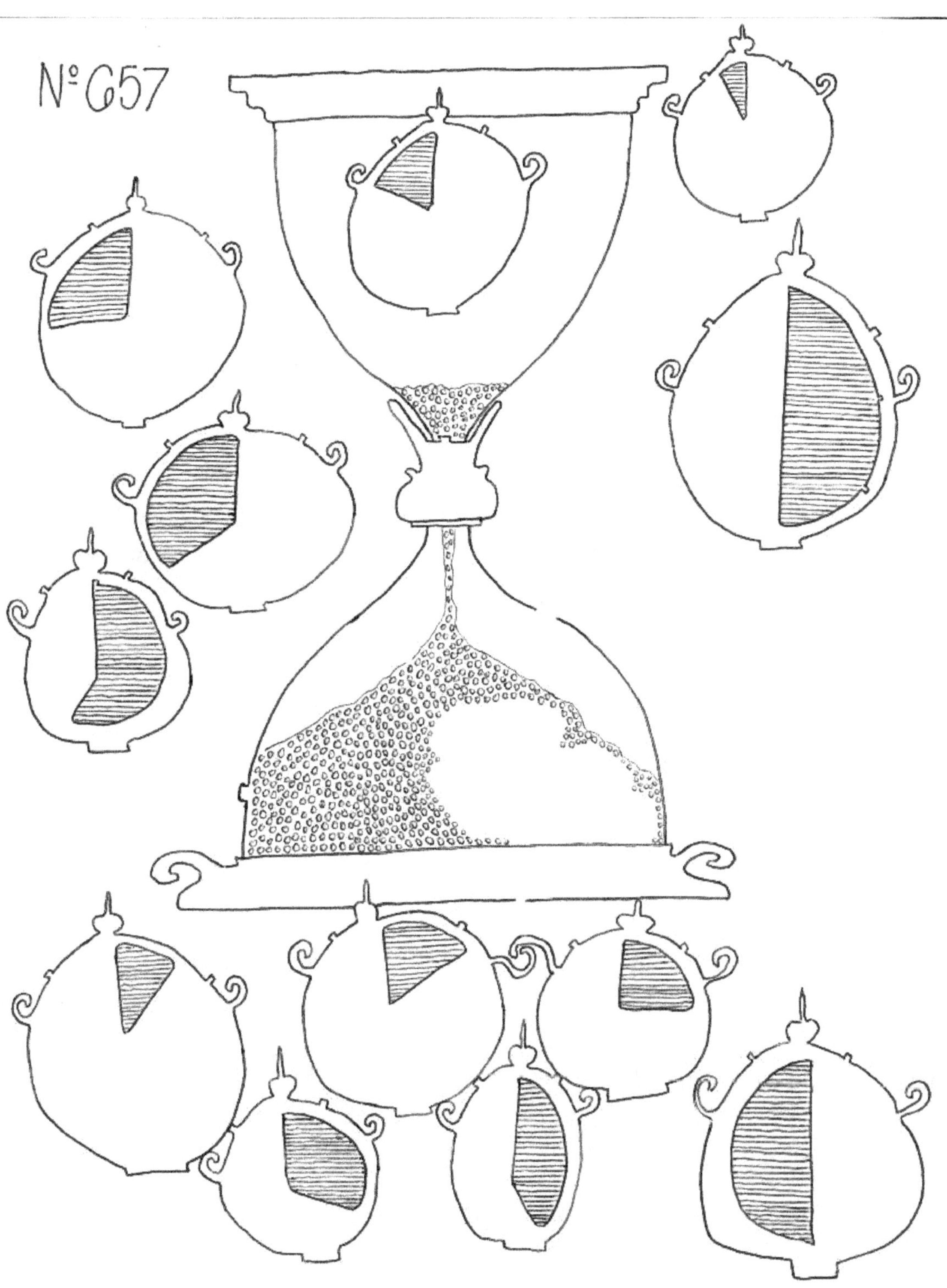
Nº 657

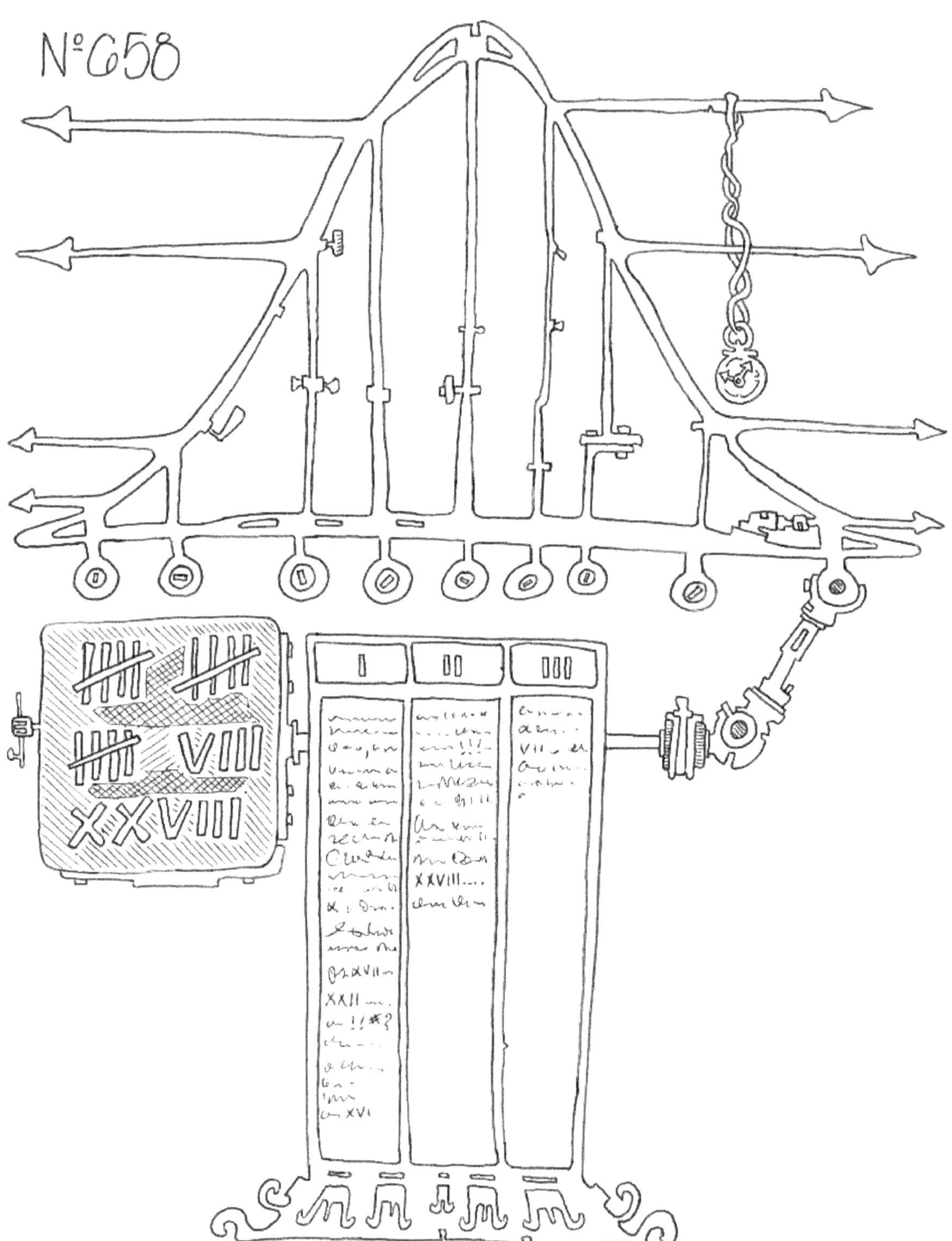

№ 658
VIII
XXVIII
I
II
III

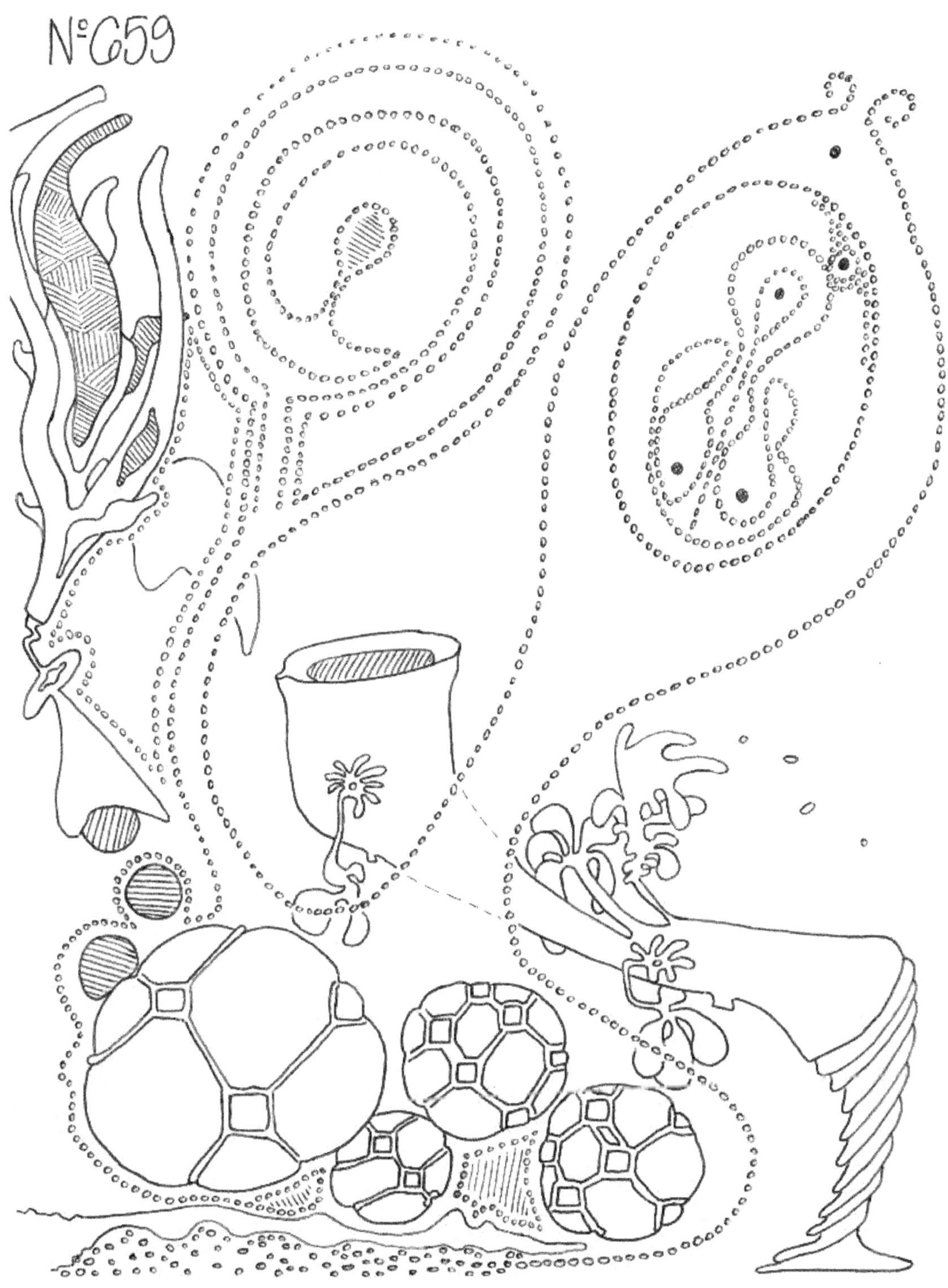
№659

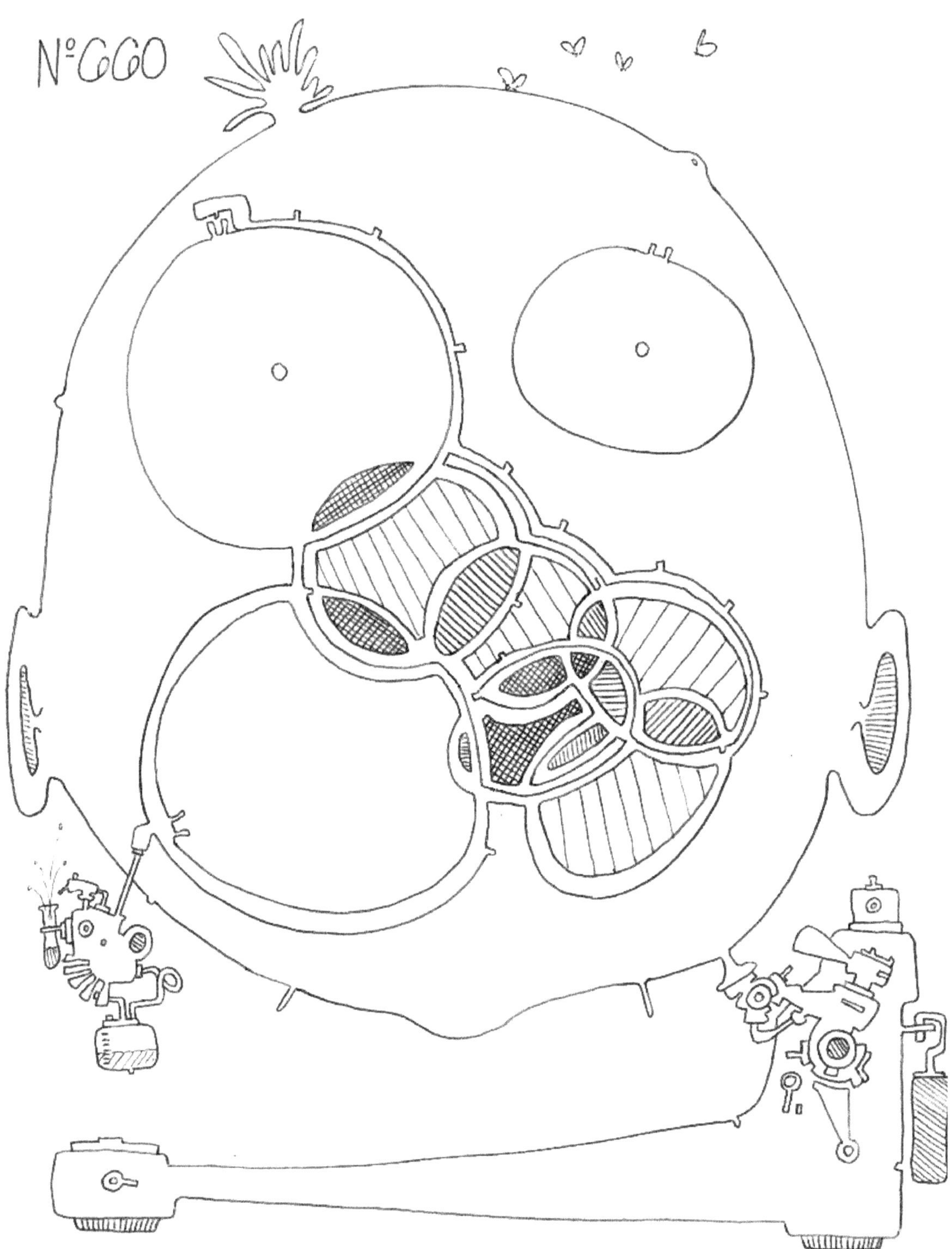
N°660

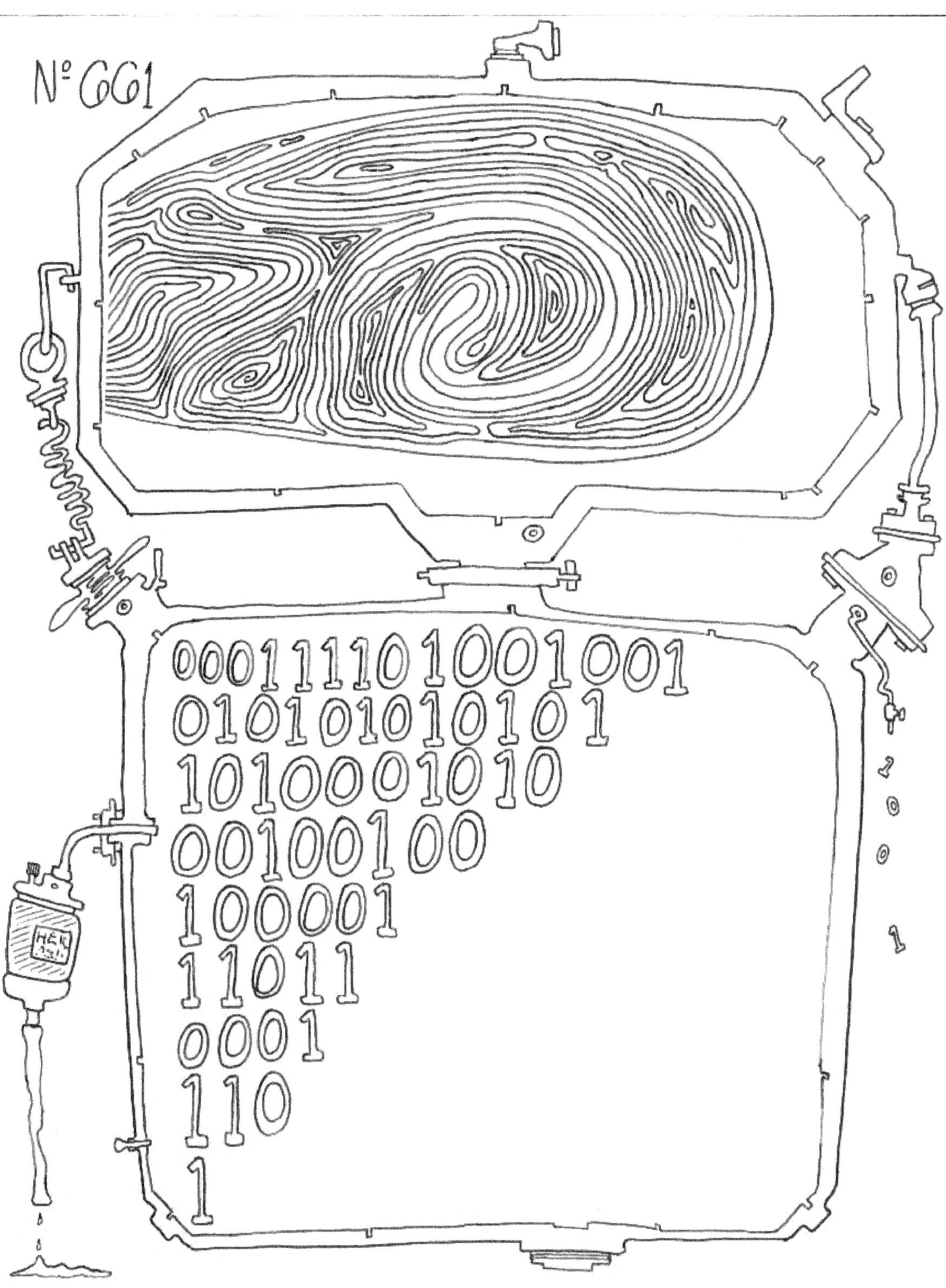
№ 661
000111101001001
010101010101
1010001010
00100100
100001
11011
0001
110
1
1
0
0
1

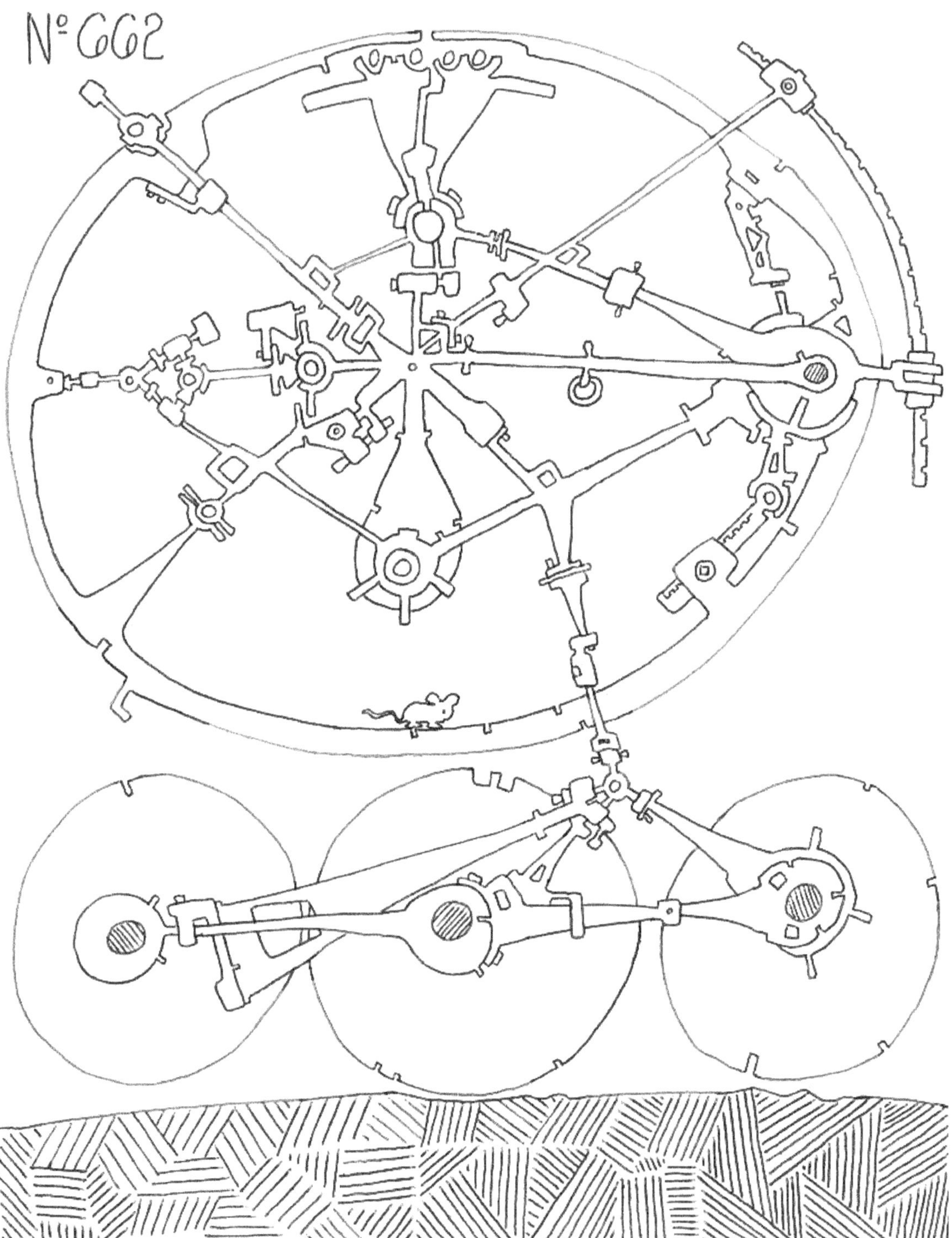
№ 662

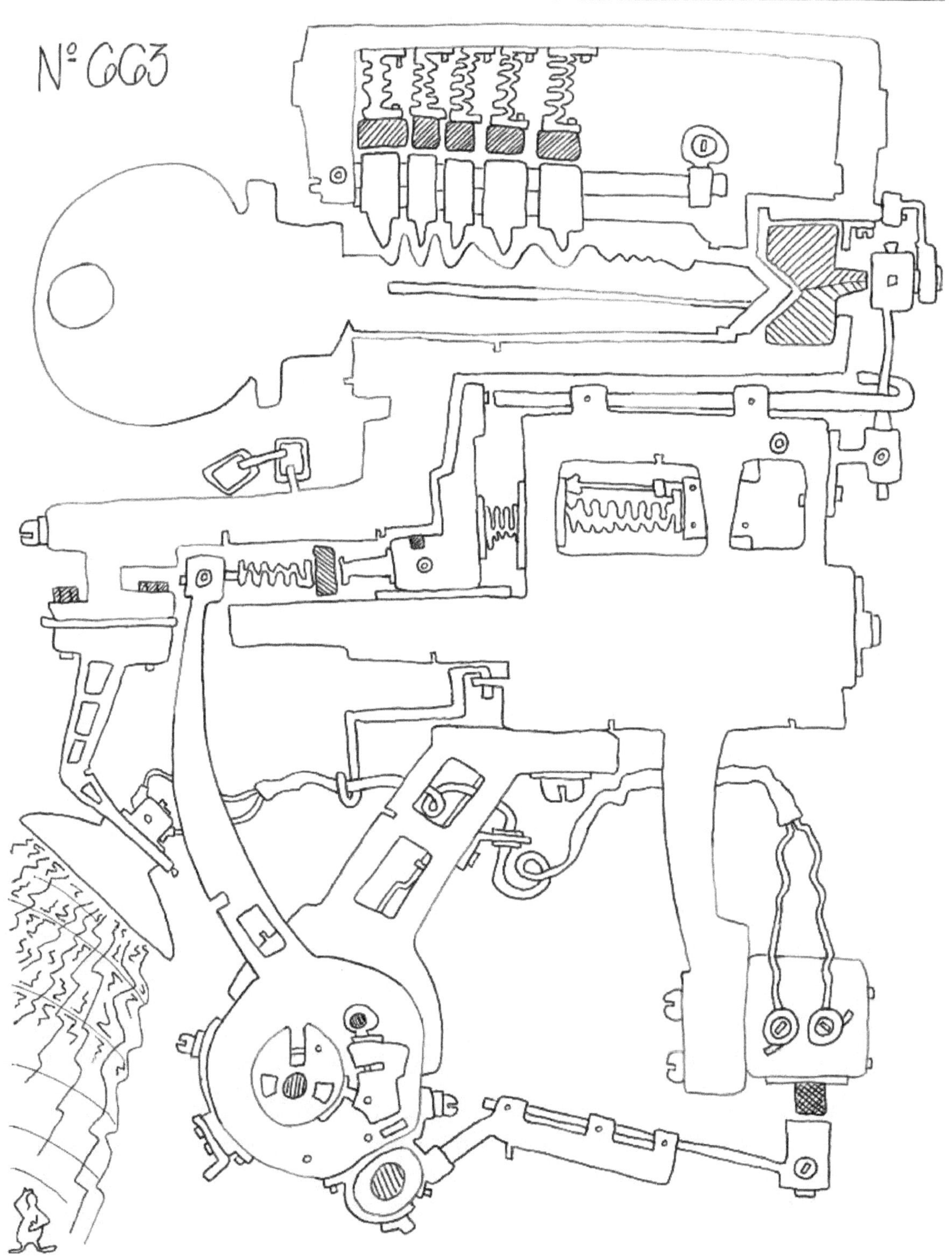
N° 663

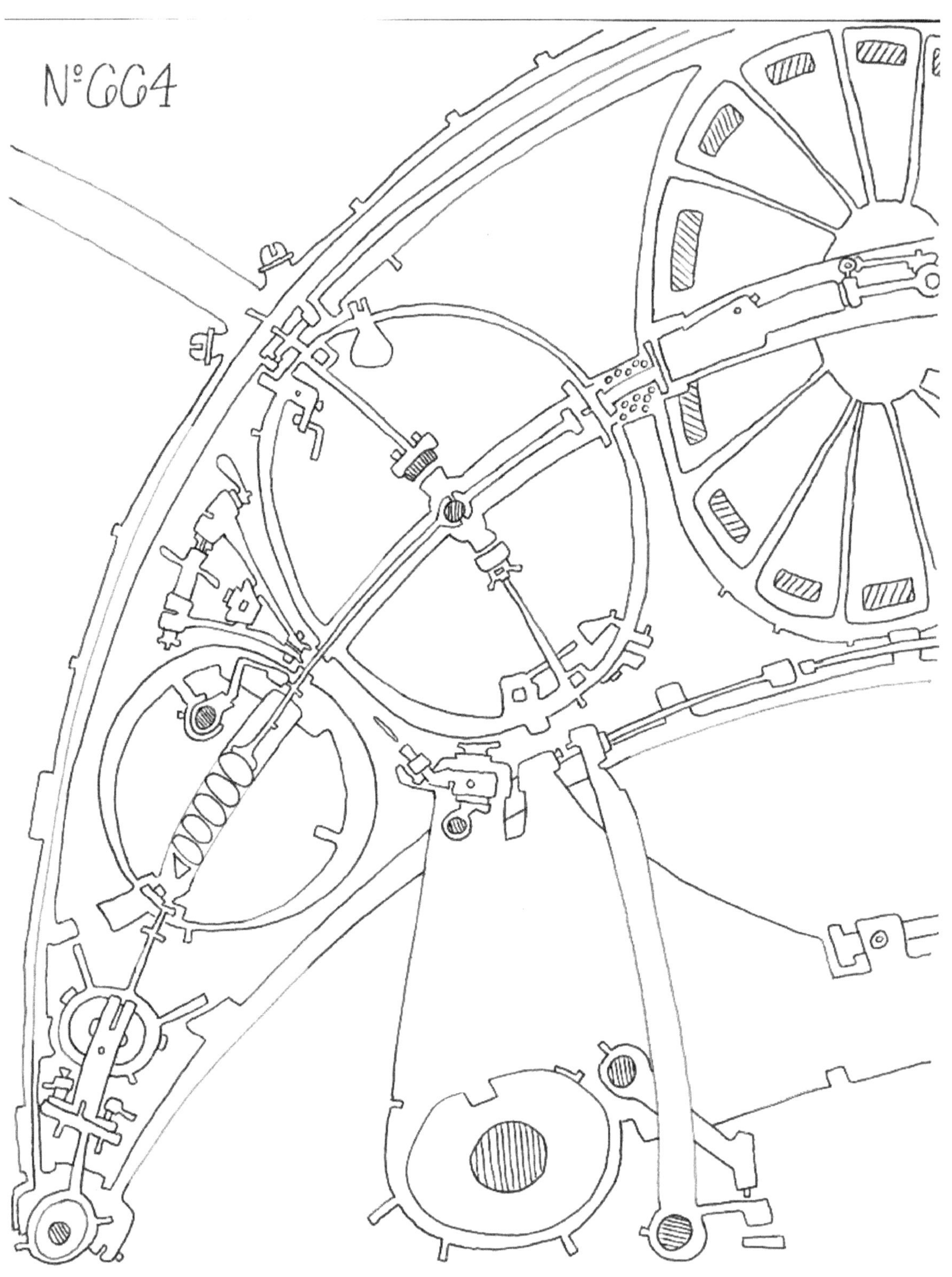
№664

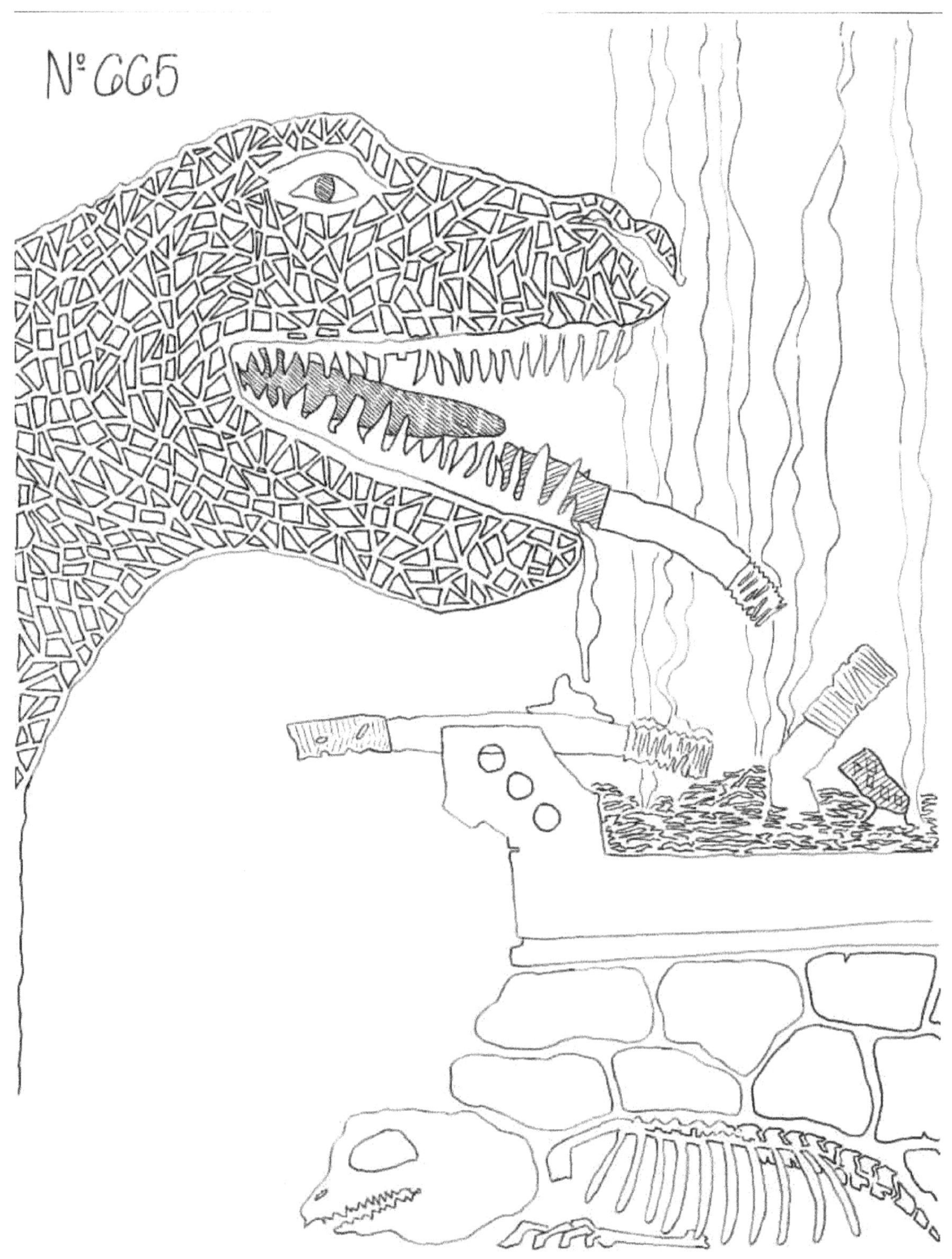
№ 665

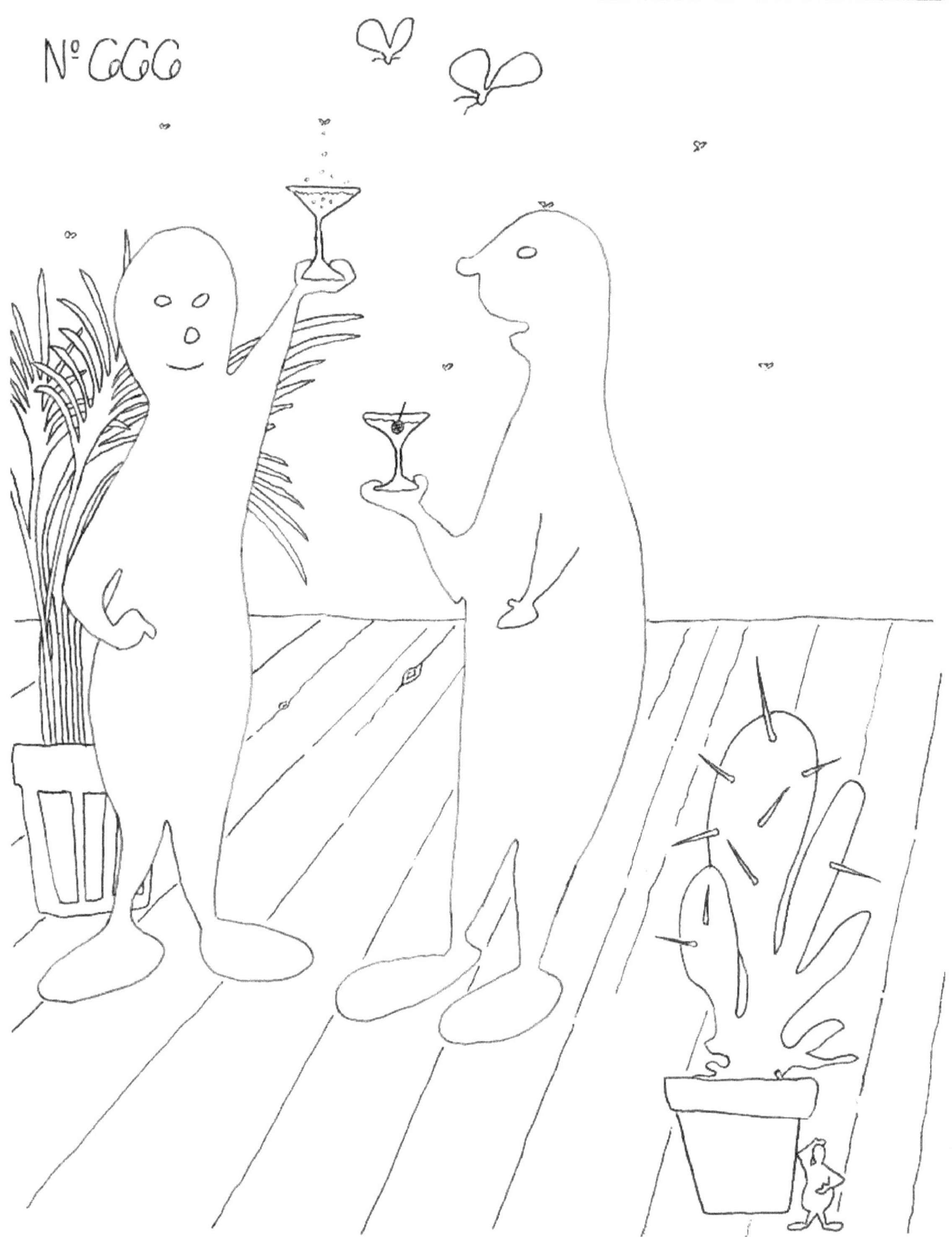
№ 6666

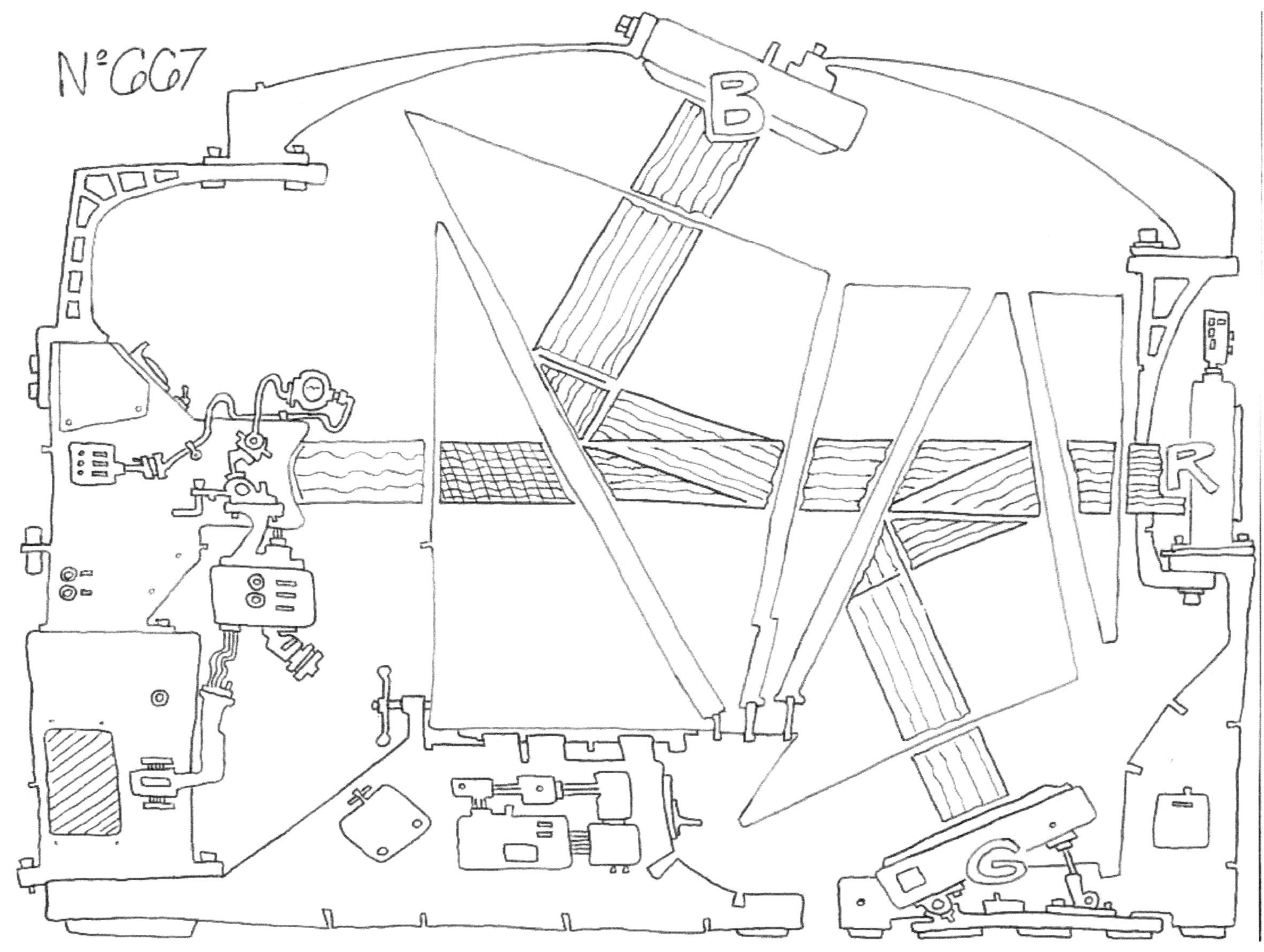
N°667
B
R
G

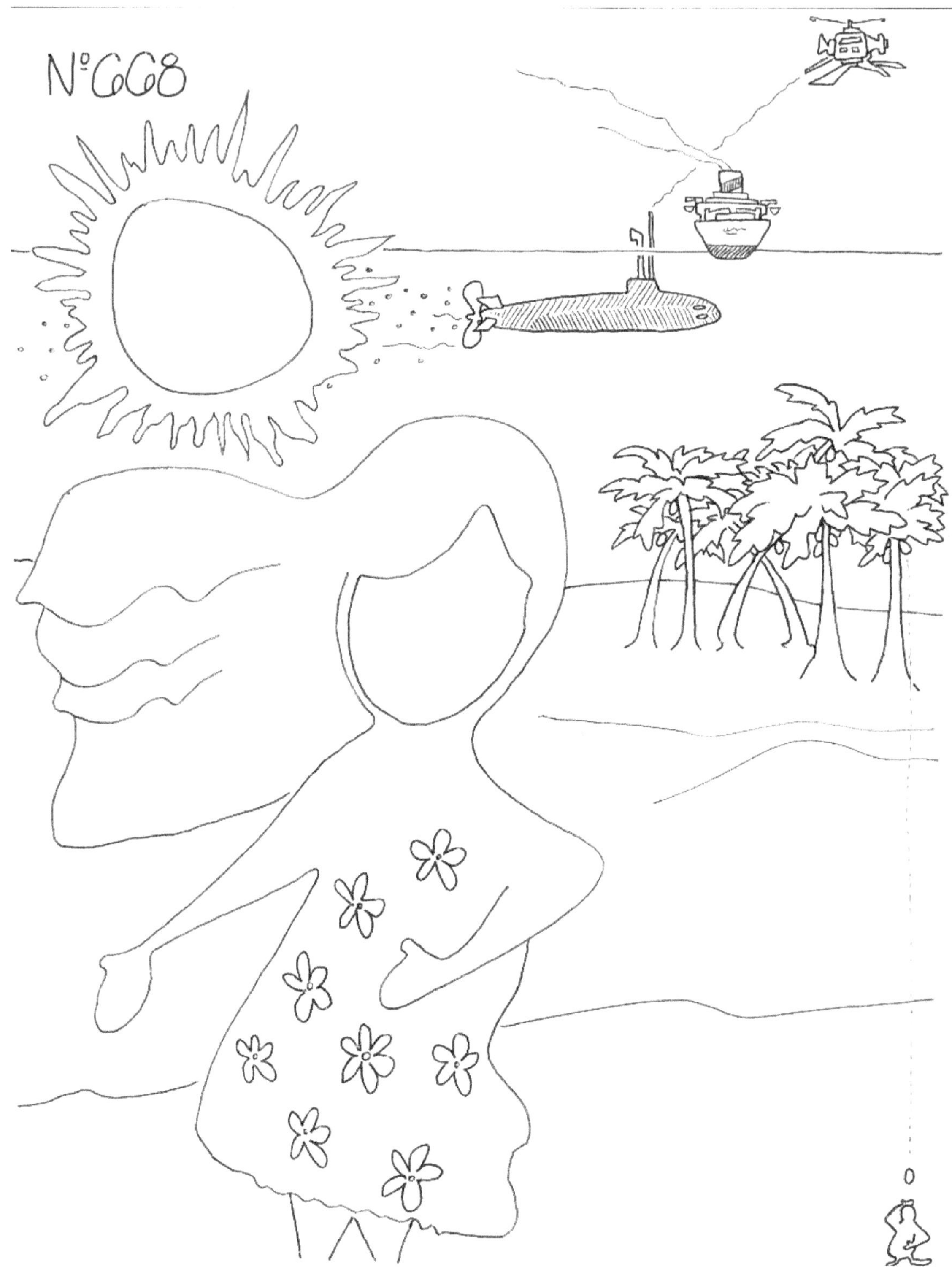
№668

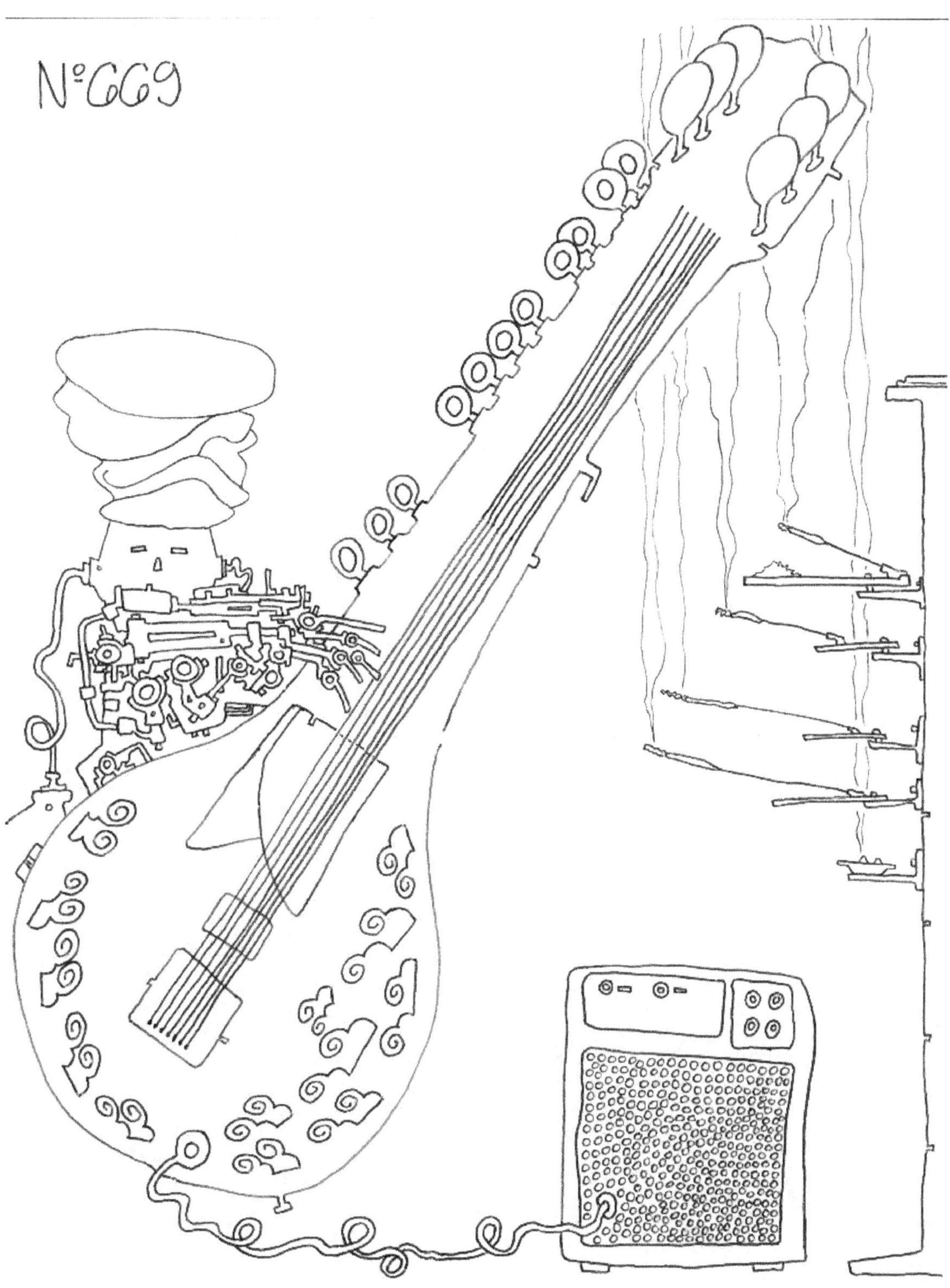
№669

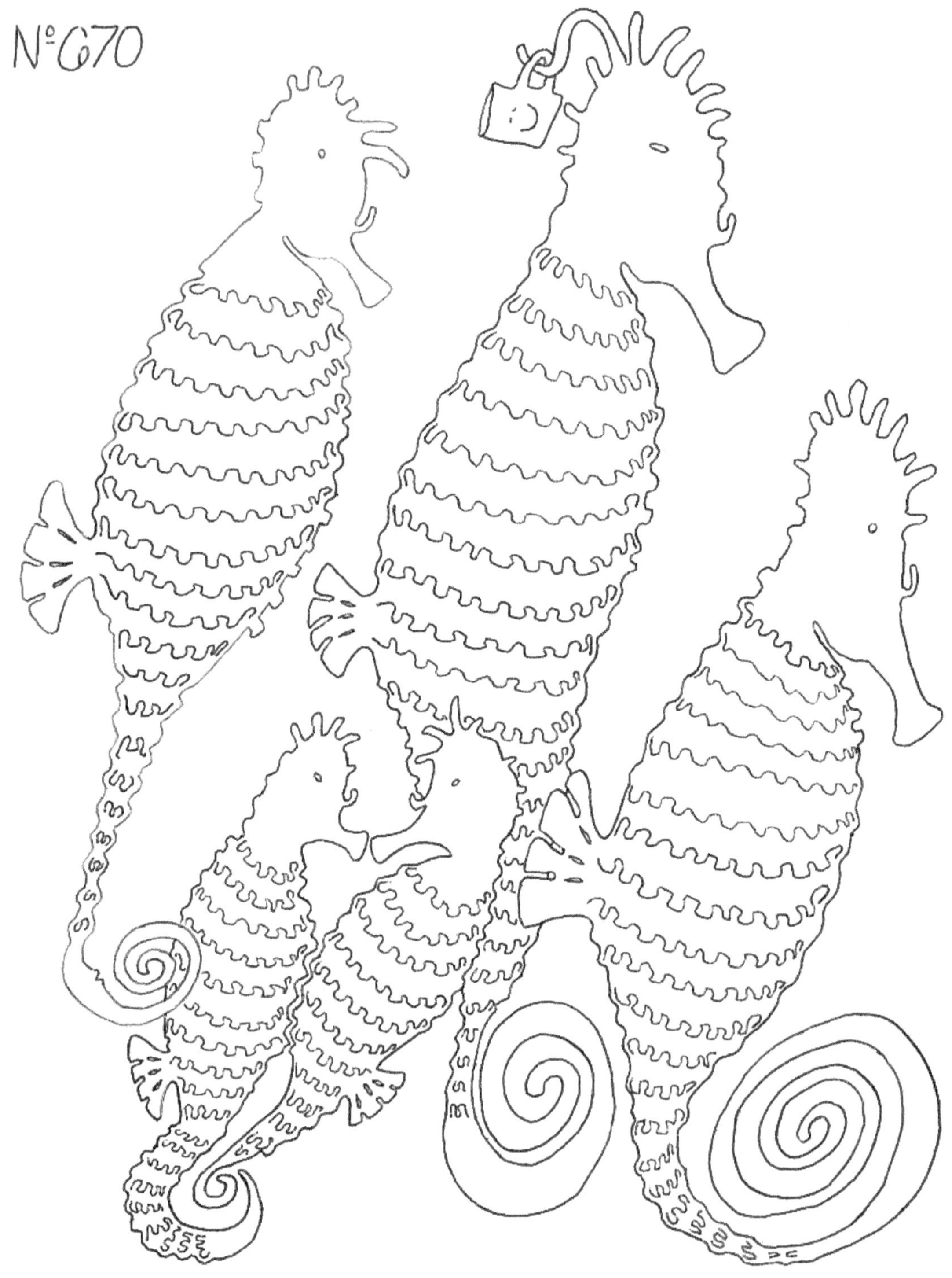
N°670

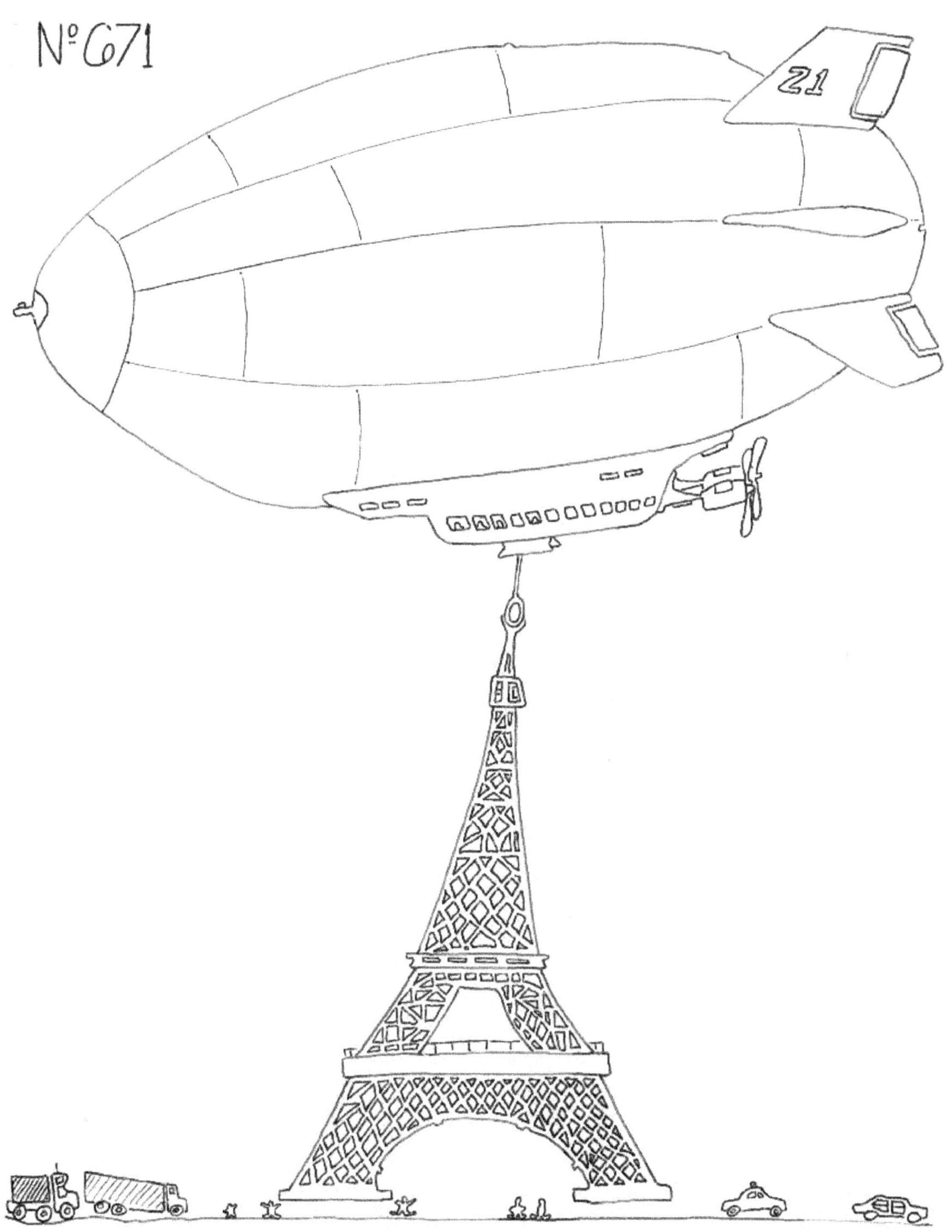
№671
21

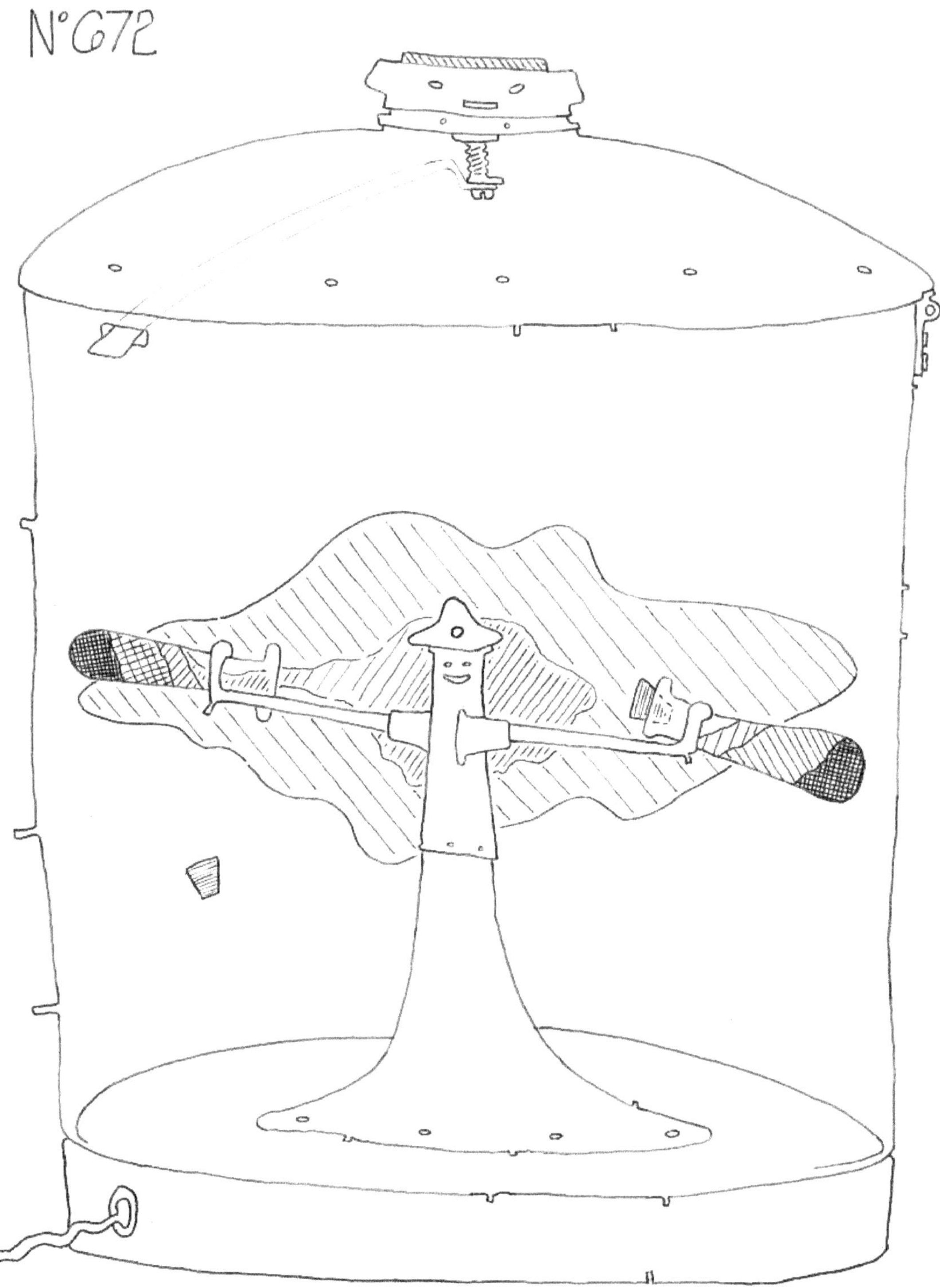
N°672

Nº 673

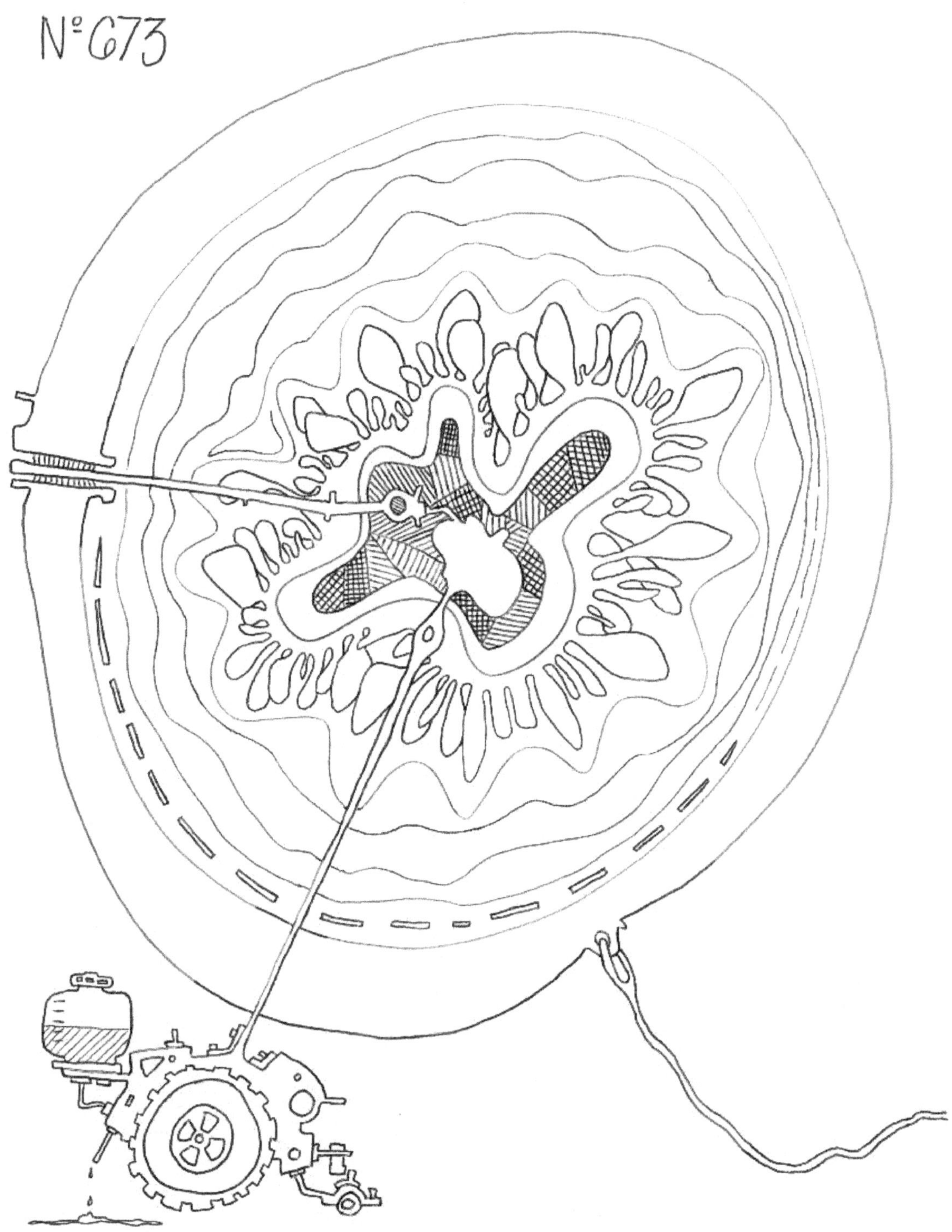

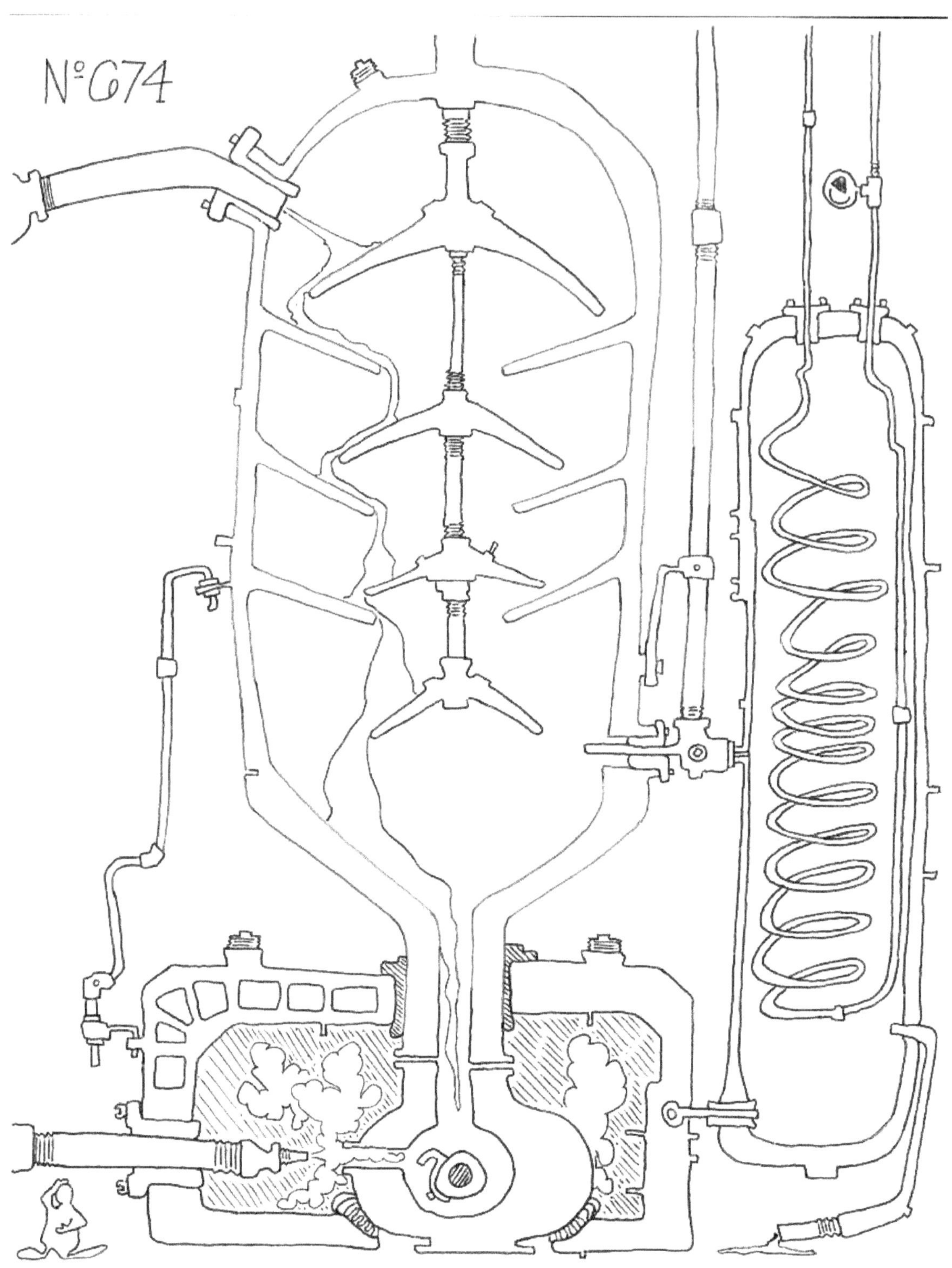
N°674

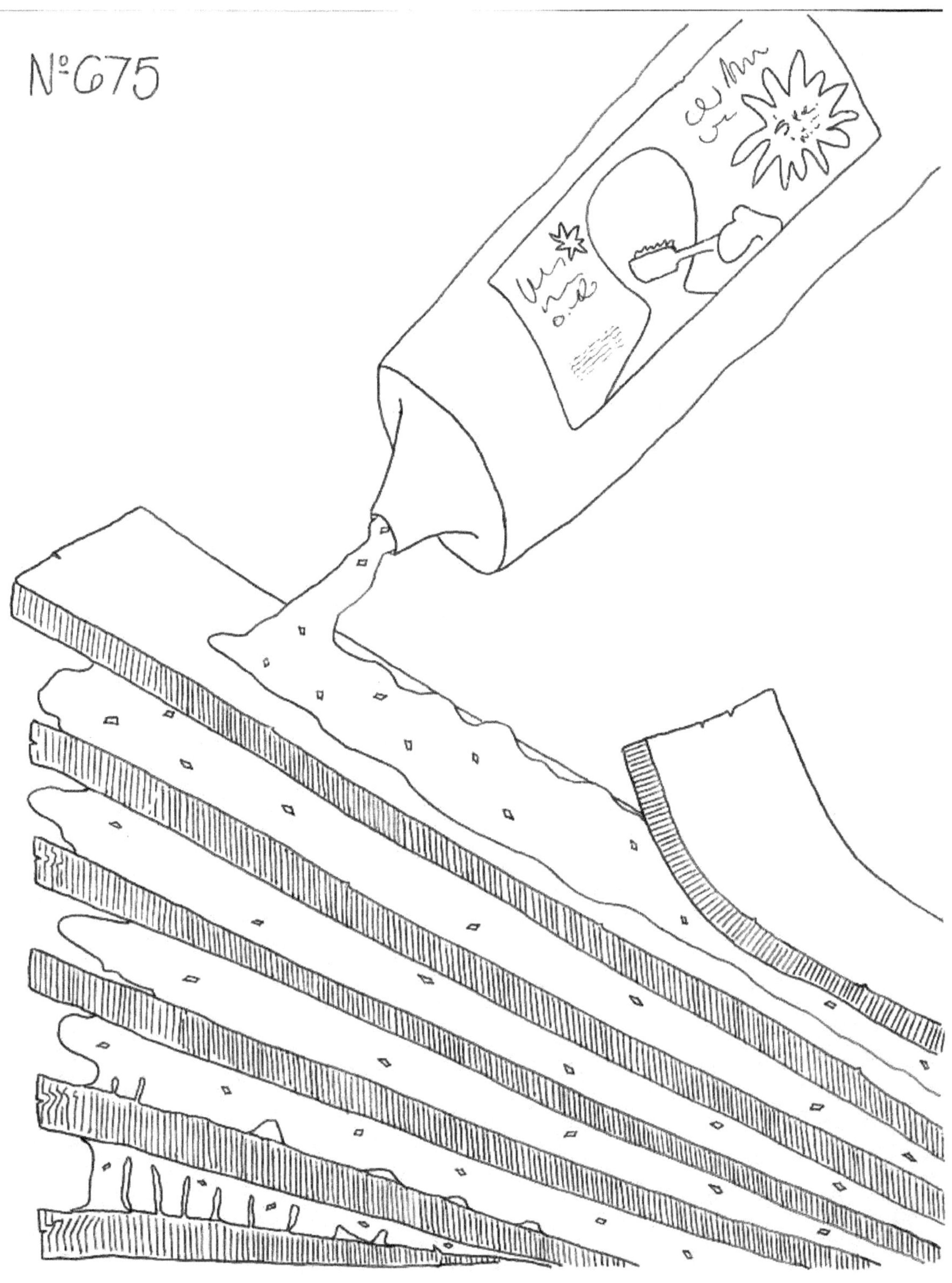
№675

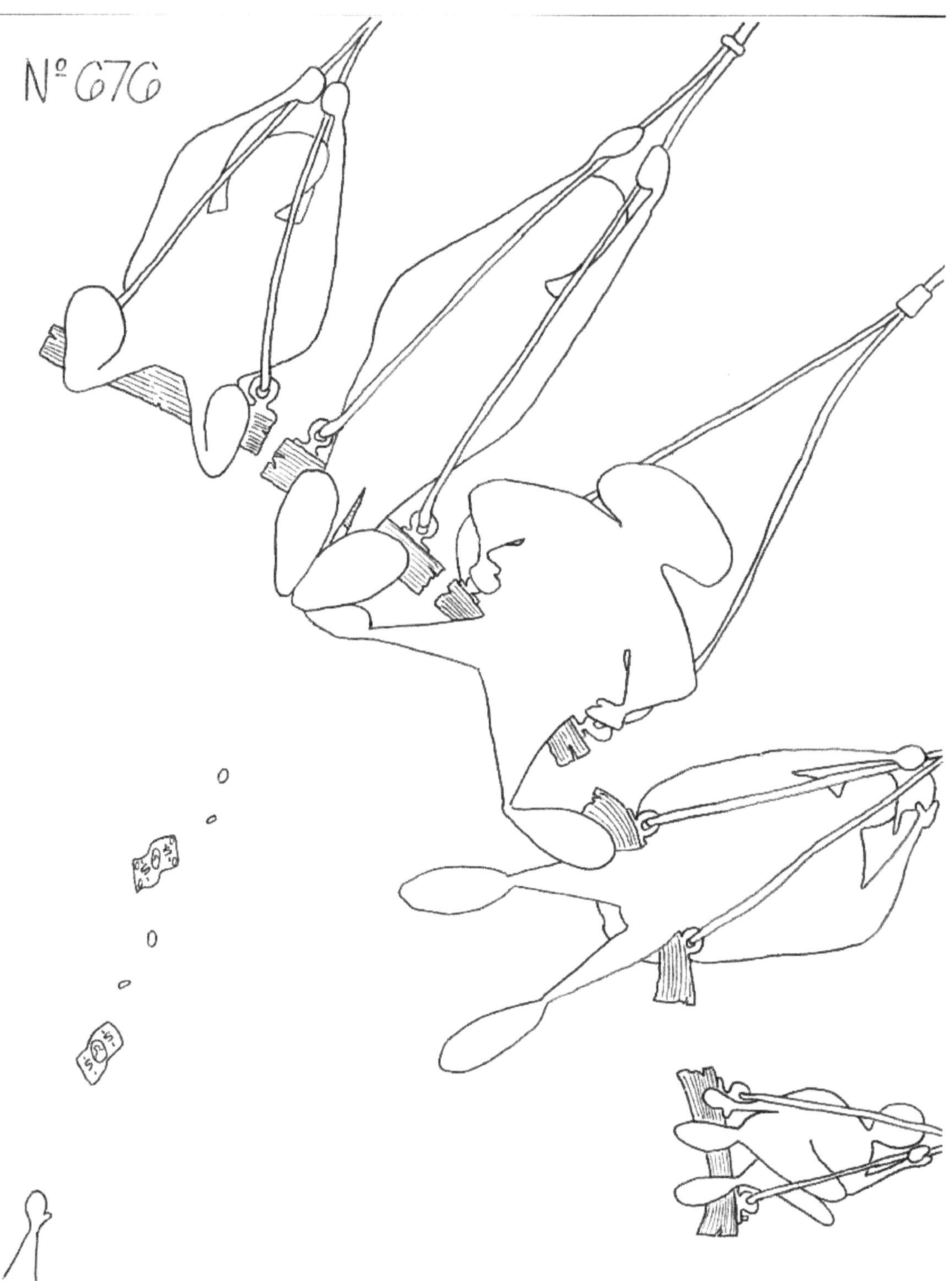
Nº 676

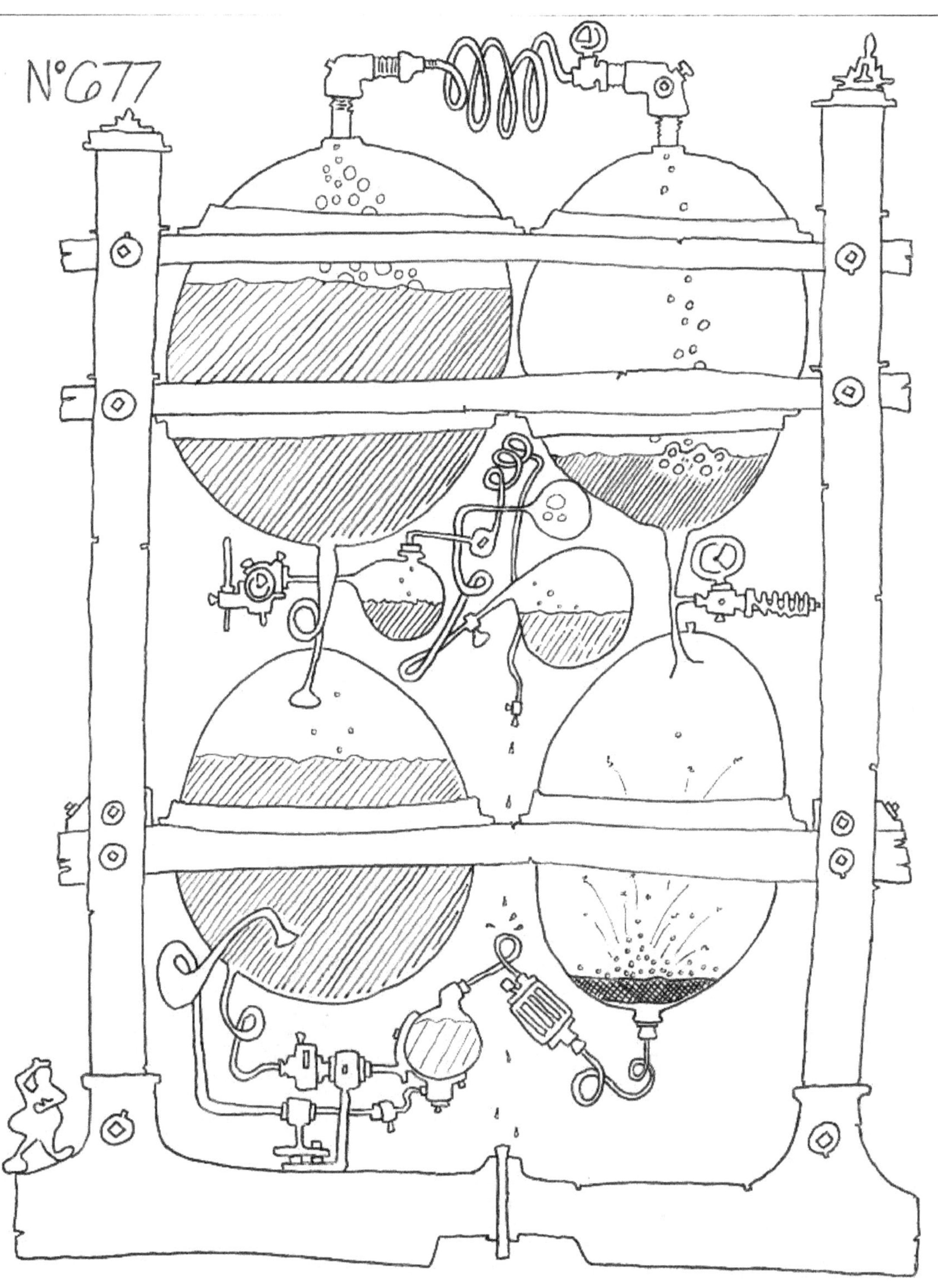
N°677

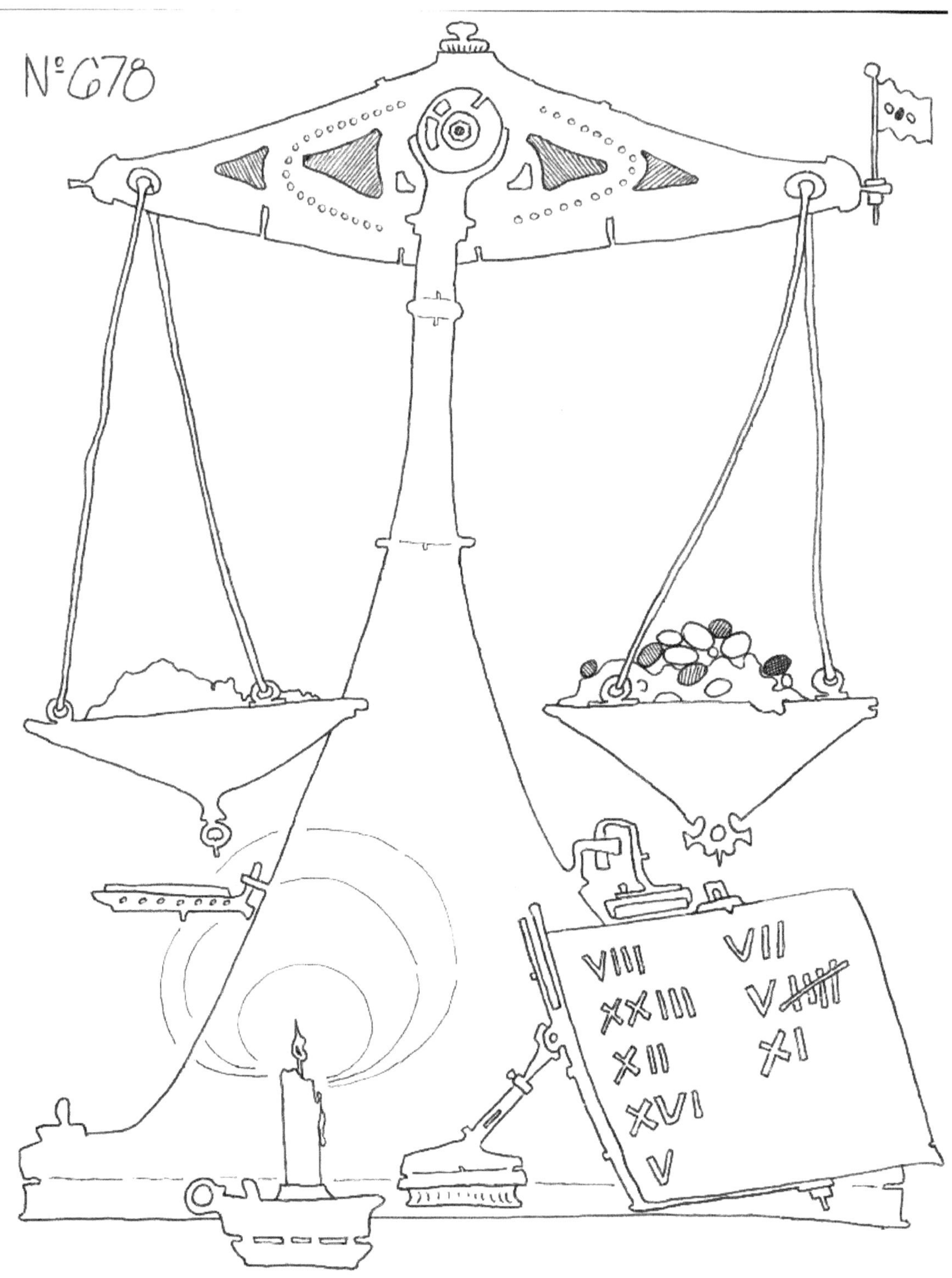

Nº678
VIII
VII
XXIII
V IIII
XII
XI
XVI
V

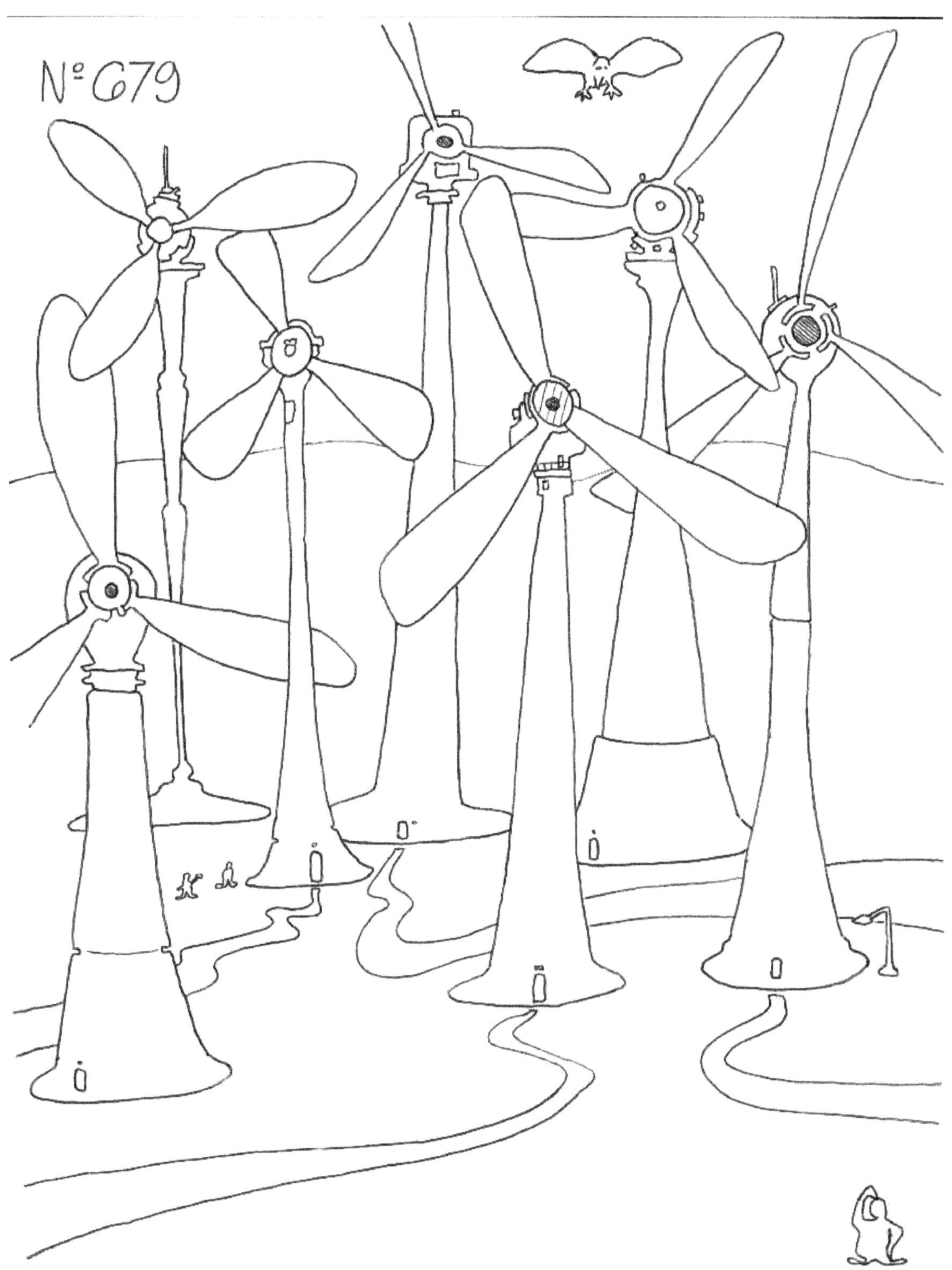
Nº 679

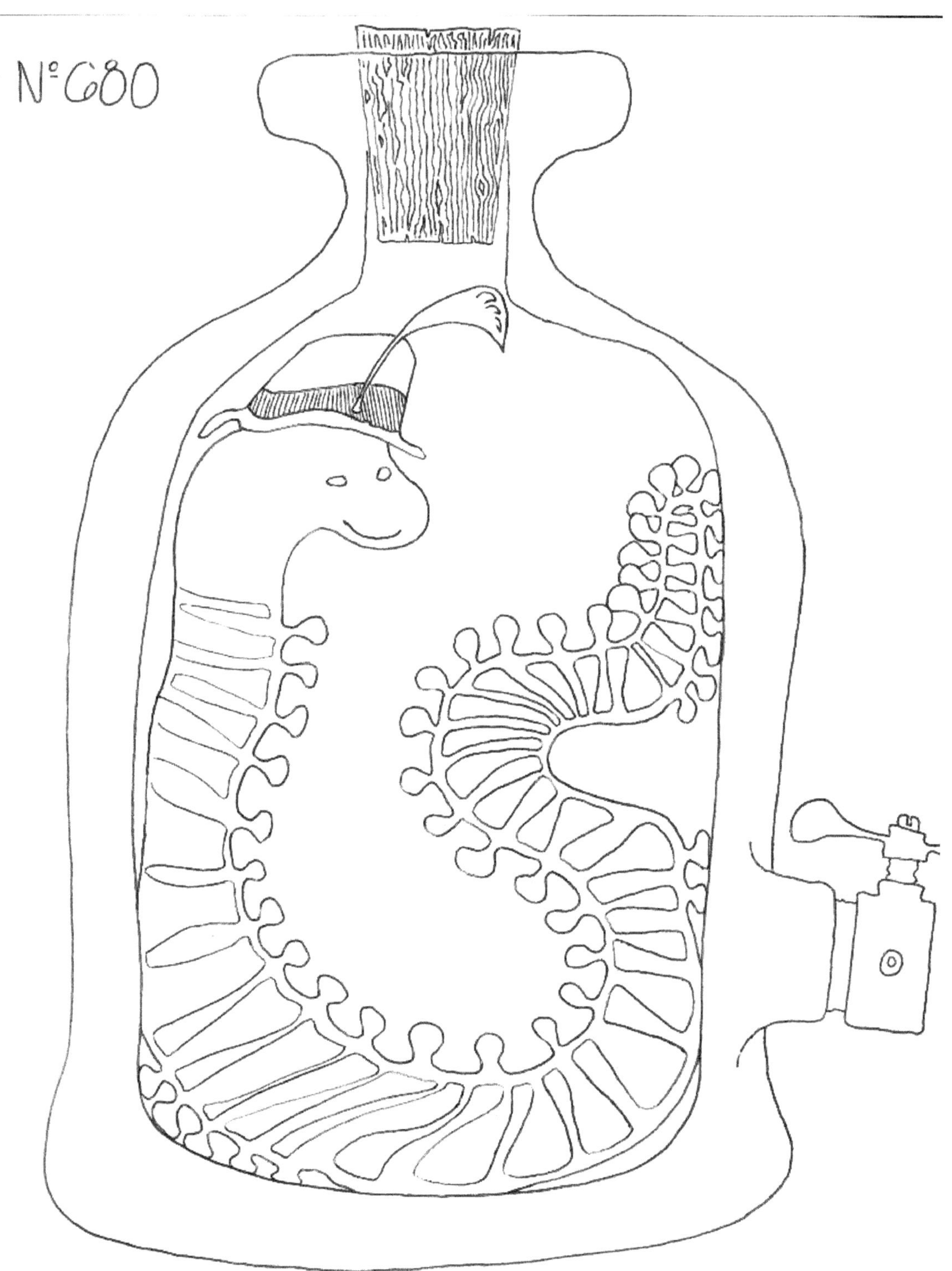
N°680

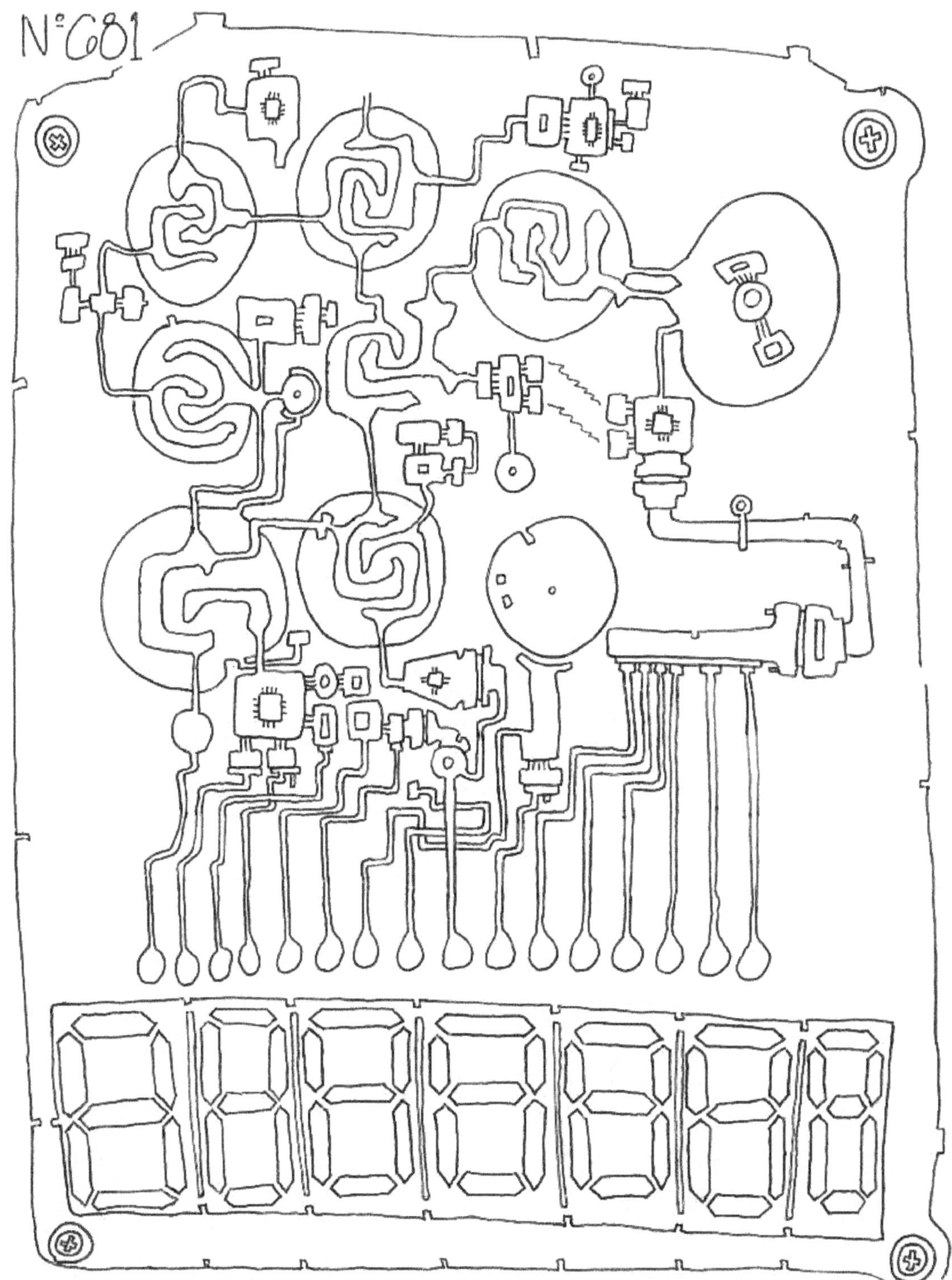
N°681

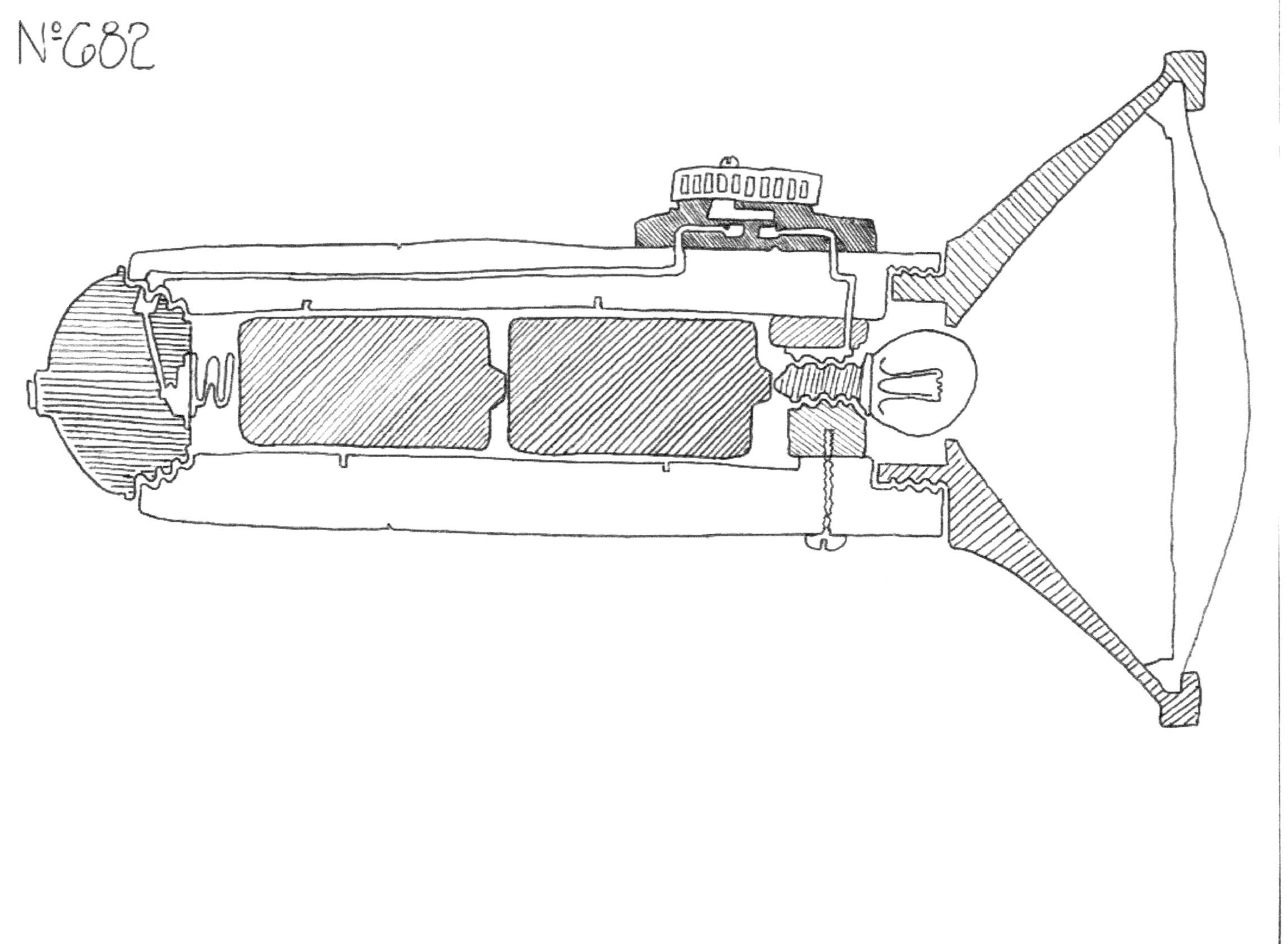
N° 682

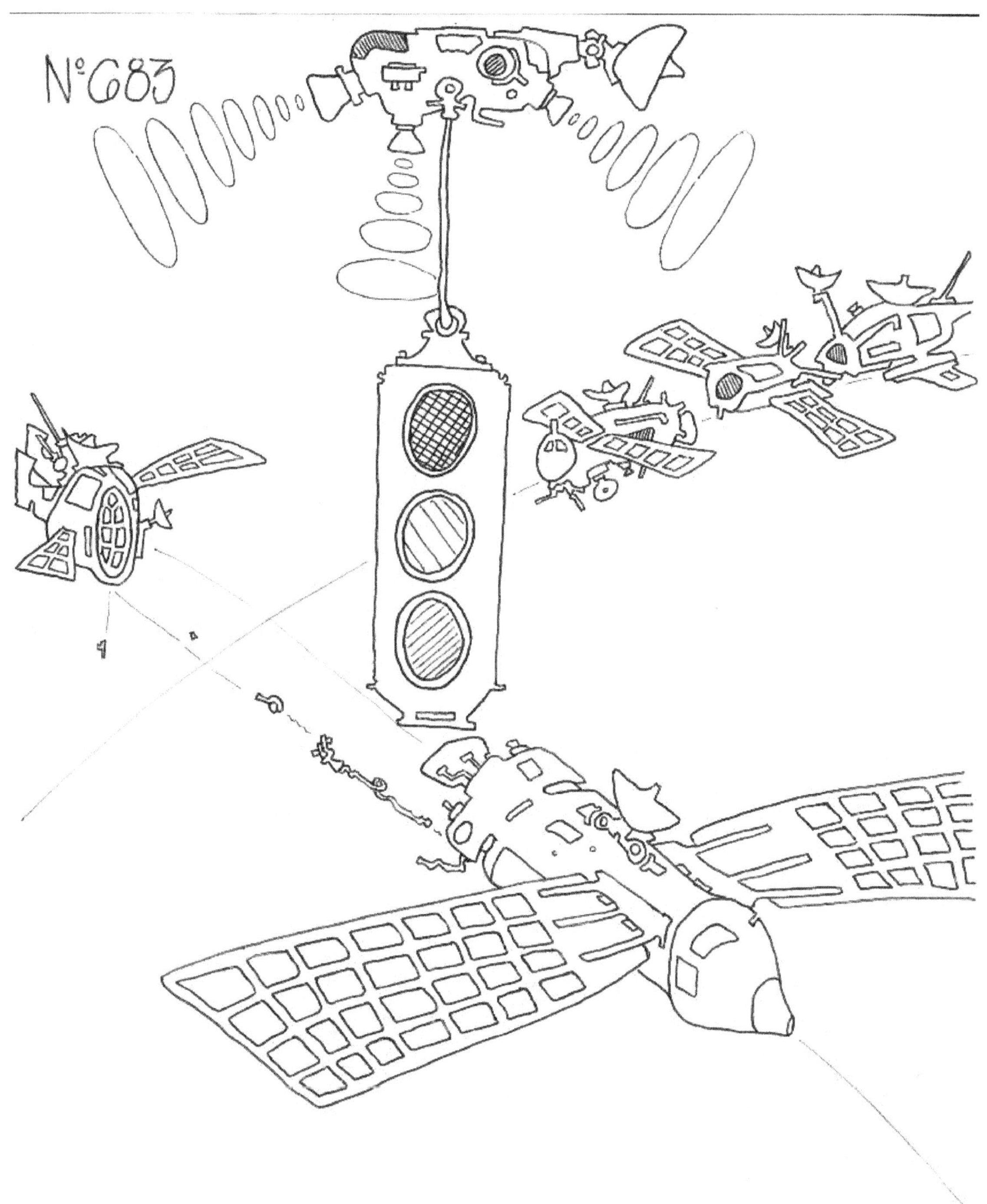
N°683

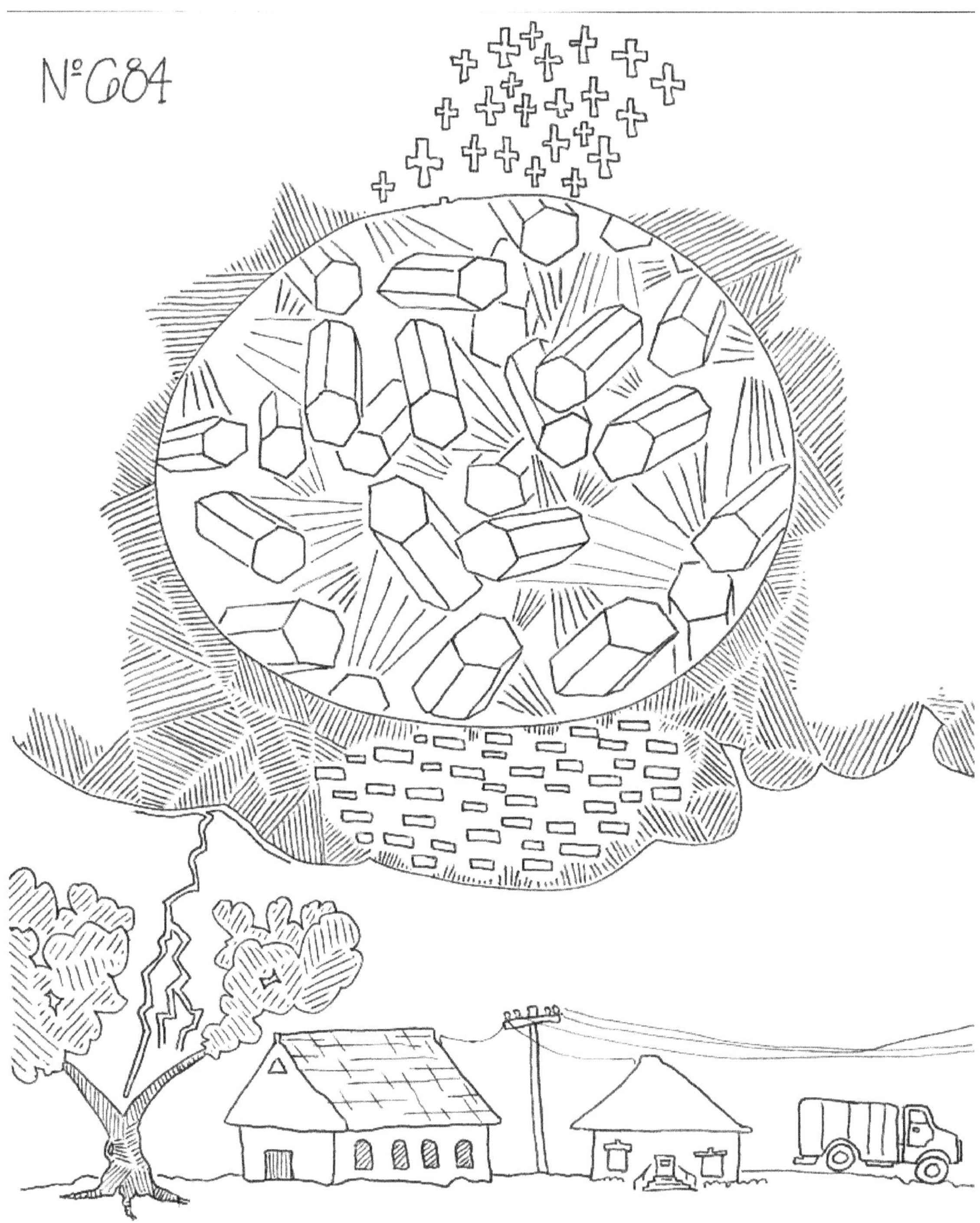
N°684

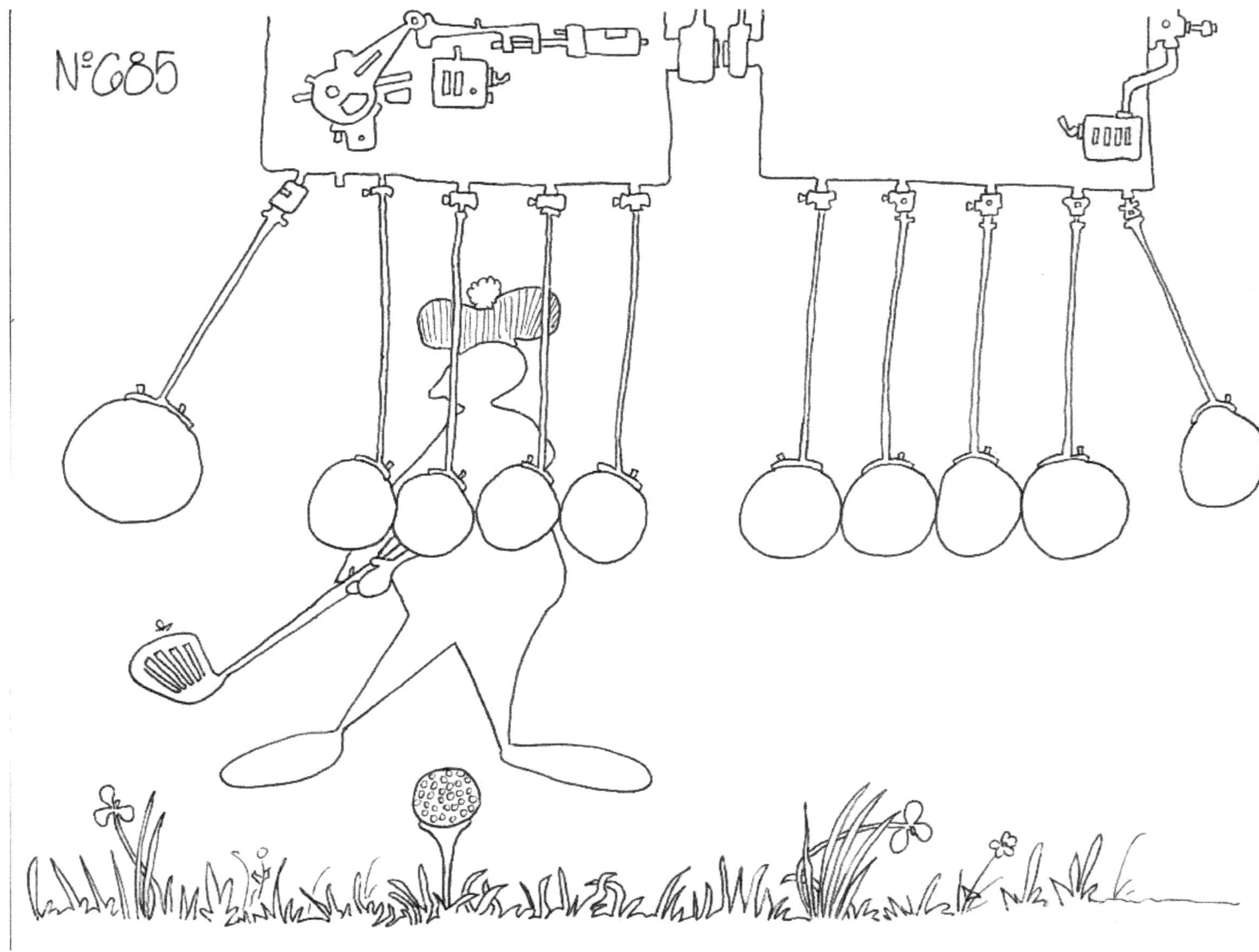
№685

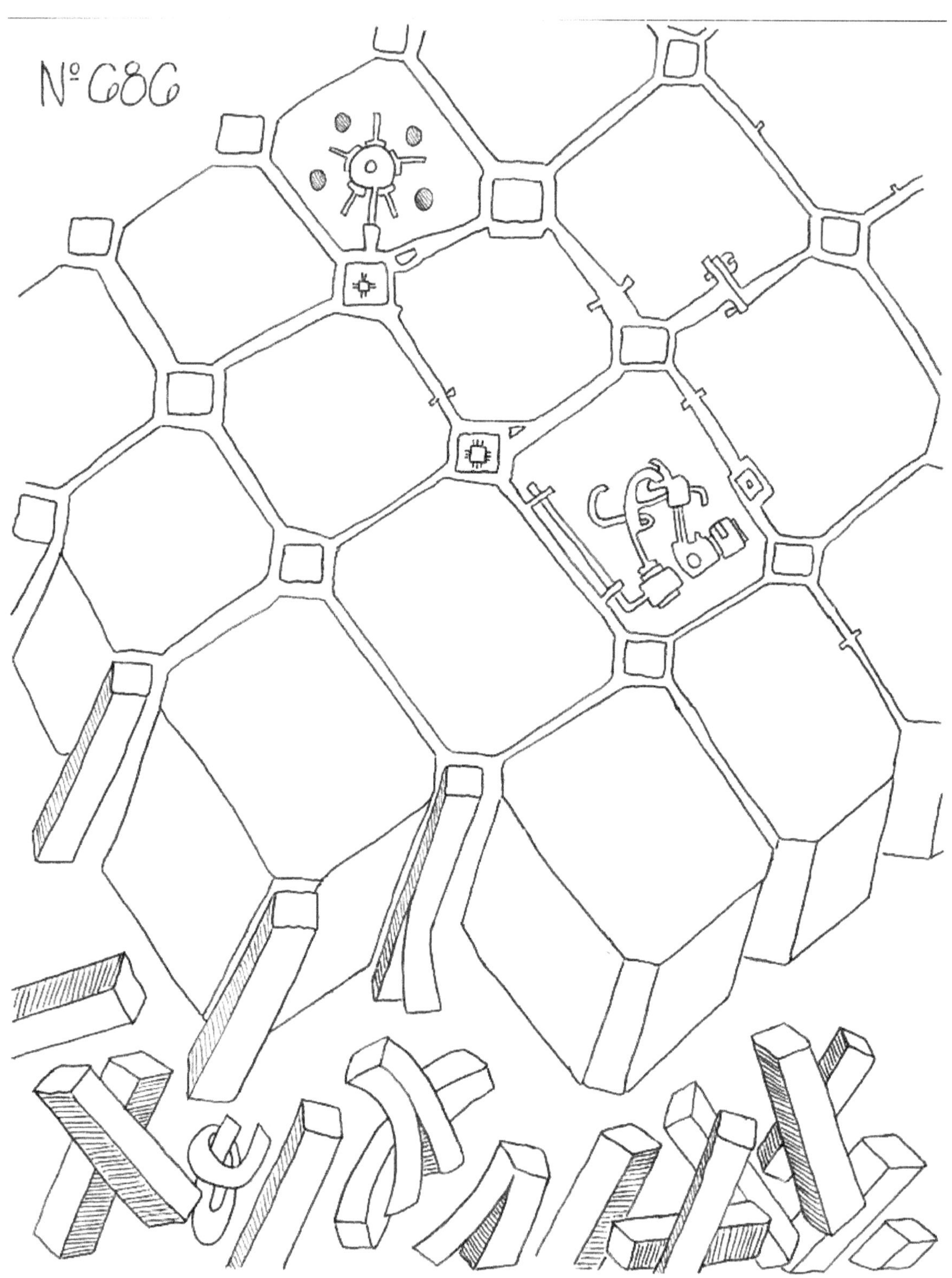
№686

№ 687

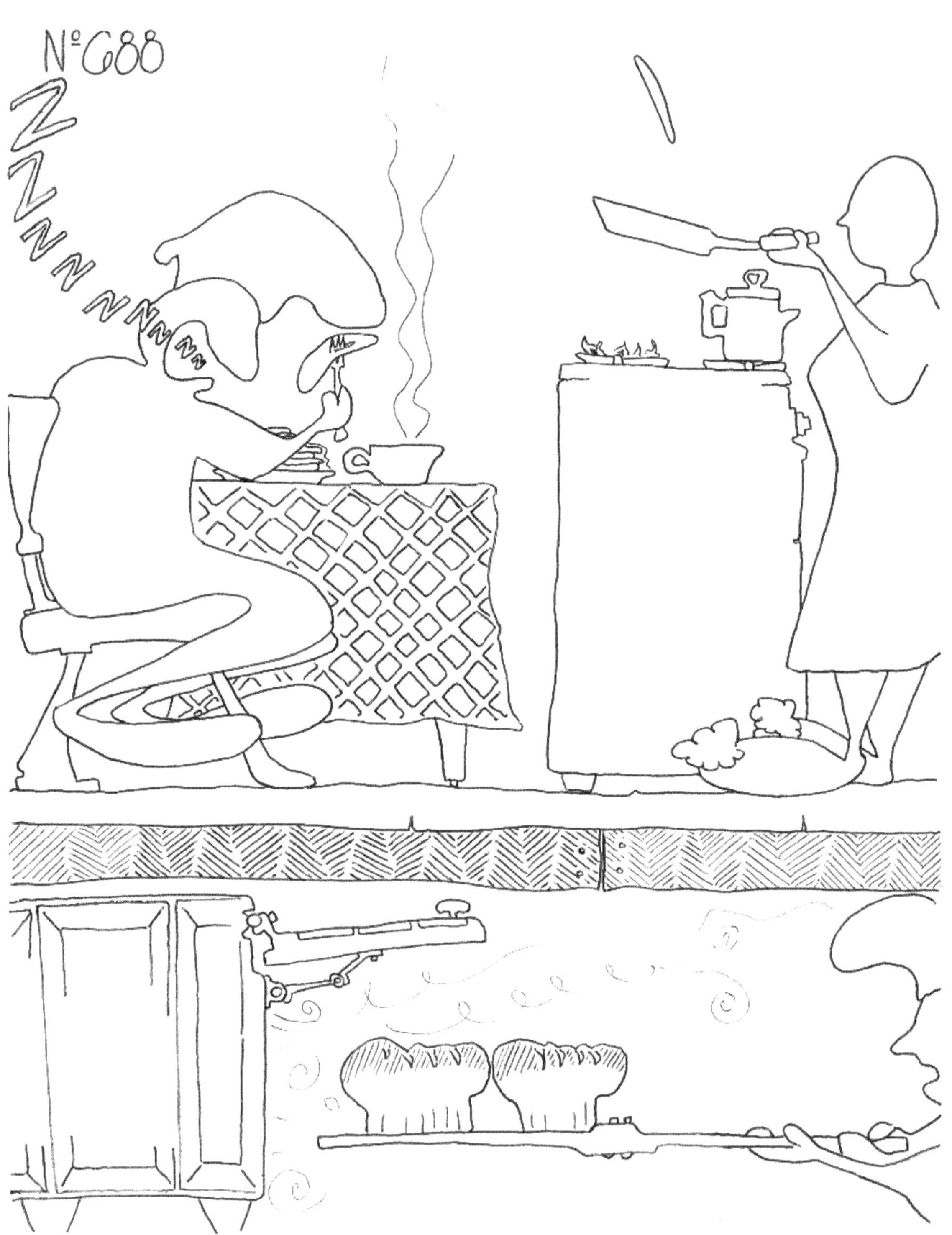
№688
ZZZZZZZZZ

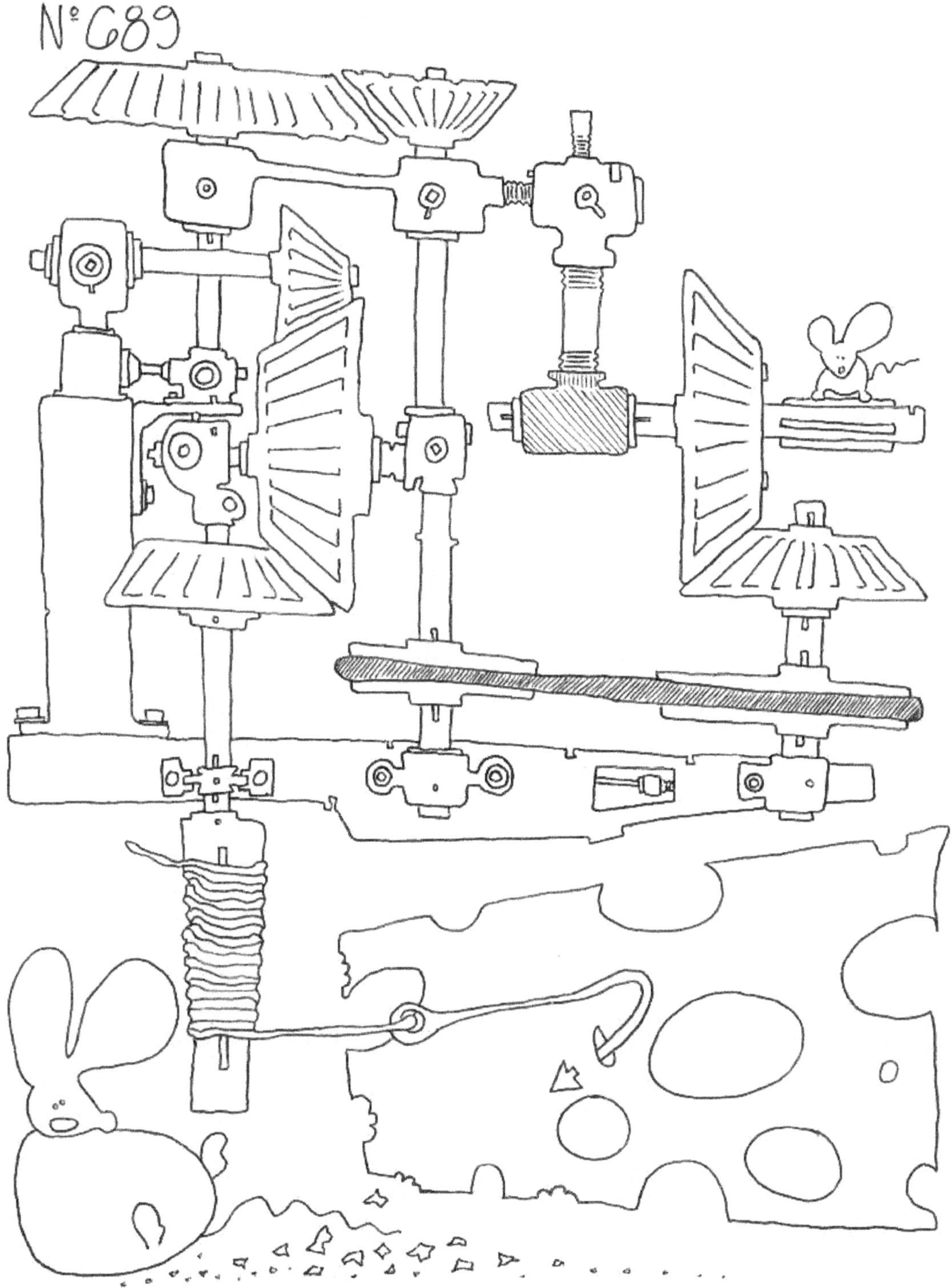
№689

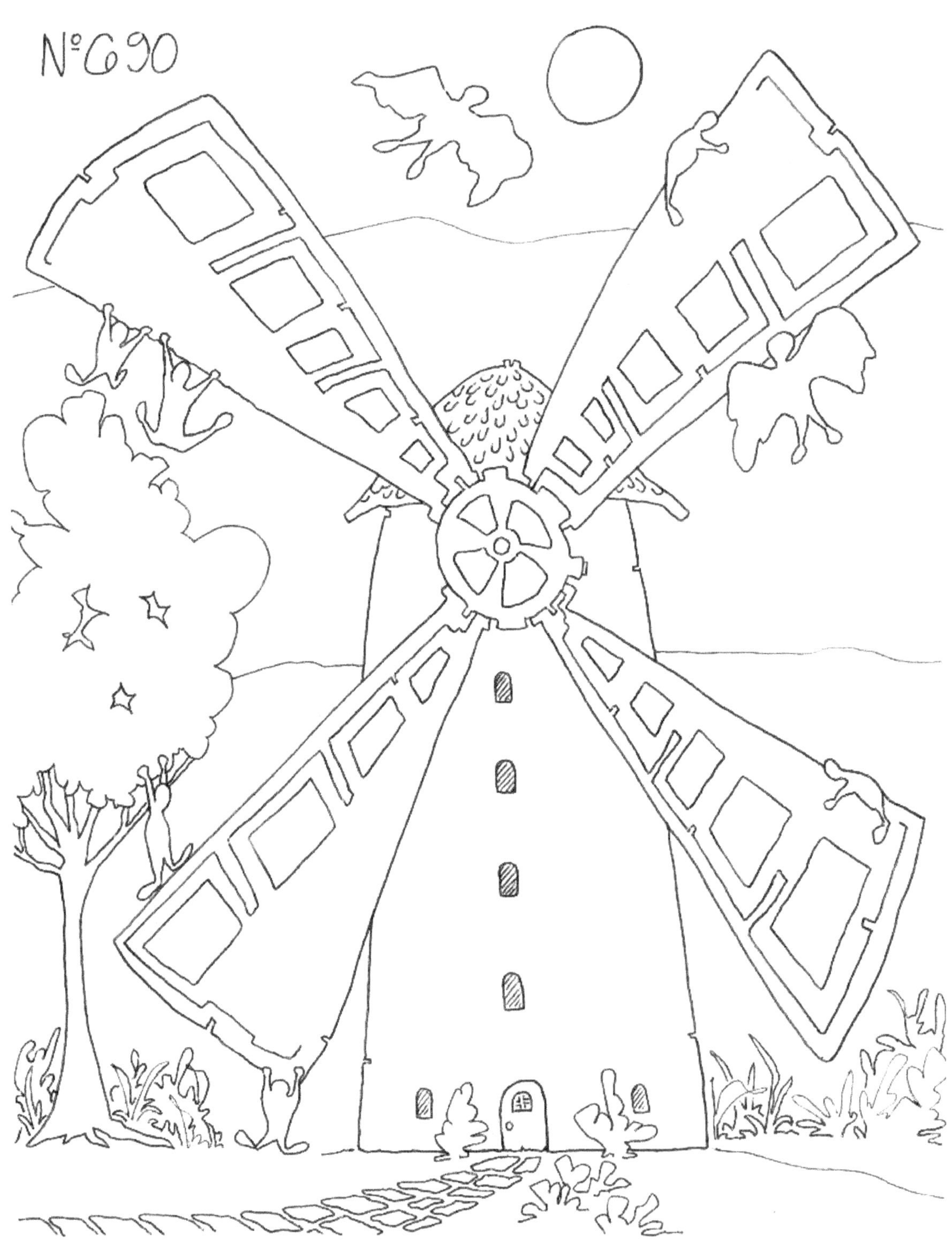
N°690

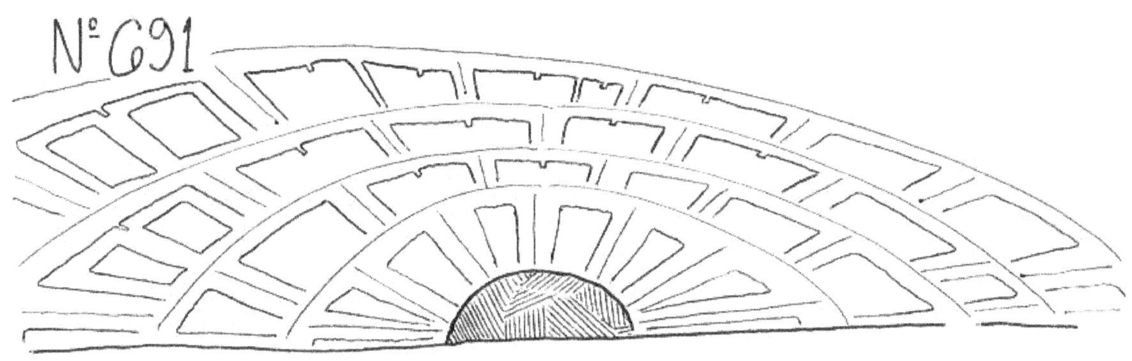
Nº 691

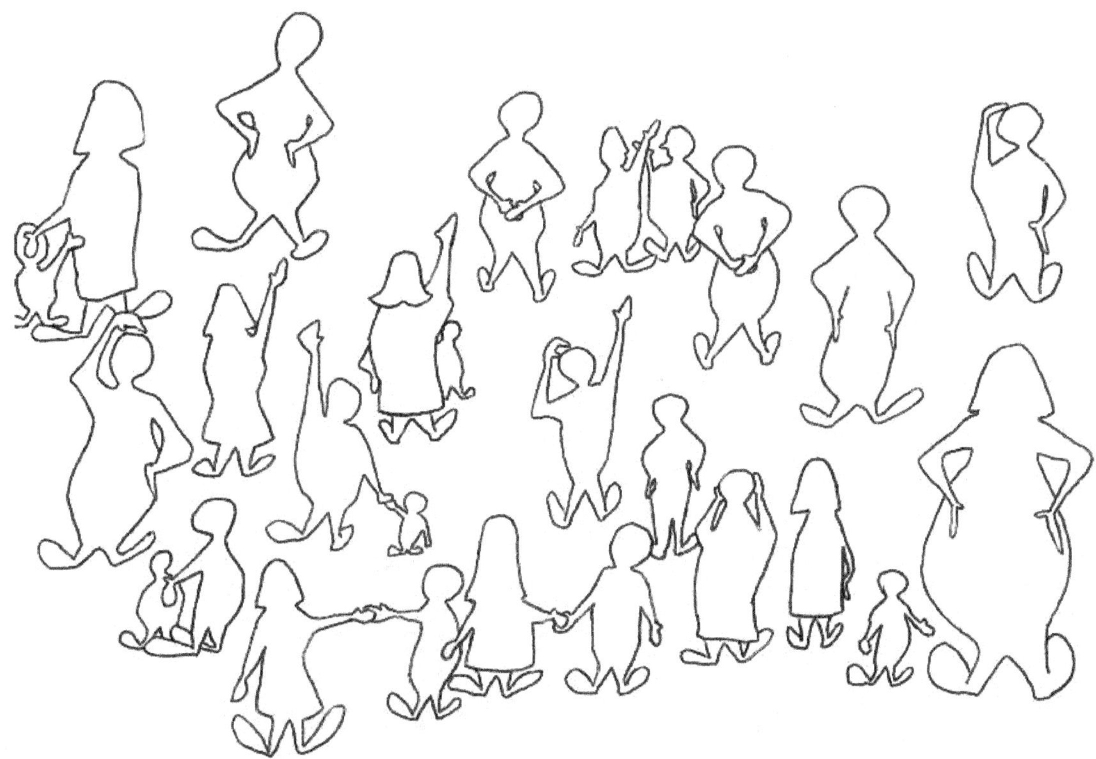

№692

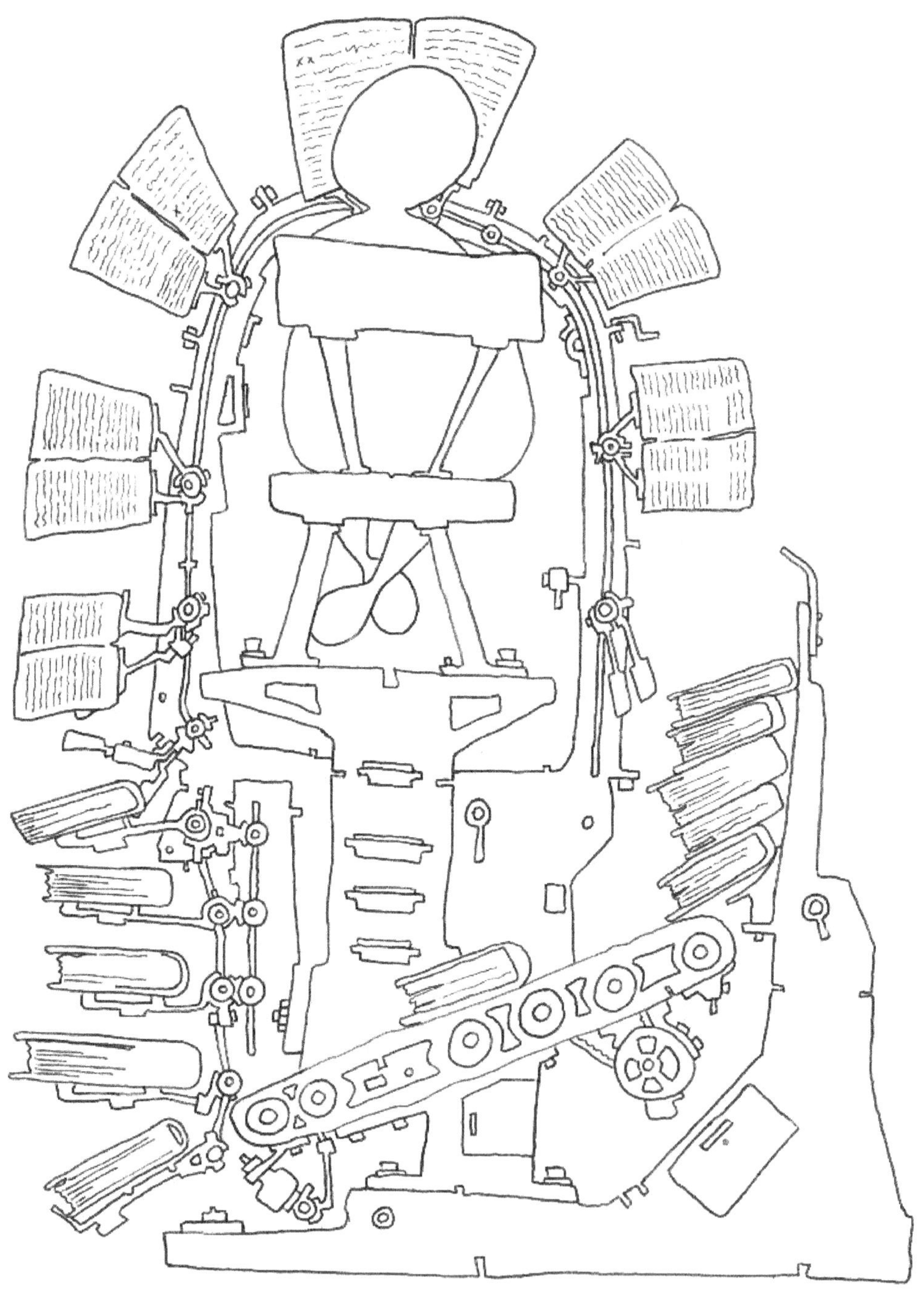

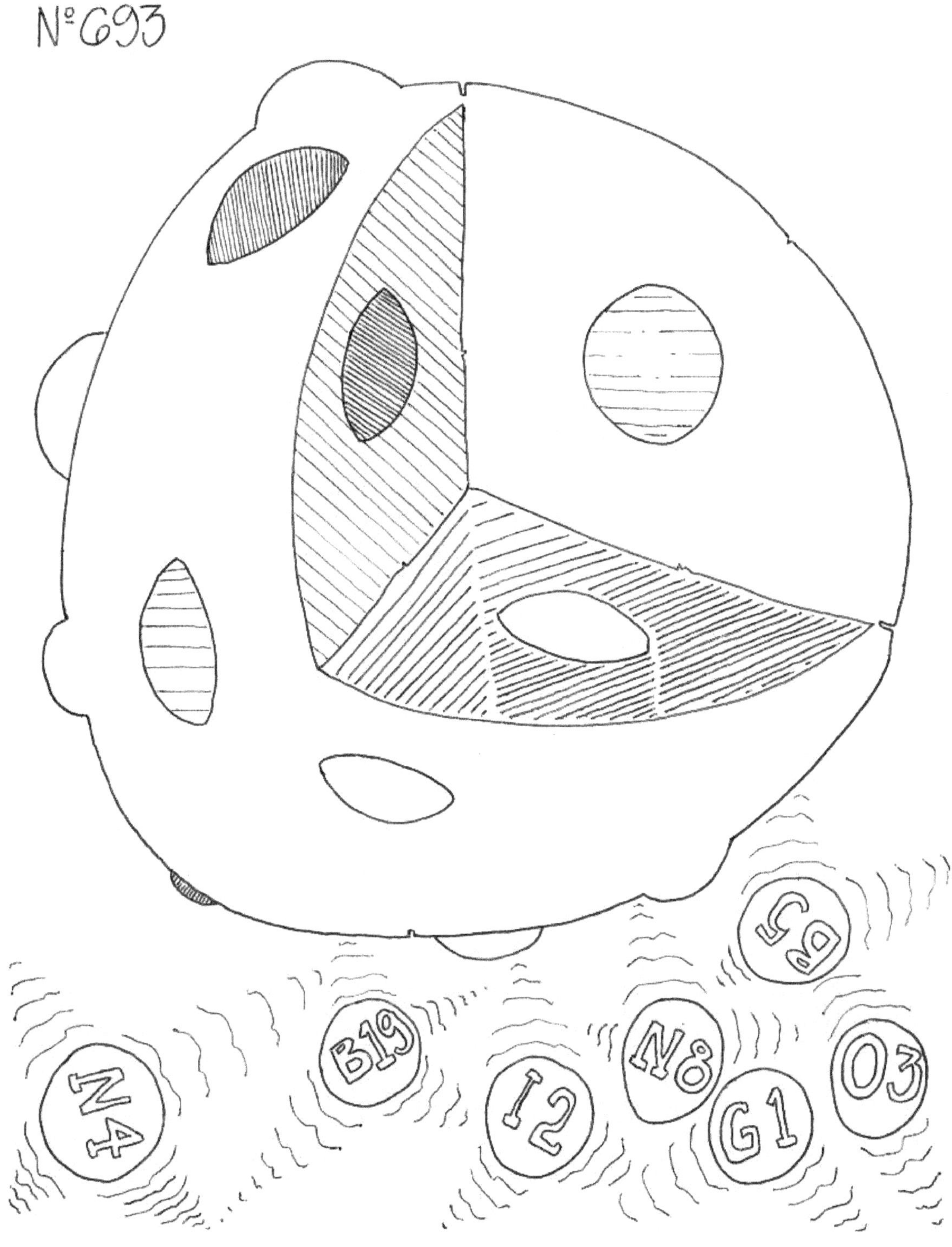
№693
G5
N4
B19
N8
O3
I2
G1

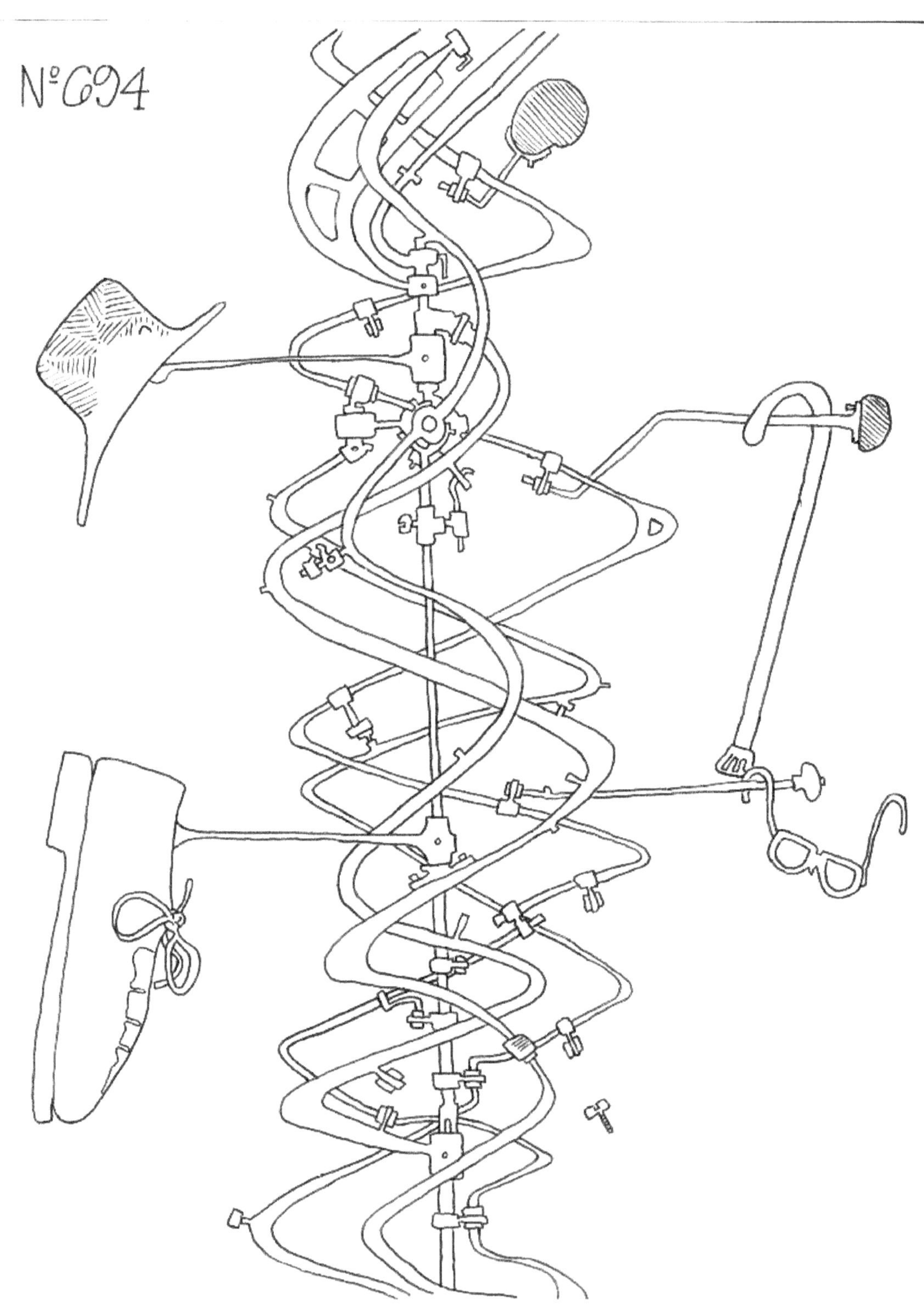

No 694

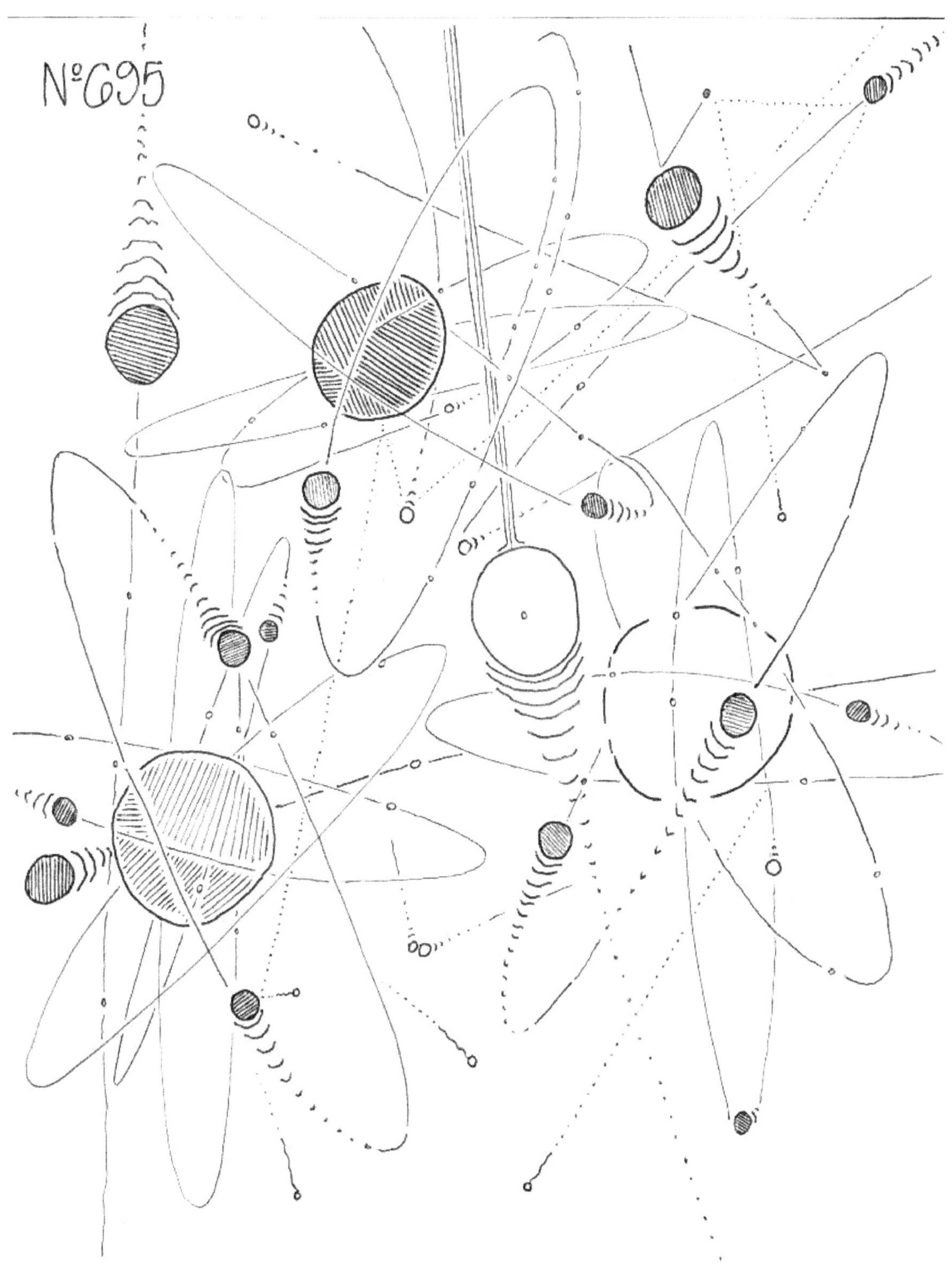
№695

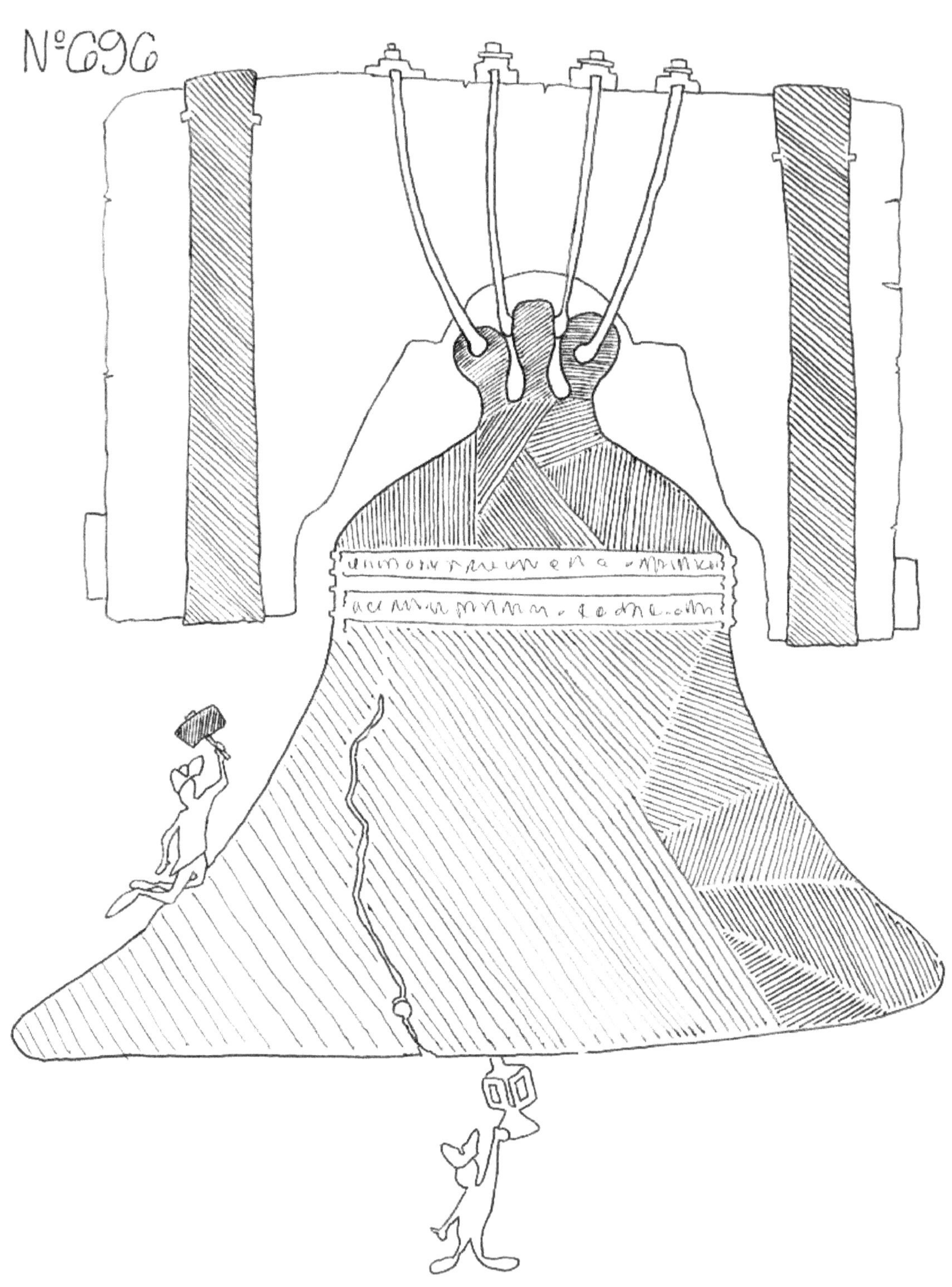
№696

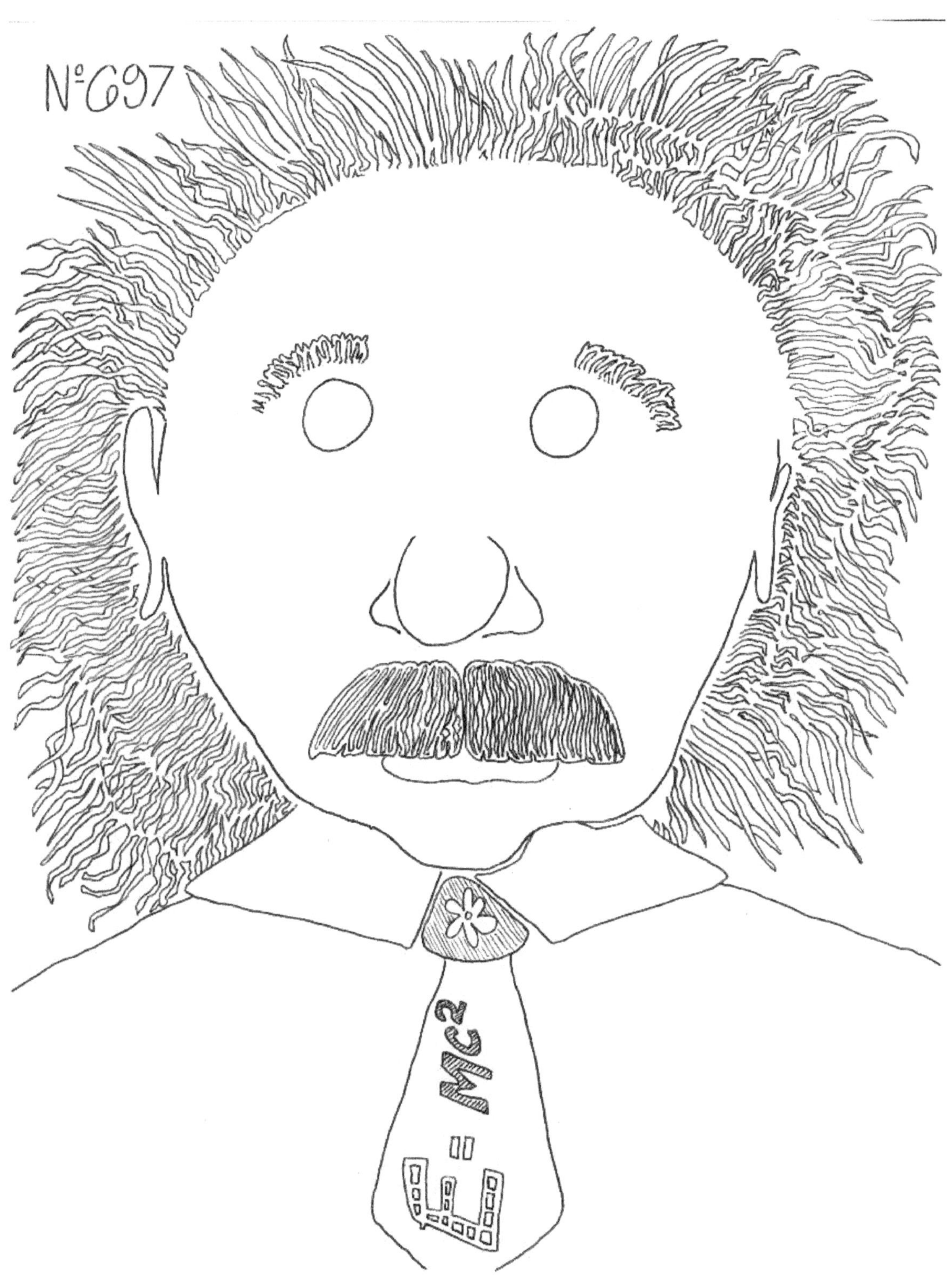

N°697
E = Mc²

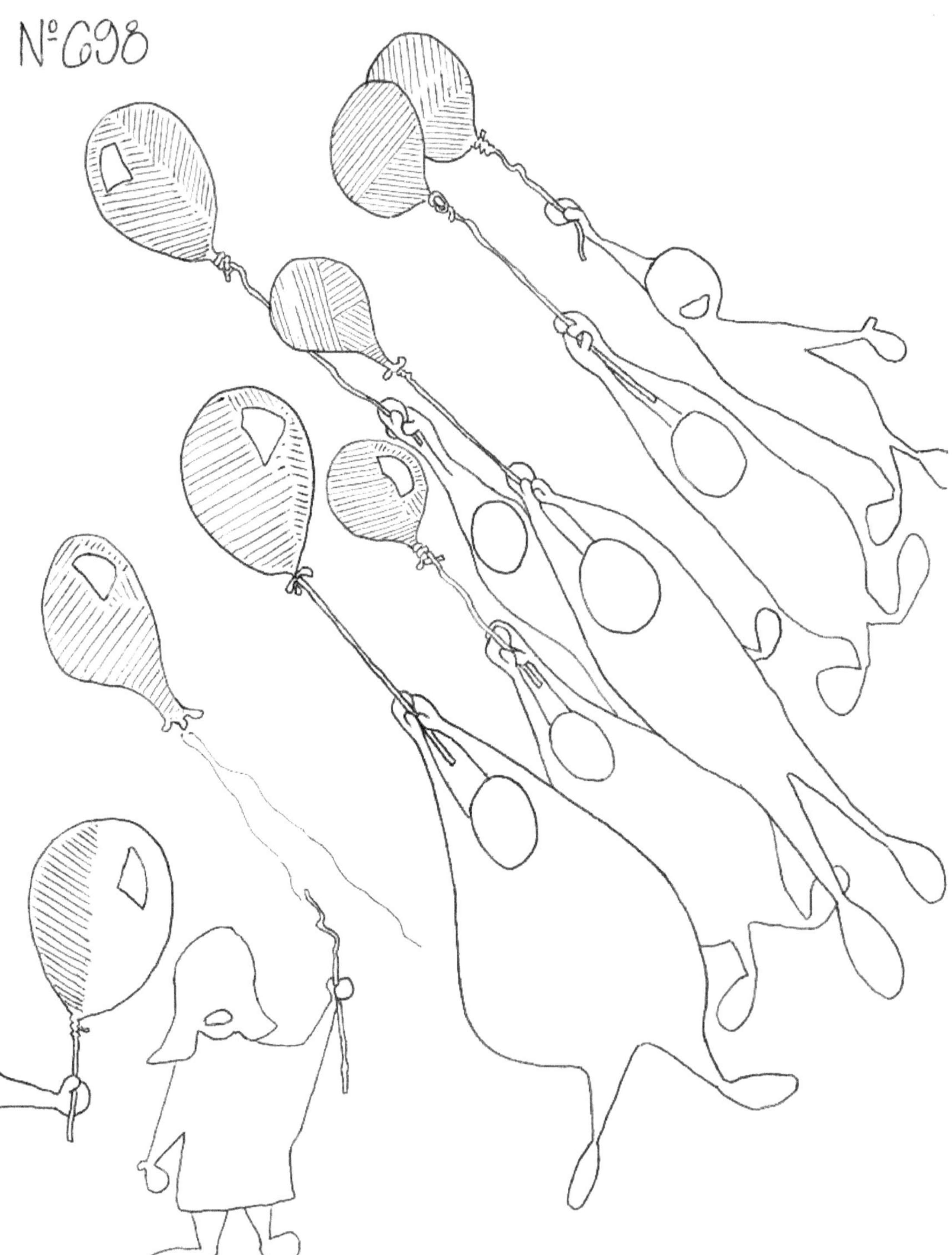
№698

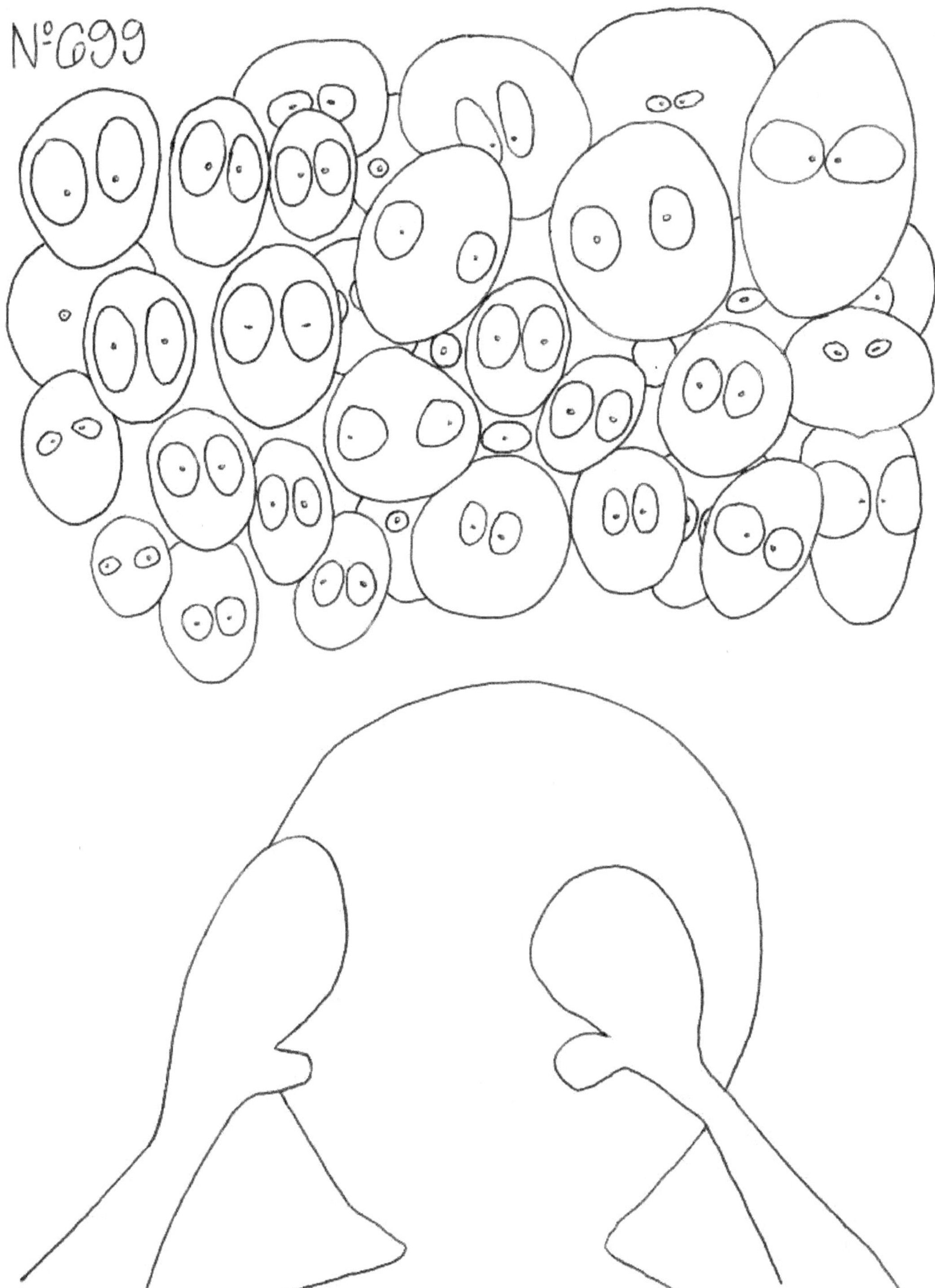
№699

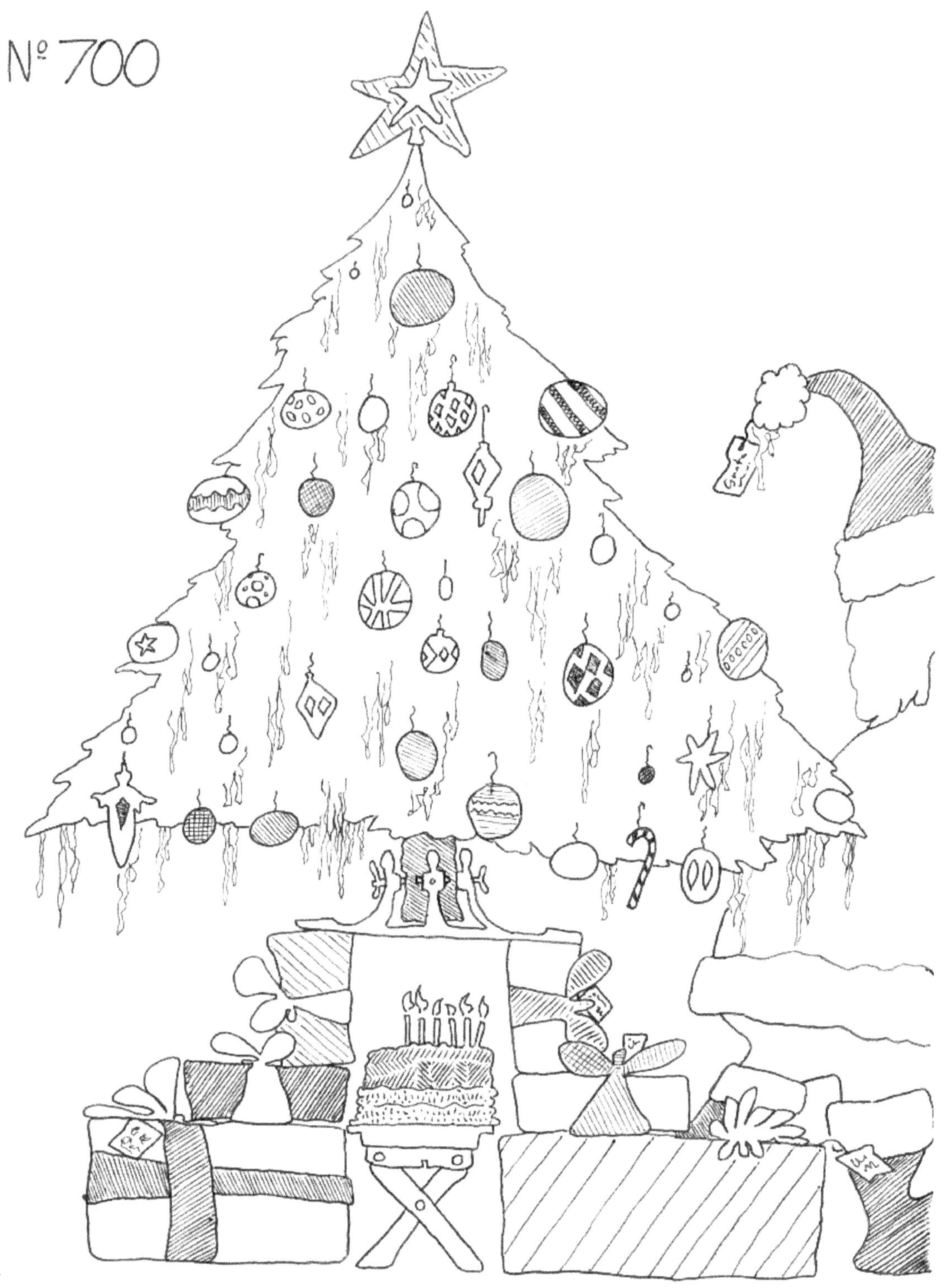
№ 700

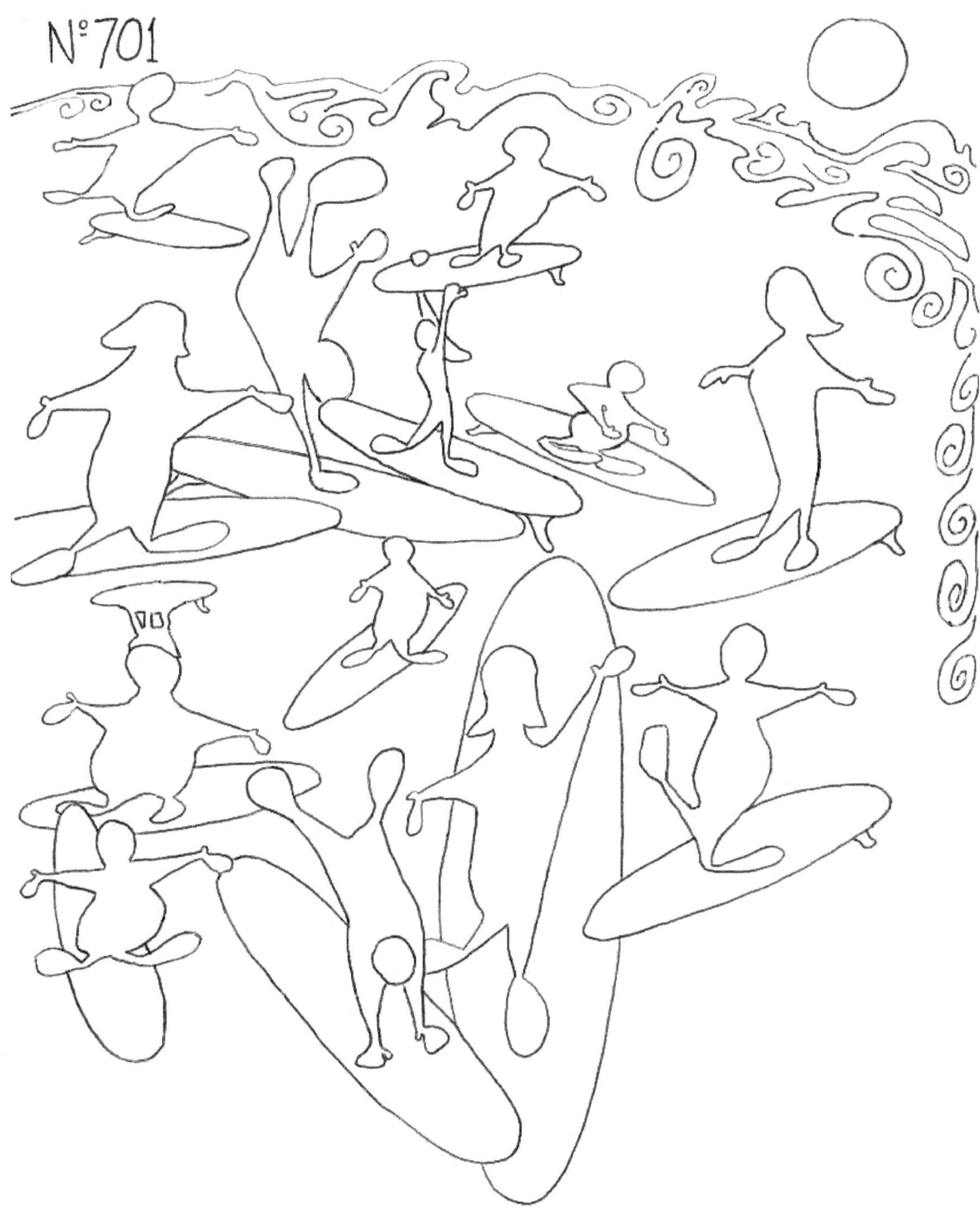
N°701

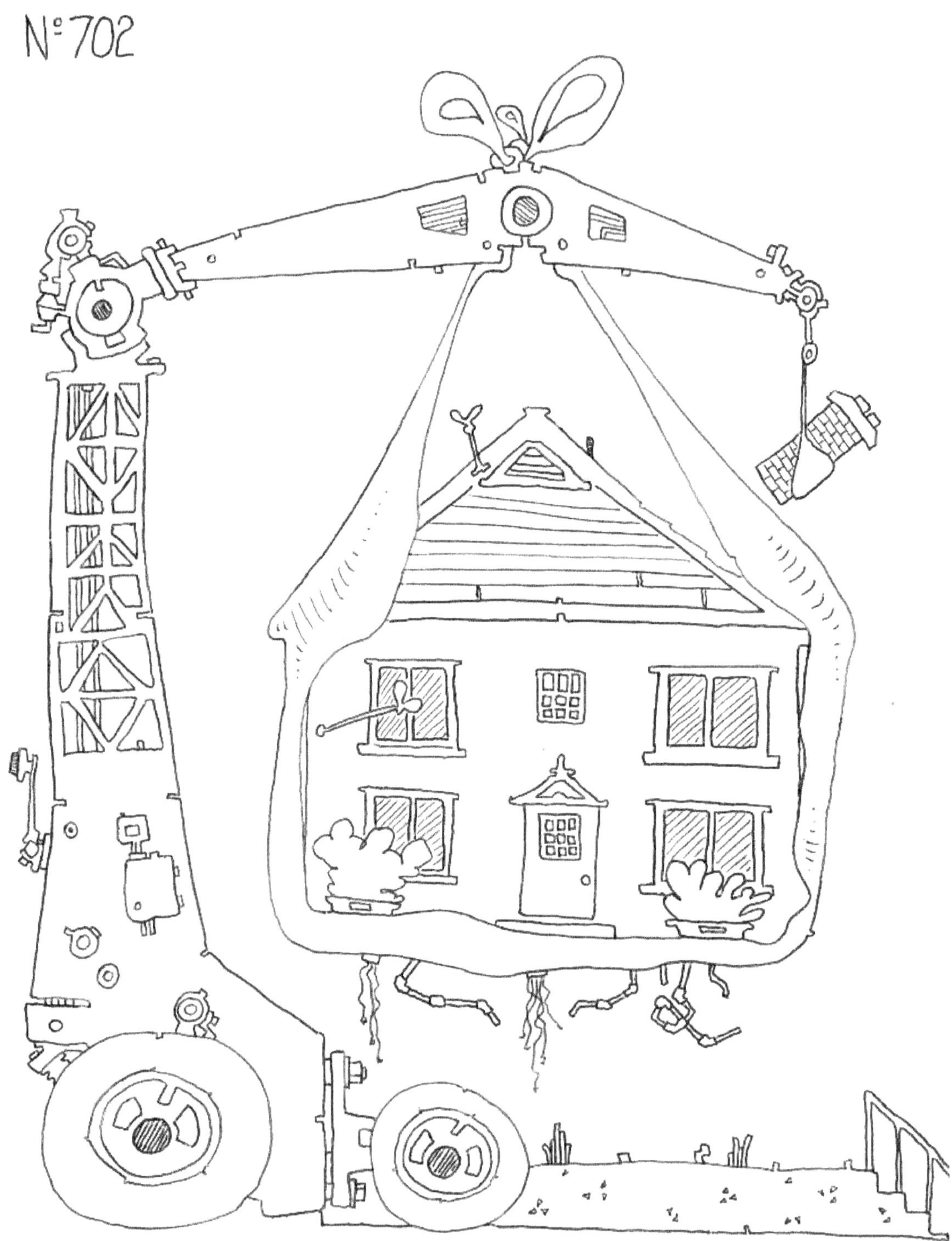
Nº702

Nº 703

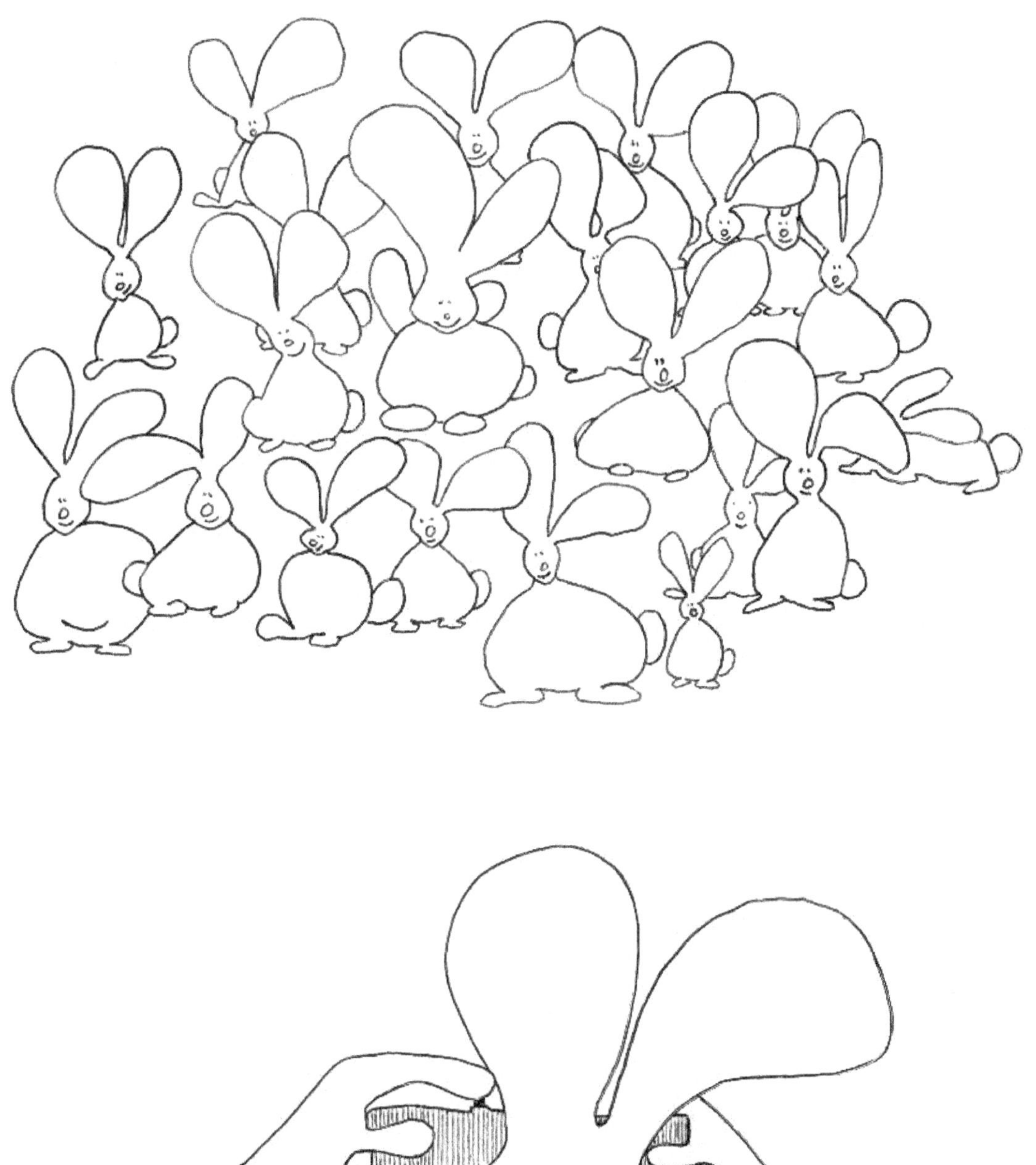

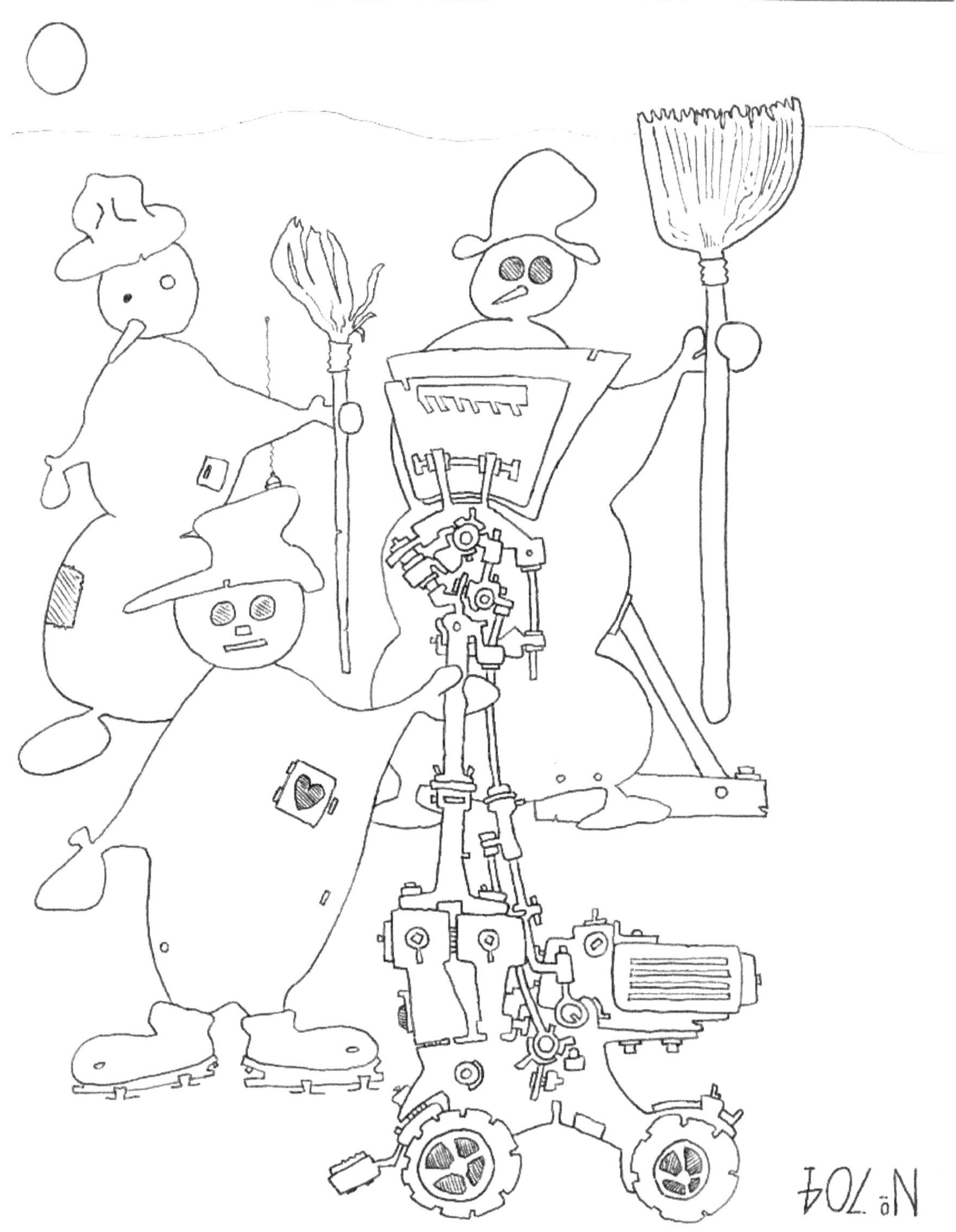
N° 704

Nº 705

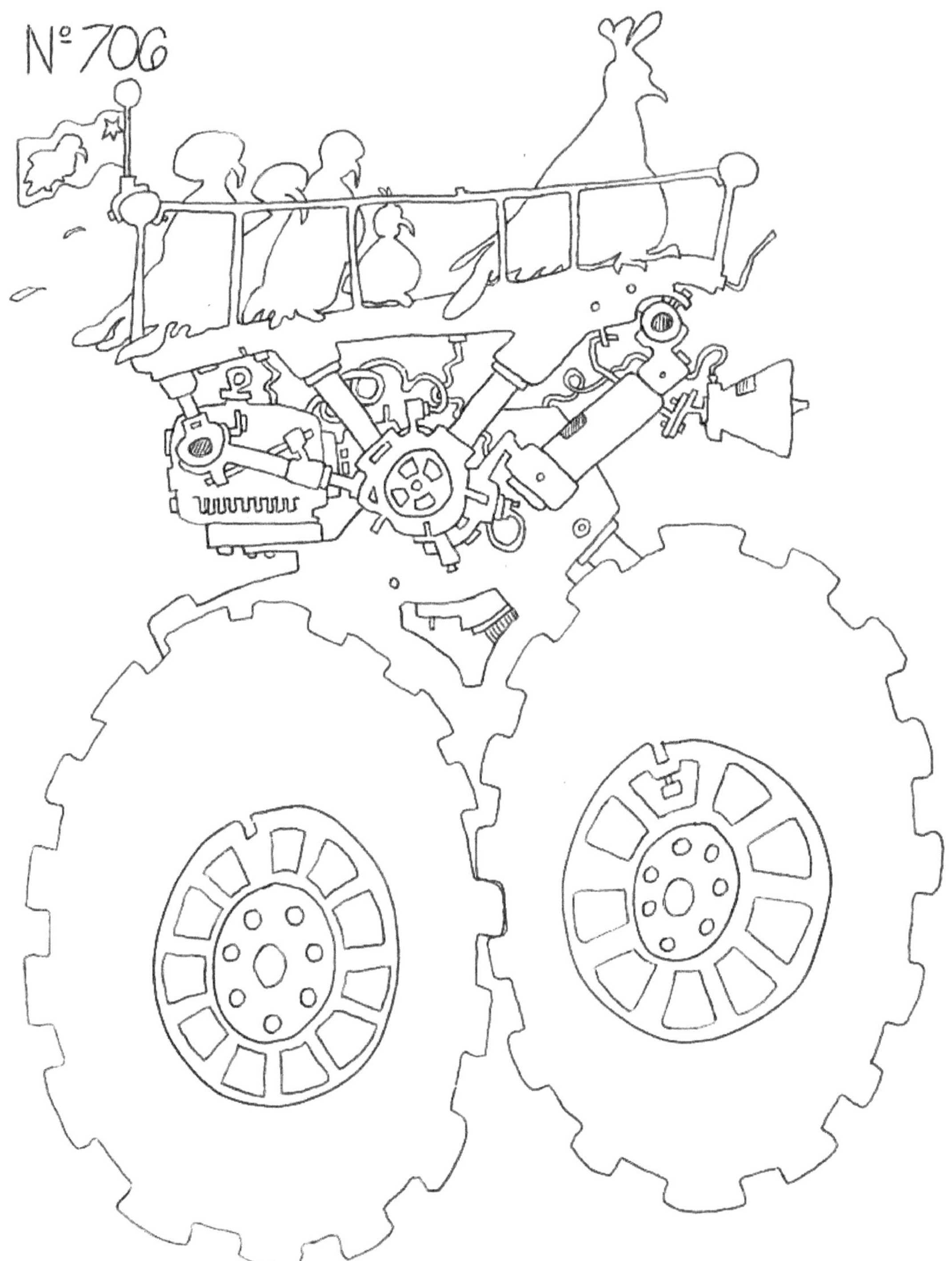
Nº706

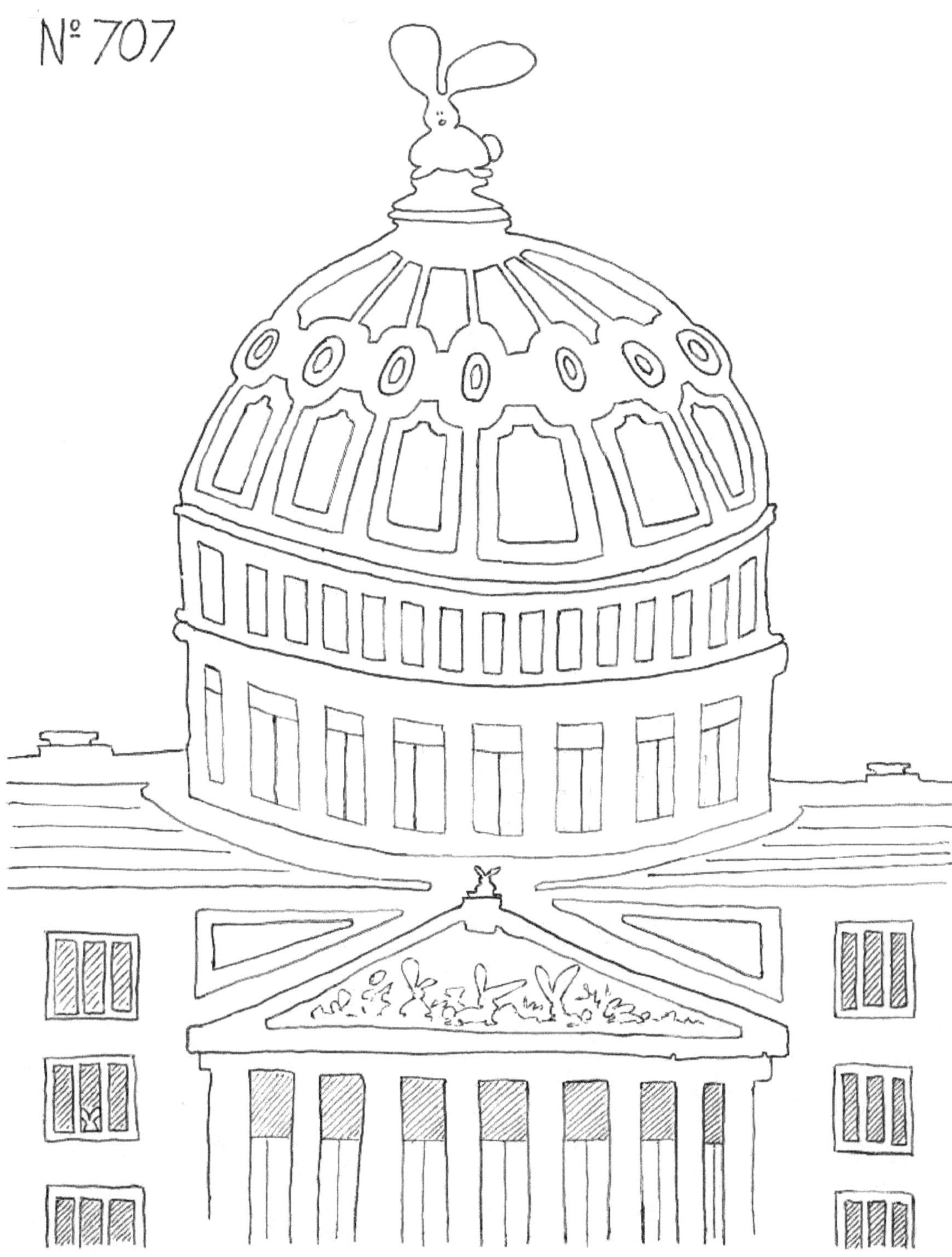
Nº 707

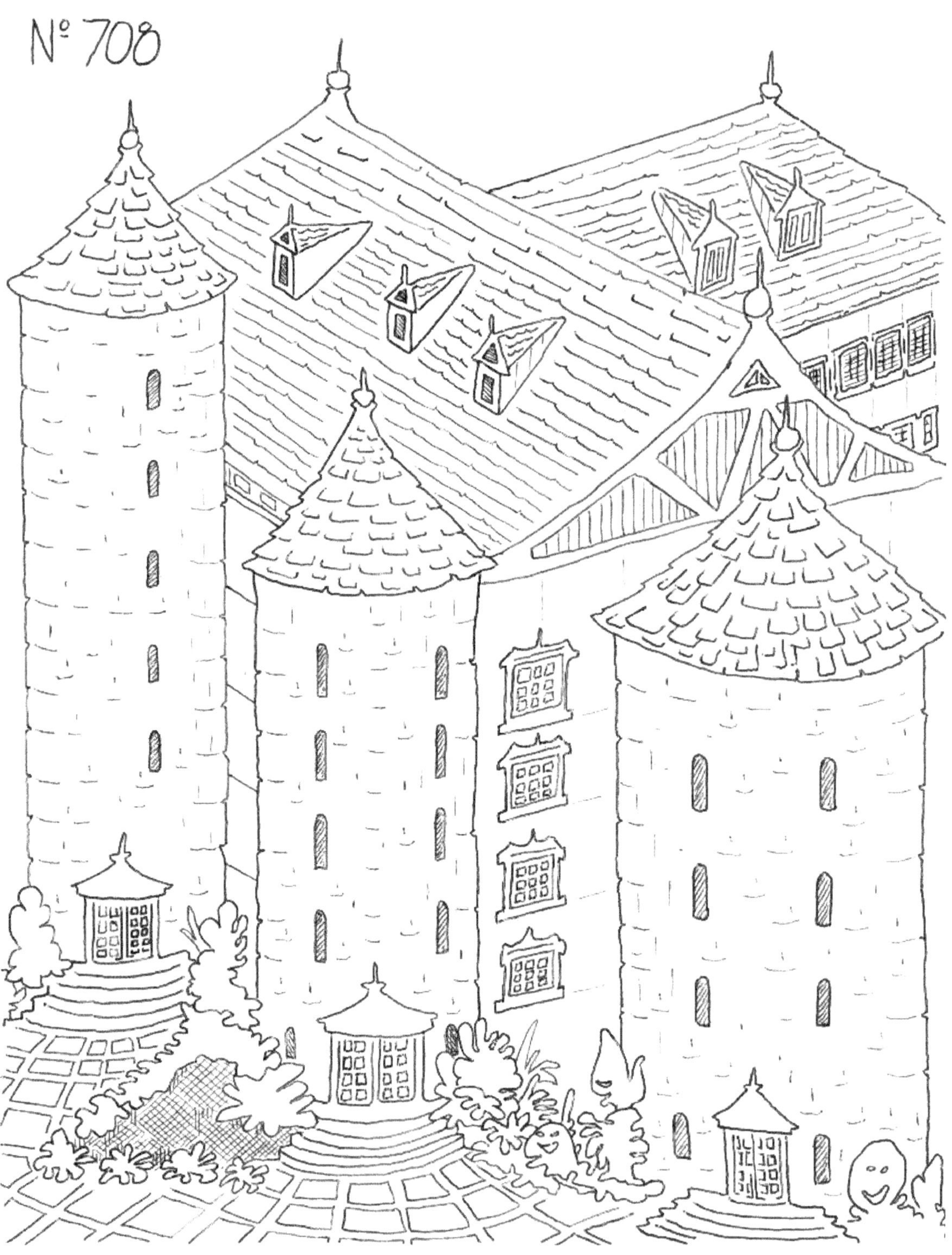
N° 708

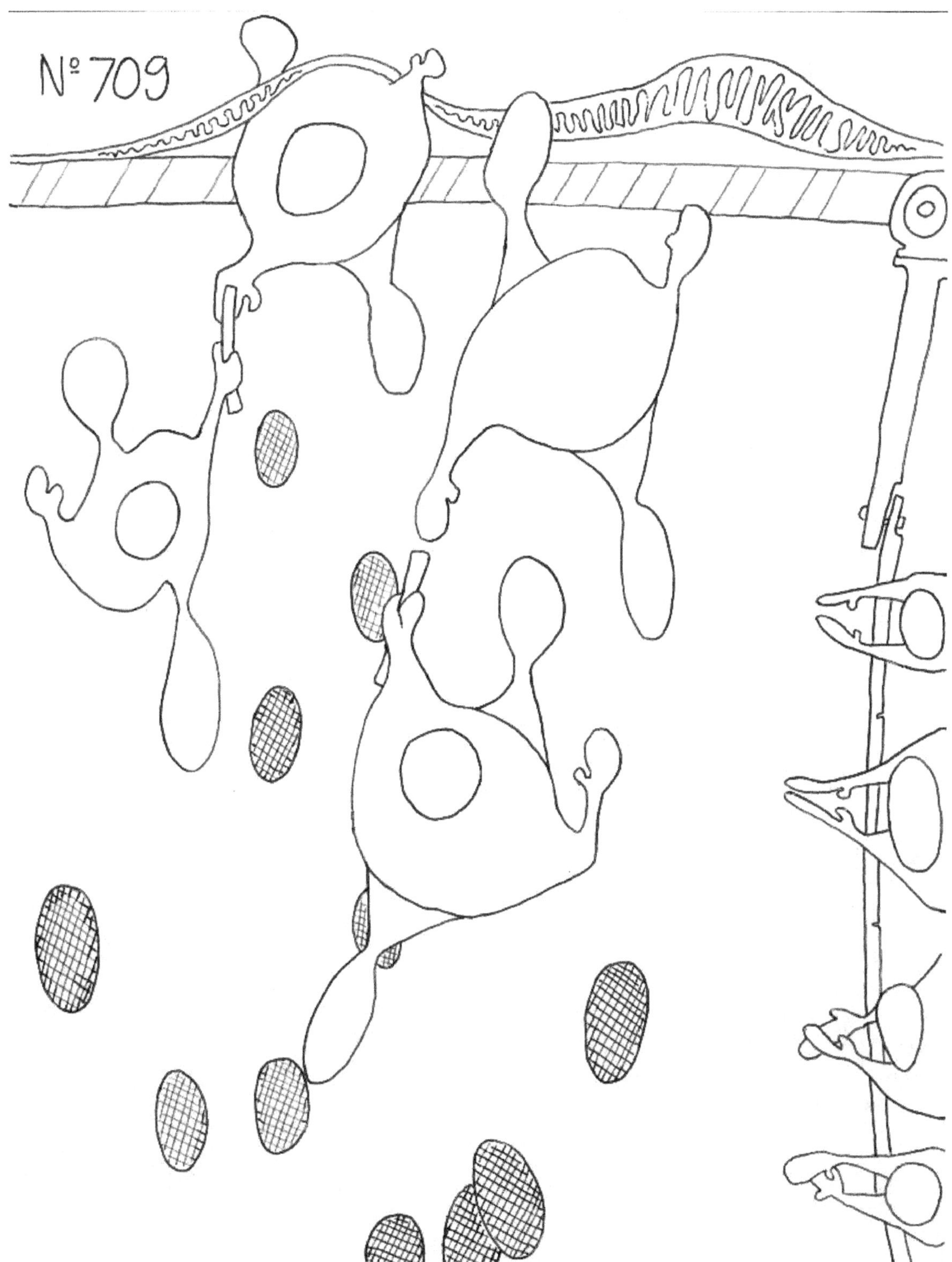
Nº709

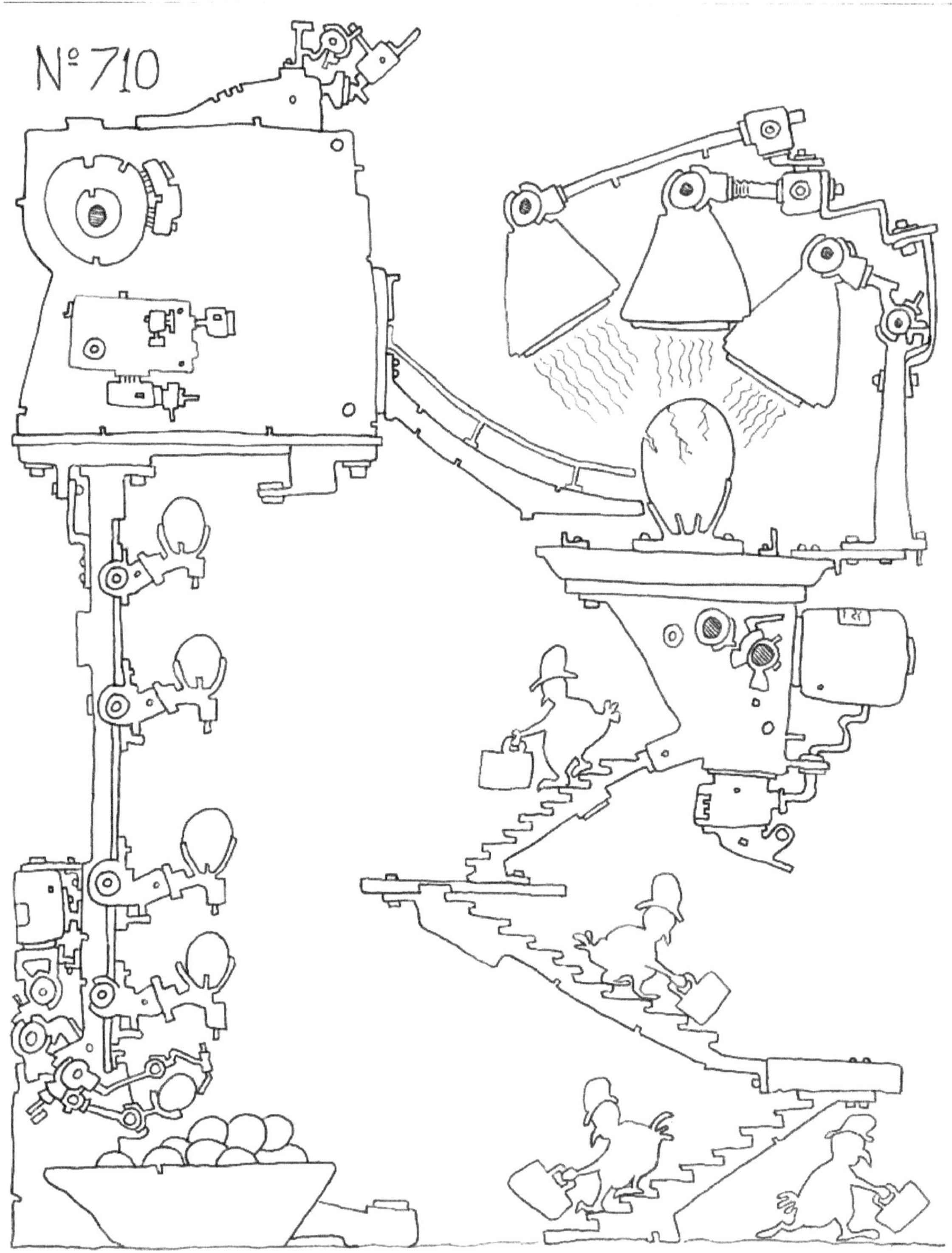
Nº 710

Nº 711

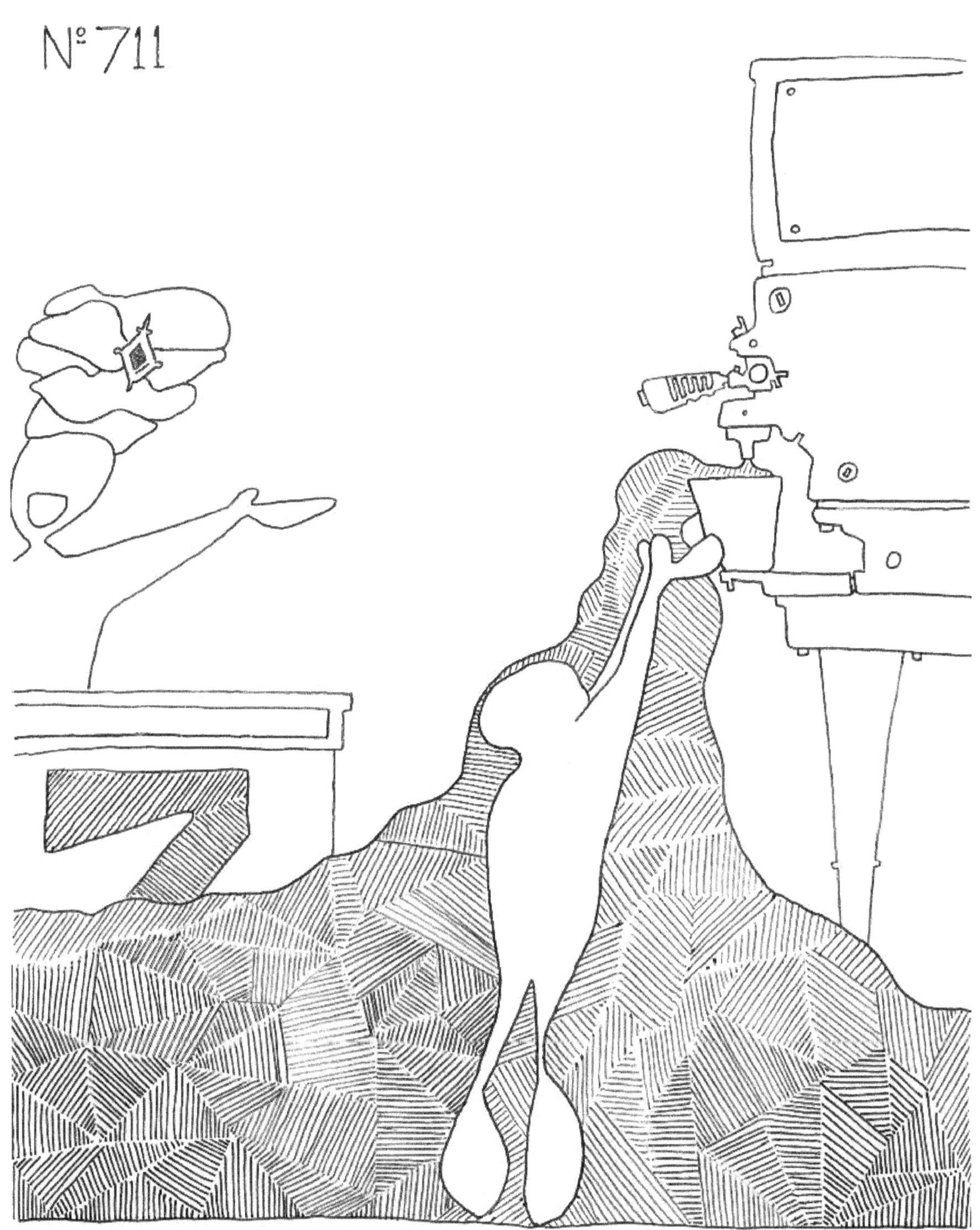

Nº 712

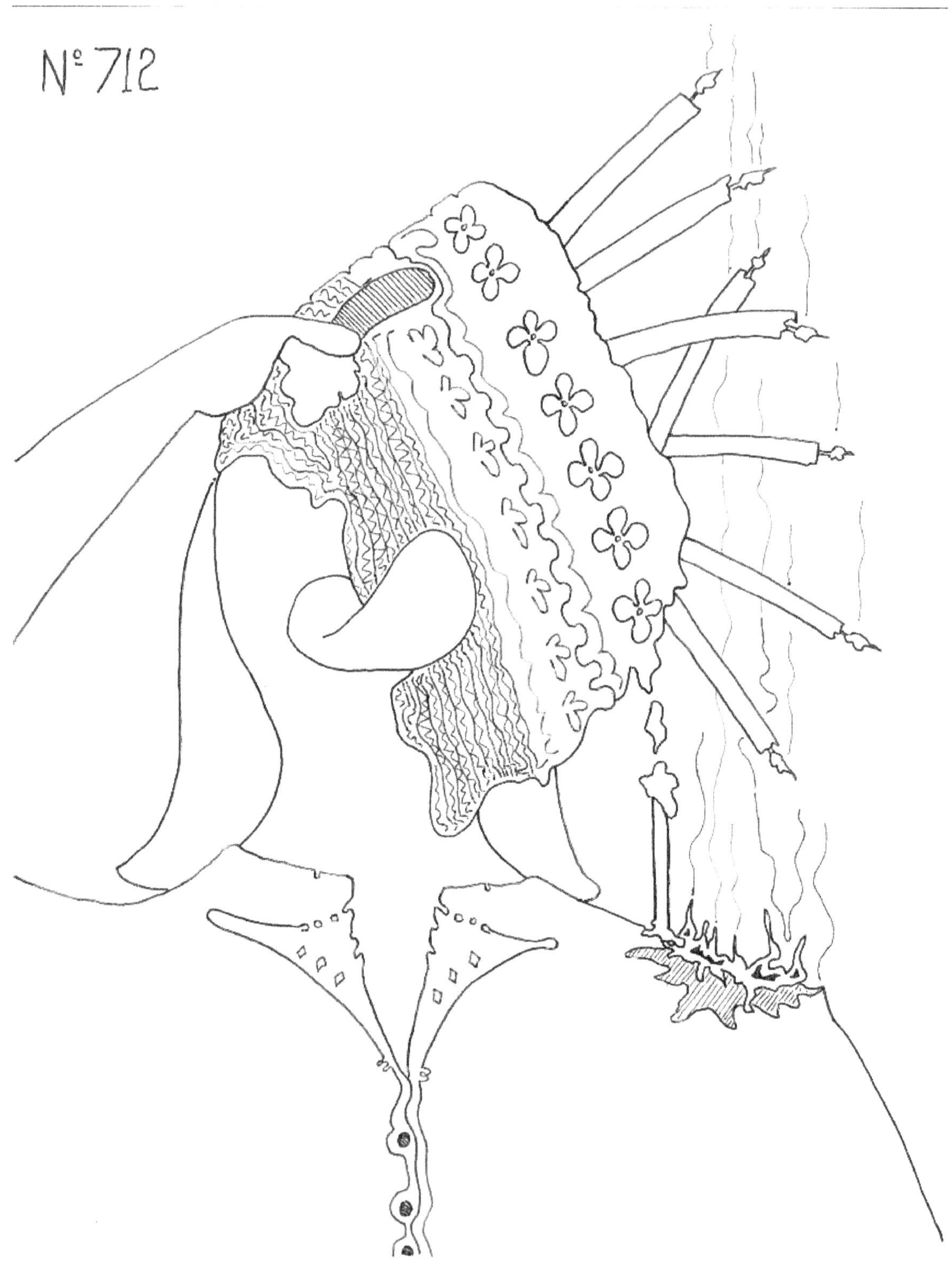

Nº 713

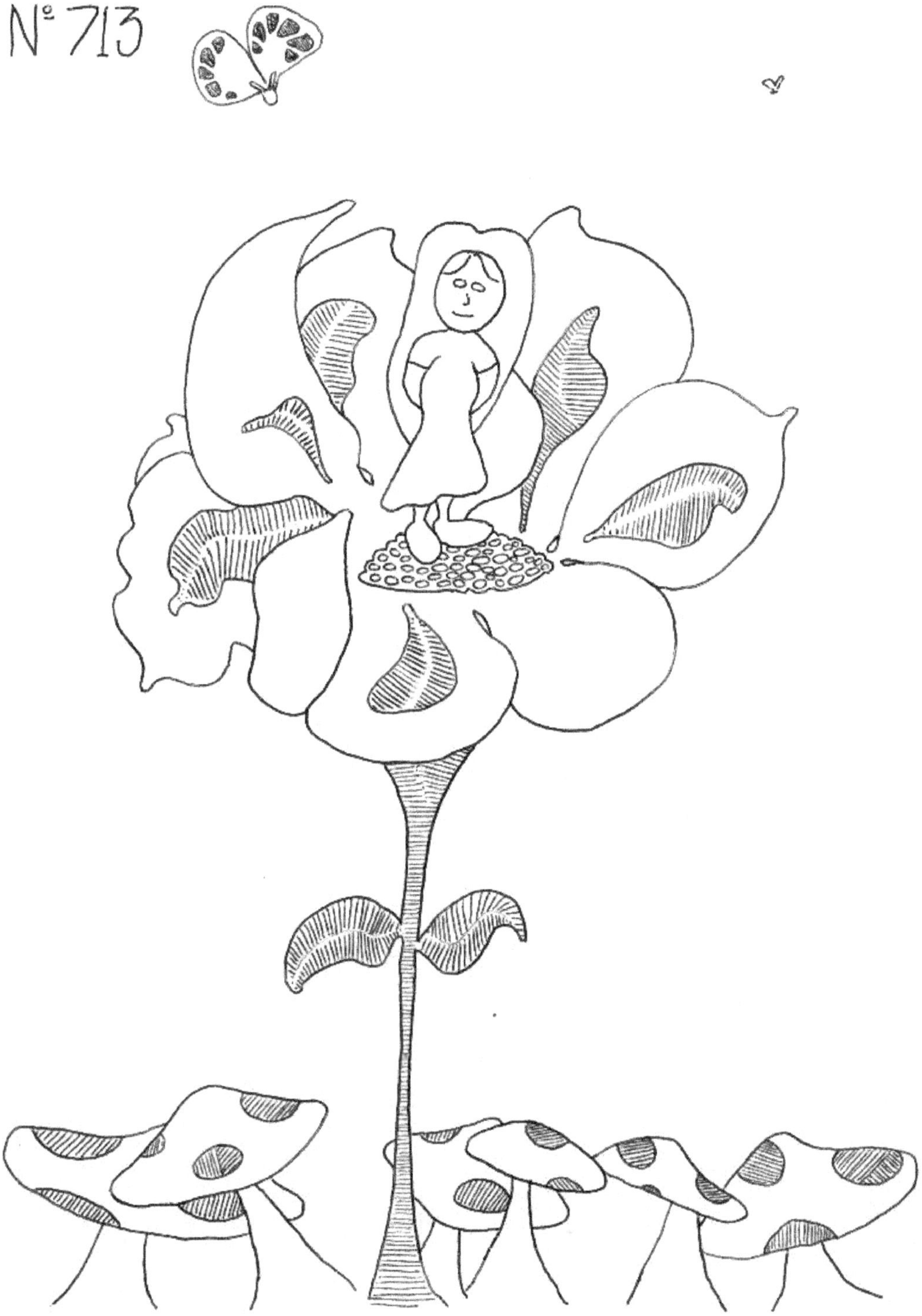

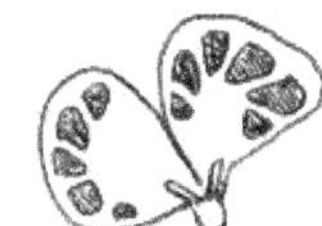

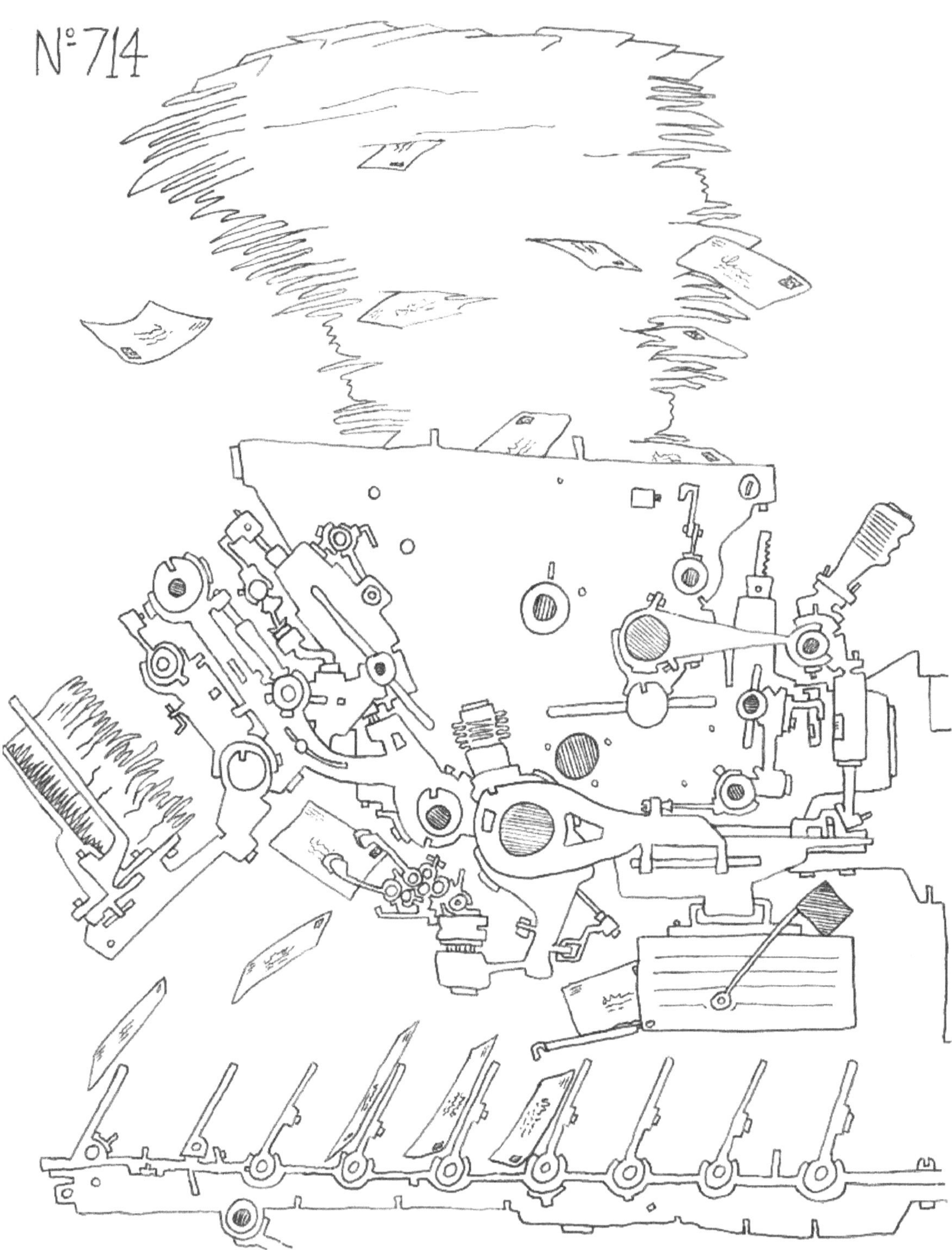
N° 714

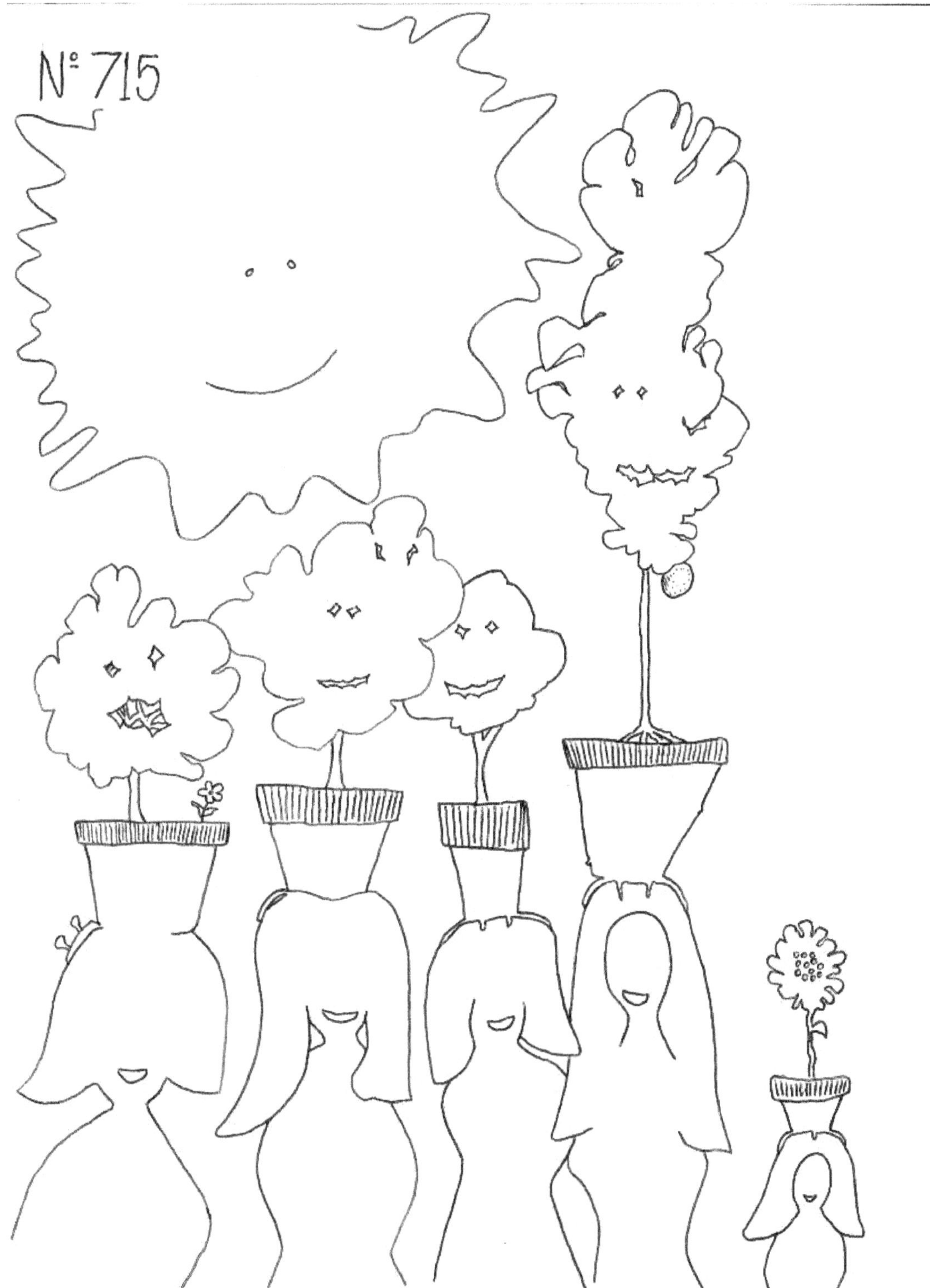
Nº 715

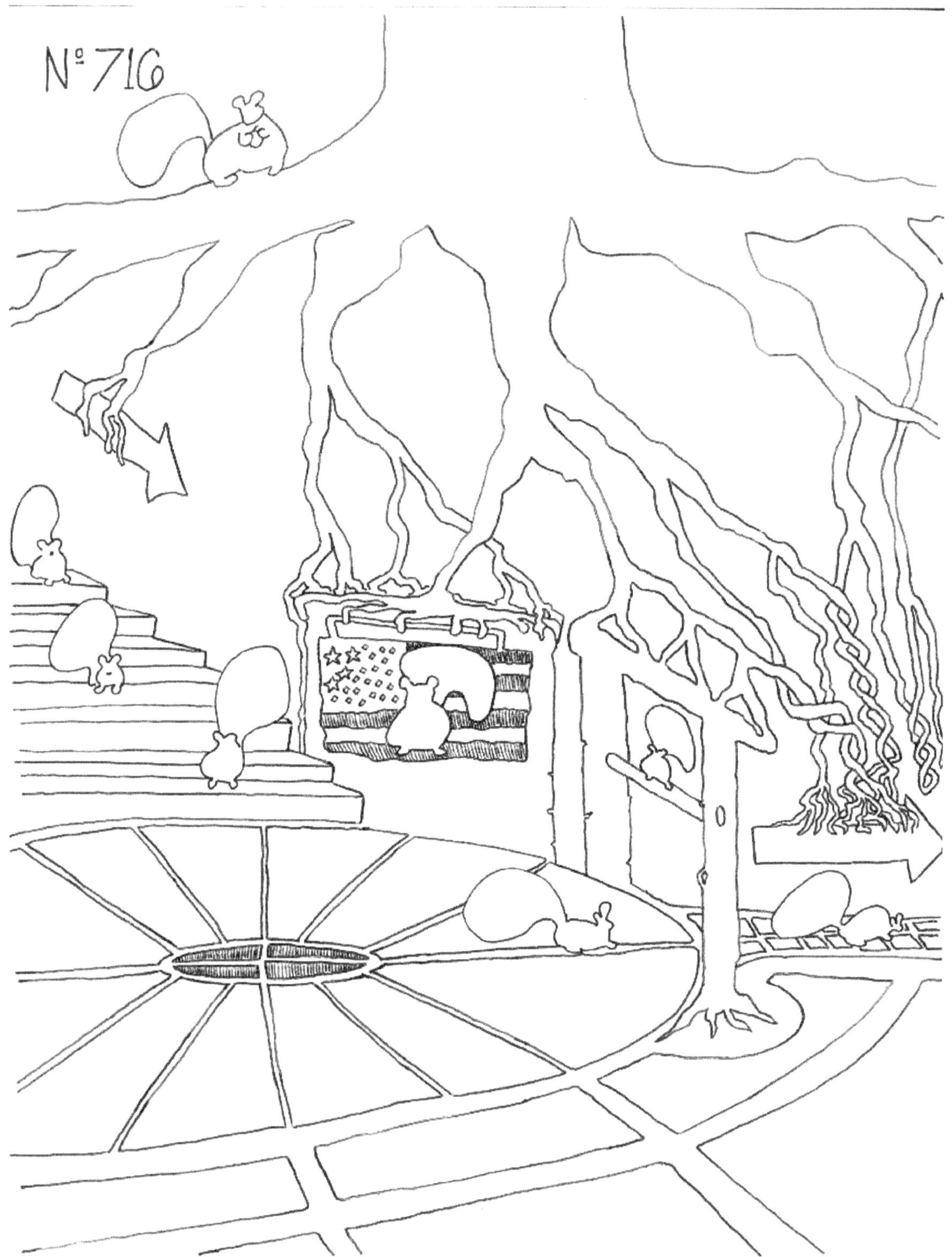
Nº 716

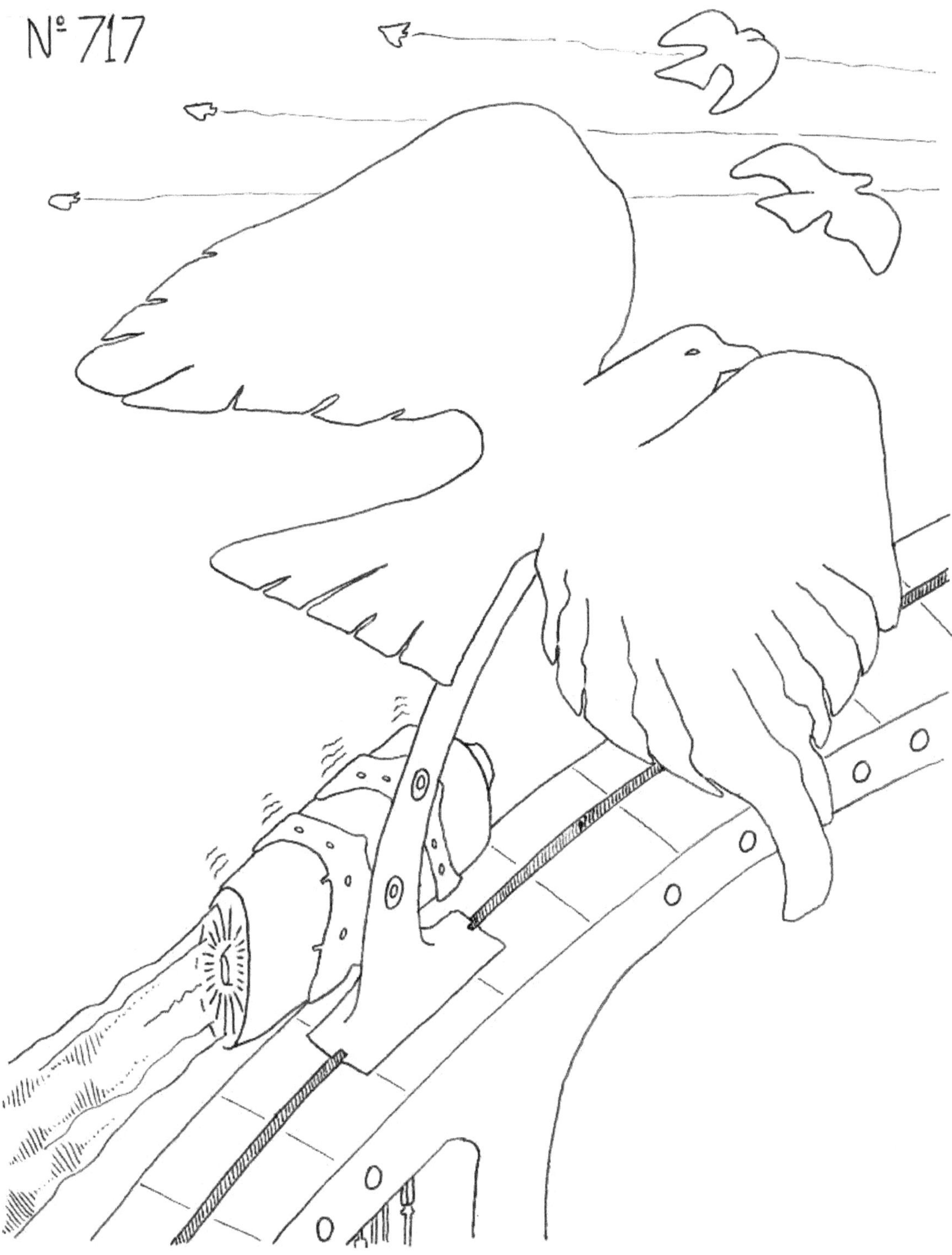
№ 717

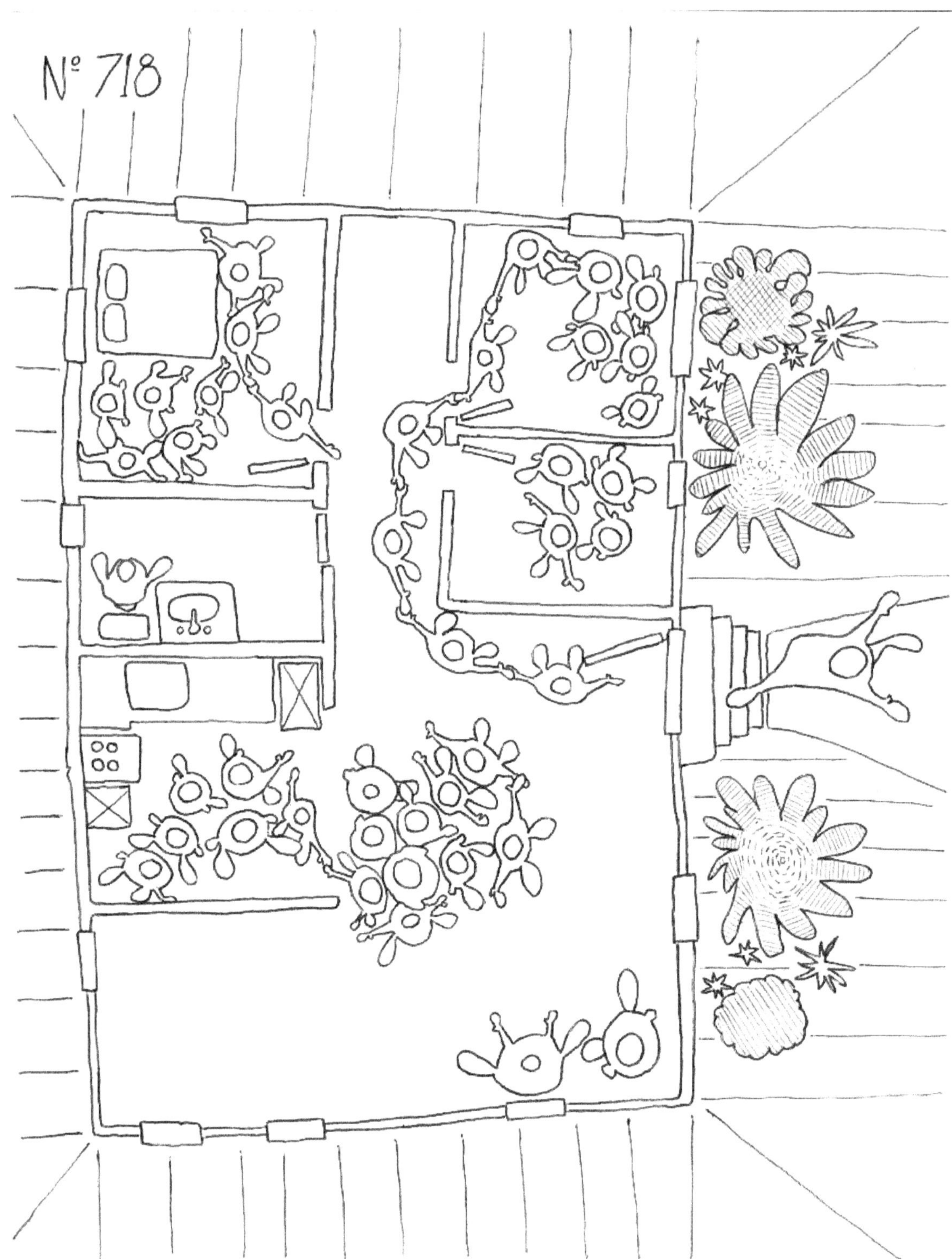
№ 718

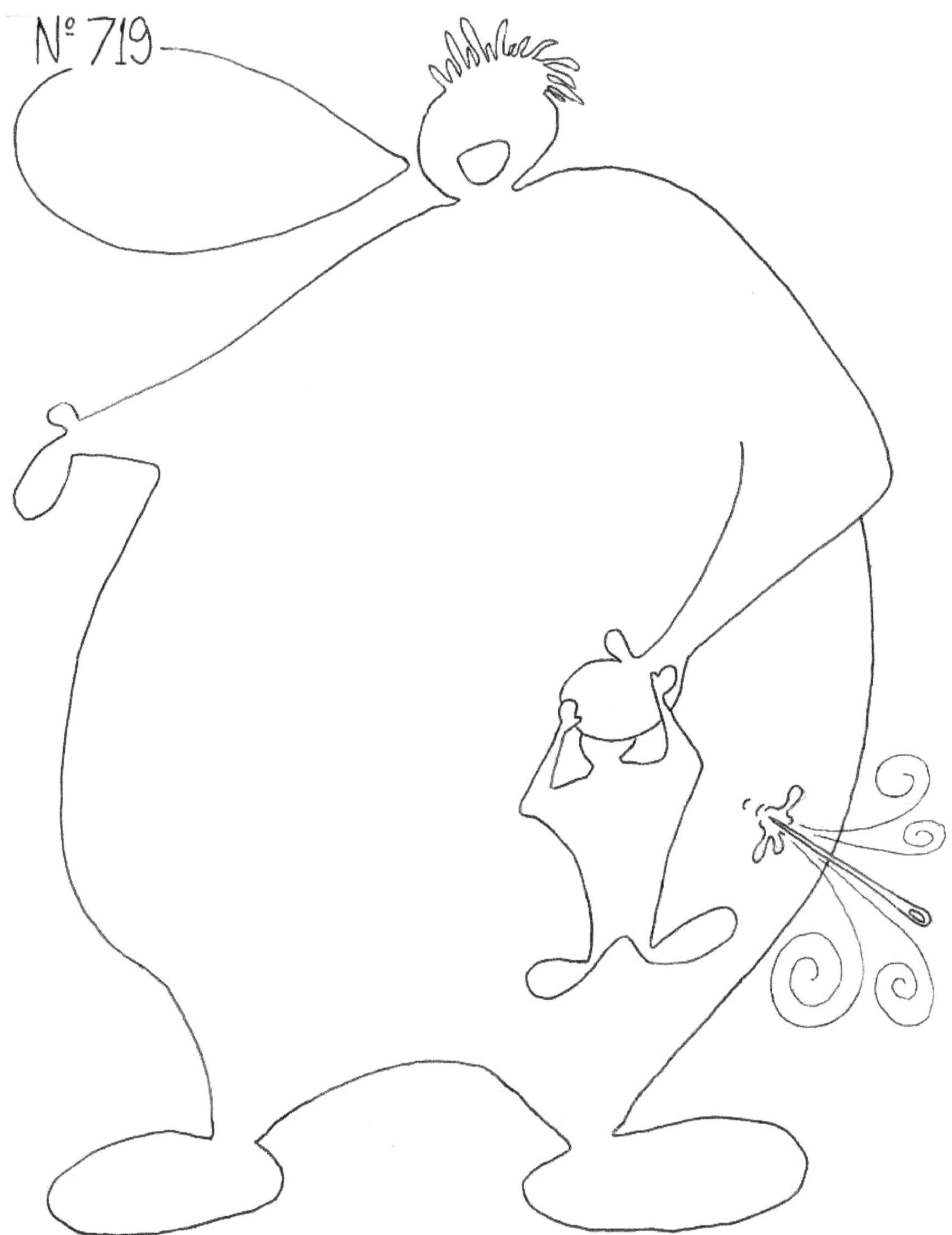
Nº 719

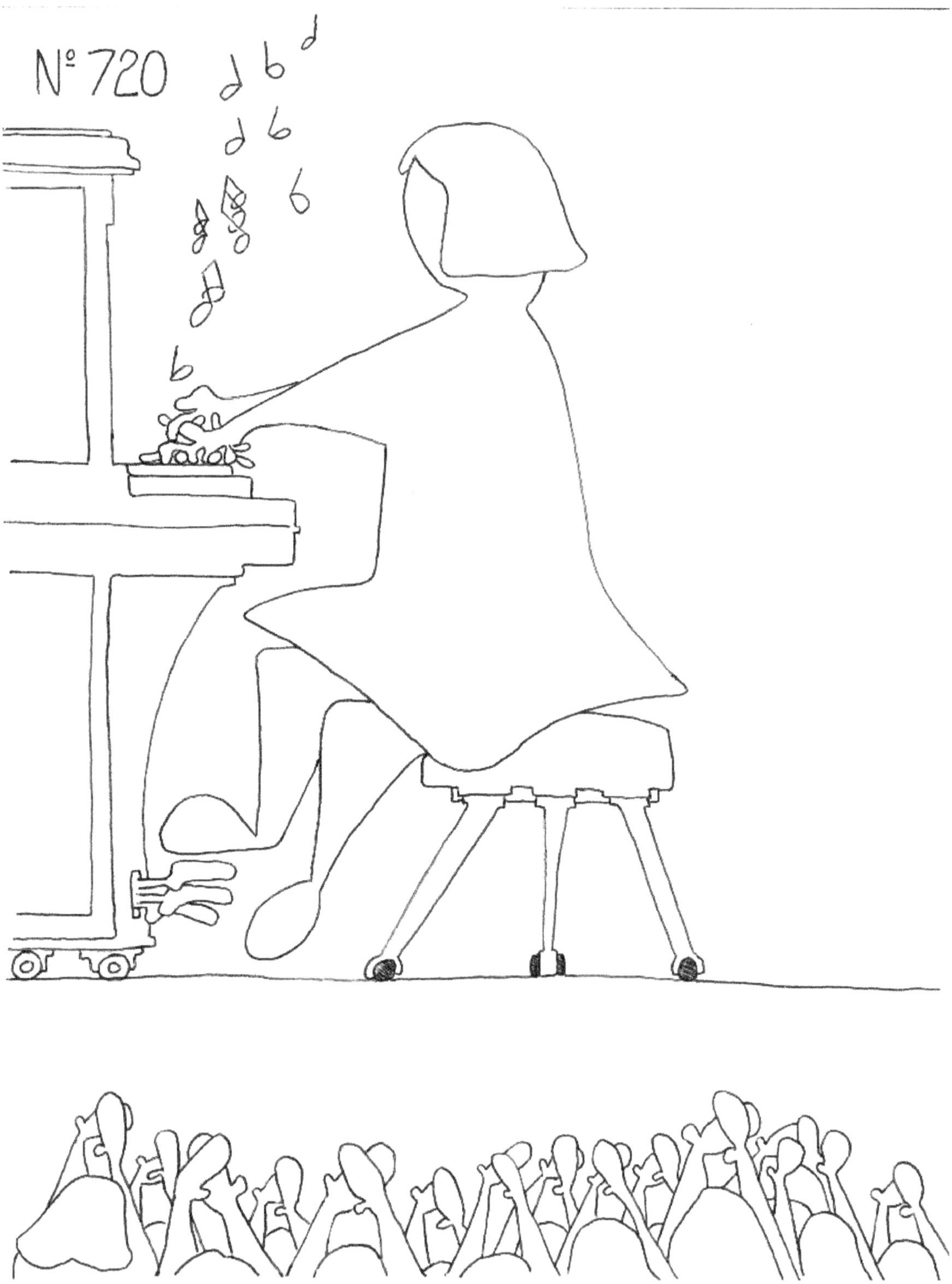

Nº 720

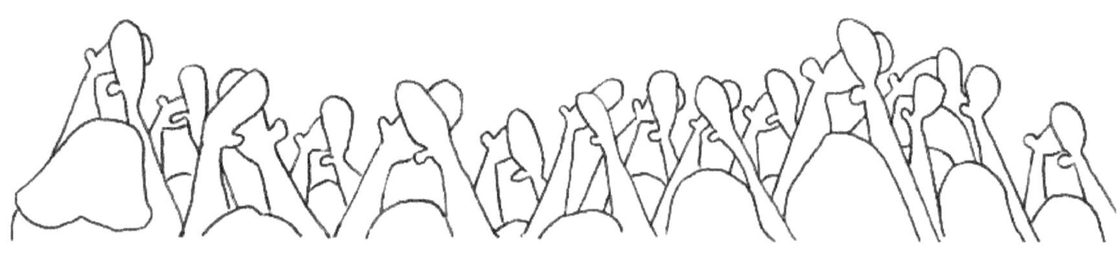

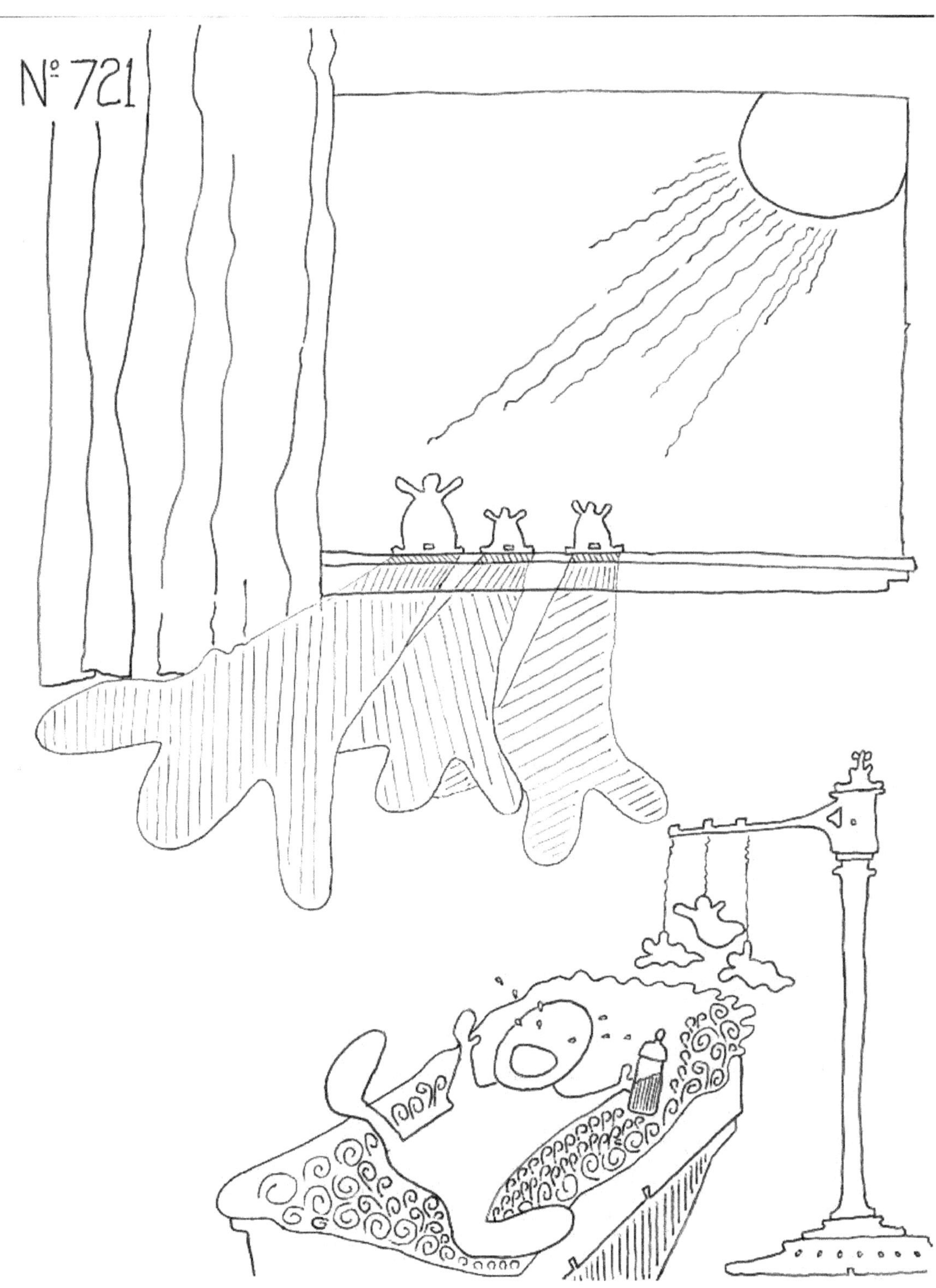
N° 721

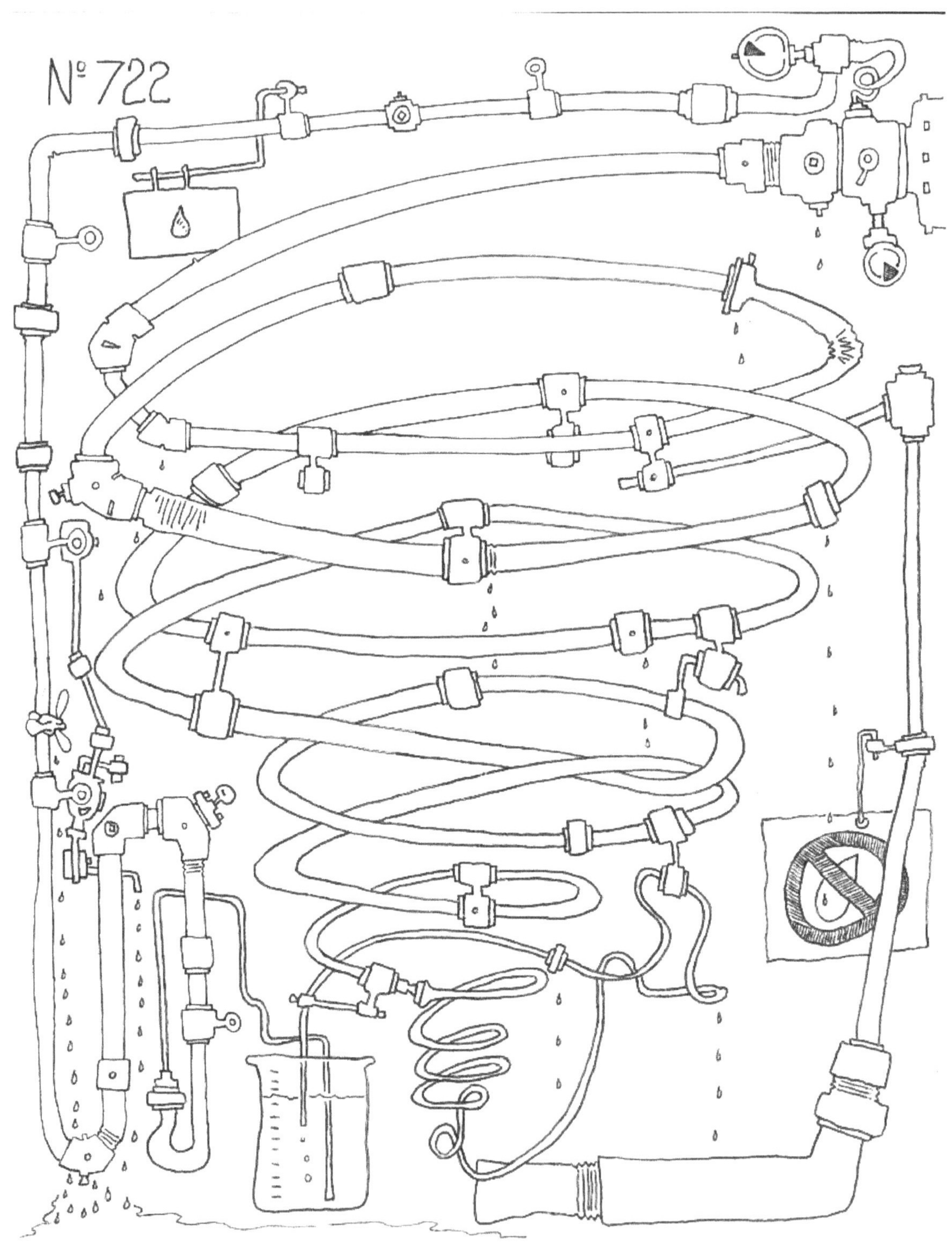
Nº 722

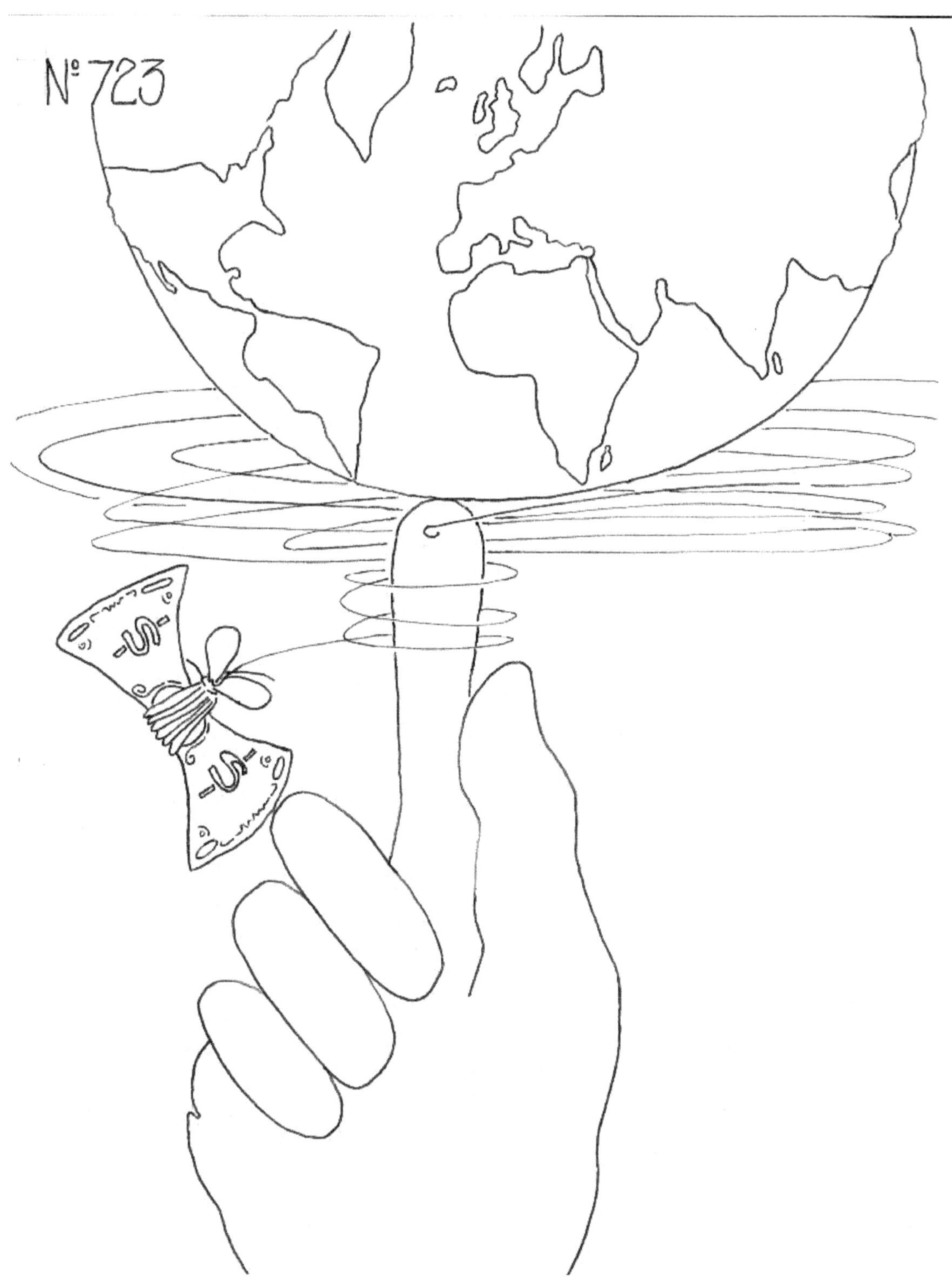
Nº 723

N° 724

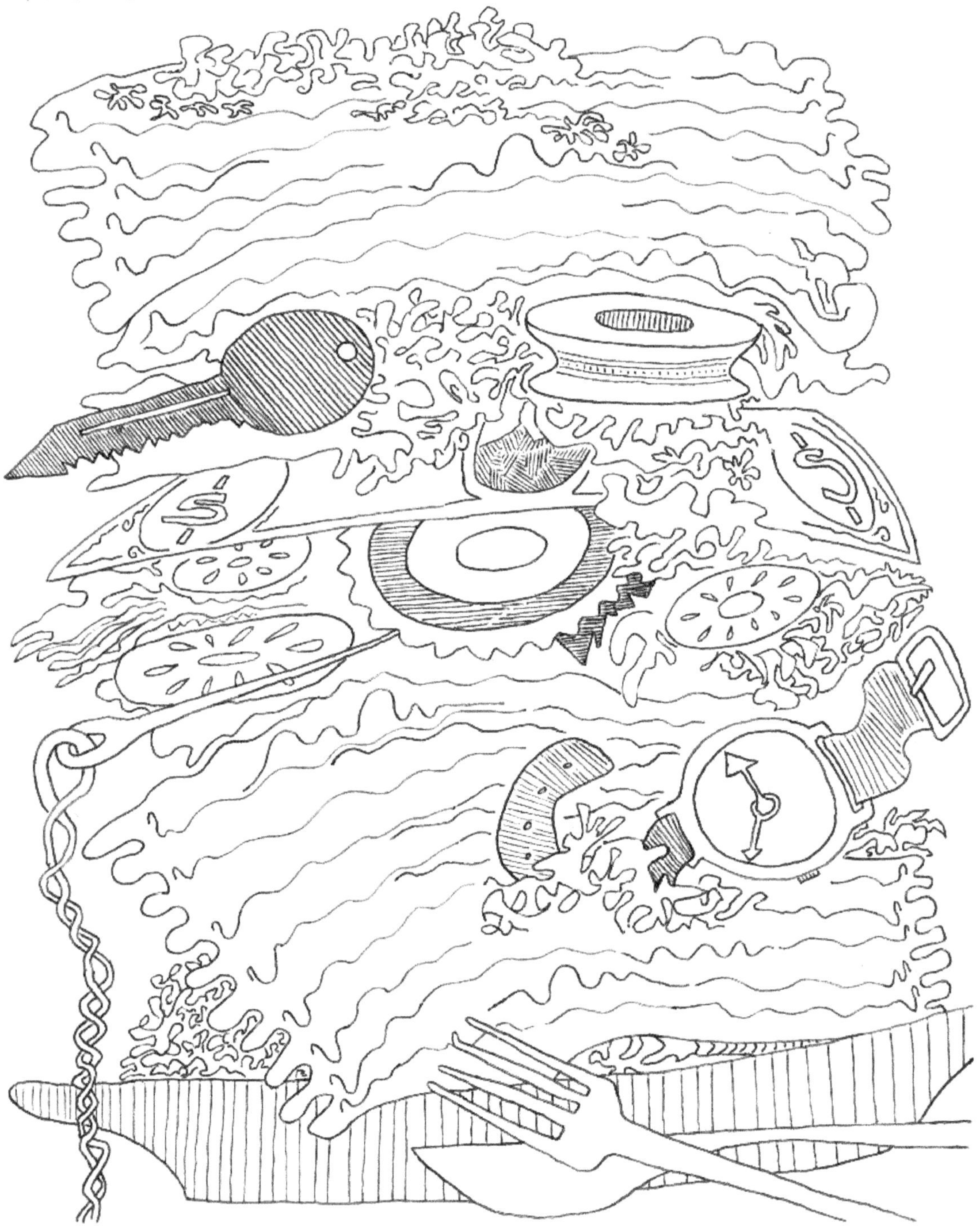

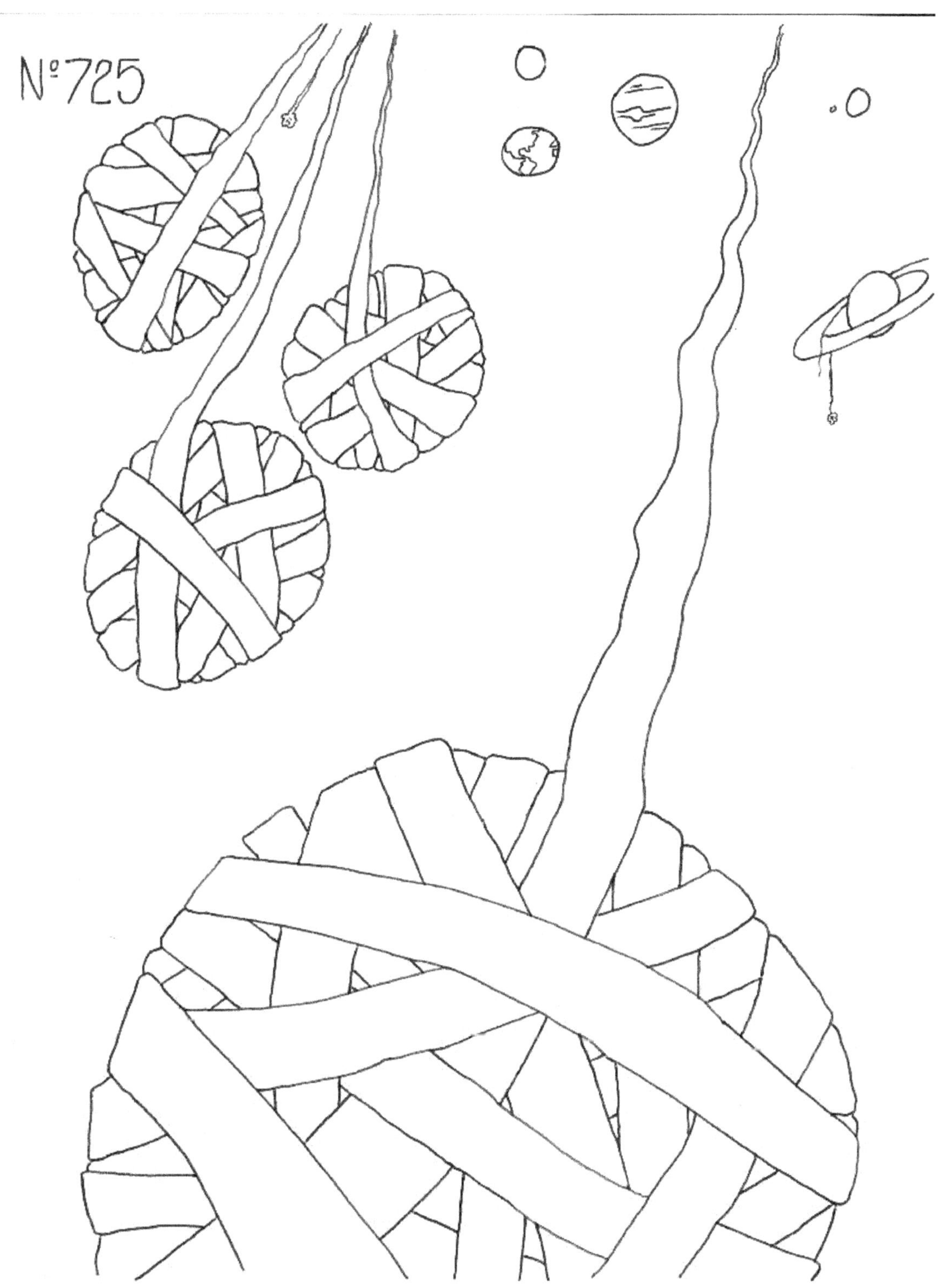
Nº725

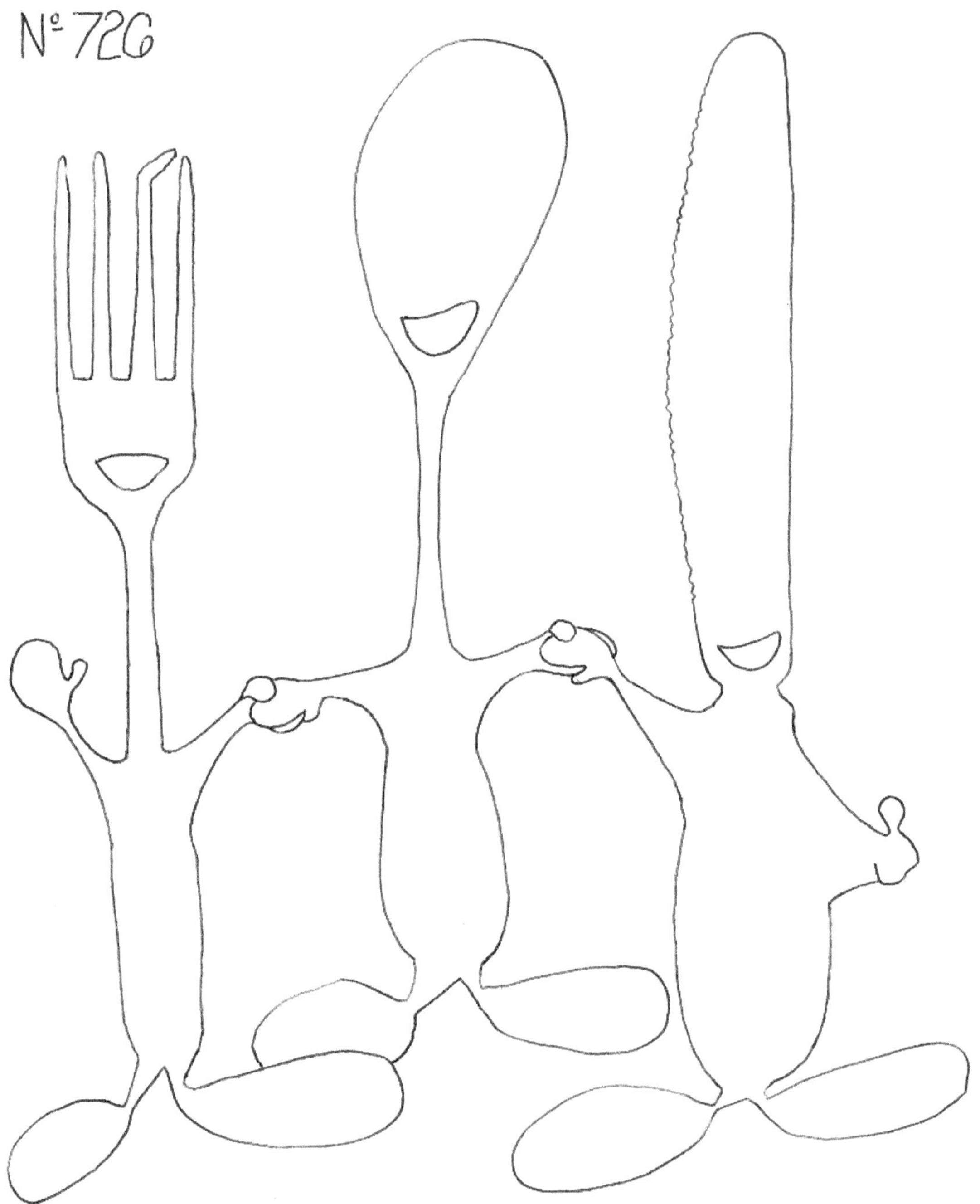
Nº 726

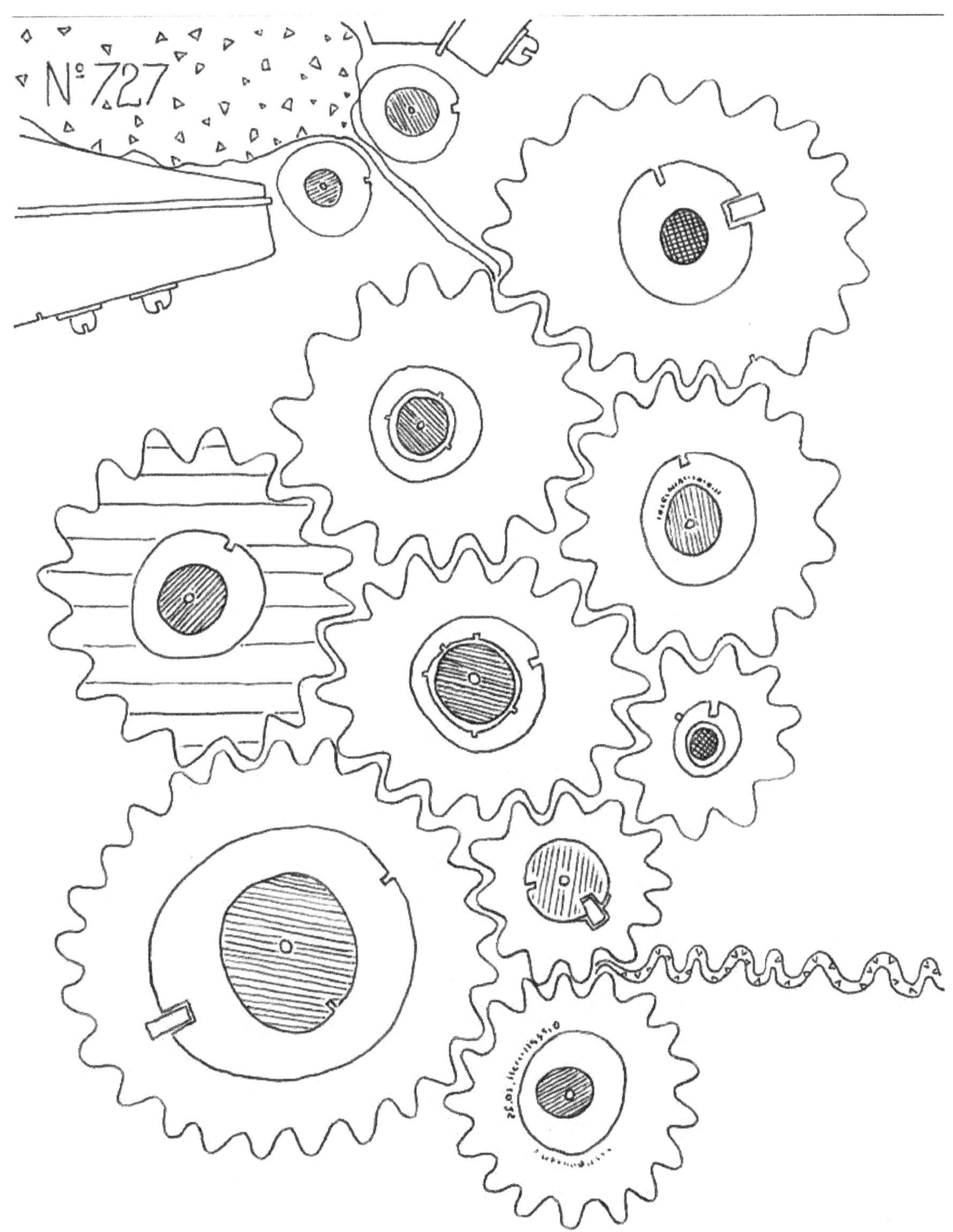
№ 727

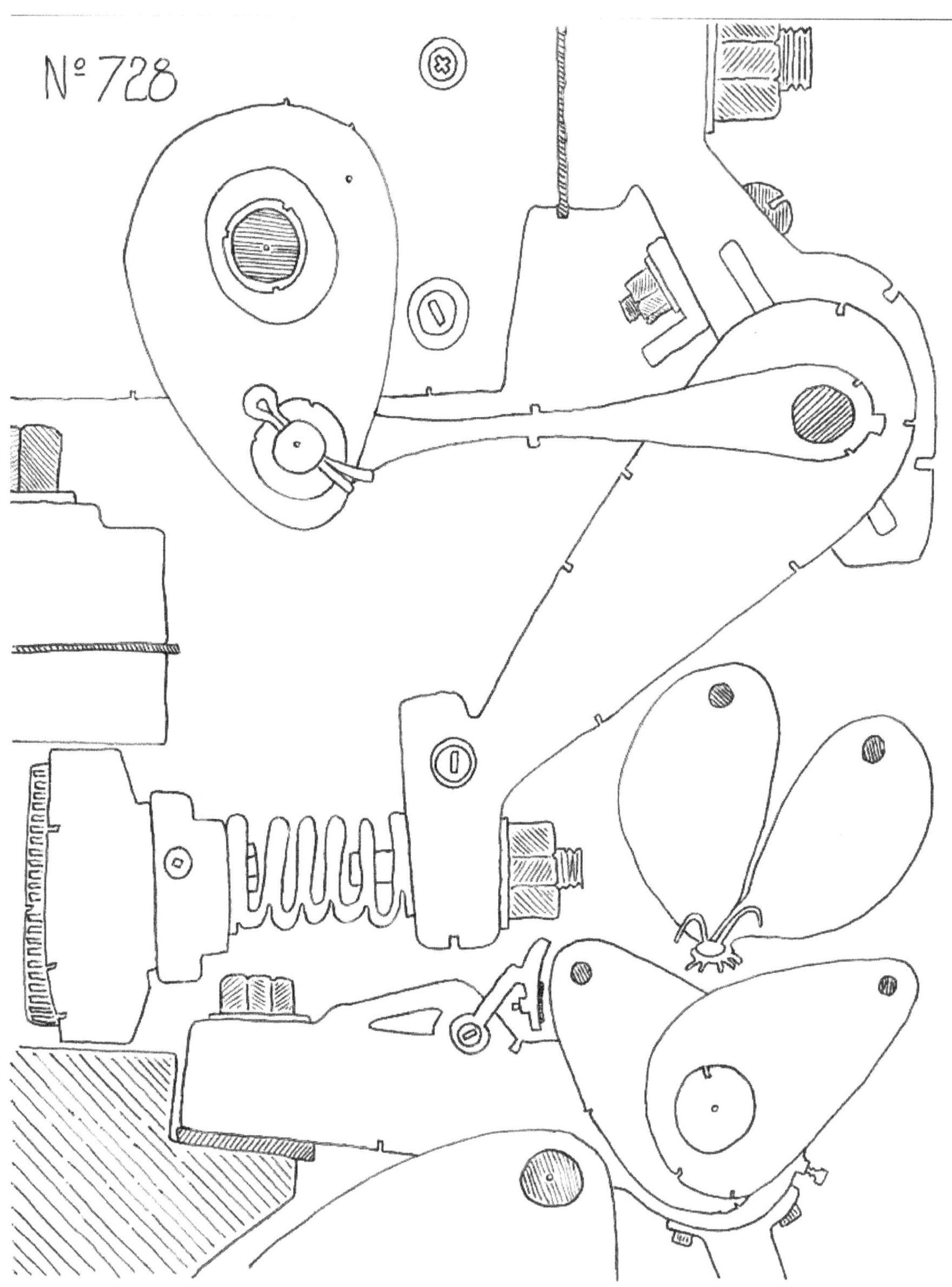
Nº 728

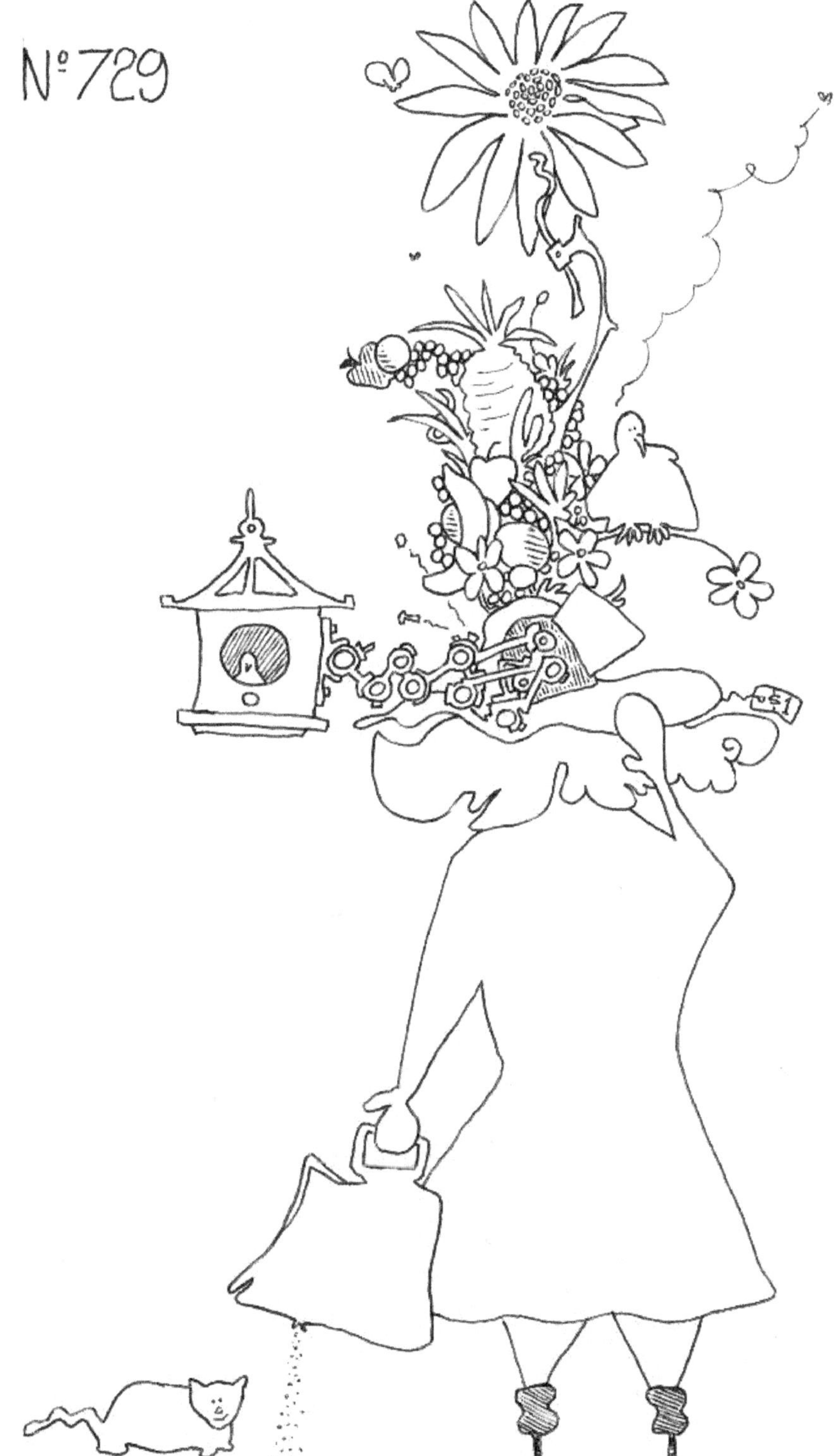
N°729

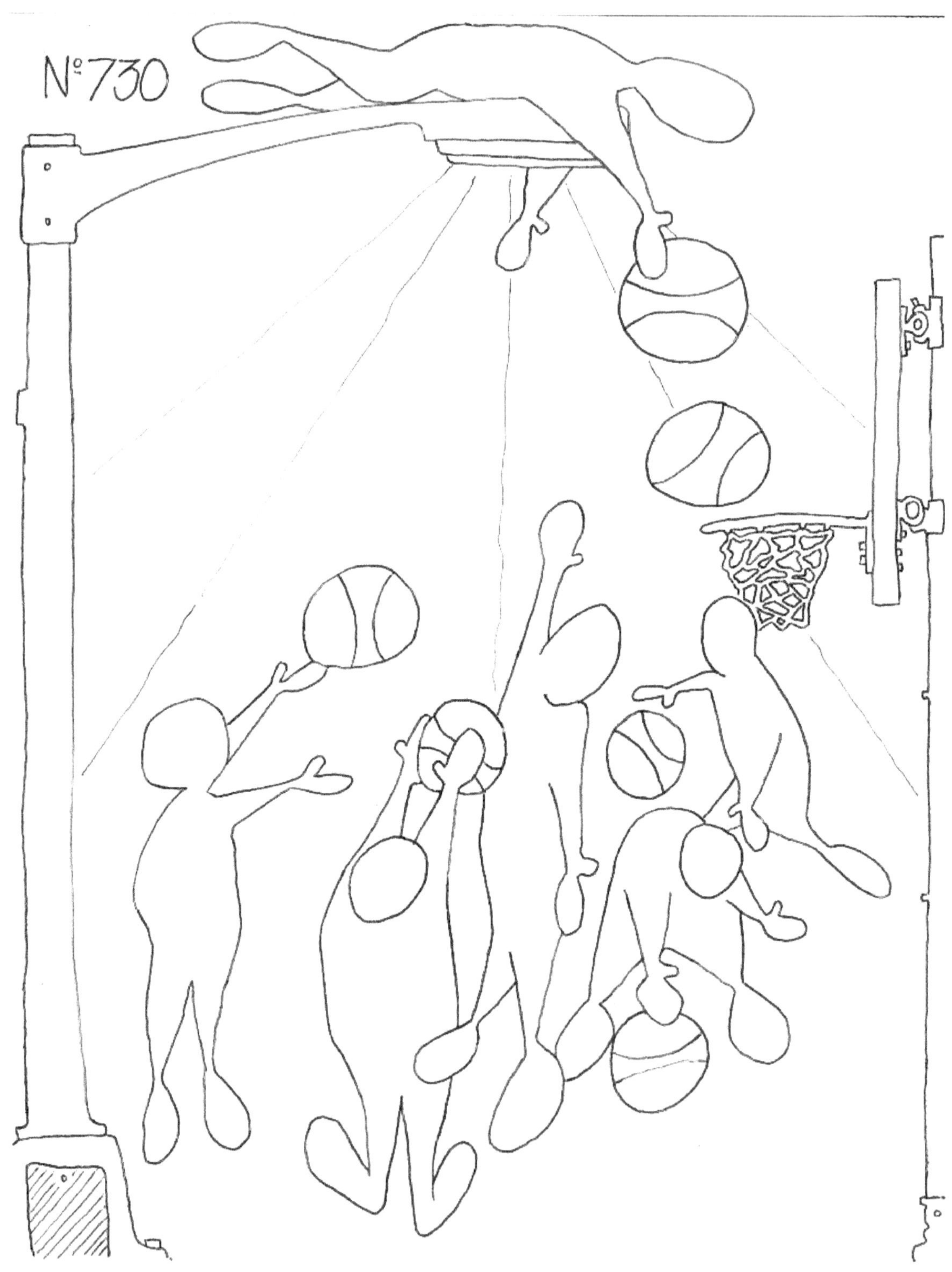
Nº730

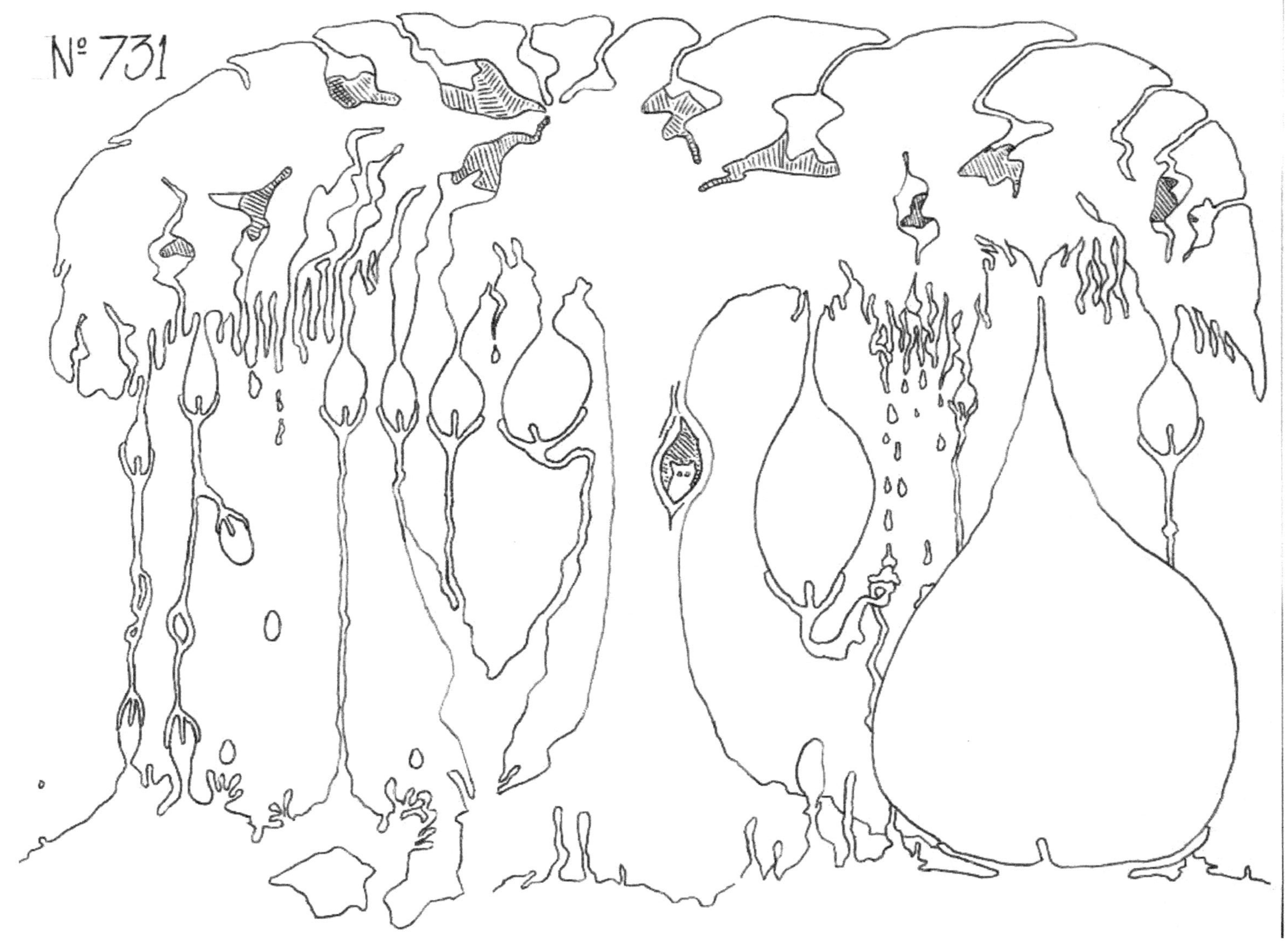
Nº 731

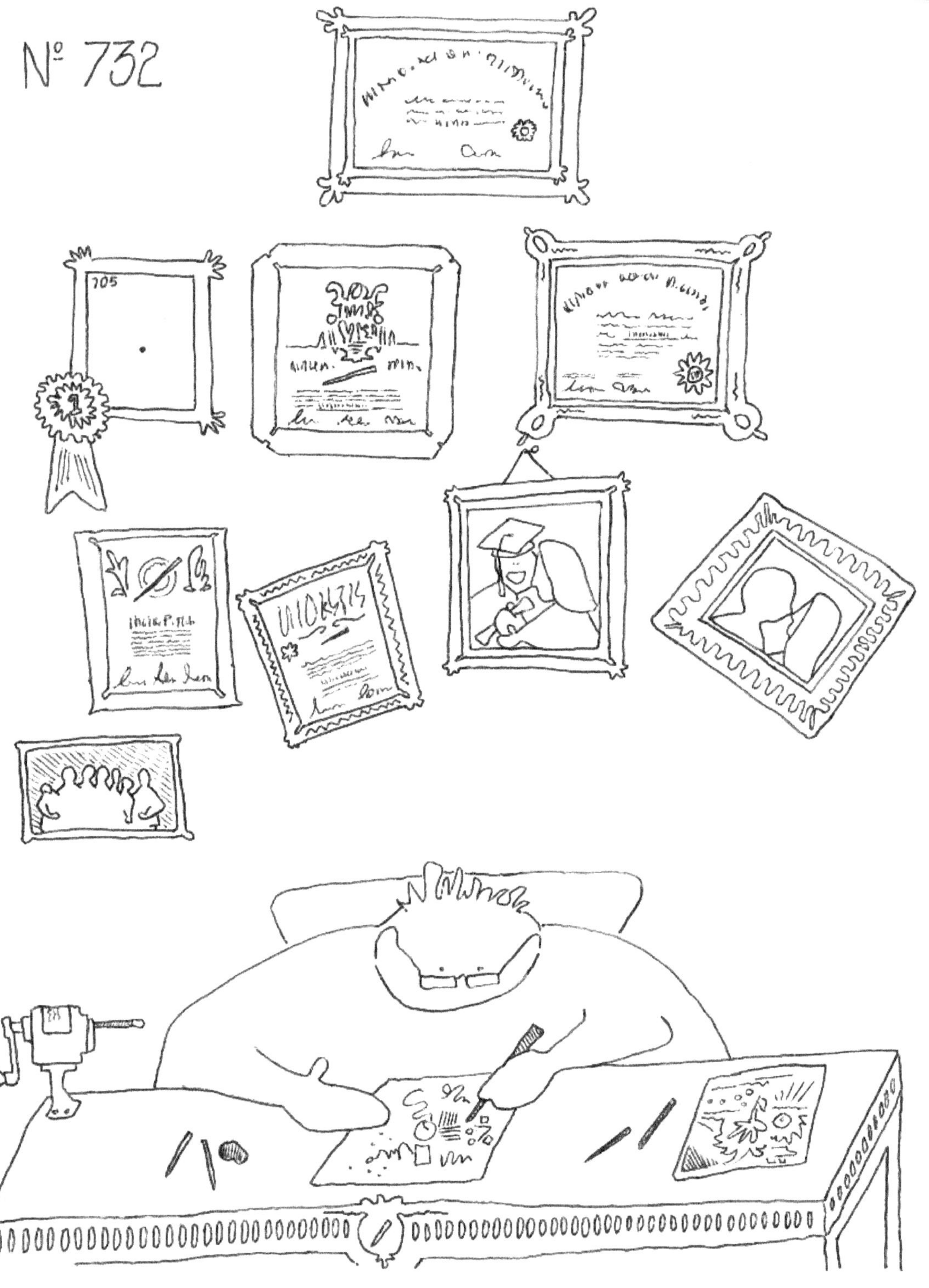
№ 732
705

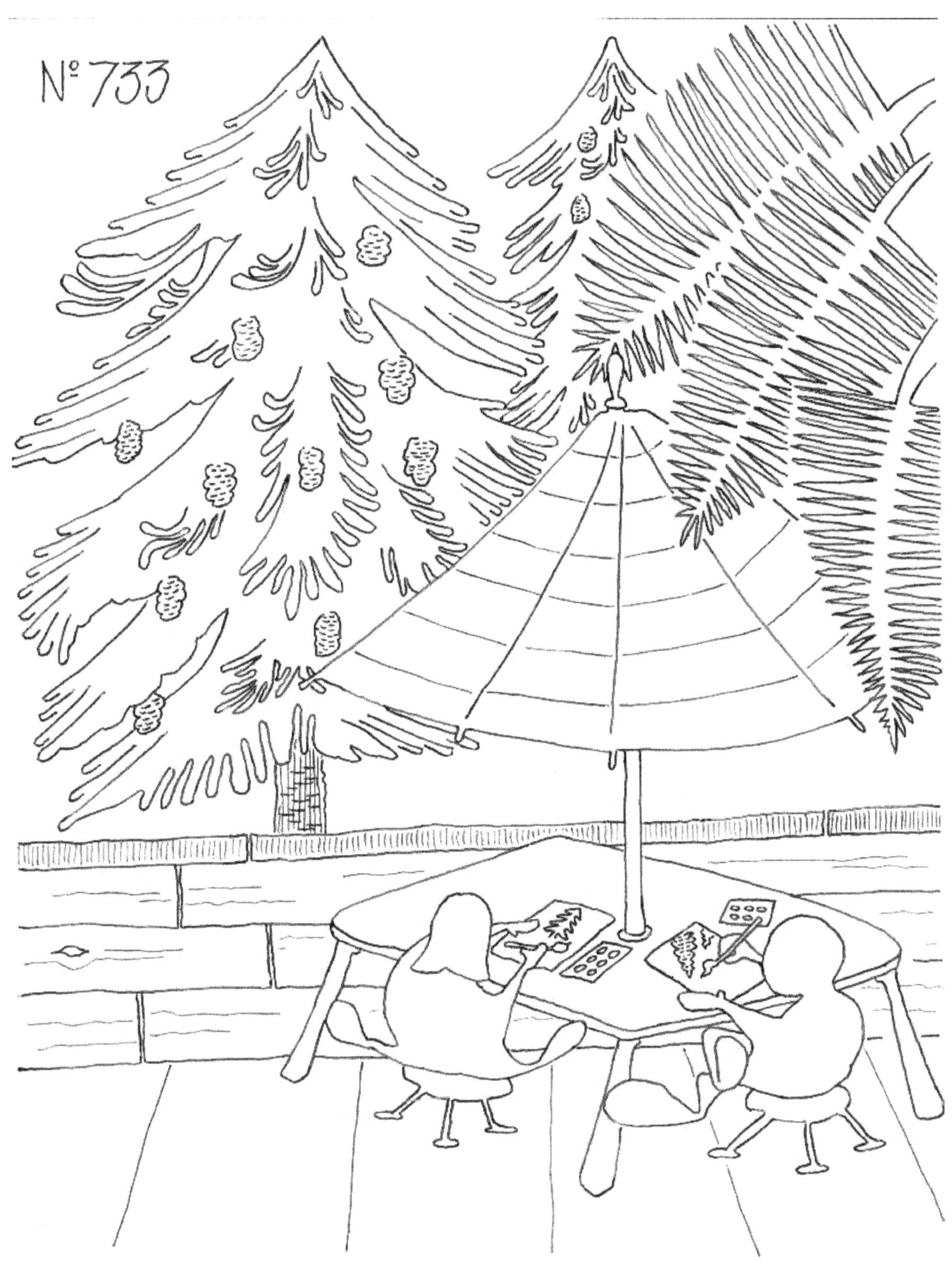
Nº 733

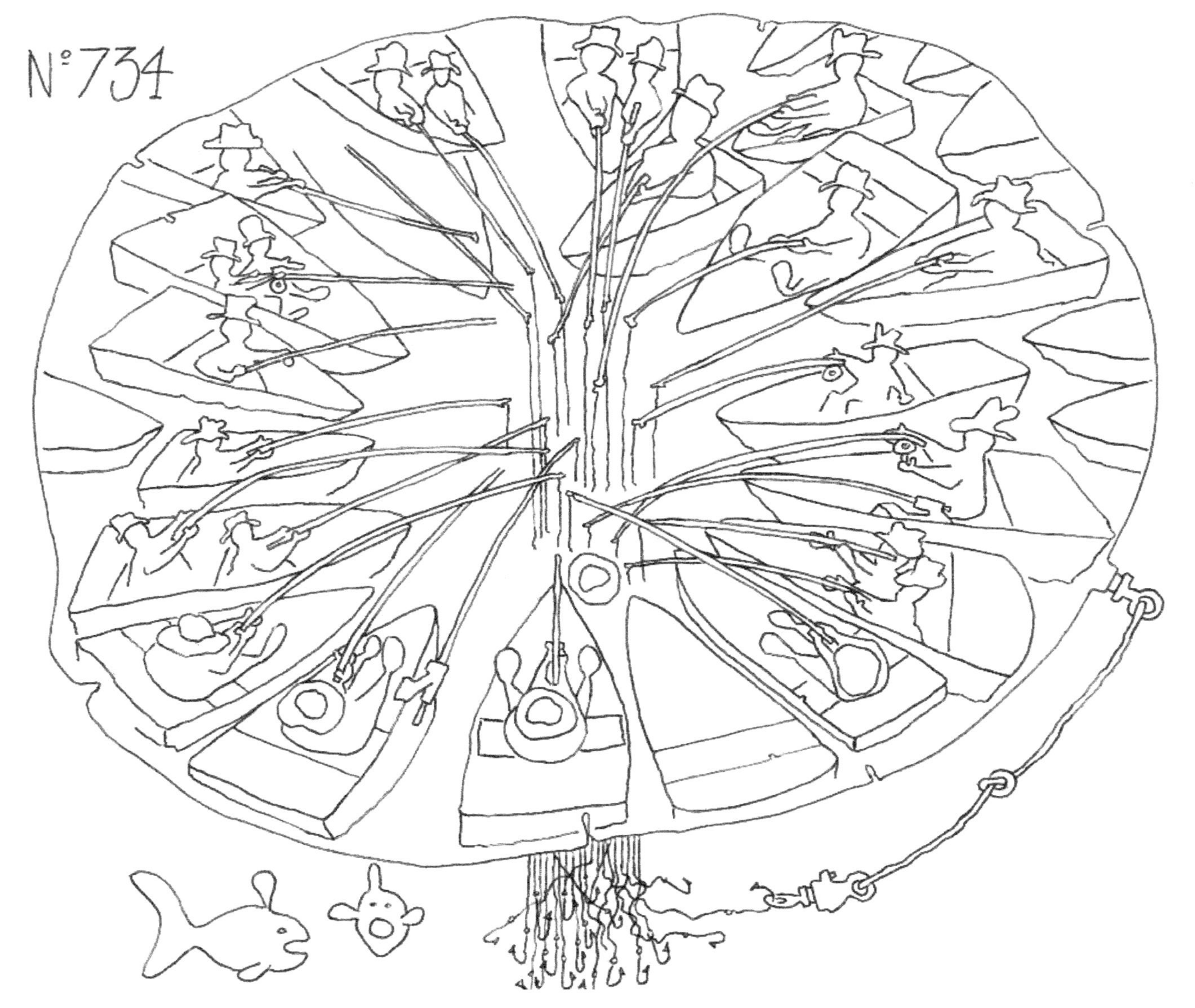
N°734

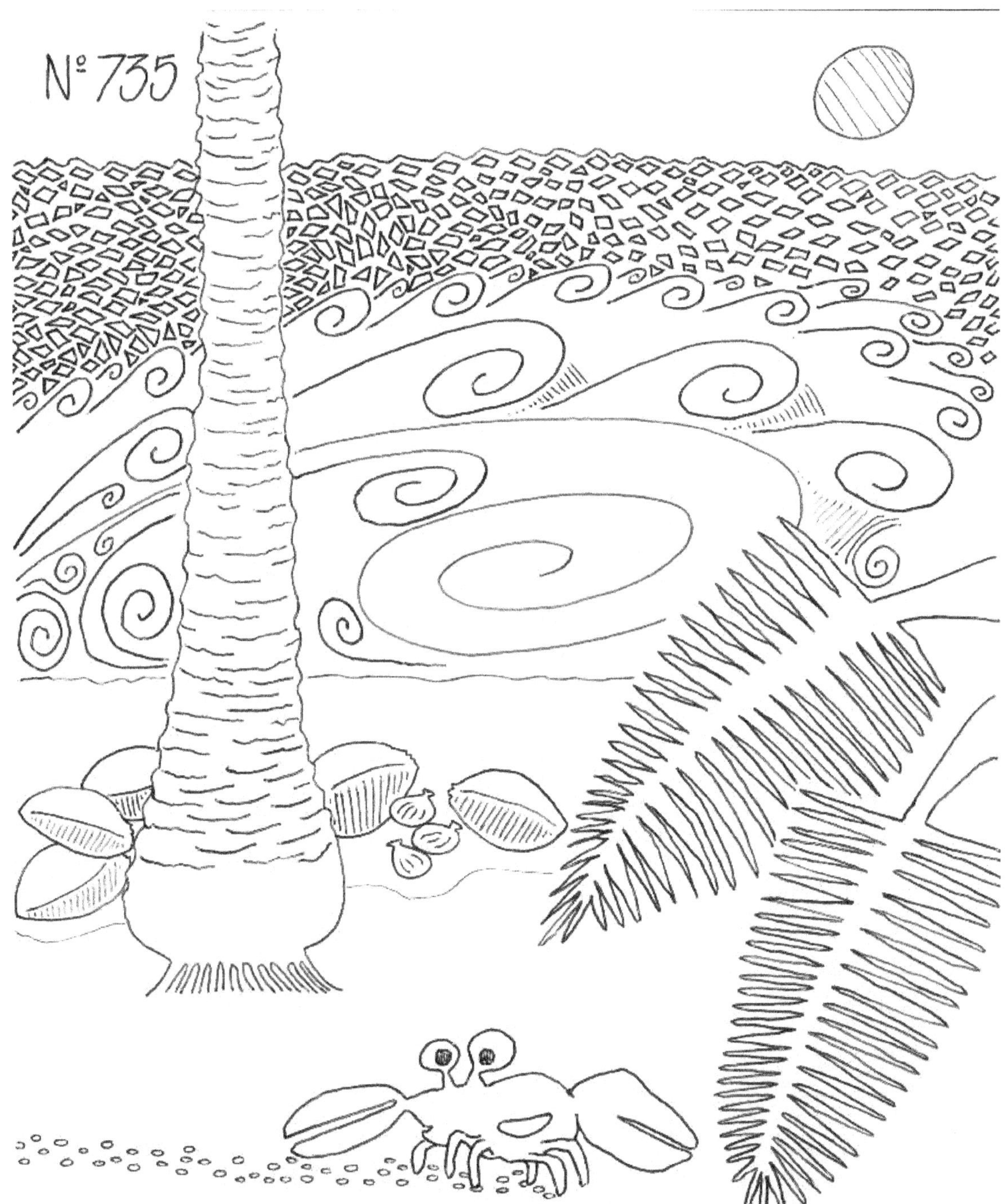
Nº 735

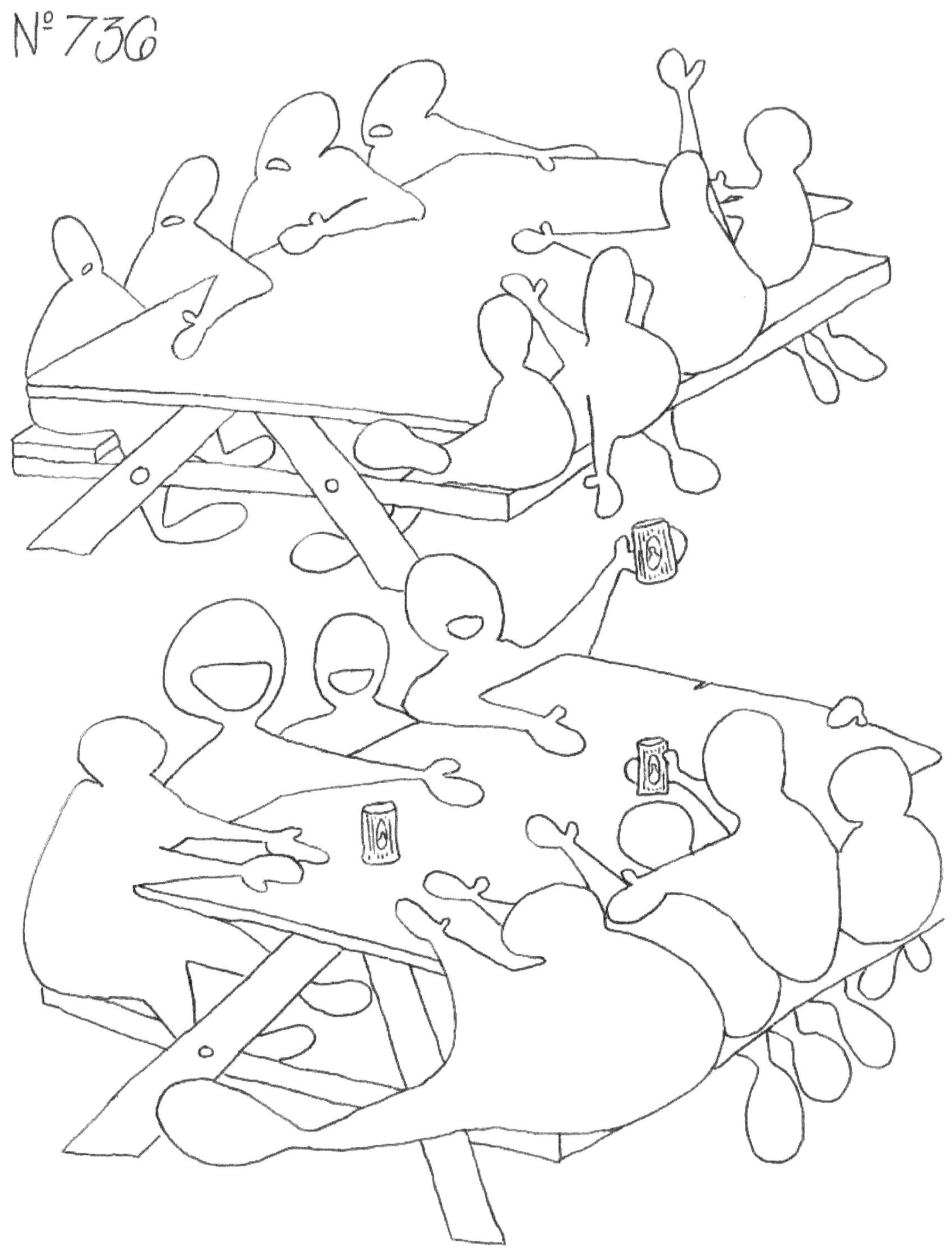
Nº 736

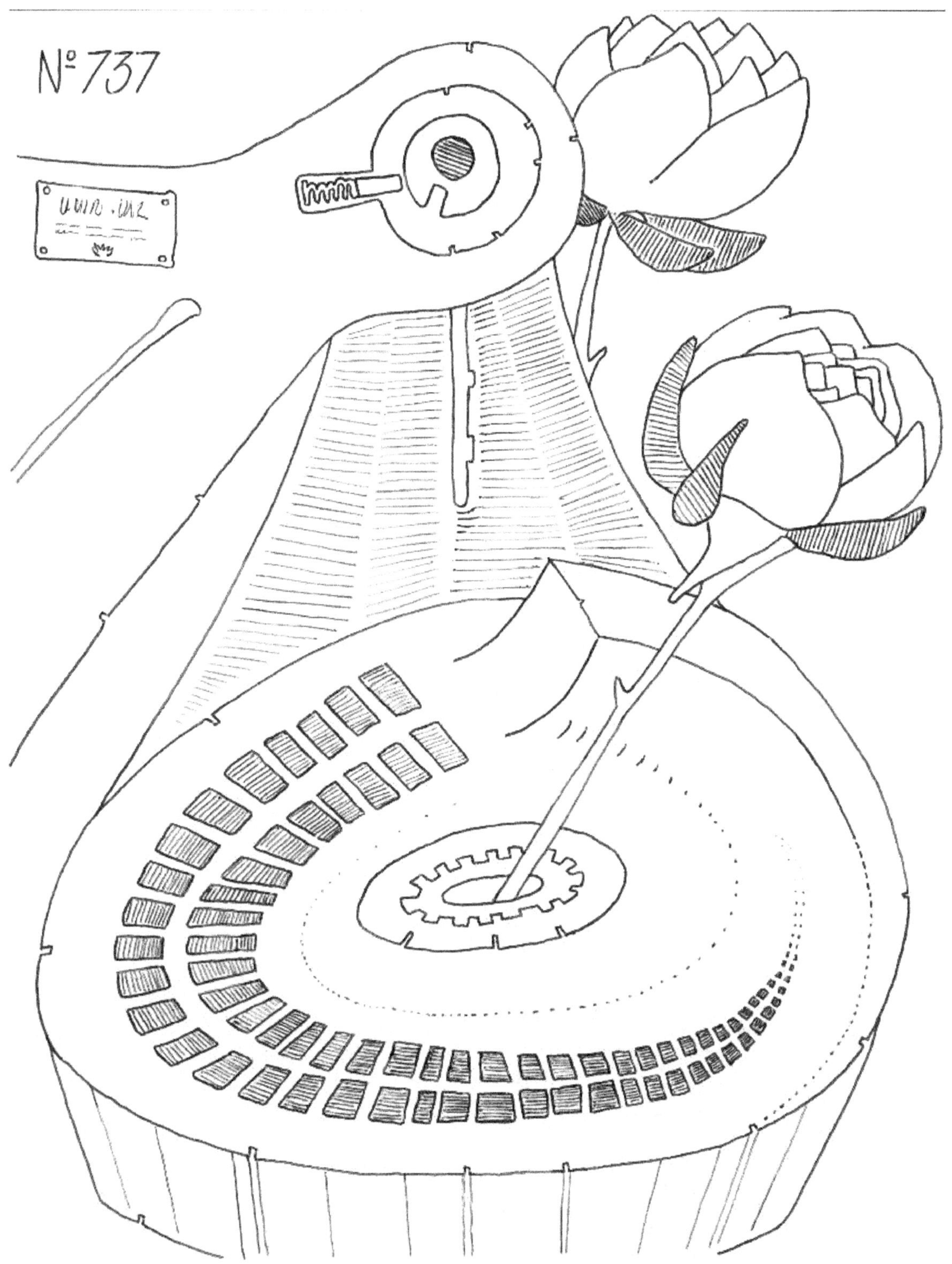
№ 737

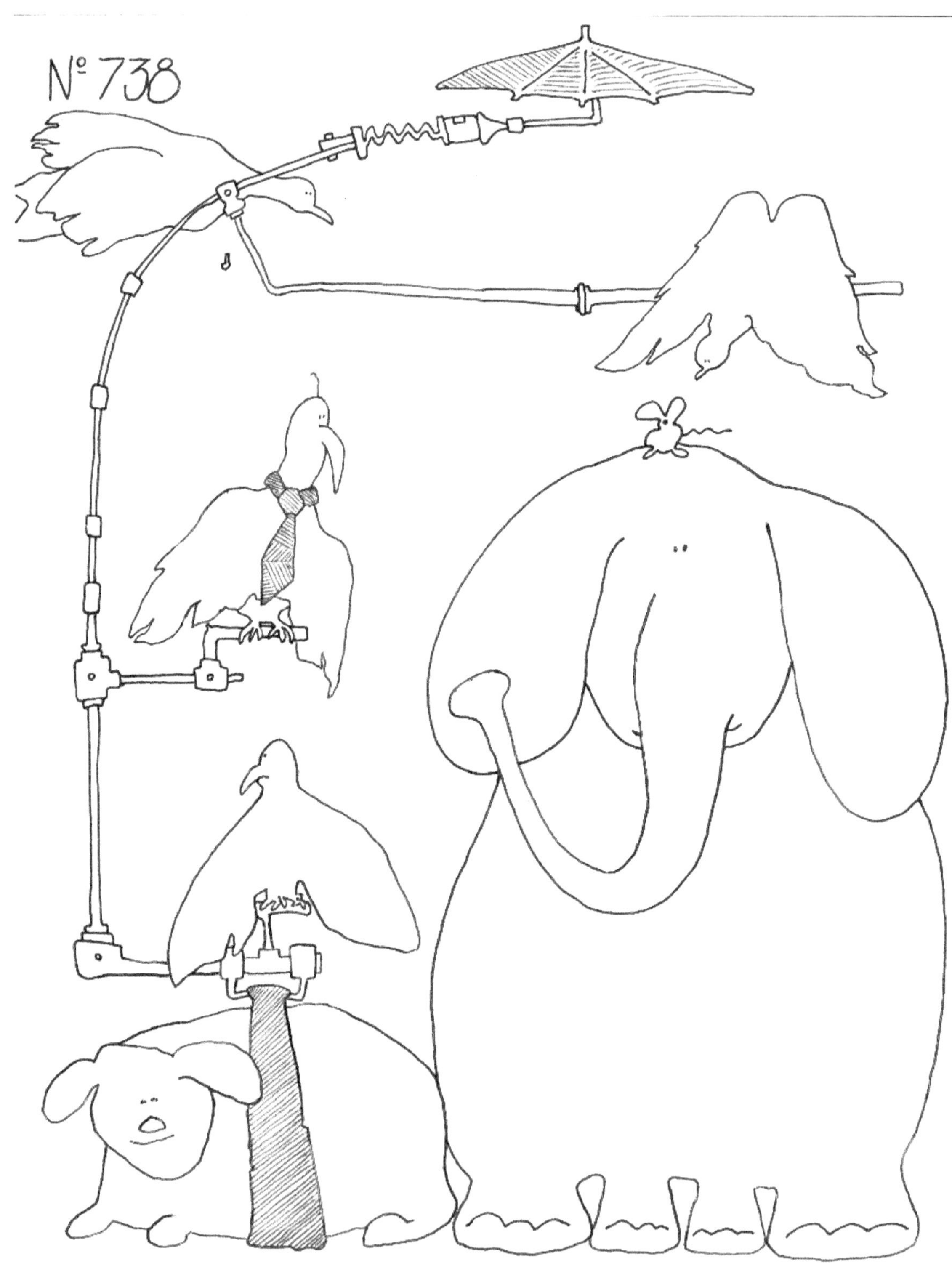
N° 738

Nº 739

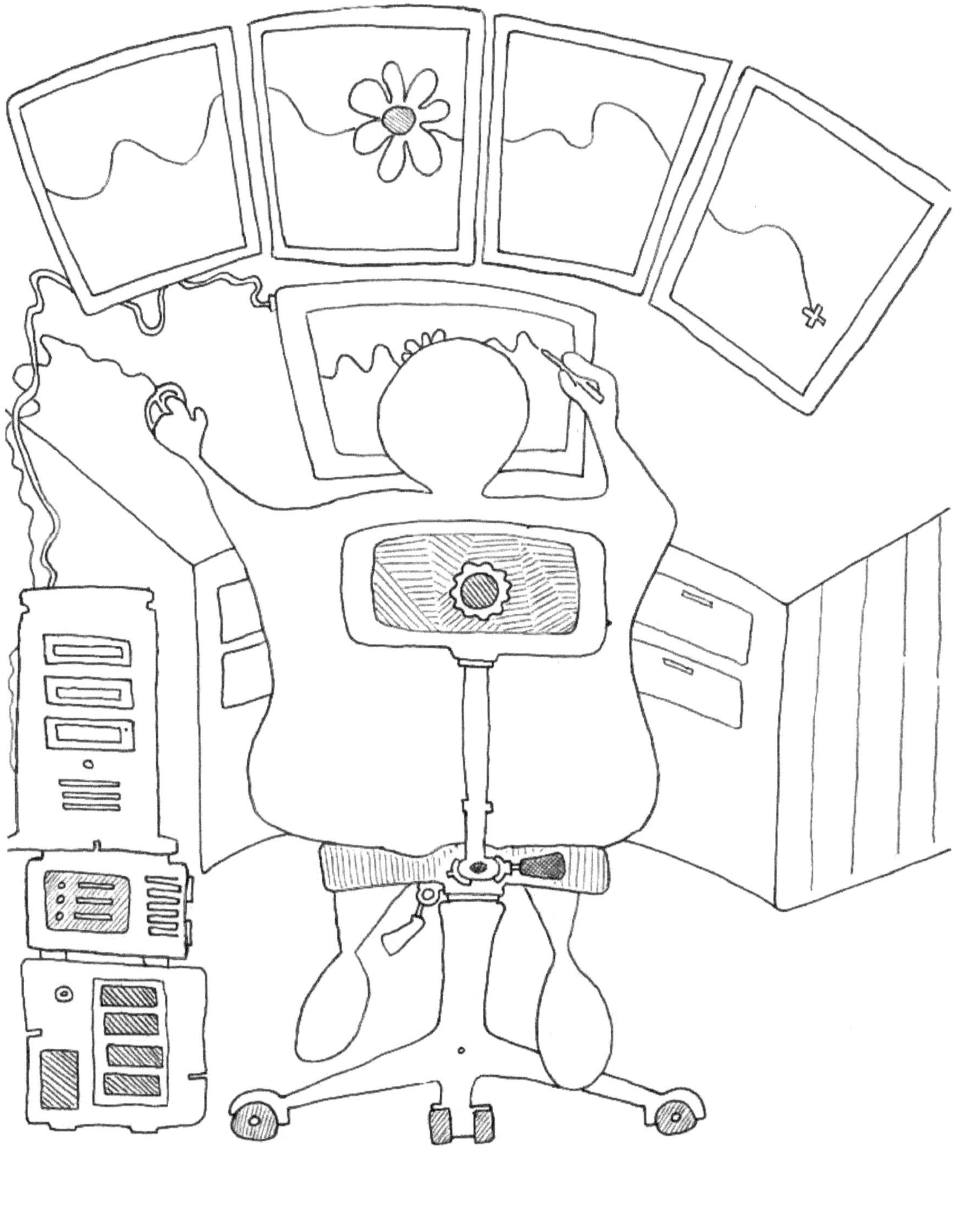

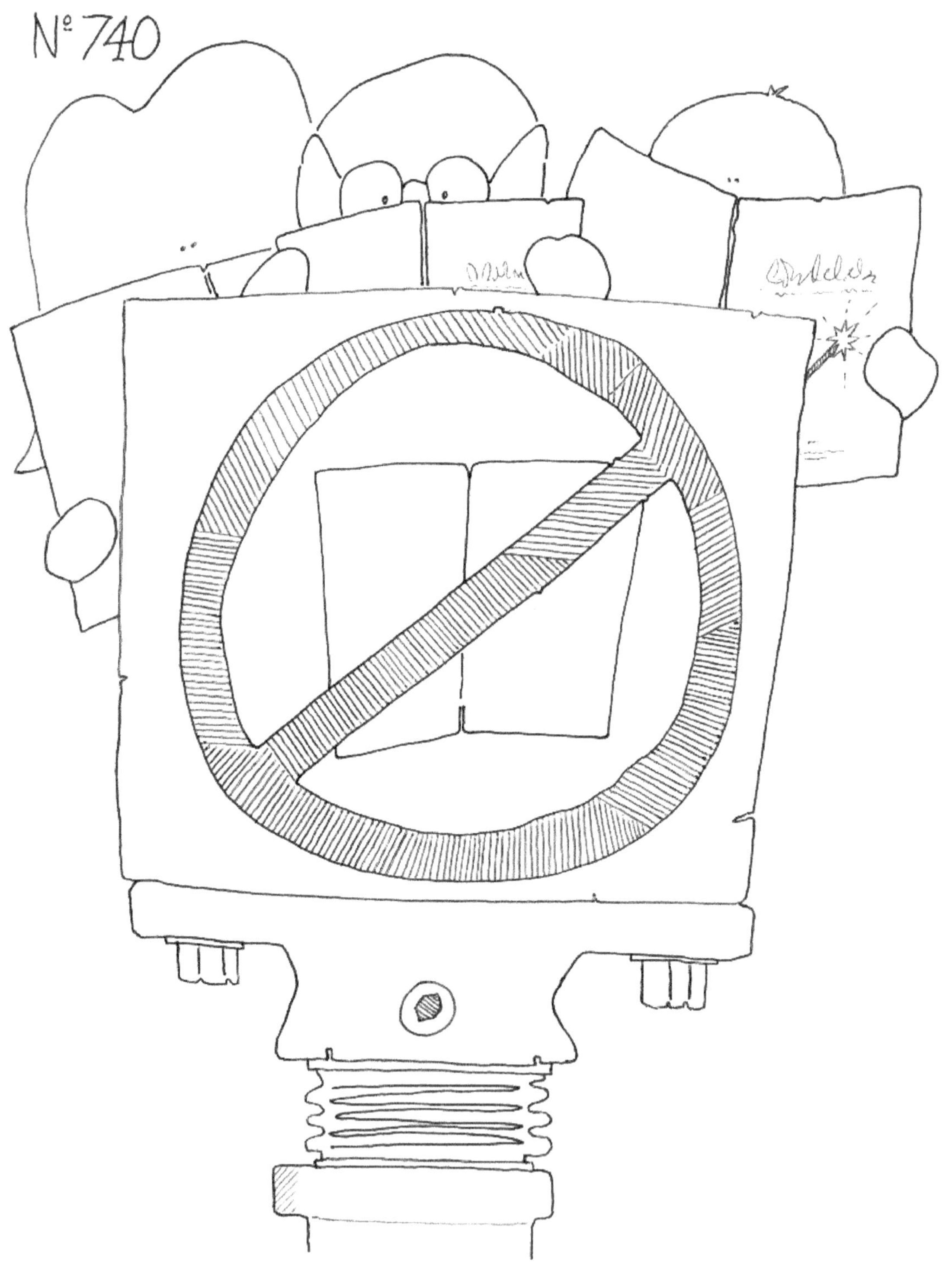
N° 740

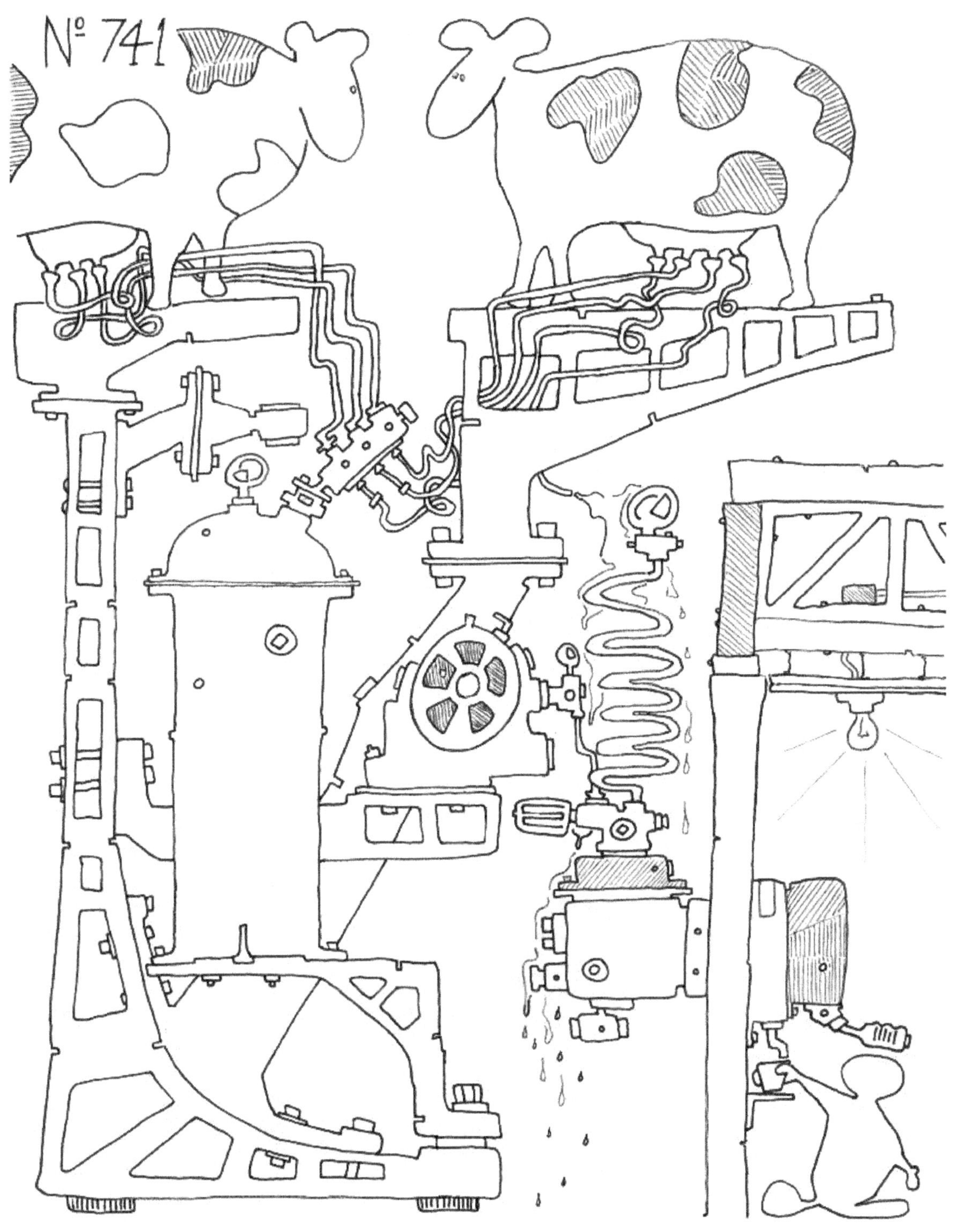

Nº 741

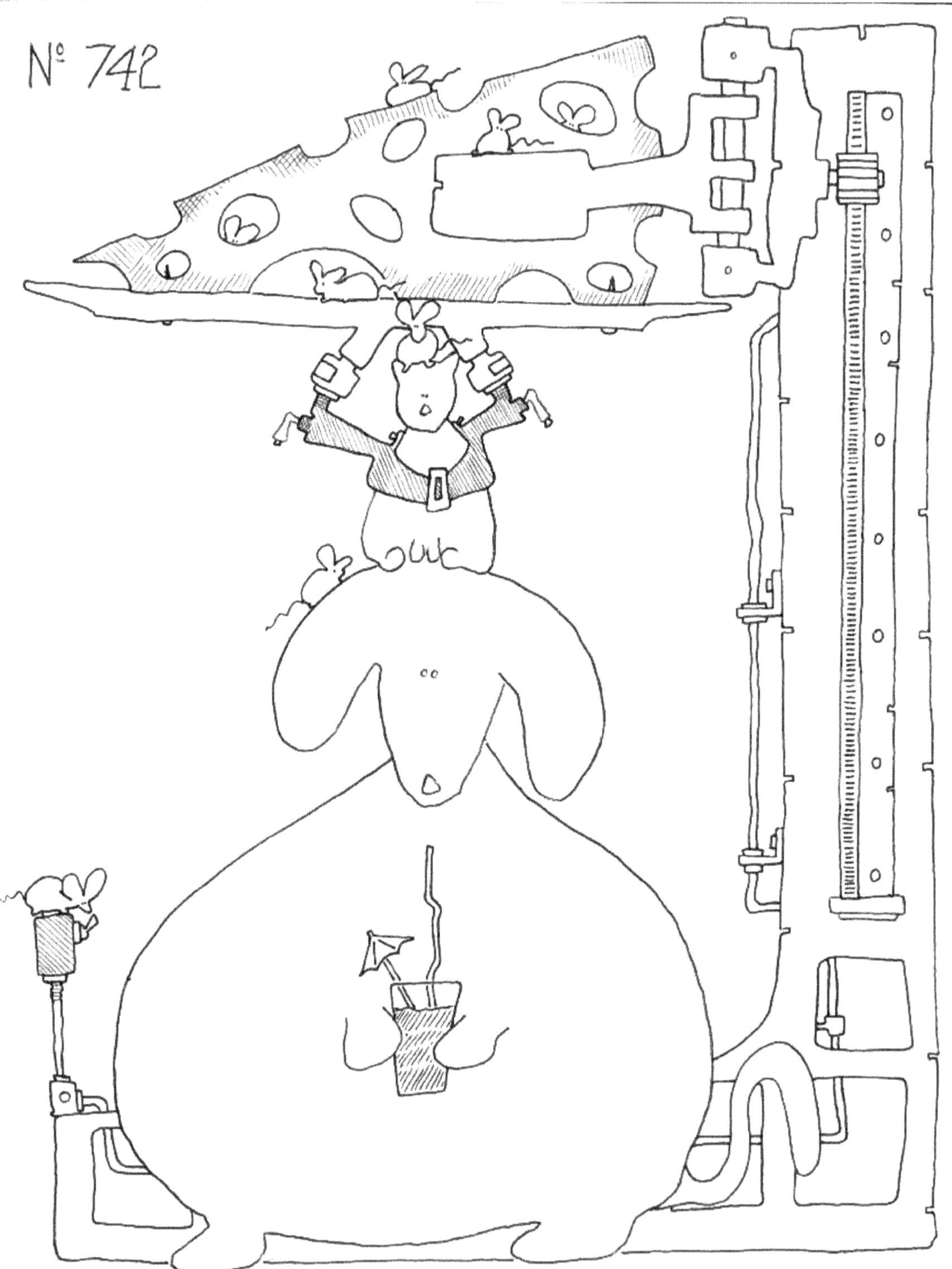
Nº 742

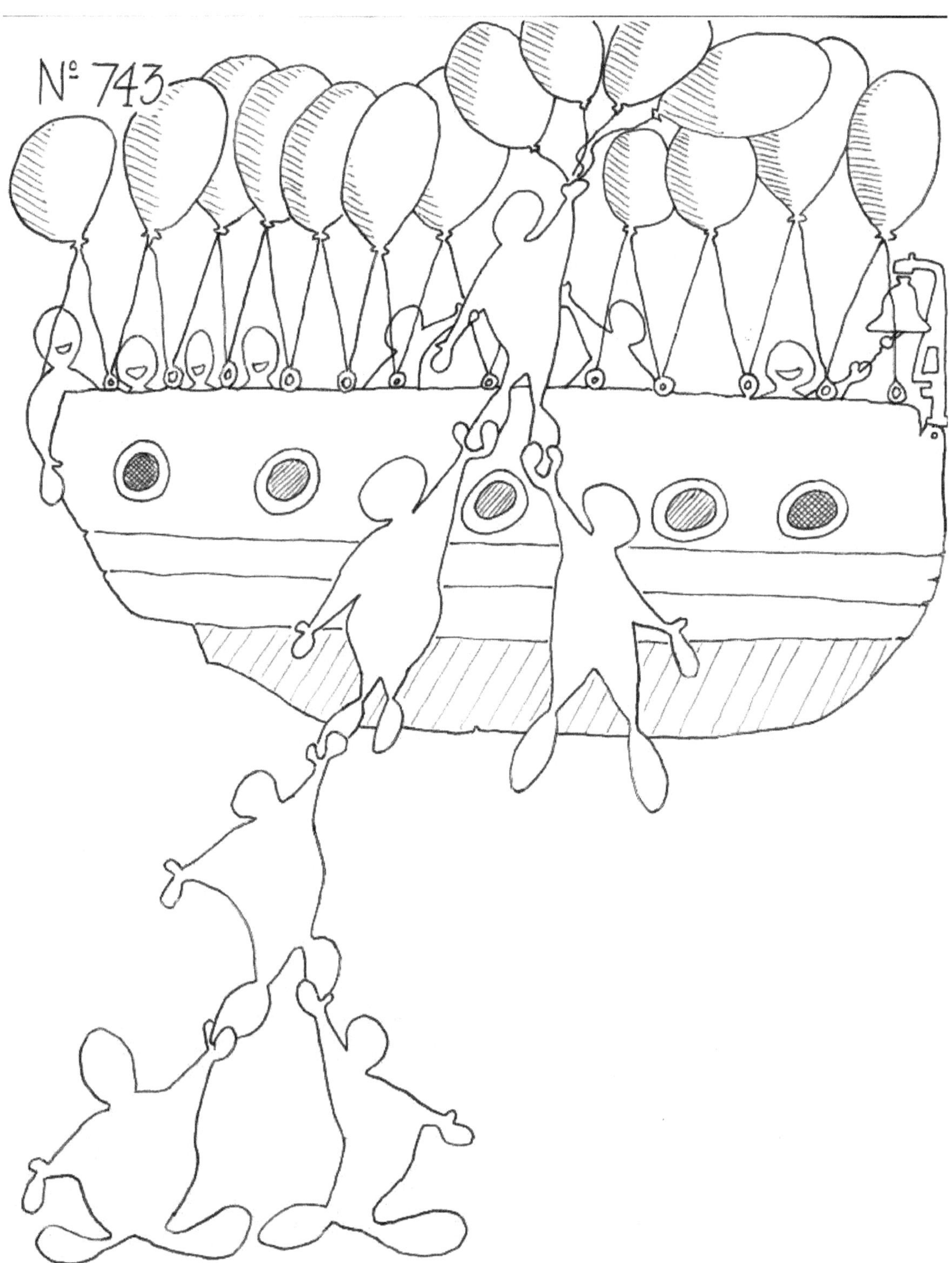
Nº 743

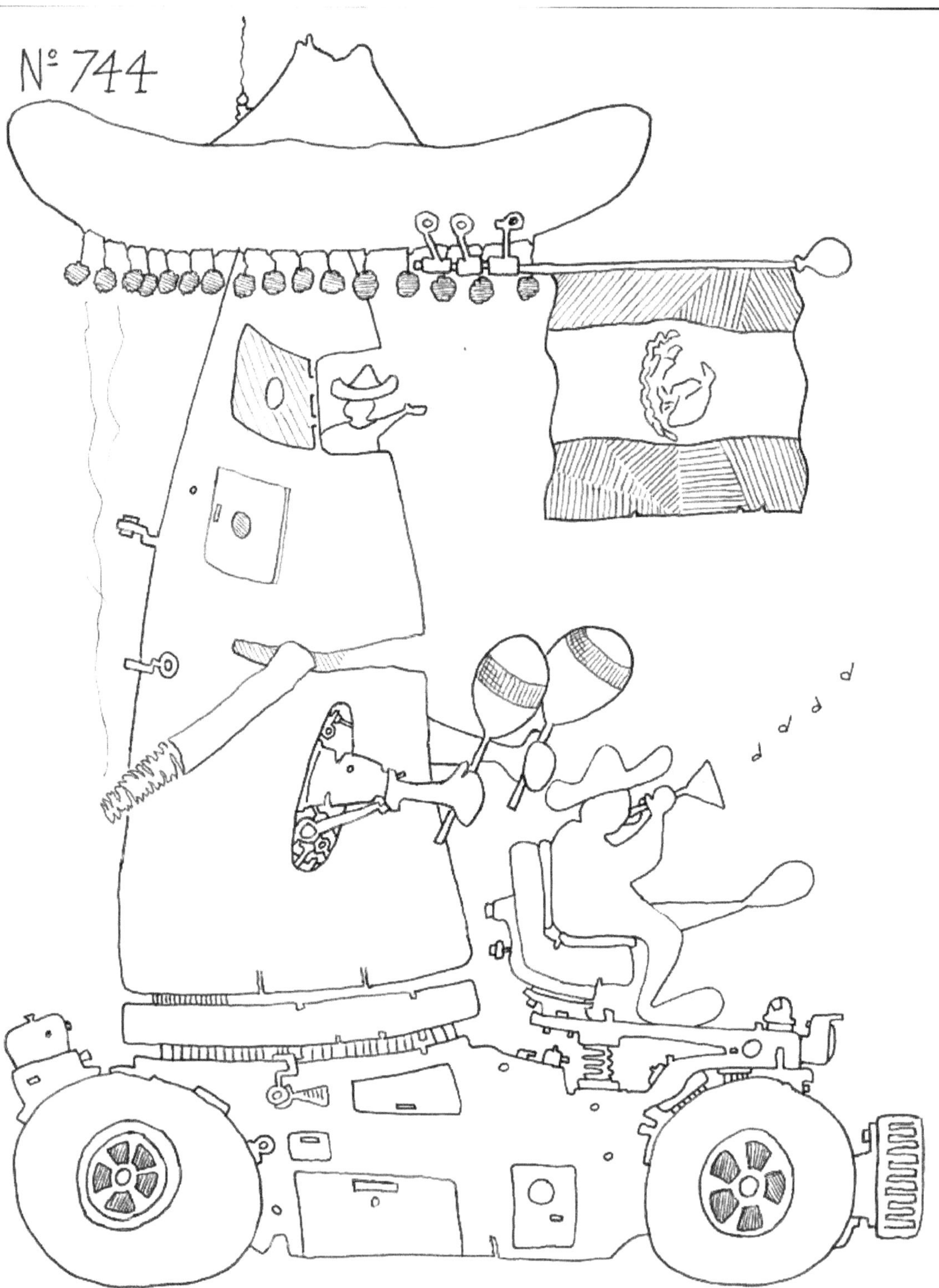
N° 744

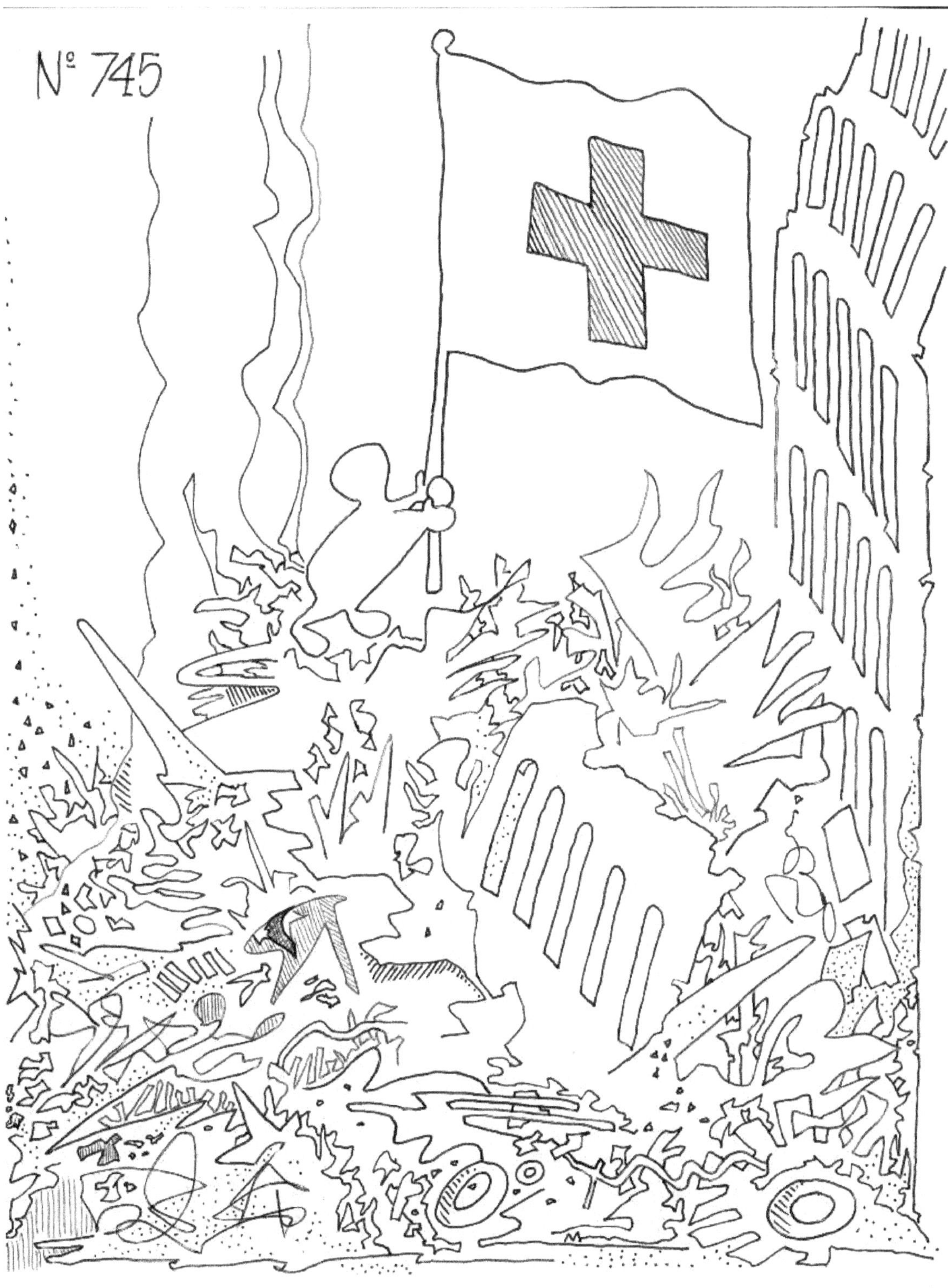
Nº 745

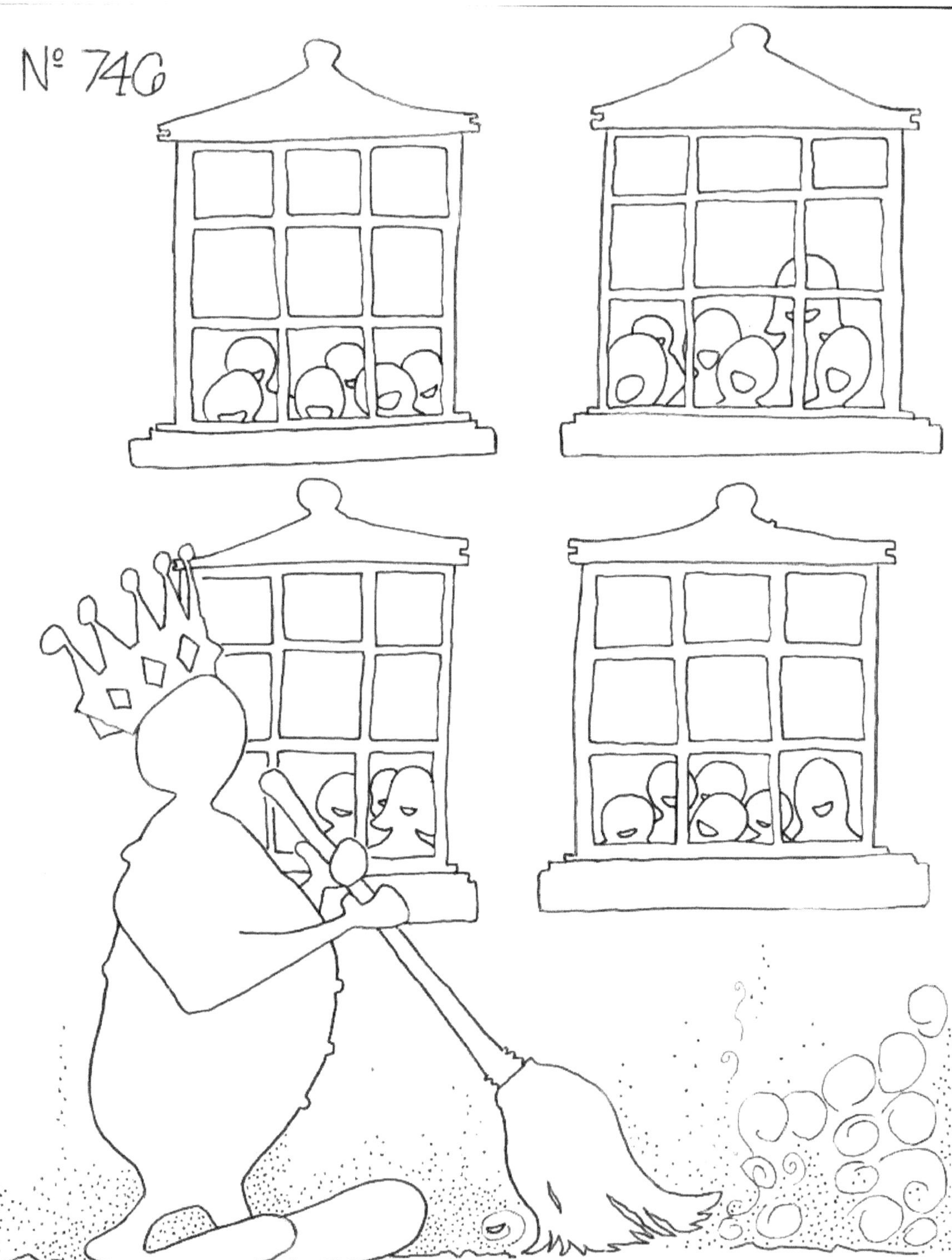
Nº 746

№ 747

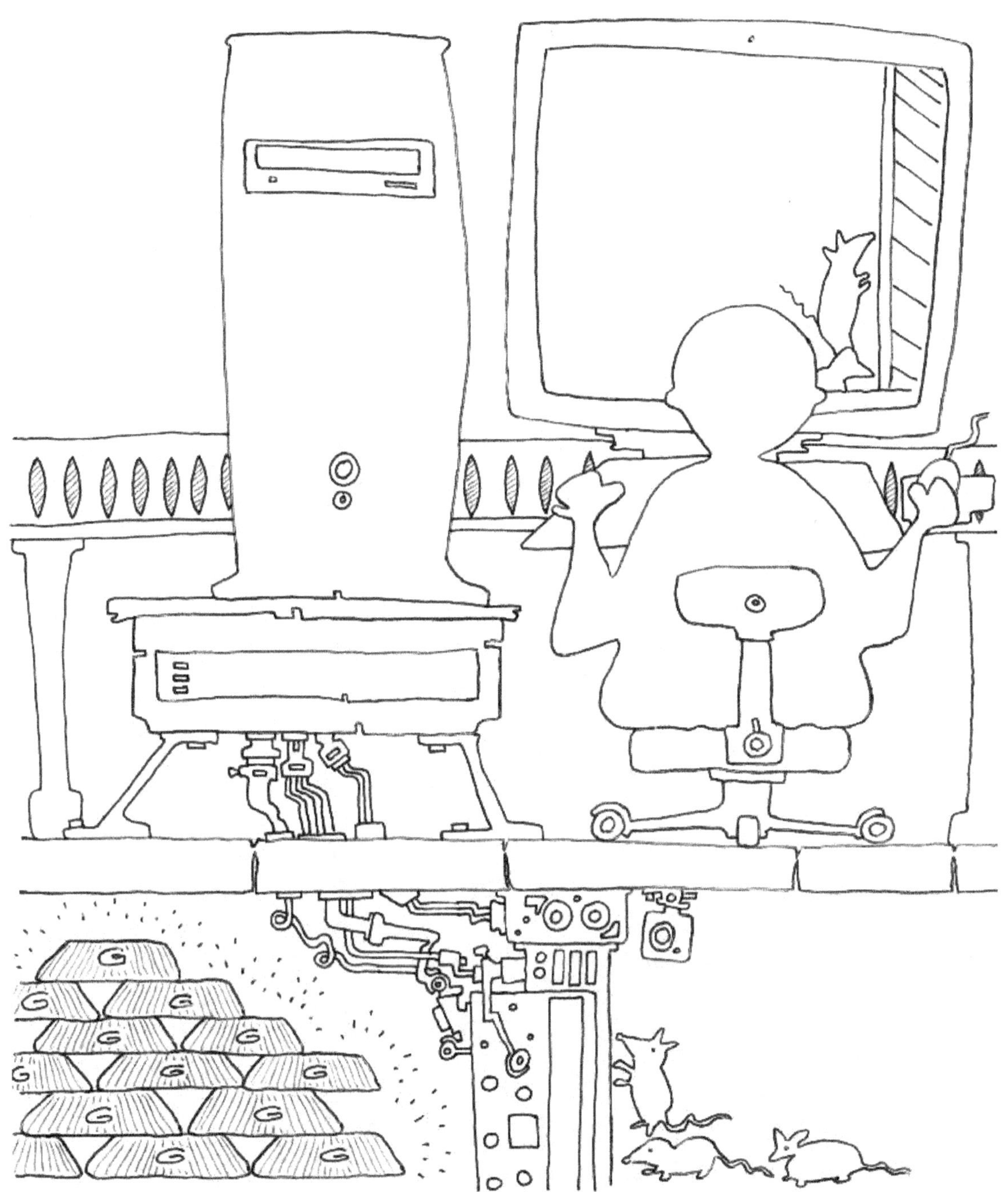

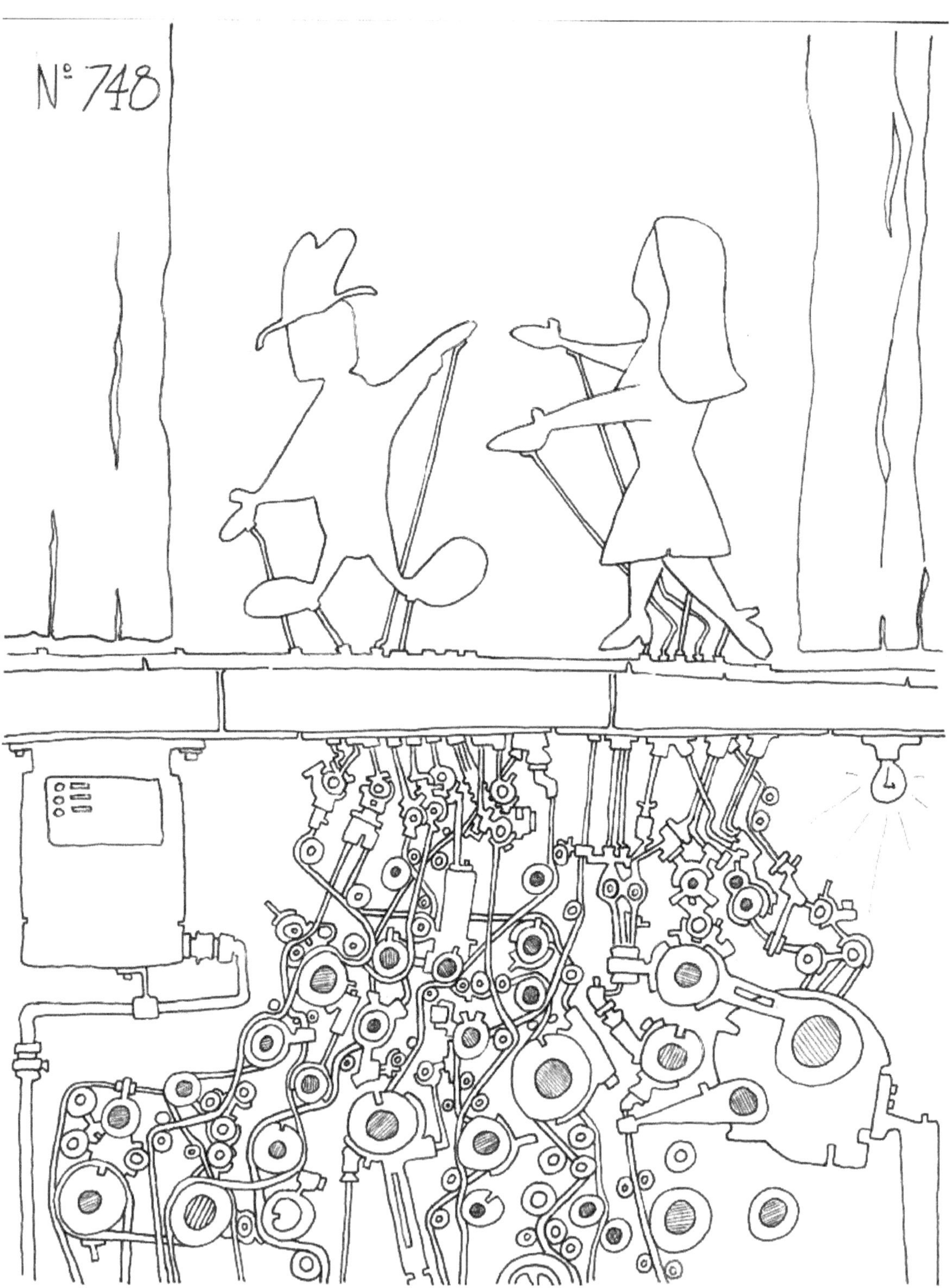

Nº 748

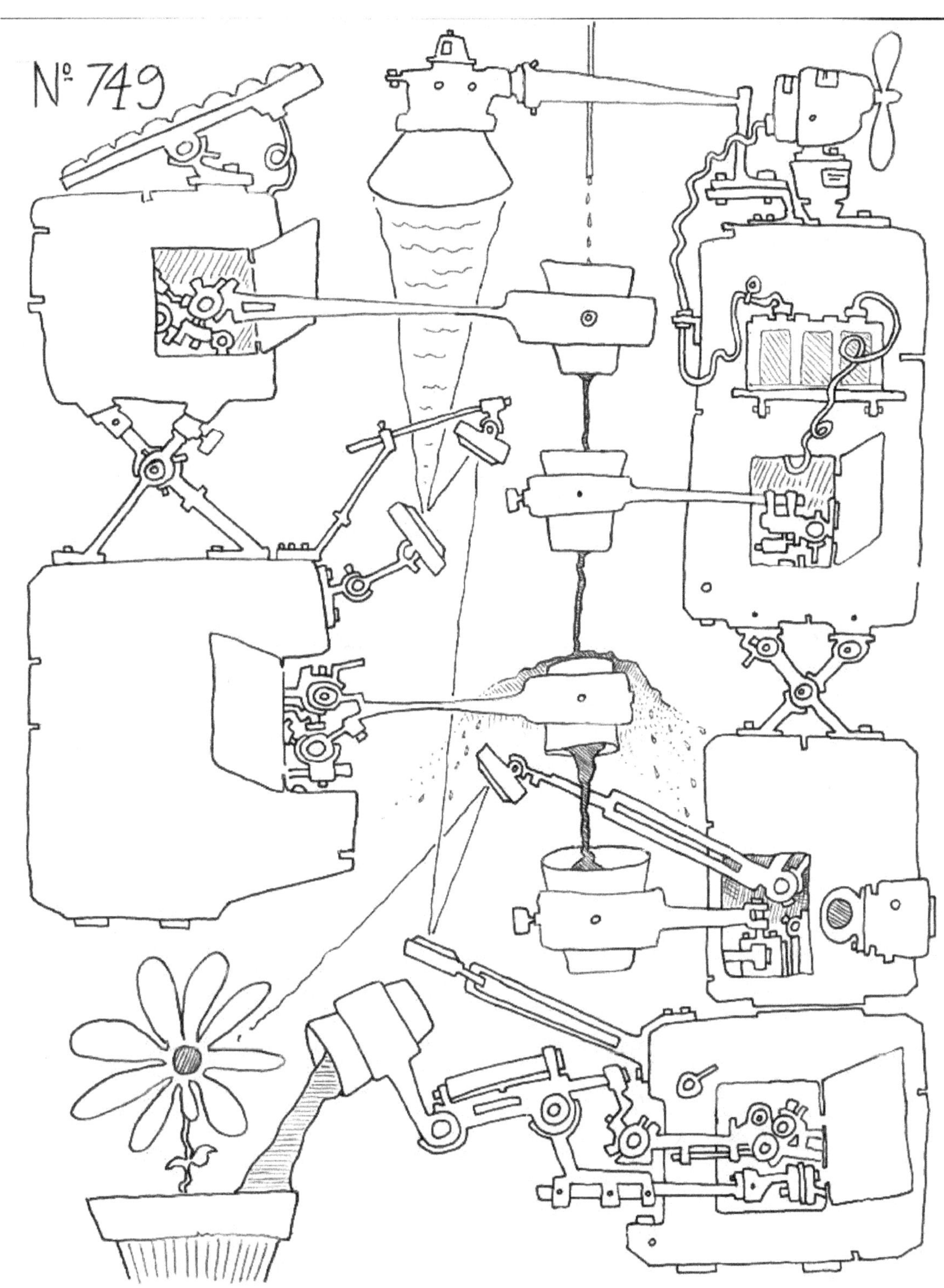
№ 749

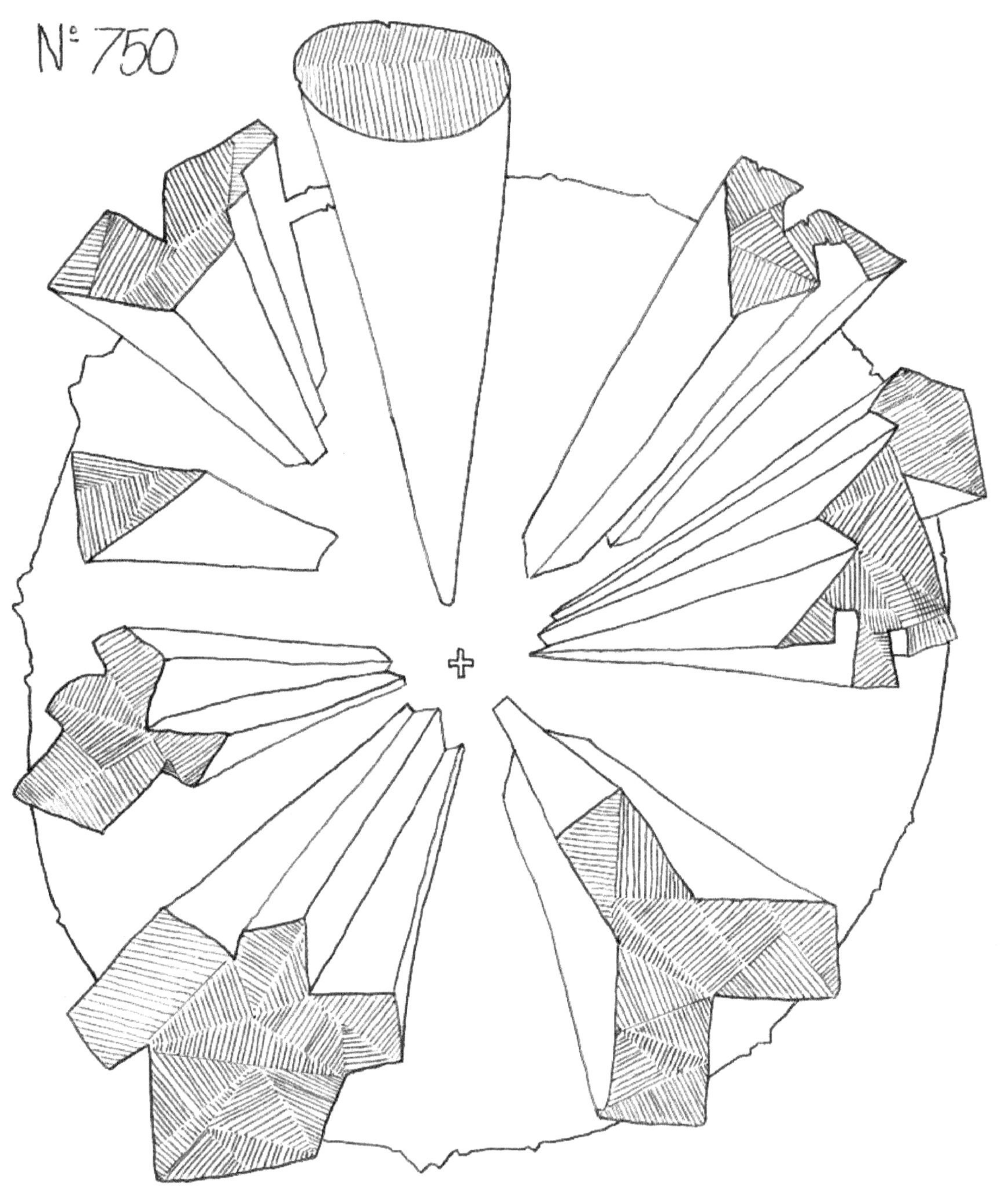

=== THE END ===